Microsoft Windows 98 Companion

Martin S. Matthews

Microsoft Windows 98 Companion

Published by **Microsoft Press**
A Division of Microsoft Corporation
One Microsoft Way
Redmond, Washington 98052-6399

Library of Congress Cataloging-in-Publication Data
Matthews, Martin S.
    Microsoft Windows 98 Companion / Martin Matthews.
        p.   cm.
    Includes index.
    ISBN 1-57231-931-3
    1. Microsoft Windows (Computer file)   2. Operating systems
(Computers)   I. Title.
    QA76.76.063M37175   1998
    005.4'46 9--dc21   98-4615
                                                                        CIP

Printed and bound in the United States of America.

1 2 3 4 5 6 7 8 9 WCWC 3 2 1 0 9 8

Distributed to the book trade in Canada by ITP Nelson, a division of Thomson Canada Limited.

A CIP catalogue record for this book is available from the British Library.

Microsoft Press books are available through booksellers and distributors worldwide. For further
information about international editions, contact your local Microsoft Corporation office or
contact Microsoft Press International directly at fax (425) 936-7329. Visit our Web site at
mspress.microsoft.com.

Acquisitions Editor: **Kim Fryer**
Project Editor: **Anne Taussig**
Technical Editor: **John Cronan**

CONTENTS *at a Glance*

CONTENTS *at a Glance*

TABLE OF CONTENTS

Acknowledgments

Many people had a part in making this book what it is, and for their assistance I am most grateful. The book is greatly improved because of their contribution. I would particularly like to thank:

Anne Taussig, whose dedication to producing a good book and much patience as project editor brought the book a great deal closer to her ideal than where it started

John Cronan, whose attention to detail and stick-to-itiveness caught a great many technical errors and inconsistencies

Harriet O'Neal and **Margaret Berson** who as copy editors with much thought and more than a little intuition figured out what I was trying to say and said it better

Sybil Ihrig of Helios Productions, who expertly guided the book through its page composition and prepress production phases

Dan Logan of The Runaway Press, who made a significant addition to the book by writing Chapters 8 and 14

Russ Madlener of Microsoft, who answered many questions, even those that were not particularly brilliant

Carole Matthews and **Michael Matthews,** my partner and our son, who put up with a lot "so dad could work on his book"

Martin Matthews
April, 1998

Introduction

The purpose of *Microsoft Windows 98 Companion* is to give you the means to quickly and fully utilize Windows 98's features and capabilities. Its objective is to go beyond just showing you how to use Windows 98 and to give you the in-depth knowledge and level of confidence needed to use Windows both practically as well as creatively. The book does this with

- Detailed explorations of the important topics in Windows 98, including what is new; setting up, customizing, and optimizing Windows 98; the user interface; file management; printing; communications; using the Internet and an intranet; e-mail; multimedia; and networking

- Detailed steps to perform hundreds of different functions

- Hundreds of tips, notes, and warnings on the many areas of Windows 98

- Many extensive tables explaining the options or alternatives in a given area

- Lavish use of screen, window, and icon illustrations

Windows 98 itself is aimed at giving both Windows 3.x and Windows 95 users an upgrade that carries them forward in a significant and useful way. Included in Windows 98 are

- Complete integration of the Internet or an intranet into the rest of the operating system

- Full use of a 32-bit file system with all of its capability to handle large disks

- Extensive support for the latest hardware innovations, including Accelerated Graphics Port (AGP), Universal Serial Bus (USB), IEEE 1394 (Firewire), and DVD

- Multiple levels of Help that take you from information on your own machine, to a server on your local area network (LAN), and to a Microsoft server over the Internet

- Sophisticated power management that knows to turn off certain devices and not others

- An Active Desktop, the entire surface of which can be used to display a Web page or a movie, or run an ActiveX control

- Networking tools that can be used with the Internet or a LAN to collaborate and share information, exchange e-mail, or create Web pages

- Enhanced multimedia that provides for the reception of broadcast TV as well as streaming audio and video, multiple display support, and more realistic gaming

Conventions Used in This Book

To make this book easier to use, the following conventions are used:

- Words or characters in **boldface** are either part of a heading or are to be typed on your keyboard.

- Words or characters in *italics* are being given special emphasis, are being defined, or are words or characters used as themselves. Also when sections of a chapter are referenced, they are in italics.

- Special keys on the keyboard are shown as bold small caps, for example, **SHIFT** or **ENTER.** If two keys are to be pressed together, they have a line joining them, as in **CTRL-ENTER.**

The Windows 98 Environment

Part 1 introduces you to the Windows 98 environment and to what is new about it. This part establishes the foundation for the rest of the book. It provides an overview of Windows 98 and serves as a guide to the more in-depth discussions that take place in the later chapters.

What's New in Windows 98

Depending on how the Windows 98 screen is set up, you may not initially see a lot of change from the Windows 95 interface. Certainly the changes are not as obvious as those between Windows 3.1 and Windows 95. The screen shown in Figure 1-1 has hyperlink-like icons on the left, the Channel bar on the right, and the Quick Launch toolbar next to the Start button. All of these can easily be turned off, and if you do turn them off, you have a plain-vanilla Windows 95 screen. Contrast this to the Active Channel Viewer screen, shown in Figure 1-2. This screen provides a totally new view that gives you full-screen Web pages to which you can subscribe.

Even though the primary interface has not changed a great deal, Windows 98 introduces a large number of very significant changes. Chapter 1 takes you through them, looking briefly at the major areas of the product and describing the changes that have been made since Windows 95.

What's New—An Overview

First look at a summary of the changes in Windows 98. These will be further described in this chapter and the remaining parts of this book.

Setting Up and Customizing Windows

■ **Simplified Setup** uses existing Windows 95 settings and applet selection, plus an automated reboot to reduce user intervention and time for installing Windows 98.

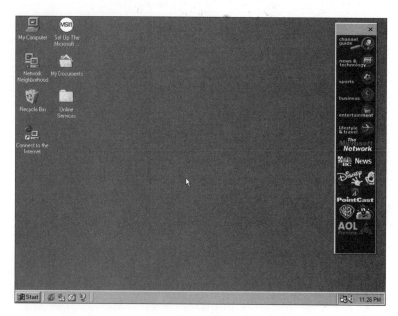

Figure 1-1.   *The default Windows 98 screen.*

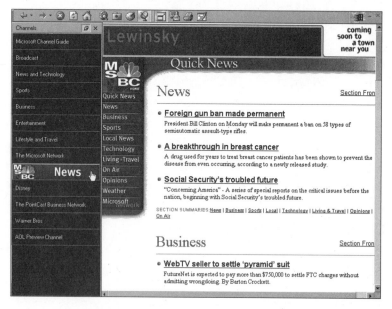

Figure 1-2.   *The Active Channel Viewer screen.*

- **Support for new hardware** provides the ability to use the Universal Serial Bus (USB) for keyboards, mice, and other serial devices; the Institute for Electrical and Electronics Engineers (IEEE) 1394 "Firewire" bus for video cameras, VCRs, and other consumer electronics; DVD, or digital video discs, for large-volume storage; and the Accelerated Graphics Port (AGP) for enhanced video and graphics performance.

- **Advanced Configuration and Power Interface** (ACPI) provides power management for devices and batteries.

- **OnNow technology** eliminates the need to boot your computer every time you want to start it up, as well as providing selective power management. This includes the ability to turn off an individual device, such as a modem, when you are not using it.

- **Win32 Driver Model** allows the creation of a single set of drivers for both Windows 98 and Windows NT.

- **Windows Update** checks for outdated files, and if necessary, gets the latest drivers and operating-system files off the Internet.

- **Windows 98 Help** provides a combination of local-disk, local-network, and Internet-based support tools to improve both the usability and timeliness of the help information that is available to you.

- **System Information utility** provides information similar to the old MSInfo utility but in a Windows Explorer-like window.

- **Year 2000 support** will help solve the many problems older software has with the change in the millennium. This includes "kicking over" the century byte in BIOSes that don't do it automatically and providing a system-wide setting for applications to use for interpreting a two-digit year.

Working with Files, Folders, and Disks

- **FAT32** allows you to have a single disk partition of over 2 TB (2048 GB), provides faster data access, and uses less disk space for files of the same size.

- **Drive Converter (FAT32)** allows you to easily convert a hard disk from 16-bit FAT (sometimes called FAT16) to FAT32.

- **Windows 98 Explorer** displays Internet and intranet Web pages as well as your disk's folders and files and includes a full set of Web navigation tools, as you can see in Figure 1-3.

- **Web-centric file handling** allows pointing at an object to select it and single-clicking to open or load it, icon highlighting, and back/forward arrows.

- **Context-sensitive toolbars** and address lists in Windows Explorer ease disk, network, and Internet navigation.

- **New Backup Utility** supports the latest tape drives and other backup devices.

- **Enhanced taskbar** can contain ActiveX controls within it, such as a stock ticker, as well as multiple toolbars, such as the Quick Launch toolbar.

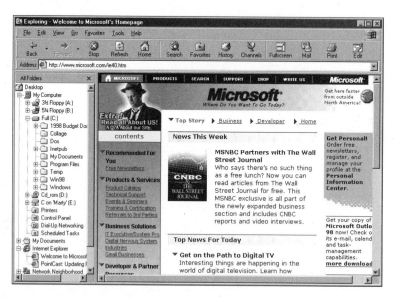

Figure 1-3. *Windows 98 Explorer displaying a Web page.*

- **Maintenance Wizard** schedules the scanning and optimization of your hard disks, as well as other reviews of your system, to make sure your system performs at its best.

- **Disk Defragmenter** notices the three applications that you use most frequently and places the related files physically together (contiguously) on your disk to minimize head movement.

- **Show Desktop,** a new taskbar button, lets you instantly minimize or restore all windows.

- **Start menu reorganization** lets you drag and drop items within the cascading menus.

- **Microsoft IntelliMouse support** allows you to use the mouse wheel to scroll compatible windows, including the Microsoft Internet Explorer, Windows Explorer, and Office 97 and 98 windows.

Using Communications and the Internet

- **Active Desktop** allows ActiveX controls as well as Web content on the desktop, and it includes additional toolbars and Web navigation.

- **Internet Explorer** is integrated with Windows 98 and provides many enhancements over Internet Explorer 3, such as the new search and favorites Explorer bar options, more secure and faster running of Java, and security zones for gauging your risks.

- **Outlook Express** handles e-mail, newsgroups, and collaboration with others.

- **FrontPage Express** helps you create and edit personal Web pages or other Hypertext Markup Language (HTML) documents.

- **NetMeeting** allows you to talk and share video over the Internet or an intranet, and NetShow allows you to listen to and view streaming audio and video.

- **Internet Connection Wizard** makes it easy to set up a connection to the Internet.

- **Updated Windows taskbar,** in addition to its original Windows 95 functions, can contain an Internet address toolbar, as well as other Internet Explorer toolbars, to serve as a frame for Web pages on the desktop.

- **Enhanced Start menu** displays the Favorites list from Internet Explorer (as do Windows Explorer and folder windows) and can take you to Internet search sites or white pages.

- **Desktop Channel bar** allows you to select and display on your desktop Web information to which you have subscribed.

- **Personal Web Server** allows you to distribute Web pages over an intranet or the Internet.

- **Multilink** provides a greater "bandwidth" connection to the Internet by linking multiple modems.

- **ISDN Connection Wizard** makes it easier to configure an Integrated Services Digital Network (ISDN) adapter and connection.

Networking

- **Client support for NetWare Directory Services (NDS)** provides all the features to log on and fully utilize a Novell NetWare 4.x server.

- **Point-to-Point Tunneling Protocol (PPTP)** allows you to create a secure virtual private network over the Internet.

- **Infrared Data Association (IrDA) 3 support** allows wireless networking among devices that have IrDA infrared capability.

- **Dial-up scripting and the Dial-Up Server,** which were part of Microsoft Plus! For Windows 95, are now part of Windows 98 and allow you to connect to and use your computer remotely.

Enjoying Multimedia

- **ActiveMovie** lets you play back streaming audio and video in ActiveMovie format, as well as the most popular multimedia file formats, such as Apple QuickTime, AVI, MPEG, and WAV.

- **Broadcast Architecture technology** allows for the reception of normal broadcast TV, as well as Web pages within the TV broadcast signal. With the addition of a TV tuner board, a PC is capable of receiving Internet content, enhanced TV shows, and other digital content.

- **TV Viewer** uses Broadcast Architecture with either streaming video over the Internet or, if you have a TV tuner board, live WebTV broadcast signals, to display TV on your system. Also, with a TV tuner board and a cable TV connection, you can use Windows 98's WaveTop Data Broadcasting to get Web content and download software and other files without using a telephone line or an ISP.

- **DirectX and Direct3D** allow multimedia applications, especially games, to take full advantage of the multimedia capabilities within your computer, including the new MMX processors, if present.

- **Multiple display support** allows you to spread the desktop over several monitors.

New Feature Details

In the following sections of this chapter, each of the new features is discussed in more detail.

Setting Up and Customizing Windows

Getting your system the way you want it has rightfully been given a high priority in Windows 98.

Running Setup

Running Windows 98 Setup, which is described in Chapter 3, is made much easier with the following new features:

- **A new Setup screen,** shown in Figure 1-4, shows where you are in the process and how much longer Setup will take.

- **Use of existing Windows 95 settings** and applets, if you are installing over Windows 95, saves installation time and user interaction.

■ **Hardware detection,** done after setting up Plug and Play devices, reduces what needs to be set up and the time it takes.

■ **An automated reboot** gives you 15 seconds to decide if you want to reboot. If you don't intervene, it reboots for you, saving you the time and attention.

■ **A Startup Disk** includes real-mode SCSI and IDE CD-ROM drivers that allow you to immediately use a compatible CD-ROM while you are restoring your hard drive.

■ **The ability to back up all system files** allows you to uninstall Windows 98 and restore Windows 95 the way it was previously installed.

Supporting the Latest Hardware

Once you have installed Windows 98, it will handle new and upgraded hardware as you add it. Windows 98 includes support for a number of hardware technologies that are just becoming available. These include the following:

■ **DVD,** the big brother to a CD, can hold a full-length motion picture as well as audio and data storage. It can replace not only data and audio CDs but also videotape, laserdiscs, and game cartridges.

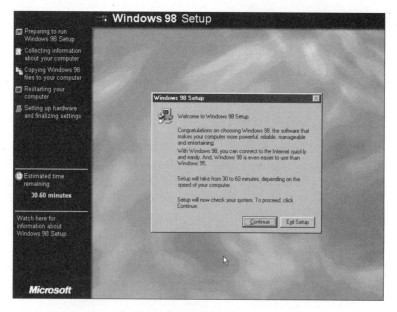

Figure 1-4.   *The new Windows 98 Setup screen.*

■ **Universal Serial Bus (USB)** provides a single, higher-speed port to which keyboards, mice, scanners, video cameras, and other input devices can be connected in a daisy chain. This will reduce the "cable clutter" behind a PC and allow you to attach and remove devices while your system is running.

■ **IEEE 1394 "Firewire"** is a high-speed serial connection for video cameras, VCRs, other consumer electronics, and even other PCs and hand-held devices.

■ **Accelerated Graphics Port (AGP)** implements Intel's specification for 3-D graphics and is utilized by Microsoft DirectDraw and the latest display adapters.

■ **Advanced Configuration and Power Interface (ACPI)** provides a single approach to power management that can be used by both the operating system and applications to turn on standard devices connected to a PC, as well as consumer electronics such as TVs and sound systems.

■ **OnNow technology** uses the ACPI to "put the computer to sleep" when it is not being used and then, almost instantly, "awaken" it when it is needed. It can be triggered not only by an on/off switch but also by the receipt of e-mail or voice mail or some other event.

■ **Advanced Power Management 1.2** handles modem wake-up and multiple batteries, as well as hard disk and PCMCIA Card modem power down.

Maintaining System Software

In addition to handling new hardware, Windows 98 must also handle new and upgraded software drivers and changes in other system software, as described in Chapters 4 and 5. Windows 98 has several new components that address this need directly:

■ **Windows Update** is a Web service, provided by Microsoft, that compares your hardware and system software to a database to determine if there are new system files available for your configuration. If so, you can have Windows download and install the files, and if needed, you can restore the original files later.

■ **Win32 Driver Model,** which allows the use of a single driver in both Windows 98 and Windows NT, and works in concert with legacy device drivers to ensure that a broad range of device-driver options is available.

Providing System Information

Besides improving the way it handles the hardware and software in your system, Windows 98 has, in several ways, improved the help and system information that is available. These improvements include:

■ **Windows 98 Help,** shown in Figure 1-5, is an HTML-based system that not only accesses HTML information on your hard disk but also goes out to the Web for further information from the Microsoft Technical Support home page, the Microsoft Knowledge Base, and Windows System Update on the Web.

■ **System Information utility** provides resource, component, and software-environment information. Included in the resource information are summaries of your DMA, I/O port, IRQ, and upper-memory usage, as shown at the top of the next page, as well as the resources and drivers used by individual components and a summary of the drivers that are in use. Also, the Tools menu provides access to a number of system utilities.

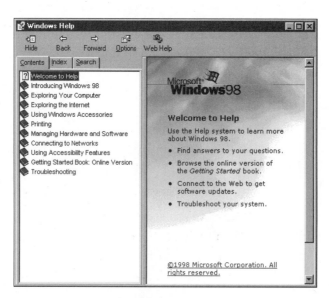

Figure 1-5. *Windows 98 Help providing both local and Web-based help.*

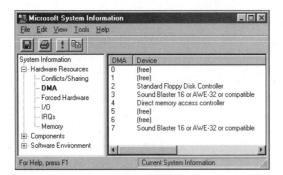

Solving Year 2000 Problems

Windows 98 includes many features to help solve the problems around switching to a new millennium. In addition, Windows 98 has undergone extensive testing to make sure that it does not contribute to the problems. Among the features that help solve Year 2000 problems are:

■ Update BIOSes for the new century if they don't automatically do it themselves. Most BIOSes store a two-digit year and a two-digit century, but many lack the code to update the century when the year goes from "99" to "00." Windows 98 will "kick over" the century the first time it notices the year has changed to "00."

■ If you enter a date in MS-DOS with a two-digit year of "00," MS-DOS in all versions prior to that in Windows 98 would assume that meant "1900." In Windows 98, all two-digit years between "00" and "79" in MS-DOS are assumed to be between "2000" and "2079." (The 1980 cut off was chosen because that is when MS-DOS first appeared.)

■ In the Date tab of the Regional Settings control panel, you can make a system-wide setting that applications can use to determine the two-digit rollover date. The default is 1930–2029. With this setting, applications can look at the year of "18" and know that it is "2018."

Working with Files, Folders, and Disks

The original and basic functions of an operating system, storing and retrieving information, have many enhancements and new features in Windows 98.

Storing Information

The system for storing information on hard disks using a File Allocation Table (FAT) has remained virtually unchanged since the earliest PC hard disks. Windows 95 OSR2 (OEM Service Release 2) changed that by introducing FAT32. Windows 98 is now making available to all Windows users FAT32 and several utilities that improve storing and retrieving information.

- **FAT32** breaks the 2-GB partition limit of FAT by allowing a single disk partition of over 2 TB (2048 GB). In addition, the FAT cluster size has been substantially reduced in FAT32. The only downside to FAT32 is that your older third-party disk utilities must be changed to support it (Windows 98 utilities do).

- **Drive Converter (FAT32)** provides an easy and safe way to convert a FAT hard disk to FAT32. The FAT32 Converter starts out with a series of wizard-like dialog boxes, then it reboots into MS-DOS for the actual conversion process. Finally, after completing the conversion and rebooting again, it runs Disk Defragmenter.

- **Maintenance Wizard** establishes the schedules for running Disk Defragmenter, running ScanDisk, and deleting unnecessary files, such as Internet cache files, from your hard disk, as shown below. The Maintenance Wizard then loads those schedules into the Task Scheduler.

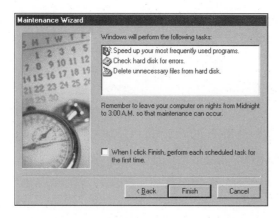

- **Disk Defragmenter** defragments your disk by not only gathering together all of the segments of files but also placing the three applications you use most frequently in the same area on the disk with their data.

- **New Backup Utility** supports the latest tape drives and other backup devices, including many SCSI devices. When you start Backup, the Backup Wizard opens and leads you through the process of determining what you want to backup, where you want to store the backup file, what options you want to use, and what you want to name the backup job. Note that Backup doesn't appear in a Typical install.

Adding Web-Centricity to File Handling

Probably the single biggest change in Windows 98 is Web-like behavior in the file and folder handling tools such as Windows Explorer, My Computer, Network Neighborhood, the Start menu, and the desktop. There are many individual changes, some insignificant and some very significant. Among them are the following:

- **Single-clicking** allows pointing at, or hovering on, a file, folder, application icon, or list entry (an "object") to select it and single-clicking to open or load it. In Windows 98, you can switch to single-clicking, or you can continue to use double-clicking, where you single-click to select an object and double-click to open or load it.

 OTE This book assumes that you are using single-clicking. To turn it on, open the View menu in My Computer, and choose Folder Options. Click Custom and then Settings in the General tab, and choose Single-Click To Open An Item in the bottom group of option buttons.

- **Web navigation tools** include icon highlighting as you point at an object, back/forward arrows with the ability to select from a list of previous locations, address toolbars with drop-down lists of previous addresses or folders, and context-sensitive toolbars for disk, network, and Internet navigation.

■ **Web View** allows any folder to contain and display a Web page along with its files and folders in order to create a custom view for that folder, as shown below for the My Documents folder. To accomplish this, Windows 98 has a Customize This Folder wizard that leads you through the process.

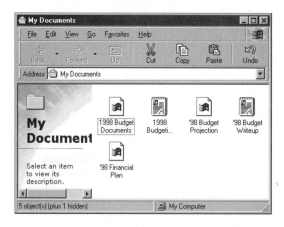

■ **Enhanced taskbar** can contain ActiveX controls, such as a stock ticker, as well as an address or another toolbar, such as the default Quick Launch toolbar. You can customize the new Quick Launch toolbar simply by dragging applications, files, folders, and Web sites to it.

■ **Enhanced Start menu** contains an option to open the new Favorites folder, similar to the option found in Windows 98 Explorer and all folder windows. The new Favorites folder can hold links to files, folders, network resources, and Web sites. The enhanced Start menu also contains an updated Find option that allows you to search for Internet sites and for people on the Internet.

Other Tools

In addition to gee-whiz Web-centricity, Windows 98 adds several other tools that provide excellent, if not equally flashy, benefits. These include the following:

■ **Show Desktop button,** which by default is in the new Quick Launch toolbar within the taskbar, lets you instantly minimize or restore all windows.

- **Microsoft IntelliMouse support** implements the IntelliMouse wheel, which can perform such functions as scrolling, panning, and zooming compatible windows and can act as a third mouse button in other windows.

- **New accessibility features** include the Accessibility Wizard, which assists in implementing various accessibility options to meet your particular needs, and the Microsoft Magnifier, which provides magnification for moderate vision impairment. Note that accessibility options are not part of a Typical install.

Networking

In addition to the well-established cabled systems (both client/server and peer-to-peer), networking is moving into wireless and dial-up systems. Windows 98 reflects this trend by incorporating most of the new networking features in those areas, including the following:

- **Dial-Up Networking enhancements** include incorporating dial-up scripting and the Dial-Up Server, which were a part of Microsoft Plus! Companion for Windows 95. In addition, the Dial-Up Networking user interface has been improved to prompt for information before dialing, to automatically redial if it receives a busy signal, and to show a confirmation dialog box after connecting.

- **Client support for Point-to-Point Tunneling Protocol** (PPTP) provides the client portion of a virtual private network (VPN) over the Internet. This gives you a secure means of remotely attaching to a server through an Internet provider, using IPX/SPX, NetBEUI, or TCP/IP protocols.

- **Infrared Data Association (IrDA) 3 support** supports wireless networking by allowing devices that have IrDA infrared capability, such as laptop computers, printers, and even desktop computers, to communicate without using cables. Windows 98 includes IrLan Access Point mode, which defines an infrared device connected to a network as a network adapter for the remote computer, communicating through the infrared device.

- **Client support for NetWare Directory Services (NDS)** allows you to connect to and use a Novell NetWare 4.x server. NDS supports processing NetWare login scripts, NDS property pages, NDS passwords, and NDS authentication, as well as browsing NDS resources, and printing to NDS print queues.

- **Client support for 32-bit Data Link Control (DLC)** allows you to use an IBM mainframe or an IBM AS/400 computer remotely. The software included in Windows 98 supports both 16-bit and 32-bit DLC. The 32-bit software conforms to Network Driver Interface Specification (NDIS) 3.1; is compatible with Ethernet, Fiber Distributed Data Interface (FDDI), and Token-Ring network adapters; and supports programs that use Controller Command Byte 2 (CCB2) and local printers.

Enjoying Multimedia

Multimedia is moving from being the icing on the cake to being the entire cake. In many areas, it is the primary focus of the work being done on a PC. Windows 98 not only recognizes that, but it is also looking ahead at the multimedia needs just around the corner. Among the new Windows 98 multimedia components are the following:

- **DirectX and Direct3D** are technologies and a set of application programming interfaces (APIs) that allow a programmer to take full advantage of all available resources for multimedia and gaming, including using MMX processors.

- **ActiveMovie** uses DirectShow technology as well as any video and audio acceleration hardware in the system to provide high-performance playback of streaming audio and video from the Internet. ActiveMovie supports files in Apple QuickTime, AVI, MPEG, and WAV multimedia formats, as well as ActiveMovie format.

- **Broadcast Architecture** is the technology that, with a TV tuner board, allows for the reception of a normal TV broadcast signal, as well as Internet and other digital content that may be contained within the broadcast signal.

- **TV Viewer** uses Broadcast Architecture to provide TV viewing on your computer using streaming video over the Internet. With a TV tuner card and Microsoft's WebTV, you can view live broadcast TV. You can access Microsoft's Guide (see Figure 1-6) for current listings, make a selection from these listings, and instantly begin viewing it. You can also use a TV tuner card and a cable-TV connection with WaveTop Data Broadcasting to get Web content and download files and software without using your telephone line and ISP.

- **Multiple display support** allows you to attach multiple monitors and PCI video adapters to a single computer and to spread the Windows desktop image over them. With the desktop spanning two or more monitors, you can drag windows from one monitor to another and better look at several things at the same time. Also, APIs that allow a program to address several monitors separately permit some interesting applications in multimedia development, desktop publishing, and games.

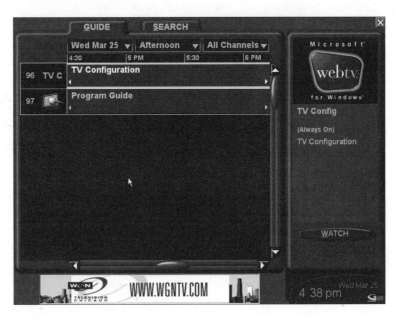

Figure 1-6.   *Accessing Microsoft's Guide for TV listings.*

- **Display settings enhancements** are a group of changes that have been added to the Display Properties dialog box Settings tab. Through the Settings tab and the Advanced Display Properties dialog box, shown in Figure 1-7, you can change the resolution and color depth without rebooting, select monitor settings, and change the hardware acceleration. Windows 98 has also implemented several display enhancements that were previously in Plus! for Windows 95, including full-window drag-and-drop, font smoothing, wallpaper stretching, large icons, and hi-color icons.

Connecting to the Internet

When Windows 95 first came out, using it to connect to the Internet was very difficult, and books devoted many pages to the subject. Plus! for Windows 95 made that process much easier, and Windows 98 continues that evolution with three significant enhancements: the Internet Connection Wizard, the ISDN Connection Wizard, and Multilink Channel Aggregation.

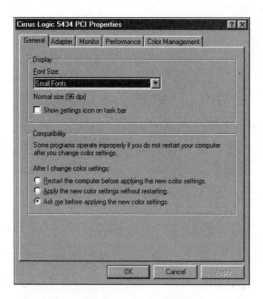

Figure 1-7.   *Display enhancements in the Advanced Display Properties dialog box.*

Internet Connection Wizard

The Internet Connection Wizard (ICW) starts when you click the Connect To The Internet icon. It configures your computer and creates a connection to the Internet using one of three options, as you can see in Figure 1-8.

- **New connection to a new account** allows you to select an Internet Service Provider (ISP) from the Microsoft Referral Service Program and then configures your computer, sets up any necessary custom software, and registers you with the selected ISP.

- **New connection with an existing account** leads you through configuring your computer and accessing existing accounts with ISPs or establishing local area network (LAN) connections to the Internet. This is similar to the Internet Setup Wizard in Plus! for Windows 95.

- **Existing connection with an existing account** identifies an existing Internet connection for use by Internet Explorer and Outlook Express.

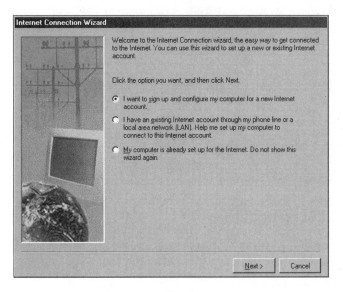

Figure 1-8.   *Internet Connection Wizard options.*

ISDN Connection Wizard

The ISDN Connection Wizard, in conjunction with Multilink Channel Aggregation, allows you to set up the hardware and the controls to manage the multiple channels of an Integrated Services Digital Network (ISDN) adapter and lines. By using one or two channels, you can switch between 64 Kbps and 128 Kbps for transmitting or receiving data without interrupting the transmission.

Multilink Channel Aggregation

Multilink Channel Aggregation allows you to link two or more modems and lines in order to combine their bandwidth for Multilink PPP connections. For example, with two 33.6-Kbps modems you would realize an effective transfer rate of something over 60 Kbps. You can use as many modem/line pairs as you have available, but they must be matched by modem/line pairs on the server, and the server must have implemented Multilink PPP. The modems can be any combination of speeds and types, including combinations of analog and digital devices such as ISDN adapters with conventional modems.

Browsing the Internet or Intranet

Windows 98 provides three ways to display both standard Web sites and those that use "push" technology. (Push sites, if you subscribe to them, send Internet content to you instead of your having to go out on the Internet and get it.) These are

- **Active Desktop,** which allows you to display Web content on your desktop, using your entire screen if you want, similar to what you see in Figure 1-9.

- **Internet Explorer,** which displays Web content in the familiar window format, along with many other Web-related functions, as shown in Figure 1-10.

- **Windows Explorer,** or "Integrated Internet Shell," which displays Web content with folder and file content in the same window, like that shown in Figure 1-11.

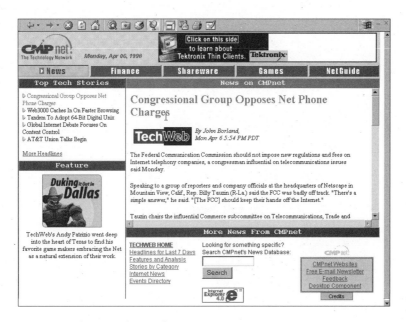

Figure 1-9. *Active Desktop with a Web view.*

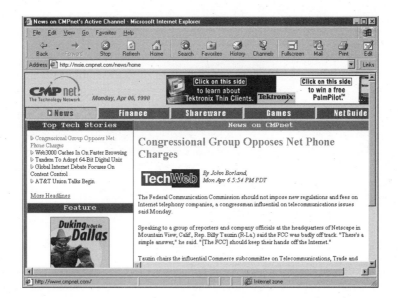

Figure 1-10. *Internet Explorer with a Web view.*

Figure 1-11. *Windows Explorer with a Web view.*

All three ways to view the Web share substantially the same set of tools for using the Internet or an intranet. This makes sense because they are all essentially Internet Explorer displayed in different ways. These tools include the new Explorer bar and other Web-related tools, support for the latest Internet content standards, performance and security enhancements, the ability to subscribe to Internet information, and the use of webcasting and channels.

 OTE   Except for title bars and other superficial elements, there is no difference between the Web components of Windows Explorer, Internet Explorer, and Active Desktop. When we speak of the capabilities of one of them, we speak of them all.

Explorer Bar

In all Web views, an Explorer bar can appear on the left of the window or screen. In the file-and-folder view of Windows Explorer, this bar is the left pane that displays drives and folders. It is called the All Folders bar. In the Web views, this bar can also be any of the following, which you select by clicking the respective toolbar button:

- A **Search bar,** which you can see in Figure 1-12, displays a search provider of the day, such as Yahoo, Lycos, Excite, or NetFind. If you

Figure 1-12. *Search bar.*

want to choose a different search engine, click that option at the top of the Search bar. The Search bar stays open as long as you want, allowing you to immediately look at and select another search "hit" without having to click the Back button.

■ A **Favorites bar,** shown in Figure 1-13, displays the same channels, Web sites, drives, folders, and files as the Favorites menu displays. You can organize this bar, along with the Favorites menu itself, by dragging the listed items to new locations. When a change occurs to a Favorites item, such as when a Web site is updated, a small red dot, called a "gleam," appears in the upper-left corner of the icon.

■ A **History bar,** like the one in Figure 1-14, allows you to go back to Web sites you have visited recently. It is organized into the days of the current week and then by week for last two weeks. Each day contains folders for the various Web sites you visited, and each folder contains an entry for each page you visited within the site.

■ A **Channel bar,** shown with one group open in Figure 1-15, allows you to access Web sites to which you can subscribe. You can display the Channel bar in Internet Explorer, Windows Explorer, or by itself on the desktop. The Channel bar contains both sites to which you

25

are not subscribed, organized into groups, and sites to which you are subscribed, listed individually. If you select a site to which you are not subscribed, you are asked whether you want to subscribe. (Subscription is free as of this writing.) If you subscribe, that site will become an individual entry on the Channel bar.

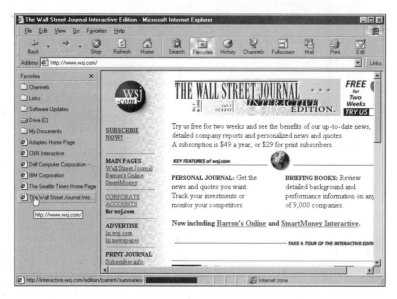

Figure 1-13. *Favorites bar.*

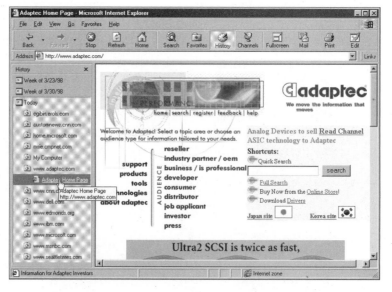

Figure 1-14. *History bar.*

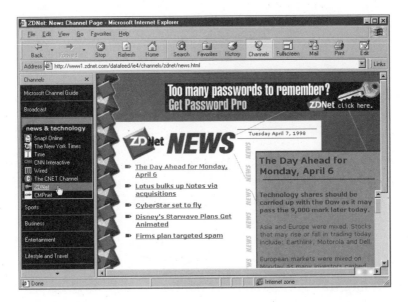

Figure 1-15. *Channel bar.*

Other New Web-Access Features

Microsoft has added a number of other features that either support the concept of making the Web available everywhere or ease the use of the Web. Both of these objectives are aimed at making your use of the Web more productive.

■ **AutoComplete** tries to complete the URL (Uniform Resource Locator or Internet address) you are typing in the Address toolbar. This feature is available in Internet Explorer, Windows Explorer, or the taskbar. If you have used a URL before, then the entry is completed automatically as soon as you have typed enough of it to make it unique. You can also right-click the portion of a URL that has been automatically filled in and get a list of variations of that URL that you have previously visited.

■ **Back and Forward history** displays drop-down lists showing the pages you have looked at, similar to the list shown at the top of the next page. This allows you to jump back to an earlier page, skipping several intermediate pages, or just to use it as a reference of what you have seen. You can access these lists by either right-clicking the Back and Forward buttons or clicking the down arrows next to them.

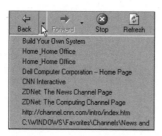

- **Enhanced printing** allows you to choose whether you want to print a selected frame, to print all frames as they are laid out on the screen, or to print all the frames individually, as shown in Figure 1-16. You can also choose to print all documents linked to the current document or to print a table of the links. The actual printing is done in the background, so you can continue browsing.

- **Improved offline support** allows you to better view and work with Web content after disconnecting from the Web. To use this feature, click the File menu's Work Offline option, and then click an entry from the Favorites menu or history list, or enter a URL in the Address toolbar.

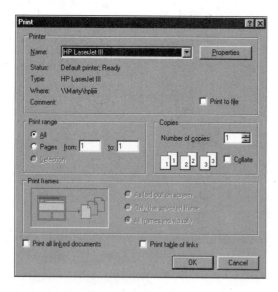

Figure 1-16. *Printing a Web page with choices for printing frames and linked documents.*

- **Start menu and taskbar Web features,** through the Favorites list, Internet site search, and Internet Address toolbar in the taskbar, provide quick ways of getting to a Web site without having to first start Internet Explorer or Windows Explorer. These features, as well as the ability to add Internet Explorer toolbars to the taskbar, support the Active Desktop, as you can see in Figure 1-17.

Support for New Internet Standards

In answer to the demand for more eye-catching, faster, and smaller Web sites, Windows 98 supports the latest in proposed Internet standards.

- **Dynamic HTML** allows you to create HTML (Hypertext Markup Language) pages that dynamically change as the viewer moves the mouse or uses the keyboard *without* the system having to go back to the server for a new page. This means that what you experience is much faster and more responsive.

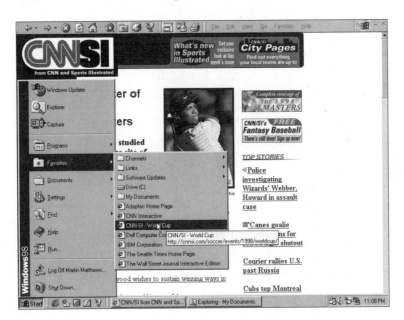

Figure 1-17. *Start menu and taskbar supporting the Active Desktop.*

- **ActiveX support** allows you to use the latest ActiveX enhancements, including VisualBasic scripts and JavaScript code, windowless controls, which operate full screen without a window border, and controls other than rectangles and ovals.

- **Java support** lets you use a full set of Java development tools and just-in-time Java compiler, so downloads are faster, and only newer class libraries are installed.

- **HTTP 1.1 support** is up to 100 percent faster than HTTP (Hypertext Transfer Protocol) 1.0 by using data compression, not resending HTTP headers, giving proxy servers better control of caching, and better supporting dynamically generated Web pages.

- **Authenticode** allows a user to irrefutably identify the publisher of a piece of software that is being downloaded and to verify that the software has not been changed by unauthorized users. Windows 98 also has the ability to verify online whether an authentication has been revoked.

- **CryptoAPI 1.0** provides the programming links developers need to build security services into their applications, including secure channels, code signing, and cryptography.

- **Microsoft Wallet** provides a secure, easily accessible place to store electronic equivalents of such things as ATM or debit cards, credit cards, driver's licenses, and cash.

- **Secure channel services** allow channel providers to utilize standard security protocols to deliver secure data.

- **Security zones** allow you to designate intranet and Internet sites as being safe or not safe and then to enable or disable their ability to download and run, for example, ActiveX controls and Java applets, based on that designation.

Subscriptions and Channels

Subscriptions schedule the delivery of information that is custom tailored to you. This saves you from having to repeatedly go to a series of Web sites to get the information you want. The information is delivered based upon your selecting schedule, notification, and delivery options, and it is then available for offline reading. Setting up and using subscriptions is as easy as opening the Favorites menu, selecting Add To Favorites, and clicking the type of subscription you want, as shown here:

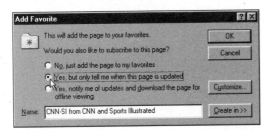

Windows 98 includes a new *webcasting* client, which automates the delivery of information that has been customized for the recipient. Webcasting handles subscriptions, as described above, as well as "true" webcasting and channels. *Channels* allow such vendors as MSNBC and PointCast to deliver push content. Channels are set apart from other subscribed sites by their use of Channel Definition Format (CDF) files, which define the Web pages, graphics, and active controls in a channel. "True" webcasting provides for the real-time delivery of Web content broadcast over an intranet or the Internet.

Internet Tools

Windows 98 provides a complete suite of tools to make the fullest use of both the Internet and an intranet. These include FrontPage Express for creating Web pages, NetMeeting for holding audio and videoconferences over the Internet or an intranet, NetShow for listening to and viewing streaming audio and video, Outlook Express for reading e-mail and newsgroups, and Personal Web Server for distributing Web pages that you create.

FrontPage Express

FrontPage Express allows you to create and edit Web pages and other HTML documents, such as pages that describe the contents of folders and give links to open files. FrontPage Express, which you can see in Figure 1-18, is based on Microsoft FrontPage and provides

- An easy-to-use WYSIWYG ("what you see is what you get") environment

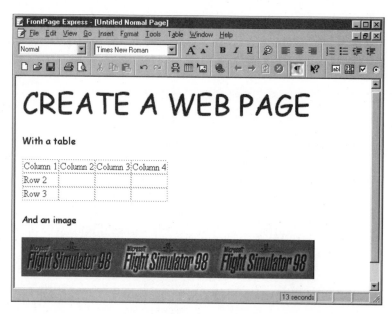

Figure 1-18. *FrontPage Express window for creating Web pages and HTML documents.*

■ The ability to easily add styles, fonts, alignment, bullets, numbering, and indentation

■ Extensive and easy table creation and formatting

■ The ability to load your new Web page directly onto the Web or to edit existing pages on the Web

■ Support for adding ActiveX controls, Visual Basic Script, JavaScript, and Java applets directly on a Web page

■ A Personal Home Page Wizard to lead you, step by step, through the process of creating your own home page

■ The ability to easily add search forms, time stamps, and include components (which allow you to place the same element on multiple pages) on a Web page

■ Form fields, where the users of the Web page you are creating can send information to you if you use a Web server that has the FrontPage Server Extensions installed

NetMeeting

NetMeeting is a full-featured audio- and videoconferencing and collaboration application. With the appropriate hardware, it provides real-time audio, video, and data communication over the Internet, an intranet, or a direct telephone connection. NetMeeting is based on and uses the broadly accepted International Telecommunications Union (ITU) standards T.120 and H.323, which allow it to work with many different types of systems and pieces of hardware. With NetMeeting, which is shown in Figure 1-19, you can

- Hold an audioconference between two or more sites using true multipoint conferencing (T.120) if you have a sound card, speakers, a microphone, and a modem that can transfer at least 28.8 Kbps

- Hold a videoconference between two or more sites if you have a video-capture card or a parallel port connection and video camera

- Share a Windows application that is running on your computer with others in a conference

- Draw and write on an electronic whiteboard, which is a collaborative drawing program

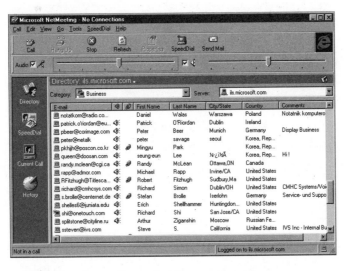

Figure 1-19. *NetMeeting for audio and video conferencing.*

- Transfer files among one or more of the conference participants using binary file transfer

- Use a text-based chat application during a conference to take notes or to have a private side conversation with another individual

NetMeeting also provides many other refinements, including high-quality audio, full-duplex support, automatic voice activation, audio muting, support for Intel MMX technology, and the ability to dedicate and then switch the audio and video among the participants.

NetShow

NetShow provides a means to easily incorporate audio and video clips as well as illustrated audio (audio synchronized with still images) in a Web site without requiring you to download large files before seeing and/or hearing the information. NetShow uses the Active Streaming Format (ASF) to transmit and display, complete with error detection and correction, a continuous stream of pictures and sound. Internet Explorer can play streamed ASF files within its window, as you can see in Figure 1-20 (in the little window on the left), in Windows Explorer, or on the desktop. Windows 98 also includes the NetShow Player, for directly playing ASF files. NetShow's playing capability can also be embedded in Netscape Navigator and custom applications. You can also purchase NetShow Server, which is a part of the Site Server on Windows NT Server 4, and a set of NetShow tools for managing NetShow content and converting existing multimedia content.

NetShow supports two different streaming techniques: multicast and unicast. Multicast is like broadcast radio and TV. A single stream is sent out at a particular time. You can connect to the server sending out the stream at the start time and see or hear the entire program, but if you connect after the start, you see or hear only the remaining material. Multicast does *not* allow for fast-forward or rewind. Unicast is like normal Web-page access in that a new copy is sent out each time someone connects and requests it. As a result, you have full control of unicast transmission: you can pause it, restart it, or skip ahead in its stream. On the negative side, unicast takes up as much network bandwidth for each transmission as multicast takes for all of its transmissions.

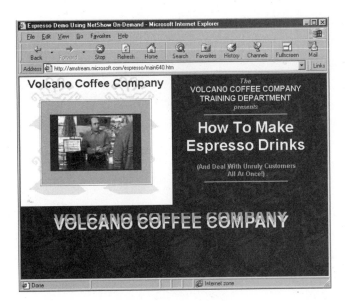

Figure 1-20. *Internet Explorer displaying a NetShow streaming video.*

Outlook Express

Outlook Express provides most of the Internet/intranet messaging capabilities of Microsoft Outlook 97. In addition, Outlook Express provides for full participation in newsgroups, as well as other enhancements over Outlook. The parts of Outlook not in Outlook Express are the nonmessaging components, including Calendar, Contacts, Tasks, Journal, and Notes. Outlook Express, which is shown in Figure 1-21, includes the following:

- Ease of use through the Outlook bar in accessing mail folders and modules; easier access to particular tasks with the Outlook Express start page; and customizable toolbars that give you the buttons, sizes, and positions that are right for you

- Ease of message creation through as many as 150 levels of undo and redo for easier changes, storage of incomplete messages in a Drafts folder to keep them visible, and a top-of-the-line spelling checker that shares custom dictionaries with Microsoft Office and Microsoft Works

- Ease of message management through multiple e-mail accounts and newsgroups, the ability to set up a hierarchical file structure and drag messages within it, a Find Message command to search for a

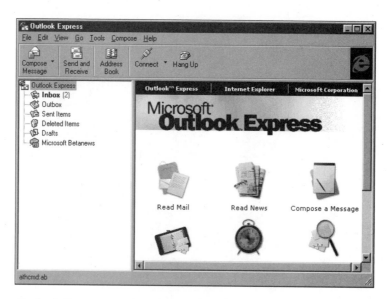

Figure 1-21. *Outlook Express mail and news client.*

particular message, and the ability to read and create e-mail and newsgroup messages offline

- Real integration with Internet Explorer through a user interface that is consistent with the other members of the Internet Explorer suite, the sharing of code for efficiency and consistency, and single-click access within the suite

- Ability to view, edit, send, and receive full HTML Web pages in an e-mail message (You just click Mail while viewing a Web page in Internet Explorer, and a mail message is created, lacking only a recipient's address.)

- Support for the latest messaging standards such as Secure Multipurpose Internet Mail Extensions (S/MIME) for encrypted and digitally signed messages, use of IMAP4 (Internet Message Access Protocol 4) servers to provide access to mail from any computer connected to the server, and LDAP (Lightweight Directory Access Protocol) directory service to link to Internet white pages to look up addresses

Personal Web Server

Microsoft Personal Web Server (PWS) allows you to distribute your Web pages over an intranet on a LAN or even over the Internet. PWS is based on the Microsoft Internet Information Server (IIS), which is bundled with Windows NT Server 4, and has most of IIS's functionality. PWS transmits HTML pages requested by a browser using HTTP. PWS can also be used as an FTP (File Transfer Protocol) server to send and receive files over the Internet or an intranet and can execute ISAPI and CGI scripts. PWS has a manager, shown in Figure 1-22, and also contains the following features:

 OTE The Microsoft Personal Web Server is not installed during Windows Setup. (The Personal Web Server option in Programs | Internet Explorer simply gives you the following information on how to install it.) It is on the Windows CD in the \Add-ons\Pws\ folder. If you open that folder on your CD and click Setup.exe, you install PWS. After installation, you find PWS on the Start | Programs menu.

- PWS can work with ODBC (open database connectivity) and ODBC32 data sources or databases and can pass through data requests and the resulting data using HTTP links to ODBC and ODBC32.

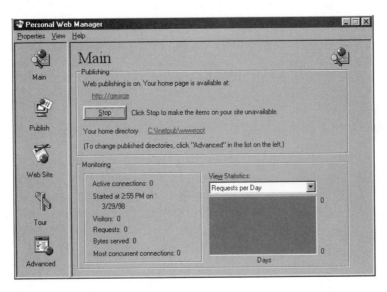

Figure 1-22. *Personal Web Server Manager.*

■ You can remotely manage PWS over the Internet or an intranet from any client using an ordinary browser, such as Microsoft Internet Explorer or Netscape Navigator.

■ PWS supports both share-level and user-level security. If you are connected to a Windows NT or a NetWare server, then you can use user-level security to create a list of user names to whom you want to allow access to PWS. This list of names is passed to the Windows NT or NetWare server, where they must also be on the accepted user list. If you are using a Windows 95 or Windows 98 based peer-to-peer network, then you are limited to share-level security. This means you can identify drives and folders to share, requiring a password for access or not, but you cannot have a specific list of allowable users.

Most of the new features in Windows 98 that have been introduced in this chapter are described in more detail in the remainder of the book. Chapter 2 describes the basic features of Windows 98. Many of them have been carried forward from Windows 95, but even here there are many new elements and enhancements. At first glance, Windows 98 does not look much different than Windows 95, but you don't have to go far to find a lot of significant change.

Windows 98 Basics

In Chapter 1, you saw many new features in Windows 98. For the most part, these are major additions to the system, such as tighter integration with the Internet. There are, of course, other components of the system whose features have been carried forward, largely intact, from Windows 95. Even these components have new elements and capabilities. This chapter will serve as an introduction to these veteran components, looking at both what is new and what has been carried forward from Windows 95. It will also serve as a way for those readers who are not as familiar with Windows 95 to acquire that foundation knowledge.

The Windows 98 Screen

The Windows 98 screen that you see in Figure 2-1 has only two primary components: the desktop, which covers the majority of the screen, and the taskbar, which is, by default, at the bottom of the screen.

The Desktop

The *desktop* is an area on which you can place items that you are working on or that await your attention. Normally, these items—such as programs that you are using or folders that you are looking at—are contained in windows. The desktop, though, can also contain icons, as well as dialog

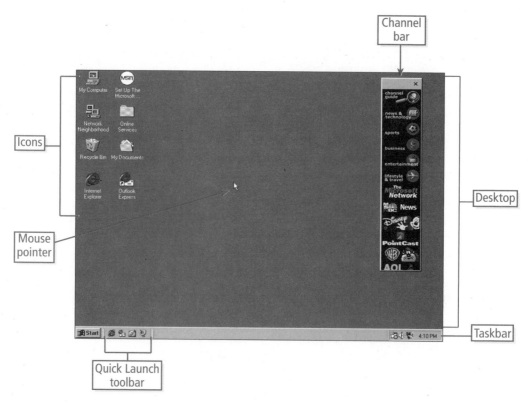

Figure 2-1.   *The Windows 98 screen.*

boxes, the mouse pointer, the Channel bar, Web pages, and toolbars, as more fully described here:

- **Icons,** such as those on the left or on the bottom of Figure 2-1, are small graphic objects that represent folders, programs, or files waiting to be used; programs running in the background; or some event that has occurred.

- **Windows** are areas of the screen with borders around them that contain the programs or folders that you are currently using. Windows also normally have menus and can be resized.

- **Dialog boxes** are areas of the screen with borders around them that contain messages to you or ask you to supply information. You cannot resize dialog boxes, and they normally do not have menus.

- The **mouse pointer** shows where the mouse is currently pointing.

- The **Channel bar** lists Web sites to which you can subscribe and display on your desktop.

- **Web pages** can use the entire screen in their display, as you saw in Chapter 1, and contain content from the Internet or an intranet.

- **Toolbars** contain buttons that you can click to launch a program, open a folder, start a process, or select a choice.

 OTE   Toolbar buttons in Windows 98 do not have borders around them. They resemble icons unless you move your mouse pointer over them.

Objects on the desktop can be moved, opened, closed, or deleted. Further discussion of the objects on the desktop and how you can handle them is provided later in this chapter and in Chapters 3, 4, and 6.

 OTE   A few icons on the desktop, such as My Computer and Network Neighborhood, cannot be easily deleted. If you really do want to delete these items, see Chapter 4.

The Taskbar

The taskbar at the bottom of the screen is the primary device for controlling Windows 98. With it, you can start a program, switch among programs already running, open Control Panel (where you can set options for many different functions), find a file, get help, shut down Windows, run MS-DOS commands, add or remove printers, and tell the current time. In addition to the Start button on the left and the clock on the right, the taskbar displays tasks—programs that are currently loaded or open file folders. The taskbar can contain toolbars, such as the Quick Launch toolbar and the Address toolbar, which you saw in Chapter 1. Also, the area containing the clock, called the *notification area,* can expand to include icons that tell you that there is information waiting to be printed or newly received e-mail, that an accessibility feature is turned on, or that a particular application is running in the background. A more fully utilized taskbar is shown here:

The tasks shown on the taskbar expand or contract to fill the space, depending on how many tasks there are. If the tasks become too small, you can expand the taskbar to make them readable. Also, if you move the mouse pointer to a task, the full task name is displayed. As you will see in this chapter, the taskbar is quite flexible. You can move it to any of the four sides of the screen, hide it, or allow it to be covered by a window.

The Start Button

The Start button opens the Start menu, which provides much of the functionality of the taskbar. The Start menu, by default, has nine *options,* or choices, from which you can select (you may also have additional items at the top of the menu). The default options and their purposes are as follows:

- **Programs** allows you to start a program.

- **Favorites** allows you to open a favorite Web site, folder, file, or disk drive.

- **Documents** allows you to open a document that you recently accessed and, in so doing, start its associated program.

- **Settings** allows you to open the Control Panel folder and other objects where you can change the settings for many Windows features.

- **Find** allows you to search for a file or folder on your computer, a computer on your network, a site on the Internet, or a person's e-mail address.

- **Help** opens the Windows Help system, where you can review topics from a table of contents, look up a word in the index, or search for words or phrases used in Help topics.

- **Run** allows you to enter the path and filename of a program, file, or folder to open or an MS-DOS command to run.

- **Log Off** allows you to log off the computer so another person, possibly with different settings, can log on. If you sign on with a password, logging off also limits access to the network until you or someone else signs on with an acceptable password.

- **Shut Down** prepares your computer to be turned off or restarted.

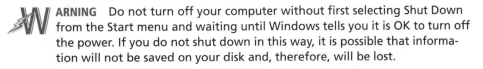

WARNING Do not turn off your computer without first selecting Shut Down from the Start menu and waiting until Windows tells you it is OK to turn off the power. If you do not shut down in this way, it is possible that information will not be saved on your disk and, therefore, will be lost.

The first five menu options have arrowheads on the right. This means that if you point at one of those options, a second menu (a submenu) will open. As Figure 2-2 shows, the Programs option can have many levels of submenus. The last three Start menu options have ellipses, or a series of three dots, after them. This means that a dialog box will open if you select one of those options. For example, if you select Run, a dialog box, like this one, opens asking you to enter the command you want to run.

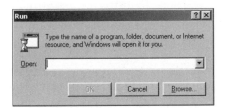

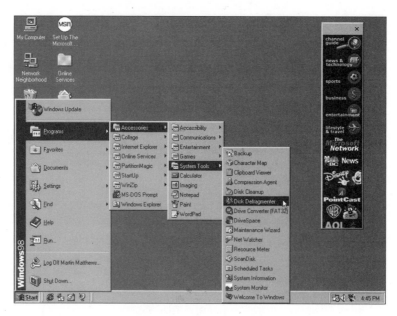

Figure 2-2.   *The Programs option with several submenus.*

Windows and Dialog Boxes

Much of what you see on the desktop appears in windows or dialog boxes. They are the containers for all that you do within the Windows interface. Dialog boxes and windows are the same in that they both define areas of the screen with borders around them, and they both present information with which you can do something. Their dissimilarities, though, are significant. Dialog boxes are a fixed size, do not have menus, and are used for getting information to or from you. Windows, on the other hand, can be resized, generally have menus, and contain programs, data files, or folders with other folders and/or files in them.

Parts of a Window

Most windows have a common set of features and controls similar to those shown in Figure 2-3. This *folder window* represents an open folder showing files and other folders within it, as you might expect. Not all folder windows have this content. Microsoft Office, Control Panel, Network Neighborhood, and My Computer are all folder windows because they share common menus and sets of toolbars, as you can see in Figure 2-4.

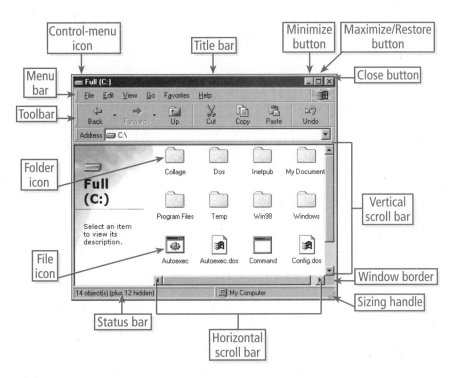

Figure 2-3. *Normal folder window.*

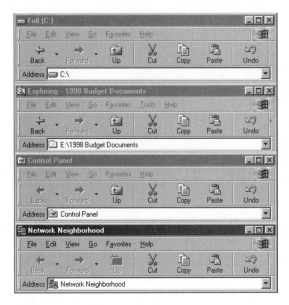

Figure 2-4. *Variety of folder windows.*

The majority of windows within Windows 98 are folder windows. There-fore, when you see the term *folder window,* we are talking about a class of windows with a common set of features. These features, some of which are in all windows, and their purposes are as follows:

 OTE   Throughout this and other chapters, folder windows are generally shown in Web style. In the Folder Options dialog box, you may choose this style, the classic style of Windows 95, or a custom style that combines elements of both. The choice of style is independent of the single/double-click choice.

- The **title bar** contains the name of the program or folder in the window. You can also drag it to move the window or double-click it to toggle the window between its maximum size and its size before being maximized.

- The **Control-menu icon** opens the Control menu, from which you can move, size, and close the window.

- The **menu bar** contains the menus that are available in the window.

- The **toolbar** contains buttons that, when clicked, perform some function on either the window or its contents.

- The **folder icon** represents a folder, which can contain other folders or files.

- The **file icon** represents a program or data file.

- The **horizontal scroll bar** contains a scroll box and arrows that you can use to move the contents of the window horizontally and see more of the window's contents.

- The **status bar** provides messages about what is displayed or selected in the window.

- The **sizing handle** allows sizing of the window in two dimensions.

- The **vertical scroll bar** contains a scroll box and arrows that you can use to move the contents of the window vertically and see more of the window's contents.

- The **window border** separates the window from the desktop and is used to size the window in one dimension by using a side border, or in two dimensions by using a corner.

- The **Close button** closes the window.

- The **Maximize/Restore button** expands the window to fill the desktop or shrinks it to its size prior to being maximized.

- The **Minimize button** hides the window so you see only the title on the taskbar.

Not all windows have all of these features, and some of them are optional. For example, in the folder window shown in Figure 2-3, you can turn the toolbar and status bar on or off.

Parts of a Dialog Box

Dialog boxes are not as standard as windows are. All dialog boxes, though, use a common set of controls, which are shown in Figures 2-5, 2-6, and 2-7. These controls and their purposes are as follows:

- The **title bar** contains the name of the dialog box and is also used to move it.

- **Tabs** allow you to select among several pages in a dialog box.

- **Option buttons** allow you to select one among mutually exclusive options.

- **List boxes** allow you to choose one or more items from lists, which may have scroll bars to move the lists so you can view additional items.

- **Check boxes** allow you to turn features on or off.

- **Command buttons** perform immediate functions, such as accepting the changes made in the dialog box and closing it (as the OK button does) or ignoring any changes in the dialog box and closing it (as the Cancel button does).

- **Drop-down list boxes** open lists of items from which you can choose. The item you chose remains visible when the list is closed.

- **Sliders** allow you to select values from sets of values.

- **Spinners** allow you to raise and lower values.

- **Text boxes** allow you to enter and edit text, including numbers.

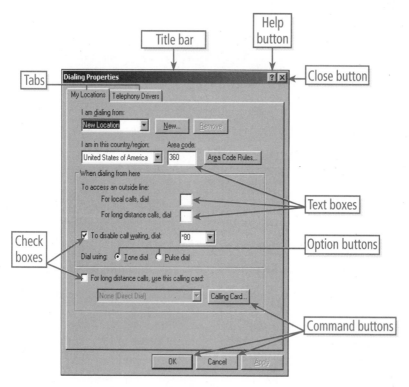

Figure 2-5. *Dialing Properties dialog box.*

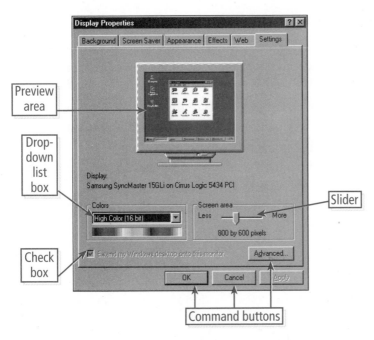

Preview area

Drop-down list box

Slider

Check box

Command buttons

Figure 2-6. *Display Properties dialog box.*

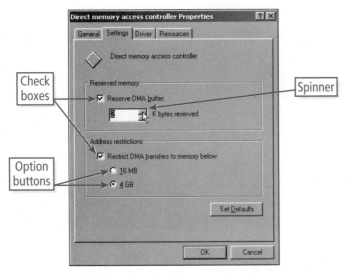

Check boxes

Spinner

Option buttons

Figure 2-7. *System Settings dialog box.*

The Mouse and the Keyboard

The parts of Windows 98 described so far represent how Windows presents information to you—how it communicates from the computer to you. The mouse and the keyboard provide the other half of the equation—how you communicate back to the computer. The mouse and the keyboard allow you to enter data as well as to control what the computer does with that data. Much of what you see on the screen, especially the controls in windows and dialog boxes, was created with the mouse in mind, but you also can use almost all of them with the keyboard.

Using the Mouse

The *mouse* is used to move the mouse pointer on the screen and to indicate a choice by pressing a button. There are a number of alternative pointing devices, including trackballs; touch pads; pointing sticks; graphic tablets, with one, two, three, or more buttons; or the new Microsoft IntelliMouse, with two buttons and a wheel. The most common, though, is a two-button mouse similar to the Microsoft Mouse, and that is what is assumed in this book. As you will see, Windows 98 requires at least two buttons to make the best use of all of its features.

You can use the mouse with either your left or right hand, and you may switch the functions of the left and right buttons to facilitate this. (Switching the functions of the buttons is done in the Mouse control panel, which you display by opening the Start menu and choosing Settings | Control Panel | Mouse—see also Chapter 4.) Typically, the right hand controls the mouse, and the left mouse button is the primary one. The left mouse button is, therefore, called the "mouse button." The right button is always called the "right mouse button." If you switch the meaning of the buttons, you will have to mentally change how you interpret these phrases.

There is also standard terminology for using the mouse. These terms and how they are used in this book and in most other sources are as follows:

- **Point at** means to move the mouse until the tip of the mouse pointer covers the object you want to select.

- **Click** means to point at an object you want to select and then quickly press and release the mouse button. This is sometimes called "single-clicking" to differentiate it from "double-clicking."

- **Right-click** means to point at an object you want to select and then quickly press and release the right mouse button.

- **Double-click** means to point at an object you want to select and then quickly press and release the mouse button twice in rapid succession.

- **Drag** means to point at an object you want to move and then press and hold the mouse button down while moving the mouse. When you get the object where you want it, release the mouse button. You can use the same technique to drag a rectangle (shown as a dotted line) around a group of objects to select them.

As you read in Chapter 1, you can choose to start a program or open a folder in Windows 98 by single-clicking or double-clicking. With single-clicking, you select an object by simply pointing at it. With double-clicking, you must click an object once to select it. When an object is selected, the object becomes *highlighted* to indicate its selection. In the following example, the My Computer icon is highlighted, whereas the Network Neighborhood icon is not.

 OTE This book assumes that you have chosen single-clicking as your method of starting programs and opening folders.

You also click to open the Start menu or select a task on the taskbar. You operate most of the controls in a window or a dialog box by simply clicking them. For example, you click tabs, option buttons, check boxes, list boxes, drop-down list boxes, sliders, spinners, scroll bars, command buttons, and the Close, Maximize, and Minimize buttons to operate them. To activate a text box, you click in it, and then enter the desired text. You drag scroll boxes and sliders. Finally, you open some of the icons on the right of the taskbar (next to the clock) by clicking or double-clicking them (even with single-clicking turned on).

Like the Start menu, all menus are opened by clicking. Once a menu is open, you select an option by clicking it. Also, while a menu is open, you can close it and open another menu by simply moving the mouse pointer to the new menu; you don't have to click until the option you want is highlighted. To open a submenu, you need only to move the mouse pointer to the submenu option. Here are other tasks that you can perform with the mouse (assuming single-clicking is enabled):

- **Start a program** by clicking its icon
- **Open a document** and start its associated program by clicking its icon
- **Open a folder** by clicking its icon
- **Select text** by dragging across it
- **Move a window** by dragging its title bar
- **Size a window** by dragging one of its sides or corners
- **Select multiple items** on the desktop or in a window or dialog-box list by dragging a rectangle, or *selection box,* around them
- **Select multiple items** in a list by holding down **CTRL** while pointing—called *Ctrl-point*
- **Select contiguous items** in a list by holding down **SHIFT** while pointing—called *Shift-point*

Using the Right Mouse Button

Prior to Windows 95, the right mouse button had very little use. Now, however, the right mouse button will open a specific *context menu* for each object you right-click. For example, right-clicking the taskbar opens the taskbar context menu shown at the top of the next page.

Almost every object on the desktop has its own context menu, as does the desktop itself. (The context menus for the desktop and for a folder are shown below.) Notice that every context menu has a Properties option. This opens a Properties dialog box, which allows you to set options for the object that you right-clicked. Figure 2-6 shows the Properties dialog box for the desktop.

 OTE Two options shown in the Folder context menu above, Add To Zip and Add To Online Services.zip, are not part of Windows 98. They are part of WinZip, a shareware program.

You can also drag an object with the right mouse button, and when you do, you will get a context menu that asks you how to interpret the drag. For example, if you drag a file from one place to another with the right mouse button, you get the context menu below, which asks what you want to do. (This operation is further discussed in Chapter 6.)

Using the Keyboard

Even though Windows 98 is designed to be used with the mouse, you can do almost everything with the keyboard. While a lot of keyboard operations are not as efficient as using the mouse, *keyboard shortcuts* (keystrokes that perform a particular function or command) are often faster than using the mouse. The shortcuts that are available in Windows 98 itself are shown in Table 2-1. Many of the Windows 98 accessories and most programs have their own sets of shortcuts, although those for Cut, Copy, and Paste are often the same from program to program. Of the shortcuts shown here, three are of particular importance: **ALT-ESC**, which allows you to switch among the programs and folders that are shown on the taskbar; **ALT-TAB**, which also allows you to switch among folders and programs on the taskbar, but does so through a dialog box and restores the folder's or program's window if it is minimized; and **CTRL-ESC**, which opens the Start menu.

Keystroke	Purpose
ALT-ENTER	Switches the active MS-DOS program between taking up the full screen and appearing in a window
ALT-ESC	Switches among the folders and the programs on the taskbar
ALT-F4	Closes the active window
ALT-PRINT SCREEN	Captures the image of the active window and places it on the Clipboard
ALT-SPACEBAR	Opens the Control menu for the active window or selected taskbar object; same as clicking the button on the far left of the active window's title bar or right-clicking a program or folder on the taskbar
ALT-TAB	Switches among programs and folders on the taskbar, using the Task Switcher dialog box
ALT-SHIFT-TAB	Switches among programs and folders on the taskbar, again using the Task Switcher dialog box but reversing the order used by **ALT-TAB**
Arrow keys	Moves the cursor in the direction of the arrow
BACKSPACE	Activates the parent folder of the active window

Table 2-1.   *Keyboard shortcuts available in Windows 98.*   *(continued)*

Table 2-1. *continued*

Keystroke	Purpose
CTRL-A	Selects all the objects in a window
CTRL-C	Copies selected objects to the Clipboard
CTRL-V	Pastes the contents of the Clipboard at the current insertion point or into the selected folder
CTRL-X	Cuts (removes) the selected objects and places them on the Clipboard
CTRL-Z	Undoes the last copy, move, delete, paste, or rename operation you performed
CTRL-ESC	Opens the Start menu
DELETE	Places the selected object in the Recycle Bin if the bin is activated; otherwise, permanently deletes the object
ENTER	Activates the selected object or menu option in the way that clicking or double-clicking would; also closes the active dialog box, implementing any changes that were made
END	Selects the last object
ESC	Closes the active menu or dialog box without making a selection
F1	Opens Windows Help
F2	Allows you to edit the name of the selected folder or file
F4	Opens the drop-down list in the Address toolbar of a folder window
F5	Refreshes the active window with the most recent information
F6 or **TAB**	Moves the selection among major areas within a window, a dialog box, or on the desktop
F10 or **ALT**	Activates the menu bar on the active window
HOME	Selects the first object
Any letter key	Selects the first object beginning with that letter
PRINT SCREEN	Captures the current image on the screen and places it on the Clipboard
SHIFT-DELETE	Deletes the selected object *without* placing it in the Recycle Bin
SHIFT-F10	Opens the context menu for the selected object (same as right-clicking on the object)

OTE *Tasks* are *loaded* programs or *open* folders. Only one task can be *active* at a time, and it will be the window on the desktop with the highlighted title bar. *Inactive* tasks may be minimized on the taskbar or a window on the desktop without a highlighted title bar. Windows, dialog boxes, and icons can be active, meaning that they are highlighted or have a highlighted title bar, and the *focus* is on them. Also, windows and dialog boxes may be open on the desktop without necessarily being active.

If you have two or more tasks that you have opened or loaded, when you press **ALT-TAB**, the Task Switcher dialog box opens, as shown below, and you can switch among tasks by holding down **ALT** while continuing to press **TAB**. If you have only one task running and it is active, then nothing happens when you press **ALT-TAB**. If you have only one task running but it is minimized on the taskbar, then **ALT-TAB** makes that task active on the desktop.

  OTE Neither **ALT-ESC** nor **ALT-TAB** takes you to the desktop. You must resize or minimize any windows that are on the desktop in order to see and thereby work on the desktop. Clicking the Show Desktop button on the Quick Launch toolbar minimizes all open windows, and clicking it again re-stores all windows. You also can use Minimize All Windows in the taskbar context menu to get to the desktop and Undo Minimize All to restore the windows you had open.

Not all of these keyboard shortcuts are available under all circumstances. You can't use **F2**, for example, on the Recycle Bin. The best way to become familiar with the keyboard is to try out the effects of various keyboard shortcuts for yourself.

Using Windows 98

To use Windows 98, you need only know how to click the Start button. The Start button opens the Start menu, from which you can start any program that has been installed in Windows 98; change the settings or defaults on most features in Windows 98; find a file, a Web site, a computer on your network, or a person on the Internet; get help; or shut down Windows. And if that isn't enough, you have the Run command, which lets you run any MS-DOS program or command. That is a lot of functionality to be gathered in one place. There are, of course, many other facets of Windows 98. The next few paragraphs introduce you to some of the other things that you can do.

Accessing Information

Along with the icons that initially may appear on your desktop, My Computer, Network Neighborhood, Recycle Bin, and My Documents provide access to the information that is stored on your computer or on other computers in your network. If you are not connected to a network, you will not have Network Neighborhood. (You may also have icons for Internet Explorer, Outlook Express, My Briefcase, Online Services, and Set Up The Microsoft Network. They will be discussed in later chapters.)

My Computer

My Computer provides access to the disk drives that are installed or defined on your computer, as shown in Figure 2-8. This includes floppy-disk drives, hard-disk drives, and CD-ROM drives that are physically attached to your computer (drives A, B, C, and D in Figure 2-8). It also includes drives physically attached to other computers on your network that have been *mapped* to drive letters on your computer. The icons for these drives are shown with a cable beneath them (drives E and F in Figure 2-8). You may have other connections, including shared folders on a server. Additionally, the My Computer window contains folders for Printers, Control Panel, Dial-Up Networking, and Scheduled Tasks. Control Panel and Printers are the same as the options with those names in the Settings option on the Start menu. Chapter 4 discusses Control Panel; Chapter 7, Printers; Chapter 12, Dial-Up Networking; and Chapter 5, Scheduled Tasks.

When you click a disk drive in the My Computer window, a new window opens and displays the files and folders that are on that disk drive. You can then click a folder to open it. If the folder you clicked contains another folder, you can keep opening folders until the final folder contains only a file or files, as shown in Figure 2-9. (You can choose to see separate windows or a single window whose contents change, as you will learn later in this chapter.) *Folders,* then, replace directories in MS-DOS and versions of Windows before Windows 95. Folders can contain files and other folders, as well as electronic mail (e-mail) and other objects. Folders are the primary containers in Windows 98.

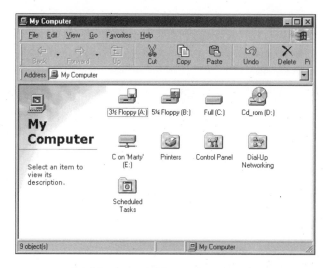

Figure 2-8.   *Drives and folders available on My Computer.*

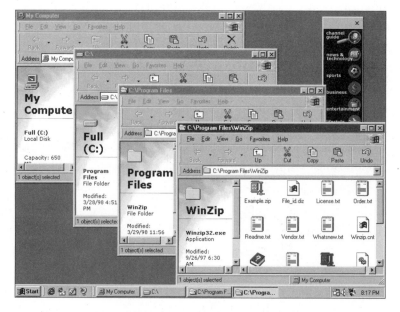

Figure 2-9.   *Opening a series of folders to find a file.*

Network Neighborhood

Network Neighborhood provides access to information located on computers to which you are connected over a network. Computers in your immediate workgroup appear as computer icons in the Network Neighborhood window (see Figure 2-10). You can use the Entire Network icon to reach computers in other workgroups connected to your network or you can gain remote access through telephone lines and a modem.

When you click a computer in your workgroup, you see the disk drives (represented by folders), folders, and printers that the computer is sharing with you. Each person on the network, as well as the network administrator, helps to determine what you see in Network Neighborhood. Opening a disk drive there begins the same process as opening a disk drive in My Computer, as you can see in Figure 2-11. Part 6 of this book contains an in-depth look at networking in Windows 98.

The Recycle Bin

The Recycle Bin provides a safety net that protects you from inadvertently deleting something you want to keep. All files and folders that you delete go into the Recycle Bin. Under the default settings, the items stay in the Recycle Bin until you "empty" it or restore the items. You can tell something is in the Recycle Bin because you can see paper sticking out of the top, like this:

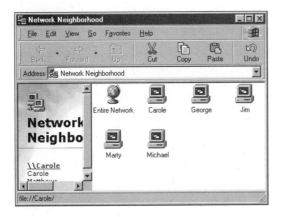

Figure 2-10.   *Network Neighborhood window.*

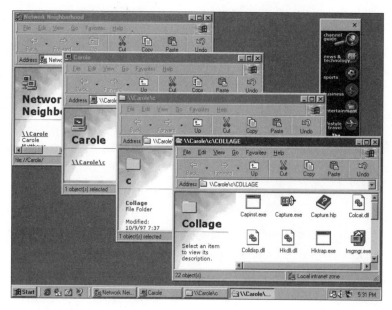

Figure 2-11. *Network Neighborhood provides access to drives, printers, folders, and files on other computers.*

You can empty the Recycle Bin by either right-clicking it and selecting Empty Recycle Bin from the context menu or by opening the Recycle Bin window and choosing Empty Recycle Bin from its File menu. Although opening the Recycle Bin window before emptying it takes a couple of extra steps, it allows you to confirm visually what it is you are permanently deleting, as you can see in Figure 2-12.

To restore (undelete) one or more objects from the Recycle Bin, you need to select the objects in the window and then choose Restore from the File menu. You can also undo the last instance of deleting, renaming, copying, or moving by pressing **CTRL-Z** or by choosing Undo from the Edit menu of any folder or Explorer window.

You do not have to use the Recycle Bin if you are comfortable working without the safety net it provides. To be able to immediately delete an object when you press **DELETE** or choose Delete or Clear from a menu, right-click the Recycle Bin, choose Properties, and then in the dialog box, click Do Not Move Files To The Recycle Bin. In this same dialog box, shown in Figure 2-13, you can select the maximum amount of disk space that you want to allocate to the Recycle Bin. It is a good idea to keep this fairly

Figure 2-12. *The Recycle Bin window.*

small so your Recycle Bin does not end up taking over your hard disk if you do not empty the bin often.

> **W**ARNING If the size of the contents of the Recycle Bin approaches the disk space allocated for it, anything else you delete that causes the Recycle Bin to exceed its allocated disk space will, without warning, immediately and irrevocably delete enough of the current contents to make room for the new deletion.

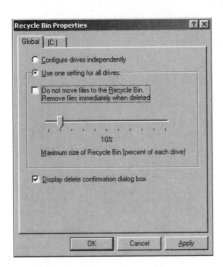

Figure 2-13. *Selecting the disk space to be used by the Recycle Bin.*

My Documents

My Documents is a folder similar to any folder you can create, which has been placed on the desktop. It is a handy place to store documents that you are currently working on, because you need only click the folder to open it and click a document to begin work. You can put documents into My Documents by saving them there from the application that created them or by dragging them to My Documents from another folder or the desktop. When you have placed some files in My Documents and opened it, you see a folder window similar to Figure 2-14.

My Documents does have two characteristics that are not in most other folders: It cannot be deleted from the desktop, and it exists in two places at once. As you can see in Figure 2-15, My Documents exists both on the desktop and within the hard disk in which you have installed Windows. In reality, the copy on the desktop is a shortcut to the folder on your hard disk, but it doesn't have the shortcut arrow. If you put a file into My Documents on your desktop, you can view and work with that file by opening the My Documents folder on your Windows hard disk. This allows programs that can see only the contents of drives to access My Documents, and it allows you fast access from the desktop.

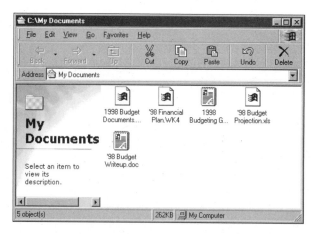

Figure 2-14.   *My Documents folder and contents.*

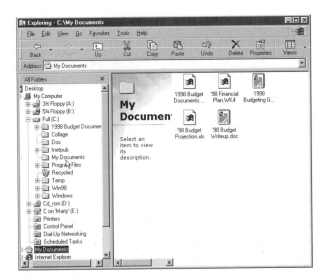

Figure 2-15.   *You have two ways of accessing My Documents.*

If you try to delete My Documents from the desktop, you get a sound indicating that it can't be deleted. You can right-click the My Documents icon on the desktop to open the context menu and select Remove From Desktop. This deletes the icon on the desktop. You can also delete the original folder on your hard disk after accepting a warning.

Using Windows and Dialog Boxes

When you open My Computer, Network Neighborhood, or any of the folders within them, you see a folder window with the same menus and controls as the ones you see in Figure 2-14. Other than windows for the programs that you run, this is the most common type of window in Windows 98.

Folder-Window Menus

The six folder-window menus—File, Edit, View, Go, Favorites, and Help—remain constant, but the options on the File menu can change, depending on what you select. If you haven't selected anything, the File menu resembles the leftmost menu in Figure 2-16. If you selected a folder, the File menu looks like the middle one in the figure, and if you selected a file, the File menu looks similar to the one on the right.

Figure 2-16.   *Three forms of the File menu of a folder window.*

 OTE   Depending on what options you installed, there might be some minor differences between your menus and those shown here. For example, the Add To Zip and Add To 1998 Budget Documents.zip options are not standard options but rather a feature of WinZip as described earlier.

The purpose of each File menu option is described in Table 2-2. In the table, you see the term *shortcut*. A shortcut, in this context, is a link to a folder or file. It allows you to open the folder or file from a location other than the folder that contains the actual folder or file. For example, if you create a shortcut to the Microsoft Access program, Msaccess.exe, you can start Access by clicking a shortcut you placed on the desktop or in another folder. If you create a shortcut for a folder, you can open the folder by clicking the shortcut. All of the Start menu Program options are shortcuts. Both Chapters 4 and 6 discuss shortcuts further.

The Edit, View, Go, Favorites, and Help menus are shown in Figure 2-17. The purpose of each option on these menus is described in Table 2-3.

Option	Purpose
New	Creates a new folder, shortcut, or file of a particular type
Open	Opens and/or loads the selected object, depending on whether it is a file, folder, or program
Explore	Opens a Windows Explorer window for the selected folder (See Chapter 6 for a discussion of Windows Explorer windows.)

Table 2-2.   *Options on the File menu of folder windows.*

(continued)

Table 2-2 *continued*

Option	Purpose
Find	Opens the same Find All Files dialog box available from the Start menu (See Chapter 1.)
Sharing	Allows you to share or to stop sharing a folder with others over a network
Send To	Copies the selected folder or file to a floppy-disk drive, the desktop, another folder, or to a fax or mail recipient
Print	Prints the selected file
Quick View	Displays the selected file on the screen, often without starting the program that created it (This option is not installed as part of a Typical install.)
Create Shortcut	Creates a shortcut for the selected object in the same folder with the original object
Delete	Deletes the selected object and places it in the Recycle Bin, if the bin is activated; otherwise, permanently deletes the object
Rename	Allows you to rename the selected object
Properties	Opens the Properties dialog box for the selected object
Work Offline	Allows you to view HTML pages stored on your hard disk but prevents you from connecting to or interacting with the Internet
Close	Closes the active window

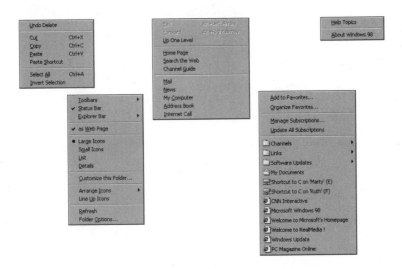

Figure 2-17. *Edit, View, Go, Favorites, and Help menus of folder windows.*

Option	Purpose
Undo	Reverses the last copy, move, delete, or rename you performed
Cut	Removes the selected object(s) from the window and places it on the Clipboard so it can be pasted elsewhere
Copy	Copies the selected object(s) to the Clipboard so it can be pasted elsewhere
Paste	Places a copy of the Clipboard contents into the active window; may be done multiple times into different windows
Paste Shortcut	Places a shortcut to the file or folder that has been copied to the Clipboard into the active window
Select All	Selects all of the objects (files and folders) in the window
Invert Selection	Selects all of the objects in the window not currently selected and deselects those that were
Toolbars	Allows the display of one or more toolbars in the active window
Status Bar	Turns on or off the status bar at the bottom of the active window
Explorer Bar	Allows the selection of an Explorer bar for display in the left pane
As Web Page	Turns on or off the display of an HTML document associated with the folder, such as the one in Figure 2-14
Large Icons	Displays the contents of the window as large icons, as shown in Figure 2-14
Small Icons	Displays the contents of the window as small icons, as shown in Figure 2-21
List	Displays the contents of the window as a brief list, as shown in Figure 2-22
Details	Displays the contents of the window as a detailed list, as shown in Figure 2-23
Customize This Folder	Starts the Customize This Folder wizard, which walks you through creating an HTML document and attaching it to the current folder
Arrange Icons	Sorts the icons in the window by name, type of file, size, or date and allows you to toggle the automatic-arrangement feature
Line Up Icons	Aligns all objects in the window to an invisible grid

Table 2-3.   *Options on the Edit, View, Go, Favorites, and Help menus*   *(continued)*
of folder windows.

Table 2-3. *continued*

Option	Purpose
Refresh	Updates the contents of the window with the latest information from the disk where the contents are stored
Folder Options	Opens the Folder Options dialog box, shown in Figures 2-18 through 2-20
Back/Forward	Displays a series of HTML pages according to the sequence in which you explored them
Up One Level	Displays the parent container of the folder
Home Page	Opens the home page that you have selected in Internet Explorer (By default, this is the Microsoft home page.)
Search The Web	Opens the Microsoft Search page, where you can select a search service (Yahoo, Excite, and so on) to look for Internet content on a particular topic
Channel Guide	Opens the Microsoft Channel Guide, where you can make channels active (See note on the next page.)
Mail/News	Opens Outlook Express for e-mail and newsgroup purposes
My Computer	Opens the My Computer window
Address Book	Opens the Address book
Internet Call	Opens NetMeeting to make a one-on-one or many-on-one voice call over the Internet
Add To Favorites	Adds the current folder, disk drive, or Web site to the Favorites folder
Organize Favorites	Opens the Favorites folder; allows you to create subfolders and move entries among folders
Manage Subscriptions	Opens the Subscriptions folder and allows you to add, delete, and update subscriptions
Update All Subscriptions	Updates content from all your subscriptions
Help Topics	Opens the Help Topics dialog box, discussed later in this chapter
About Windows 98	Opens a message window that, among other things, tells you the amount of physical memory and system resources your system has left

OTE Channels, as used in Table 2-3, are a way to have Internet content sent to you (using what is called "push technology") instead of your having to go to the site to get it. For a channel to work, you must make it active, giving details about what content you want and when you want to receive it. Not all Web sites have this capability, but you can receive updated content automatically from non-channel sites by subscribing to them.

 IP If you want to select all but a few objects in a folder window, select the objects you *do not want* to select, and choose Invert Selection from the Edit menu.

The Folder Options dialog box, which you open by choosing Folder Options from the View menu, has three tabs. The first, General, shown in Figure 2-18, lets you specify if you want your windows to be Web style, classic (Windows 95) style, or a style that combines elements of both. If you choose Custom and click Settings, the Custom Settings dialog box opens with a number of options, as you saw in Chapter 1. The most important of these is whether to use single-clicking or double-clicking.

The second tab, View, allows you to specify the types of files you want to display and how you want to display them, as you can see in Figure 2-19.

Figure 2-18.   *Folder Options dialog box, General tab.*

The third tab, File Types, shows you the registered file types and the programs that open them, as well as allowing you to add or remove types, as shown in Figure 2-20.

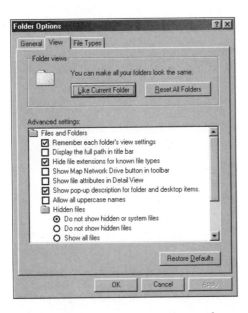

Figure 2-19. *Folder Options dialog box, View tab.*

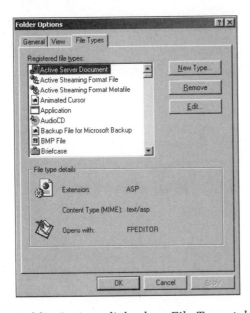

Figure 2-20. *Folder Options dialog box, File Types tab.*

The difference between Small Icons view (Figure 2-21) and List view (Figure 2-22) is that, in Small Icons view, you scroll vertically and, in List view, you scroll horizontally. The icons and the information shown are the same. In Details view (Figure 2-23), you can sort the objects by clicking the heading for the column by which you want to sort. For example, if you want to sort by size (from smallest to largest), click the Size heading; if you want to sort from largest to smallest, click the Size heading again. In other words, you get an ascending sort the first time you click a heading and a descending sort the second time. If you want to change the width of a column in Details view, drag the vertical line between the headings. When you point at a vertical line between headings, the mouse pointer becomes a vertical line with a horizontal, double-headed arrow running through it, like this:

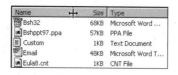

 TIP If your Details view columns get completely messed up and you just want to return them to the default size, you can quickly do that. Click in the right pane of Windows Explorer to establish the focus, and press and hold **CTRL** while pressing the **+** in the numeric keypad.

You can also resize a column to its "best fit" width by double-clicking (even with single-clicking as your default) the vertical line to the right of its heading.

 TIP With Windows 98, you can rearrange columns by dragging headings left or right.

Folder-Window Toolbar and Controls

If you select Toolbars from the View menu of a folder window, a submenu appears like the following:

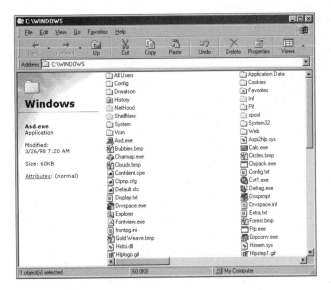

Figure 2-21. *Folder window in Small Icons view.*

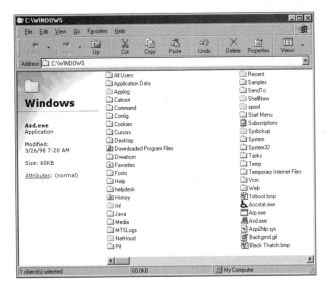

Figure 2-22. *Folder window in List view.*

Figure 2-23.   *Folder window in Details view.*

The Toolbars submenu allows you to turn on or off three toolbars—Standard, Address, and Links—and to turn on or off the text labels on the Standard toolbar. With all three toolbars and text labels turned on, the top of a folder window looks like this:

The drop-down list box of the Address toolbar lets you quickly open any drive or drive-level folder on your computer, while the Standard-toolbar buttons perform the functions described in Table 2-4. The Links toolbar is normally used when you access the Internet or an intranet, but you can also use it to quickly get to any drive or folder by simply dragging it to the Links toolbar.

The drop-down list box on the Address toolbar, shown on the next page, is the most versatile and, therefore, the most valuable of the toolbar elements. It always shows the hierarchy of folders from the folder you are viewing to the drive that contains it, as well as all the drives and folders that you have available. This places information on even a large network only a few clicks away. The default folders, at the same level as disk drives, are Control Panel, Printers, Dial-Up Networking, and Scheduled Tasks. But, as you will see in Chapter 4, you can place other folders at either the My Computer or desktop level (where My Documents and Online Services reside).

Using Help

Windows 98 has a Help system, shown in Figure 2-24, which is formatted in HTML and provides additional help over the Internet. This Help system is opened by selecting Help from the Start menu or by selecting Help Topics from the Help menu in any folder window. You can also open Help by selecting an object (drive, folder, or file) in the folder window and then pressing **F1**.

Button	Name	Description
	Back	Displays the contents of the folder, drive, or Web page you most recently displayed
	Forward	Displays the contents of the folder, drive, or Web page you displayed before using the Back function
	Up	Displays the parent container of the folder
	Map Network Drive	Connects a shared folder or drive on another computer to your computer and assigns a drive letter to the connection (not on the default toolbar)
	Disconnect Net Drive	Disconnects a shared folder or drive on another computer from your computer (not on the default toolbar)

Table 2-4.   *Buttons on the folder-window toolbar.*   *(continued)*

Table 2-4. *continued*

Button	Name	Description
	Cut	Removes the selected object(s) from the window and places it on the Clipboard so it can be pasted elsewhere
	Copy	Copies the selected object(s) to the Clipboard so it can be pasted elsewhere
	Paste	Places a copy of the Clipboard contents into the active window; may be done multiple times into different windows
	Undo	Reverses the last copy, move, delete, or rename you performed
	Delete	Removes the selected object(s) from the window and places it in the Recycle Bin, if the bin is activated; otherwise, permanently deletes the object(s)
	Properties	Opens the Properties dialog box for the selected object
	Views	Changes the view displayed in the window each time the button is clicked, from Large Icons to Small Icons to List to Details

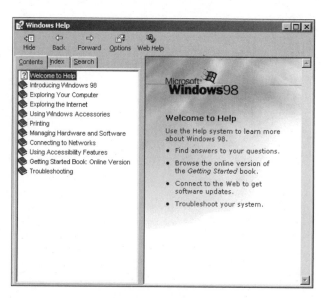

Figure 2-24. *HTML-based Help window.*

The Help window has two panes. In the left pane, you use one of three methods to select a Help topic, while the right pane displays the information available about the topic. The three selection methods are implemented through three tabs, as follows:

■ In the **Contents tab,** you can look through a hierarchical list for the subject on which you want help.

■ In the **Index tab,** you can look up a word or phrase in an alphabetical list to find either a series of steps that tell you how to do something or a topic about the subject on which you want help.

■ In the **Search tab,** you can look for specific words or phrases in help topics.

Help Contents Tab

In the Contents tab, shown in Figure 2-24, you can click a heading to see related subheadings and then click subheadings until you eventually see a list of topics with the question-mark icons. Clicking a topic may display information, a list of topics for more detailed information, or both, as you can see in Figure 2-25.

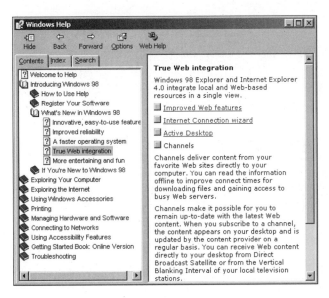

Figure 2-25.   *Information on a Help topic displayed in the right pane.*

Help Index Tab

If you select the Index tab, you can type one or more characters or use the scroll bar to display a particular index entry. When you see the entry you want, click it and then click Display (or double-click the entry, even with single-click set as your default). If there are several topics related to an entry, a Topics Found dialog box opens, as shown in Figure 2-26. Here you can choose a topic to display in the right pane. The topic often has a button you can click to access related topics.

Help Search Tab

In the Search tab, you type the word or phrase you want to search for, click List Topics, select a topic, and then click Display, with the results of a search for "subscriptions" shown in Figure 2-27.

 OTE   The Help Index tab lists topics that define particular terms. The Search tab, on the other hand, lists all topics in which particular terms appear, regardless of whether those topics contain definitions.

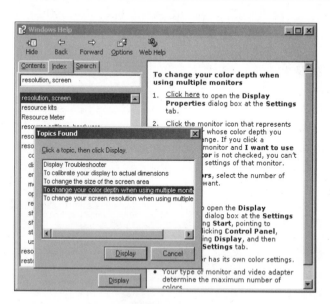

Figure 2-26.   *Displaying an index entry.*

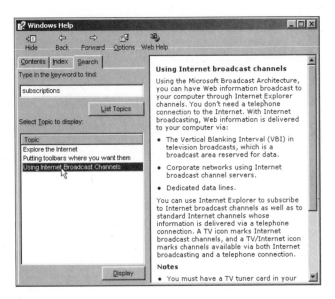

Figure 2-27. *Searching for a word in Help.*

Windows 98 Applets

Windows 98 comes with a large number of small programs, or *applets*, many of which are discussed in other chapters of this book. The following tables give you an overview of them. You can start most of these applets from the Programs Accessories option on the Start menu. To give this list some organization, the applets are divided into categories: file management, printing, networking, Internet and intranet, communication, multimedia, productivity, system, and games. Each of the table entries shows an icon, gives a brief description of the applet, tells how to start it, and refers to the chapter in the book in which it is discussed. Several of these applets are not installed during a Typical setup; you need to install them separately, using Control Panel's Add/Remove Programs | Windows Setup dialog box.

Icon	Name	Description
	Windows Explorer	Provides access to all folders and files; started from Start I Programs; discussed in Chapter 6
	Backup	Backs up folders and files to disks or tape; started from Start I Programs I Accessories I System Tools; discussed in Chapter 6
	Briefcase	Synchronizes files with the same name on two computers; started from the desktop; discussed in Chapter 6
	Drive Converter (FAT32)	Converts a FAT drive to FAT32; started from Start I Programs I Accessories I System Tools; discussed in Chapter 6
	Compression Agent	Allows specification of how you want particular files compressed if you are running DriveSpace 3; started from Start I Programs I Accessories I System Tools; discussed in Chapter 6
	Disk Defragmenter	Optimizes file storage on hard disks; started from Start I Programs I Accessories I System Tools; discussed in Chapter 6
	DriveSpace 3	Compresses files stored on disks and manages those compressed disks; started from Start I Programs I Accessories I System Tools; discussed in Chapter 6
	Disk Cleanup	Searches for and allows you to delete temporary files; started by clicking Disk Cleanup in a disk's Properties dialog box; discussed in Chapter 6
	ScanDisk	Checks for and repairs disk errors; started from Start I Programs I Accessories I System Tools; discussed in Chapter 6
	System File Checker	Checks whether your system files are the latest versions and not corrupted; started from Start I Programs I Accessories I System Tools I System Information I Tools menu; discussed in Chapter 6

Table 2-5.   *File-management programs.*

Icon	Name	Description
	Printers	Allows adding and deleting of printers and managing of print queues; started from Start	Settings; discussed in Chapter 7
	Fonts	Allows adding and deleting fonts; started from Start	Settings	Control Panel; discussed in Chapter 8

Table 2-6.   *Printing programs.*

Icon	Name	Description
	Dial-Up Networking	Allows access to a computer and a network from a remote computer over phone lines; started from Start	Programs	Accessories	Communications; discussed in Chapters 11 and 16
	WinPopup	Allows a two-way conversation over a network; started with Winpopup.exe from the Windows folder; discussed in Chapter 16
	Net Watcher	Provides control over who is connected to your computer and the folders and files that you share; started from Start	Programs	Accessories	System Tools; discussed in Chapter 16

Table 2-7.   *Networking programs.*

Icon	Name	Description
	Address Book	Allows storage of contact information; started from Start	Programs	Internet Explorer; discussed in Chapter 12
	Microsoft Chat	Allows conversation over the Internet; started from Start	Programs	Internet Explorer; discussed in Chapter 14

Table 2-8.   *Internet and intranet programs.*   *(continued)*

Table 2-8. *continued*

Icon	Name	Description
	FrontPage Express	Allows creation and revision of Web pages; started from Start	Programs	Internet Explorer
	Internet Explorer	Allows exploration of the Web; started from the desktop; discussed in Chapter 11
	NetMeeting	Allows audio communication and videoconferencing over the Internet or an intranet; started from Start	Programs	Internet Explorer; discussed in Chapter 14
	NetShow Player	Allows the reception and display of streaming audio and video data over the Internet or an intranet; started from Start	Programs	Internet Explorer; discussed in Chapter 14
	Outlook Express	Allows creation, delivery, and storage of messages; started from the desktop; discussed in Chapter 12
	Personal Web Server	Allows the publishing of Web pages from your computer; started from Start	Programs	Internet Explorer

Icon	Name	Description
	Direct Cable Connection	Allows transfer of files and folders over a serial connection or parallel cable; started from Start	Programs	Accessories	Communications; discussed in Chapter 9
	HyperTerminal	Allows transfer of files and messages with a modem; started from Start	Programs	Accessories	Communications; discussed in Chapter 10

Table 2-9.   *Communications programs.*

Table 2-9. *continued*

Icon	Name	Description
	ISDN Configuration Wizard	Sets up ISDN communications using a standard, two-channel ISDN connection; started from Start I Programs I Accessories I Communications; discussed in Chapter 10
	Phone Dialer	Allows the computer to dial a phone number for you; started from Start I Programs I Accessories I Communications; discussed in Chapter 10

Icon	Name	Description
	ActiveMovie Control	Allows playing of several digital video formats; started from Start I Programs I Accessories I Entertainment; discussed in Chapter 13
	CD Player	Allows playing of audio CDs; started from Start I Programs I Accessories I Entertainment; discussed in Chapter 13
	DVD Player	Allows playing of DVDs; started from Start I Programs I Accessories I Entertainment; discussed in Chapter 13
	Media Player	Allows control of playing digital audio and video clips; started from Start I Programs I Accessories I Entertainment; discussed in Chapter 13
	Sound Recorder	Allows digital recording of sound with the appropriate hardware; started from Start I Programs I Accessories I Entertainment; discussed in Chapter 13
	Volume Control	Allows control of sound volume; started from Start I Programs I Accessories I Entertainment; discussed in Chapter 13
	Web TV for Windows	Allows the reception of broadcast TV, with the appropriate hardware; started from Quick Launch toolbar; discussed in Chapter 3

Table 2-10.   *Multimedia programs.*

Icon	Name	Description
	Calculator	Provides the functions of either a simple or scientific calculator; started from Start I Programs I Accessories; discussed in Chapter 9
	Character Map	Provides access to all of the special characters in all of the fonts on your computer; started from Start I Programs I Accessories I System Tools; discussed in Chapter 8
	Clipboard Viewer	Allows viewing and saving of the Clipboard's contents; started from Start I Programs I Accessories I System Tools; discussed in Chapter 9
	Imaging	Provides a means of displaying and editing bitmap images; started from Start I Programs I Accessories; discussed in Chapter 9
	Magnifier	Allows magnification of segments of the screen; started from Start I Programs I Accessories I Accessibility; discussed in Chapter 1
	Notepad	Provides an editor for plain-text files; started from Start I Programs I Accessories; discussed in Chapter 9
	Paint	Provides bitmap drawing; started from Start I Programs I Accessories; discussed in Chapter 9
	WordPad	Provides basic word processing; started from Start I Programs I Accessories; discussed in Chapter 9

Table 2-11. *Productivity programs.*

Icon	Name	Description
	Regedit	Allows viewing and editing of Windows Registry; started with Regedit.exe in the Windows folder; discussed in Chapter 5
	Resource Meter	Displays the system resources that are free on your computer; started from Start I Programs I Accessories I System Tools; discussed in Chapter 5

Table 2-12. *System programs.*

Table 2-12. *continued*

Icon	Name	Description
	Maintenance Wizard	Looks for, recommends, and schedules various optimization procedures; started from Start ׀ Programs ׀ Accessories ׀ System Tools; discussed in Chapter 6
	Scheduled Tasks	Manages a schedule of tasks to be repeatedly performed; started from Start ׀ Programs ׀ Accessories ׀ System Tools; discussed in Chapter 6
	Sysedit	Allows viewing and editing of Autoexec.bat, Config.sys, Win.ini, System.ini, and other files; started with Sysedit.exe in the Windows\System folder; discussed in Chapter 4
	System Information	Displays system information, including resources, components, and software; started from Start ׀ Programs ׀ Accessories ׀ System Tools; discussed in Chapter 4
	System Monitor	Allows monitoring of system-resource usage; started from Start ׀ Programs ׀ Accessories ׀ System Tools; discussed in Chapter 5

Icon	Name	Description
	FreeCell	A solitary card game of logic and skill; started from Start ׀ Programs ׀ Accessories ׀ Games; discussed in Chapter 9
	Hearts	A card game for play over a network; started from Start ׀ Programs ׀ Accessories ׀ Games; discussed in Chapter 16
	Minesweeper	A game of figuring out where the mines are; started from Start ׀ Programs ׀ Accessories ׀ Games; discussed in Chapter 9
	Solitaire	A card game of luck and skill; started from Start ׀ Programs ׀ Accessories ׀ Games; discussed in Chapter 9

Table 2-13. *Game programs.*

Getting the Most Out of Windows 98

Getting the best performance from Windows 98, while making Windows look and operate the way you want it to, is the subject of Part 2 of this book. This part is valuable to almost every reader. It includes clear, step-by-step instructions and the examples you need to get all you can out of your system.

Installing Windows 98

The actual process of installing Windows 98 is easy. But before you rush off and install it, take a minute to plan and prepare, examining the decisions you will make as you progress through the installation. This chapter guides you through that process. Here is a summary of the steps that we will use:

1. Look at the system requirements for Windows 98, and compare them to your current system. In addition, print out your system settings, such as which devices use which interrupts (IRQs) and I/O port addresses, so that this information is available should it be necessary during installation.

2. Back up your data and configuration files so you are prepared for the unlikely event that you lose the contents of your hard disk or so you can reformat your hard disk.

3. Create a bootable floppy disk for MS-DOS 6.x/Windows 3.x or Windows 95 with the driver software for your CD-ROM drive so you can reload your current system from a CD, if necessary.

4. Remove any unneeded files and folders from your hard disk; then optimize and check it for errors to make sure that the disk drive onto which you are installing is in the best condition possible.

5. Review the questions you will be asked during installation so you will have the answers that are correct for you.

6. Review the different types of installations, and decide which to use.

7. Carry out the installation and any post-installation tasks.

Let's begin this process by looking at the system requirements for Windows 98.

Requirements for Windows 98

Windows 98 will run on a large number of the computers in use today, although it will run better on some systems than it will on others. Microsoft says that Windows 98 will run on a system with a 486/66 processor with 16 MB of RAM and 200 MB of available hard-disk space. While that may be literally true, such a setup will not allow you to do much with Windows 98. Table 3-1 shows both the minimum and recommended system requirements. In addition, you can upgrade from either Windows 3.*x* or Windows 95.

Although Table 3-1 recommends an Intel Pentium 120 processor, there is no requirement for an Intel chip; Windows 98 will run fine on AMD and

Component	Minimum	Recommended
Processor	Intel 486DX, 66 MHz or faster	Intel Pentium, 120 MHz or faster
Memory	16 MB	32 MB or more
Free conventional memory	500 KB	500 KB
Available hard-disk space for Windows Setup	200 MB	300 MB or more
Video display and adapter	VGA (640 × 480, 256 colors)	SVGA (800 × 600, High Color-16 bit) or higher
CD-ROM	2× or above	12× or above
Audio board	None	16 bit
Modem	None	33.6 Kbps fax modem
Mouse	Microsoft or compatible mouse	Any pointing device

Table 3-1.   *System requirements for Windows 98.*

Cyrix processors. After the processor, the next most important component of your system is memory; the more you have, the faster Windows 98 will operate. With 16 MB of memory, Windows 98 will perform reasonably. Keeping the same processor and doubling the memory to 32 MB will give you good performance. At today's memory prices, you should not skimp on memory.

When you calculate disk space, remember that most of the space used by your current version of Windows will be reused by Windows 98, so you can subtract that space from the total needed. (You can use RipSPACE, a shareware program, to determine how much space your current Windows files occupy.)

What Do You Currently Have?

Your next step in installing Windows 98 is to identify the hardware and software components of your current system. You may already know what you have, and if so, you can skip this step. If you don't know, there are a couple of ways to find out. One of the best is to open the Windows 95 Device Manager and print your System Summary, which might be useful during installation. Use these steps to do that from Windows 95:

 OTE In the other chapters of this book, we assume you use the Windows 98 single-clicking convention, where you point at an object to select it and click an object to open or load it. In this chapter, however, we assume that you are upgrading from Windows 3.x or Windows 95, and therefore, we have reverted back to the double-click convention, where you click to select and double-click to load or open. If you have installed Internet Explorer 4 and have already switched to the single-click convention, you need to adjust the instructions.

---

1. Either right-click the My Computer icon, and select Properties; or open the Start menu, choose Settings, and click Control Panel. In Control Panel, double-click System. The System Properties dialog box opens.

2. Click the Device Manager tab. Here you can see what hardware components you have, as shown in Figure 3-1. If you select a particular item and click Properties, you can see the settings for that item.

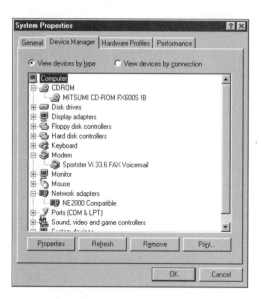

Figure 3-1.   *Getting information about your system from Device Manager.*

3. After looking at Device Manager, click Print. Select System Summary, and click OK. After you are done printing, click OK again to close the System Properties dialog box.

The report that you printed using the above steps gives you a wealth of information. Among the most important data are the interrupt, or IRQ, usage and the I/O port addresses. If your installation does not run smoothly and you have to set up some of your hardware manually, it will be handy to have this information. Often the only other way to find these settings is to physically open your computer and look at the switch settings on the adapter cards and motherboard.

Another way to find out about your system is to use an MS-DOS program called Msd.exe, which is on the Windows 95 CD in the \Other\Msd folder and which was available in MS-DOS version 6.0 and later. You can run this from Windows 95 by opening the Start menu, choosing Run, typing **d:\other\msd\msd** (where *d* is the drive letter of your CD-ROM), and pressing **ENTER.** If you are running an operating system that precedes Windows 95, you could run Msd.exe from an MS-DOS prompt by typing **msd.** Finally, the source of last resort is to ask the dealer who sold you the system.

Preparing for Installation

The installation of a new operating system is a milestone that you can ignore or use as a reason to do some major housecleaning. At the very least, you should back up your data files and your Windows configuration files. Because you will need a lot of disk space for the new operating system, it would also be a good time to remove files, folders, and programs you no longer use.

If you have been using Windows for some time and have added and removed a lot of programs, you probably have many files in your Windows directories that you are not using. Because these files do not belong to Windows, Windows 98 will not replace them when you install it. To recover this space, you can do one of two things: You can buy an uninstall program, such as CleanSweep, that looks for files no longer in use; or you can wipe out all of your Windows directories before installing Windows 98. While the latter is a drastic step and should not be underestimated, it is the most thorough way to clean up your hard disk. You will be amazed at how much disk space you will recover.

 OTE The terms "directories" and "folders" are synonymous and used interchangeably.

 ARNING If you delete your Windows directories, you will need to reinstall your Windows applications, and you will lose your Windows settings.

Backing Up Files

No matter what else you do, use the excuse of installing Windows 98 to back up all of your data files (the files you created with your word processor, spreadsheet, database, and other programs). If you have all of your program files on the floppy disks or CDs from which you loaded them, you do not have to back up these files.

If you don't choose to delete your Windows directories, you should back up your Windows configuration files in addition to your data files. The configuration files include the following, which are all in your Windows directory:

.ini (initialization files)

.dat (Registry data files)

.pwl (password files)

You should also back up your Config.sys and Autoexec.bat files in your root directory, as well as all the files they reference. To see the Config.sys and Autoexec.bat files, use Notepad in Windows or Edit in MS-DOS. If you are connected to a network, you also need to back up your network-configuration files and any logon scripts that you use.

Backing Up Data Files

An easy way to back up your data, configuration, and startup files is to use the Windows 95 Backup program. Although Windows 98 Backup is different, it restores files backed up with Windows 95 Backup. Follow these instructions to back up your files:

 OTE   Neither Windows 95 nor Windows 98 backup utilities restore files backed up with Windows 3.x or MS-DOS 6.x. You can use a third-party backup utility that works on both Windows 3.x and Windows 98 files. If you are on a network, you can use a network backup utility or simply copy your files to another computer on the network.

---

1. In Windows Explorer or My Computer, right-click your hard disk (any one of your hard disks, if you have more than one), and choose Properties.

2. In the drive's Properties dialog box, click the Tools tab, and then click Backup Now. If you get a message that Backup is not installed, follow the instructions to install it, and then click Backup Now again.

3. If you get the Welcome screen, click OK. Also click OK to acknowledge the existence of the Full System Backup file set (even though you don't want to use it), and if you don't have a tape drive, click OK to acknowledge that you don't have one. Finally you see the Backup window, similar to Figure 3-2.

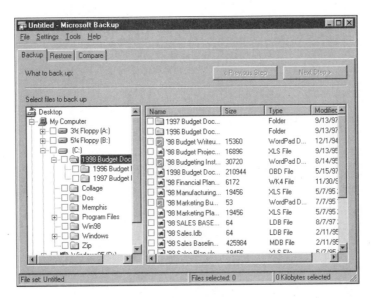

Figure 3-2. *Windows 95 Backup window for selecting folders and files.*

4. In the left pane of Backup, locate the folder that contains the files you want to back up. Then, in the right pane, click those files to select them. Besides the application-data files already mentioned, here are some other, not-so-obvious files that you should consider backing up:

■ If you use Microsoft Exchange, look in your Exchange folder for your Mailbox.pst, with all your e-mail, and Mailbox.pab, with your Address Book. (If you have installed Office 97 with Outlook, look in your Windows folder for more .pst and .pab files.)

■ If you use Microsoft Office 95 or 97, look in \Msoffice\Templates (Office 95) or \Program Files\Microsoft Office\Templates (Office 97) for templates, as well as \Program Files\Common Files\Microsoft Shared\Proof for custom dictionaries.

■ Look in the folders of other applications for configuration and data files. For example, the CompuServe address book and file cabinet reside in your Cserv folder, and the Federal Express address book and shipping history reside in your Ship folder, if you have these applications.

■ Look in your Windows folder for your Recent and Fonts folders, as well as (if you use Internet Explorer) your Favorites, Cookies, and History folders.

 IP One quick way to find configuration and data files among application files is to sort the contents of a folder by date. To do this, click the Modified column header in the Details view of Windows Explorer. The most recent files are typically the ones you want to back up.

---

5. After you have selected all the files and folders that you want to back up, click Next Step.

6. Select the device to which you want to back up, and click Start Backup. Enter the name you want to give to the backup set, and click OK. Backup starts and tells you where it is in the process. When the operation is complete, Backup notifies you. Click OK twice, and then close the Backup window.

Backing Up Configuration Files

Windows 95 came with two utilities just for backing up your system and configuration files. These are ERU (Emergency Recovery Utility) and Cfgback (Configuration Backup), which are on the Windows 95 CD in the \Other\Misc\Eru and \Other\Misc\Cfgback folders, respectively. (If you don't have a Windows 95 CD, you can download it from http://www.microsoft.com/windows95/info/otherutils.htm.) ERU backs up all of your configuration and settings files, including .ini, .dat, and root-directory files (Autoexec.bat, Config.sys, Io.sys, Msdos.sys, and Command.Com). Cfgback, on the other hand, backs up only your Registry (User.dat and System.dat). Use the following instructions to open and run Eru.exe (if you run ERU, you don't need to run Cfgback):

1. Place your Windows 98 CD in the drive, and click No when you're asked to run Setup. (If that doesn't close the Windows 98 Autorun window, click Close.)

2. In Windows Explorer, open the CD in the left pane, and open the \Tools\Misc\Eru folder. Double-click Eru.exe. The Welcome mes-

sage appears and tells you that ERU will save the most valuable configuration information. Click Next.

3. Select either your floppy drive or Other Directory to contain the backup file. If you choose Other Directory, another dialog box appears asking you to enter a drive and directory to contain the backup. In that case, type the drive and directory, and click Next. If you choose your floppy drive, you are told to insert a formatted system disk in Drive A (assuming that is the floppy drive you picked) and label it Emergency Recovery Disk.

4. ERU next displays a list of files to be saved. If you want to change this list, click Custom; otherwise, click Next. Clicking Custom gives you a complete list of all the files this program can back up, as you can see in Figure 3-3.

5. If you clicked Custom, select the files that you want to back up, click OK, and then click Next. ERU tells you about the progress of the copying operation and when it is complete. The final message box tells you how to restore the files by running A:\Erd\Erd.exe (assuming you backed up to your A: drive). Click OK.

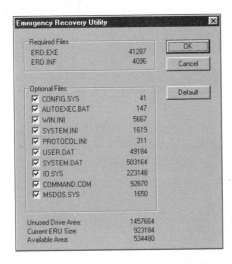

Figure 3-3.   *Files that can be backed up with ERU.*

Creating a Startup Floppy

Another precaution you should take prior to installing Windows 98 is to create a startup floppy for Windows 3.x or Windows 95 (if you don't already have one). This startup floppy should contain files to access your CD-ROM so you can get to a Windows CD. If something prevents you from booting from your hard disk, you can still boot your computer from a floppy and see what is happening on your hard disk.

 OTE   While installing Windows 98, you will make a startup floppy for Windows 98. That should not prevent you from also creating a startup floppy for your current installation.

From Windows 95

To make a startup floppy from Windows 95, follow these instructions:

1. Place your Windows 95 CD in your CD-ROM drive, and insert into your floppy drive either a new floppy disk or one that can be erased.

2. Open the Start menu, choose Settings, and click Control Panel. In Control Panel, double-click Add/Remove Programs.

3. Click the Startup Disk tab, and then click Create Disk. You are informed of the progress as the floppy is formatted and the startup files are copied to it. Then the Startup Disk tab appears. Click Close.

From Windows 3.x

To make a startup floppy from Windows 3.x, follow these instructions:

1. Insert into your floppy drive either a new floppy disk or one that can be erased.

2. Start File Manager, open the Disk menu, and choose Format Disk. Select your floppy disk and its capacity, click Make System Disk, and click OK. If the Format Confirmation dialog box appears, click Yes. Click No when asked if you want to format another disk.

3. In File Manager, open your Dos directory, and drag the following files to your floppy drive: Attrib.exe, Chkdsk.exe, Deltree.exe, Diskcopy.com, Doskey.com, Drvspace.sys, Drvspace.bin, Edit.com, Emm386.exe, Expand.exe, Fdisk.exe, Format.com, Himem.sys,

Mem.exe, Mouse.sys, Mouse.com, Mscdex.exe, Msd.exe, Power.exe
(if you are using a laptop), Qbasic.exe (so you can use Edit),
Scandisk.exe, Setver.exe, Smartdrv.exe, and Xcopy.exe.

In Either Windows 3.*x* or Windows 95

In either operating system, continue with these instructions to provide the
files needed to initialize your CD-ROM drive:

1. In either Windows Explorer or File Manager, look at the contents of
   your newly created startup disk. Figure 3-4 shows an example of
   such a disk created in Windows 95. Yours may differ slightly.

2. Look in the root directory of your hard disk to see if you have the
   files Config.dos and Autoexec.dos. These files start your computer
   in MS-DOS mode, and they should have the commands necessary to
   let you access your CD-ROM drive. You can see my .dos files below,
   which are for a Mitsumi CD-ROM drive. If you don't have .dos files,
   see if you have Config.sys and Autoexec.bat files, which assist in
   your normal startup and may have the commands you want.

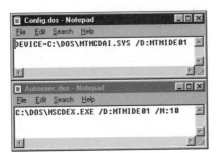

Look at your Config.sys and Autoexec.bat files, if they exist, to identify and locate the commands and their related files you need to
copy to the startup floppy you just created. You need the commands
and files that enable you to use your CD-ROM drive. You are interested in only one command in each file. In your Config file, you
need a command that loads the appropriate driver and assigns a
drive letter to your CD-ROM drive. (This command uses the
Mtmcdai.sys file in the previous illustration; yours will probably be
different.) In your Autoexec.bat file, you need a command that starts
the controller for the CD-ROM and assigns the drive defined in the

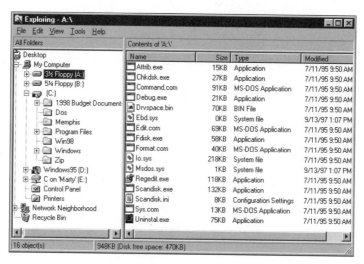

Figure 3-4. *Windows 95 Startup disk contents.*

Config.sys file to the controller. (Mscdex.exe is the controller in the previous illustration; yours should be the same.) The Mscdex.exe file is in your \Windows\Command folder in Windows 95 and in your Dos folder in Windows 3.*x*. The driver file is probably either in your root directory or in a folder related to your CD-ROM drive. (The previous illustration shows Mscdex.exe in the Dos folder, because that is where it will be on a clean hard disk without Windows, as discussed later in this chapter. Copy it from your Windows folder to your startup floppy now so, later, you can format your hard disk and copy it back to the Dos folder on your hard disk.)

3. In Windows Explorer or File Manager, drag your Config.dos and Autoexec.dos files, if you have them (or your Config.sys and Autoexec.bat files, if you don't), to your startup floppy.

4. Locate the CD-ROM driver, which will have a .sys extension, and the Mscdex.exe file, and drag them both to your floppy. (Mscdex.exe was in the above list of files to be copied from the Dos directory in Windows 3.*x*.)

5. In Windows Explorer, right-click the Config file, choose Open With, and select Notepad. In File Manager, click Config.sys, open the File menu, choose Run, press **HOME** to go to the left end of the command line, type **edit** (with a space after *edit*), and click OK. Edit the com-

mand that loads the CD-ROM driver so that it looks for the file on your startup floppy. Mine changes to this:

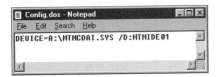

If there are other commands in your Config file, the easiest approach is to delete them. If you keep these commands, you will have to make sure that the files they use are on your startup floppy. The only purpose of this floppy is to start your system and enable you to use the CD-ROM drive so you can install or reinstall Windows. It does not perform any other function.

6. Save your changed Config file as Config.sys, open your Autoexec file, change the path to Mscdex.exe so it points to your floppy drive, delete any other commands, and save the file as Autoexec.bat. Close Notepad or your Editor.

7. Restart your computer with your startup floppy in its drive. Your system should boot, your CD-ROM driver should load, and the CD-ROM drive should be attached to the Mscdex controller. If you get error messages, use the information they contain to help cure the problem, possibly by reopening the Config.sys and Autoexec.bat files on your startup floppy or by replacing the driver file on your startup floppy. If you did not take all the other commands out of your Config.sys and Autoexec.bat files, you may need to do that; if you took them all off, you may need to add one or more back. Look carefully at the original files on your hard disk to figure this out.

8. When your system has properly booted and you are at the MS-DOS prompt, put a disc in your CD-ROM drive, type **d:** (if d is the drive letter for your CD-ROM drive), and press **ENTER.** The prompt switches to the drive letter of your CD-ROM drive. Type **dir** and press **ENTER.** You should see a list of the folders and files in the root directory of the CD in the drive. If this did not happen, you need to go back to Step 1 and figure out what went wrong.

9. When you can access your CD-ROM, you have a fully functioning emergency startup disk to protect you. Remove the startup floppy from its drive, label it, store it in a safe place, and reboot your system normally to bring Windows back up.

Cleaning Up Your Hard Disk

The first step in cleaning up your hard disk is to remove all of the files that you no longer use. For most people this is an almost impossible task— "How do I know which files I no longer use?" The easy answer is to back up all your data files, remove all your files by reformatting your hard disk, install Windows 98, and then reinstall the applications you know you need and restore the data files you know you need. Yes, this process takes a lot of time and work, but the alternative of sleuthing through your files, trying to figure out what to remove, can take even longer and generally is not as successful. A third option—to leave all your files—burdens your system with all the unused files on your hard disk. This virtually ensures that your system will not perform at the level of which it is capable, therefore taking even more time than the other alternatives by slowing down everything that you do.

TIP Give serious consideration to reformatting your hard disk, even though you will have to reinstall all your applications afterward. No other method cleans up your hard disk as well, giving you lots of free space and making your system much more efficient.

After you have removed all of the files that you want to remove from your hard disk, it is worthwhile to check the disk for errors (by running ScanDisk) and to defragment or optimize the disk. ScanDisk looks both for problems with your current files and for problems with your hard disk itself. It fixes many of the problems and alerts you to any problems that remain. During normal disk usage, files are broken into segments, and the segments may be scattered around the disk. Defragmentation gathers all of the segments pertaining to a single file onto one contiguous area of the disk, which greatly speeds up disk reading.

Both disk-error checking and defragmentation are available in Windows 95 on the Tools tab of a disk's Properties dialog box, as you can see in Figure 3-5.

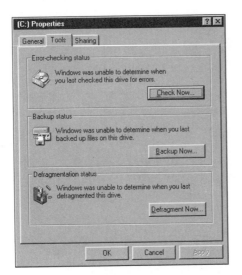

Figure 3-5. *ScanDisk and defragmentation options.*

 IP It is strongly recommended that you run the ScanDisk Thorough option and then run the defragmenter on your hard disk before running Windows 98 Setup. This may take over an hour, but when you are done, you will have the cleanest, safest, and fastest disk possible.

From Windows 95

To run ScanDisk and the defragmenter from Windows 95, follow these instructions:

1. Start either My Computer or Windows Explorer, right-click your hard disk, and choose Properties in the context menu that opens.

2. Click the Tools tab, and then click Check Now to start ScanDisk. After the ScanDisk dialog box opens, make sure your hard disk is selected, click the Thorough option and the Automatically Fix Errors check box, and then click Start. If ScanDisk restarts often, you need to disable your screen saver. Its starting may cause ScanDisk to restart.

3. When ScanDisk has finished, you are shown a status report for your hard disk, similar to the one in Figure 3-6. Click Close on the report, and then click Close again on the ScanDisk dialog box.

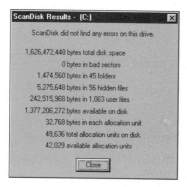

Figure 3-6. *Results of running ScanDisk.*

4. Back in your hard disk's Properties Tools tab, click Defragment Now. A dialog box opens telling you how badly your hard disk is fragmented and giving a recommendation on whether you need to defragment it.

5. Click Start to defragment the disk; otherwise click Exit. If you go ahead, a message box indicates the percent completed and informs you when the disk is defragmented. Click Yes to close the Disk Defragmenter, and then close your hard disk's Properties dialog box.

From Windows 3.*x* and MS-DOS

To run ScanDisk and the defragmenter from Windows 3.*x* and MS-DOS, follow these instructions (which assume that your hard disk is C):

1. If you are in Windows, exit to MS-DOS. At the MS-DOS prompt, type **scandisk c:** and press **ENTER.**

2. When ScanDisk completes its basic scan, you are asked if you want to perform a surface scan. Type **y** for Yes. This will take some time. When it is done, you are told of any problems with the disk and given options for fixing them. When you are satisfied with your disk, type **x** for Exit.

3. Again at the MS-DOS prompt, type **defrag c:** and press **ENTER.** You are told the percentage of the drive that is fragmented and given a recommendation on optimization. To accept the recommendation, press **ENTER**; otherwise, type **c** to configure the defragmenter, and

then select the option you want, or type **x** to exit. If you go ahead with the optimization, you will be told of the progress made.

4. You are told when the process is complete. Press **ENTER** to accept the message. You can then defragment another drive or type **x** to Exit.

Checking Your Current System

One final step before actually running Windows 98 Setup is to look at your current system and make sure that it, including networking hardware and software, is the way you want it. This includes reading the Windows 98 Readme.txt file in the root directory of the Windows 98 CD to see if any notes apply to your hardware or software, especially those that relate to networking.

A second aspect of checking your current system is to look at your Config.sys and Autoexec.bat files and remove any commands other than those that are absolutely necessary for hard-disk control or partitioning, for networking, and as device drivers for your CD-ROM. No other programs or utilities should be started by Config.sys, Autoexec.bat, or your \Windows\Start Menu folder or by your StartUp group (in Windows 3.*x*).

Making Installation Decisions

When you install Windows 98, you have one major decision and one subsidiary decision to make. These are:

- Whether to run Setup from Windows 3.*x* or Windows 95, or to reformat your hard disk and run Setup from a startup floppy disk

- Whether to use the Typical, Portable, Compact, or Custom installation

Running Setup from Windows 3.*x*, Windows 95, or from a Startup Floppy

Running the Windows 98 Setup program from Windows 3.*x* or Windows 95 allows you to preserve the settings in your Registry and other configuration files. Also, your Start menu and desktop setup, as well as the application files in your Windows folders, are preserved, so you do not have to reinstall your applications.

On the other hand, as mentioned earlier in this chapter, installing from a startup floppy has the benefit of allowing you to erase all of your old Windows files and do a major housecleaning of your hard disk. While it may sound scary to erase your settings and all your files, these functions are reasonably easy to restore. It is admittedly a pain to flip all the floppies and CDs necessary to reinstall your Windows applications, but the gain in efficiency and hard-disk space is generally worth it.

There is another reason for installing from a startup disk—getting a new hard disk. With the recent demands for huge amounts of disk space (Microsoft Office 97 can easily use well over 200 MB) and the great disk prices that are available, you may well decide to install a new, large hard disk.

Preparing a New or Reformatted Hard Disk

If you have decided to reformat your hard disk or install a new one, then you need to prepare that disk. To do that, make the startup floppy described above, carefully back up your hard disk, and physically install your new hard disk. Then use the following instructions to format the new disk or to reformat your old disk and to put the minimum number of boot files on that disk. When you are done, you will be ready to install Windows 98.

 ARNING   The following instructions irrevocably remove all information on your hard disk. Do not use these instructions unless you have successfully backed up all the files you believe necessary and are prepared to lose other files.

 ARNING   If you are installing the Windows 98 upgrade after formatting or reformatting your hard disk, you must have Windows 95 or Windows 3.*x* *floppy* Disk 1 to get through the piracy protection scheme. The Windows 95 CD will *not* work.

---

1. Put your startup disk in your floppy drive, and turn on, or boot, your computer.

2. At the MS-DOS prompt, type **fdisk** and press **ENTER.** When the Fdisk screen appears, type **3** and press **ENTER** to delete the current partition; type **1** and press **ENTER** to delete the primary DOS partition; press **ENTER** to confirm your choice; type a volume label, and

press **ENTER**; type **y** and press **ENTER** to once again confirm that you want to delete the partition.

3. After you confirm the deletion, press **ESC** to return to the original Fdisk screen. Type **1,** press **ENTER**, type **1,** and press **ENTER** again to create a new primary DOS partition. Type **y** and press **ENTER** to confirm that you want to use the maximum available size for the primary DOS partition. After creating the new partition, reboot your computer.

4. At the MS-DOS prompt, type **format c:/s** and press **ENTER.** This formats the drive and places the MS-DOS system files on it. Type **y** and press **ENTER** to confirm that you want to remove all the contents of the hard disk. After formatting is complete, type a volume label if you want one, and press **ENTER.**

5. When you are again at the MS-DOS prompt, type **c:** and press **ENTER,** and then type **md\DOS** and press **ENTER** to make a directory named Dos.

6. Type **copy a:*.* \dos** and press **ENTER** to copy the files you put on the startup floppy to your newly formatted hard disk.

7. If you had Config.dos and Autoexec.dos on your previous hard disk or installation, they are now in your Dos directory. Copy these files to the root directory of your newly formatted hard disk, and rename them by typing **copy \dos\config.dos \config.sys** and pressing **ENTER,** followed by typing **copy \dos\autoexec.dos \autoexec.bat** and pressing **ENTER.**

8. If you do not have Config.dos and Autoexec.dos, copy your Config.sys and Autoexec.bat files to the root directory of your hard disk by typing **copy \dos\config.sys** and pressing **ENTER,** followed by typing **copy \dos\autoexec.bat** and pressing **ENTER.** If you type **dir** at this point, your system should list three visible files (Command.com, Config.sys, and Autoexec.bat) and one directory (Dos).

9. Open the newly copied Config.sys and Autoexec.bat files by typing **\dos\edit config.sys** or **\dos\edit autoexec.bat** and pressing **ENTER.** Edit these files as discussed under *Creating a Startup Floppy* so that

the paths now point to your hard disk. For example, your Autoexec.bat file should contain a command similar to

C:\Dos\Mscdex.exe /:Mtmide01 /M:10

and your Config.sys should contain a command similar to

Device=C:\Dos\Mtmcdai.sys /D:Mtmide01.

10. When you have prepared your newly formatted hard disk, remove the startup floppy, and then reboot from the hard disk. Try to access your CD-ROM drive by inserting the Windows 98 CD, typing the drive letter of your CD-ROM drive, and pressing **ENTER,** followed by typing **dir** and pressing **ENTER.** You should see a list of files on your Windows 98 CD. If you have problems, review the Config.sys and Autoexec.bat files and the files that they use to make sure they are correct and in the correct folder.

Using Typical, Portable, Compact, or Custom Setup

If you choose to reformat your hard disk or install a new hard disk, the remaining question in Windows 98 Setup is which type of setup you want to perform. You have four types to choose from, which will determine the Windows 98 features and options that you install and the amount of disk space that they use. Table 3-2 describes these types, and Table 3-3 shows the Windows 98 options that are available in each.

Most of the options can also be installed after you have Windows 98 installed and you have had a chance to read the rest of this book and learn what the options do. Windows 98's Control Panel has an Add/Remove Programs capability that allows you to do that. Therefore, the decision on which options to install during the initial setup is not critical.

Because you can add many of the options after the installation and the Typical installation is so much easier, that is the recommended choice. Study Table 3-3 to see what is not included in the Typical installation, and then use Add/Remove Programs in Control Panel to add the missing programs after you have finished installing Windows 98.

Type of Setup	Description
Typical	Installs what Microsoft believes are the most commonly selected options in a manner that requires the least amount of interaction with you. It is the default and what is assumed in this book.
Portable	Installs the options typically selected by users of portable, or mobile, computers. This type of installation combines lower disk-space usage with features needed in a mobile environment.
Compact	Installs the minimum number of files needed to run Windows 98.
Custom	Allows you to choose the options you want to install and to confirm the configuration settings as they are made. This gives you the most flexibility, but it also requires the most knowledge about your system.

Table 3-2.   *Types of Windows 98 Setup.*

Setup Option	Typical	Portable	Compact
Accessibility			
Accessibility Wizard			
Microsoft Magnifier			
Accessories			
Briefcase		Yes	
Calculator	Yes		
Desktop Wallpaper			
Document Templates	Yes		
Games			
Imaging	Yes		
Mouse Pointers			
Notepad	Yes	Yes	Yes
Online Guide			
Paint	Yes		
Quick View			
Screen Saver	Yes (1)		
Windows Scripting Host	Yes	Yes	

Table 3-3.   *Options available in different types of setup.*   *(continued)*

Table 3-3. *continued*

Setup Option	Typical	Portable	Compact
WordPad	Yes	Yes	
Communications			
Dial-Up Networking	Yes	Yes	Yes
Dial-Up Server			
Direct Cable Conn.		Yes	
HyperTerminal		Yes	
Infrared			
ISDN Configuration Wizard			
Microsoft Chat 2.0			
Microsoft NetMeeting	Yes		
Phone Dialer	Yes	Yes	
Virtual Private Networking		Yes	
Desktop Themes			
Internet Tools			
Microsoft FrontPage Express	Yes	Yes	
Microsoft Outlook Express	Yes	Yes	
Microsoft VRML 2.0 Viewer	Yes	Yes	
Microsoft Wallet			
Personal Web Server	Yes	Yes	
Real Audio Player 4.0			
Web Publishing Wizard			
Web-Based Enterpise			
Multilingual Support			
Multimedia			
Audio Compression	(2)	(2)	
CD Player	(3)	(3)	(3)
DVD Player	(3)	(3)	(3)
Macromedia Shockwave Director	Yes		
Macromedia Shockwave Flash	Yes		

(continued)

Table 3-3. *continued*

Setup Option	Typical	Portable	Compact
Media Player	Yes	Yes	
Microsoft NetShow Player 2.0			
Multimedia Sounds Schemes			
Sample Sounds			
Sound Recorder	(2)	(2)	
TV Viewer			
Video Compression	Yes	Yes	
Volume Control	(2)	(2)	
Online Services			
AOL	Yes	Yes	Yes
AT&T WorldNet Service	Yes	Yes	Yes
CompuServe	Yes	Yes	Yes
Prodigy Internet	Yes	Yes	Yes
The Microsoft Network	Yes	Yes	Yes
System Tools			
Backup			
Character Map			
Clipboard Viewer			
Compression Agent	Yes	Yes	
Disk Cleanup	Yes	Yes	Yes
Disk Defragmenter(4)	Yes	Yes	Yes
Drive Converter (FAT32)	Yes	Yes	
DriveSpace 3	(5)	(5)	(5)
Group Policies			
Net Watcher			
Resource Meter			
ScanDisk (4)	Yes	Yes	Yes
Scheduled Tasks	Yes	Yes	Yes
System File Checker			

(continued)

Table 3-3. *continued*

Setup Option	Typical	Portable	Compact
System Information			
System Monitor			
Welcome To Windows	Yes	Yes	Yes
Maintenance Wizard	Yes	Yes	
Windows Update	Yes	Yes	Yes
WinPopup	(6)	(6)	
CD-Tools Directory			
Batch 98			
Old MS-DOS Utilities			
Policy Editor			
Resource Kit			
Tweak UI			
Windows 95 Exchange and Fax			
CD-Add-ons Directory			
Personal Web Server			

Notes on Table 3-3

All of the options in Table 3-3 are included on the Windows 98 CD. The options down through System Tools can be selected for installation in a Custom install. The only exceptions to that are ScanDisk and Defrag, which are automatically installed in all cases. If you want to install the options beginning with CD-Tools Directory and going to the end of the table, you must copy them from the CD by dragging them in Windows Explorer after installation. A "Yes" under Typical, Portable, or Compact means that the option is automatically installed in that setup type. A blank space in a column is the same as a "No." Other notes on Table 3-3 are as follows:

1. Only some of the screen savers are installed in a Typical setup. Other screen savers are available on the CD and can be installed in a Custom setup or by using Add/Remove Programs after completing installation.
2. Installed only if a sound card is detected.
3. Installed only if a drive is detected.
4. Automatically installed in all situations.
5. Only installed if DoubleSpace or DriveSpace is detected.
6. Only installed if networking capability is detected and other networking software is installed.

Running Windows 98 Setup

After all the preparatory work to get ready to install Windows 98, running Windows 98 Setup is definitely anticlimactic. You have already made the tough decision: whether you are going to install from Windows 95, Windows 3.*x*, or from a new or newly formatted hard disk. That decision leads you to one or the other of the next two sections. (Because installing from Windows 3.*x* is very similar to installing on a new hard disk, both are discussed together.) Independent of that choice, you also have the option of installing Windows 98 using a script and files across a network, as described at the end of this section.

Running Windows 98 Setup from Windows 95

If you install Windows 98 from Windows 95, all your settings and configurations in Windows 95 automatically transfer to Windows 98. This includes your choice of features and applets. Windows 98 installs them without asking you if want to choose other applets or features.

Use the following instructions to install Windows 98 from Windows 95:

 WARNING   Make sure no other programs or utilities are running.

---

1. Reboot your computer to make sure that you have a clean environment and that nothing is running besides Windows 95.

2. Insert your Windows 98 CD in the drive.

3. The CD automatically loads and appears on your screen with the following message, asking if you want to upgrade to a newer version of Windows.

4. Click Yes. You will see a Welcome message. Click Continue. Setup prepares your system for the installation.

5. If Setup detects any other programs running, a message appears telling you to use **ALT-TAB** to switch to those other programs and close them. Do that if prompted, and then click OK to continue with Setup.

6. The License Agreement will appear. You can scroll through the License Agreement by using the scroll bar or by pressing **PAGE DOWN**. When ready, click I Accept The Agreement, and then click Next.

7. After Windows 98 verifies your settings and available hard-disk space, you are asked if you want to save your old system files (taking approximately 50 MB); doing so allows you to uninstall Windows 98 later, if you want. I recommend that you choose the default, Yes, to save the files and click Next. (You can always delete the files when you are sure that you won't need them—see *Getting Rid of Saved System Files* later in this chapter.)

8. Next a message indicates that Setup will create a Startup Disk. You are not given a choice. If you click Cancel, you abort the installation. Click Next. After the files are gathered, you are told to label a floppy disk, insert it into your floppy drive, and click OK. Do this. The information is then copied to the disk. When this process is finished, you are so informed and told to remove the disk. Do so and click OK.

9. Setup tells you it is about to begin copying the Windows 98 files to your hard disk (see Figure 3-7). At this point, you can still look at and make changes to your earlier settings by clicking Back. If you are ready to begin copying files, click Next.

10. Setup then copies all the necessary files to your computer. When it is done, your computer restarts, and then Windows 98 is set up for your hardware. The system configurations and settings, including Control Panel, the Start menu, and the desktop, are then built.

11. Finally the computer reboots, and the Windows 98 screen appears.

Figure 3-7. *Windows 98 Setup ready to copy files.*

Running Windows 98 Setup from Windows 3.*x* or a New or Newly Formatted Disk

You can also install Windows 98 from Windows 3.*x* or on a freshly formatted hard disk that you have prepared with system files so you can access your CD-ROM drive, as described in *Preparing a New or Reformatted Hard Disk*, earlier in this chapter.

If you install Windows 98 from Windows 3.*x*, unlike installing from Windows 95, you can choose either a Typical, Custom, Portable, or Compact installation; and if you choose Custom, you can select the applets and features that you want installed.

To install Windows 98 from Windows 3.*x* or on a new or newly formatted hard disk, use these instructions:

 OTE You can boot your system and run Setup from a floppy drive, but you must be able to boot your hard disk by itself so that Setup can restart itself.

---

1. With nothing in the floppy drive, reboot your computer to make sure that you have a clean, bootable environment with nothing else running except Windows 3.*x*, if it is available.

2. On a new or newly formatted hard disk, at the MS-DOS prompt, type **d:\setup** (assuming that your hard disk is C:, your CD-ROM is D:, and the Windows 98 CD is in the CD-ROM drive), and press **ENTER.**

3. If you are running Windows 3.*x*, in either File Manager or Program Manager, open the File menu, choose Run, type **d:\setup,** and click OK.

4. You see a message telling you that Setup is going to perform a routine check of your system (running ScanDisk without the Thorough option). Press **ENTER** again to continue. ScanDisk will run; and given no problems, press **x** for Exit, and Setup will start and display a Welcome message.

 OTE If you are installing the Upgrade version of Windows 98 on a new or newly formatted hard disk, you need to have Disk 1 from Windows 95 or Windows 3.*x* handy to get through the piracy-protection scheme.

---

5. Click Continue. The Setup Wizard starts and prepares your system to run Windows 98 Setup. The License Agreement appears. You can scroll through the License Agreement by using the scroll bar or by pressing **PAGE DOWN.**

6. When ready, click I Accept The Agreement, and then click Next. You will be asked to choose the folder in which you want Windows 98 installed, with a choice of Windows or another folder name. After making the choice, click Next.

 IP I recommend that you use the default Windows folder. It is assumed by just about everybody, including this book, and will be one less thing to worry about.

---

7. If you chose Other, you are asked to enter the name of the folder you want to use. Do so, and then click Next once again.

8. The Setup Options dialog box opens, asking if you want a Typical, Portable, Compact, or Custom install. Make your choice, and click Next.

IP If you are using a portable computer, choose Portable; if you know you want an option that is only in Custom, choose Custom; otherwise, choose Typical. (Note that a Compact install needs over 170 MB, while a Portable install requires 220 MB, and a Typical install needs 205 MB.)

---

9. Enter your name and your company name when asked, and click Next.

10. If you chose Custom, you are asked to select the components you want to install. Most of the components have several subcomponents. To see those subcomponents, select the parent and click Details. Select the subcomponents and components that you want, and then click Next.

11. If you chose Typical or Portable, you are given a chance to look at the components that were chosen for you. You can make changes by selecting Show Me The List Of Components and clicking Next. This takes you to the same dialog box that was described in Step 8. Make the changes in components that you want, and click Next.

12. If you are on a network, you are asked to enter a computer name, your workgroup name, and a description of your computer. When you are done, click Next.

13. Select the country whose set of Internet channels (for use in the Channel bar) you want on your computer, and click Next.

14. A message now indicates that Setup will create a Startup Disk. You are not given a choice. If you click Cancel, you abort the installation. Click Next. After the files are gathered, you are told to label a disk, insert it into your floppy drive, and click OK. The information is then copied to the disk. When it is done, you are so informed and told to remove the disk. Do so and click OK.

15. Setup tells you it is about to begin copying the Windows 98 files to your hard disk. At this point, you can still look at or make changes to your earlier settings by clicking Back. If you are ready to start copying files, click Next.

16. Setup then copies all the necessary files to your computer. When it is done, your computer restarts, and then Windows 98 is set up for your hardware. If you are on a network, you may be asked to enter

the Interrupt (IRQ) and I/O address of your network adapter if Setup can't detect it. If so prompted, do this and click OK.

17. The system configurations and settings, including Control Panel, the Start menu, and the desktop, are then built. During that process, you will be asked to confirm that the time zone is correct.

18. Finally the computer reboots, you are asked to enter a username and password, and the Welcome to Windows 98 window appears. Click any of the options, or click the Close button to see the Windows 98 screen.

Running Windows 98 Setup Across a Network

If you are connected to a network, the Windows 98 Setup programs and files may reside on a network server's hard disk or on a CD accessible over the network. In that case, you can still install Windows 98 from Windows 95 or Windows for Workgroups across the network. Replace Steps 2 and 3 in *Running Windows 98 Setup from Windows 95* or Step 3 in *Running Windows 98 Setup from Windows 3.x or on a New or Newly Formatted Hard Disk*, found earlier in this chapter, with the following steps:

 ARNING If you install over a network, sometimes the network connection is lost during one of the reboots, and the installation cannot be completed. In most circumstances, all of the files have already been downloaded, and only the hardware needs to be set up. You should be able to reboot into Safe mode and to set up your hardware manually. Begin by trying to reestablish your network connection. One way to prevent this from happening, if you have enough disk space (assume 130 MB in addition to the average 250 MB for Windows 98), is to copy the Win98 folder from the CD onto your hard disk and then to run Setup from there.

1. Using Windows Explorer in Windows 95 or the File Manager in Windows for Workgroups, locate the drive and folder (probably named Win98) on the network that contains the Windows 98 Setup.exe program.

2. Double-click Setup.exe to start the process and see the Welcome message. Click Continue. Setup prepares your system for the installation.

3. Continue with Step 4 in the *Running Windows 98 Setup from Windows 95* section of this chapter.

 OTE   If you install from a network server, Windows 98 will automatically go there for any optional files or device drivers that you need in the future. This can be very handy and can save you from having to keep track of many sets of disks in even a modest-size organization.

Using Scripts to Automate Windows 98 Setup

You can completely automate running Windows 98 Setup, or you can allow just the user interaction that you want. This is particularly useful if you have a number of machines on which you want the same settings. By preparing a script (or batch program) once, you can run Setup on all the machines, getting the same installation by entering and executing a single command on all the machines. To automate Setup, you use a program called Microsoft Batch 98, which leads you through the questions in Setup and then creates a script file called Bsetup.inf. Setup uses this script file to replace all of the user input. The batch-file creation program is on your Windows 98 CD in the \Tools\Reskit\Batch folder and must be installed separately using Add/Remove Programs in Control Panel. See how to install these programs, create a script, and run Setup using a script with these steps:

1. In the Windows Explorer open your CD-ROM drive and Tools\Reskit\Batch folder. Double-click Setup.exe. Follow the instructions on your screen to complete the installation of Batch 98.

2. Open the Start menu, and choose Programs | Microsoft Batch 98. The Microsoft Batch 98 window opens, as you can see in Figure 3-8.

3. Click Gather Now. This picks up all the information in your Registry and uses it to fill in as much of the script as possible.

4. Click General Setup Options, Network Options, then Optional Components, and finally Advanced Options; in each, go through the many tabs and options to create the setup that is correct for your computer. Figure 3-9 gives you an example of one of the dialog boxes.

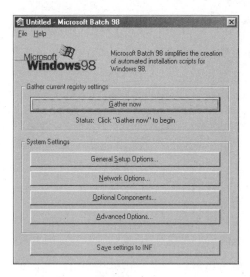

Figure 3-8. *Batch Setup window for creating a batch file.*

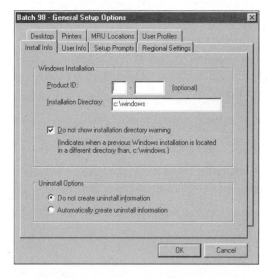

Figure 3-9. *Some of the many options used to script Setup.*

5. When you are finished, click Save Settings To INF. A dialog box appears, asking where you want to save the .inf file. Probably the best choice is the root directory of your hard disk. Select the path and click Save. Click Close to close the Microsoft Batch 98 dialog box.

IP You can look at and manually edit your batch file by simply opening it in Notepad. For example, mine is shown in Figure 3-10. If you want to edit the file with more certainty, you can also reopen it with File menu Open option of Batch 98.

6. Run Setup with the script by opening the Start menu, choosing Run, typing (for example, if the Windows 98 CD is in your D: drive, and the script is in the root directory of your C: drive) **d:\win98\setup c:\msbatch.inf,** and finally pressing **ENTER.**

Setup should start as it normally does. If you appropriately answered all of the questions, it runs through to completion without your intervention. In my case, I was asked to shut down another program, to accept the License Agreement, to insert a floppy disk for the Startup Disk, and to remove the floppy. While not completely automatic, it was a lot better than a manual install. The key here is that I did not have to make any decisions as Setup ran; they were already made.

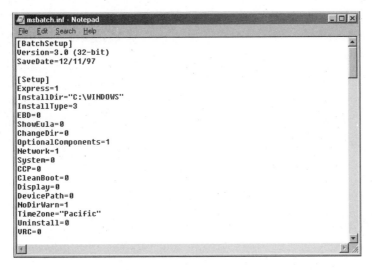

Figure 3-10. *Looking at a batch setup file.*

Uninstalling Windows 98

If you decide that Windows 98 is not right for you and you would like to return to Windows 95, you may, in fact, do that if all of the following conditions hold true for you:

■ You installed Windows 98 as an upgrade from Windows 3.x or Windows 95.

■ You backed up the Windows 3.x or Windows 95 system files as prompted during Windows 98 Setup.

■ You have not compressed your primary partition.

To uninstall Windows 98 and return to Windows 95 or Windows 3.x:

1. Open My Computer or Windows Explorer, and locate the \Windows\Command\Uninstal.exe program.

2. Double-click Uninstal.exe. Click Yes, you do want to uninstall Windows 98. Click Yes again to run ScanDisk.

3. Click Yes to proceed with the uninstall. Uninstall exits to MS-DOS and restores your directories and files. It looks for deleted files and modified files.

4. When Uninstall is done, it tells you to remove any disks in your floppy drives and to press **ENTER,** and then it reboots your system. Windows 95 or Windows 3.x then reappears.

5. If you have some Windows 98 items still on your desktop, simply delete them.

Getting Rid of Saved System Files

If you saved the system files during setup so you could uninstall Windows 98 but have now decided that you want to stay with Windows 98, you can delete the files and recover up to 50 MB of hard-disk space. The files to do this are named Winundo.dat and Winundo.ini, and they are in your root directory. They are read-only and hidden, so you may not see them, and when you delete them, you are asked to confirm their deletion. If you cannot see the files, open the View menu in either My Computer or Windows Explorer; choose Folder Options; and on the View tab, click Show All Files under Hidden Files in the Advanced Settings box. Click OK to return to My Computer or Windows Explorer. Then select the two files you want to delete, and press **SHIFT-DELETE** to delete them permanently.

Setting Up and Customizing Windows 98

Windows 98 is designed with a great deal of flexibility to allow you to tailor it to behave the way you want it to. Of course, you must take the time to learn how to do that and then do it. The purpose of this chapter is to identify what you can customize, to describe what your options are, and to show you how to customize Windows 98.

Setting Up Windows 98

You can tailor Windows 98 in two broad ways: by setting up and organizing your screen, disk, folders, and files the way you want them; and by customizing the many settings available in Control Panel. In this section, we will look at setting up and organizing your screen and files; in the next major section, we will examine customizing Windows 98 using Control Panel.

Arranging Your Screen

The first place to tailor your system is the Windows 98 screen. When you start Windows 98, your screen looks approximately like the one shown in Figure 4-1. (Yours may have more or fewer icons on the left, depending on what Windows options you have installed and whether you upgraded from Windows 3.x or Windows 95. You may or may not still see the Welcome to

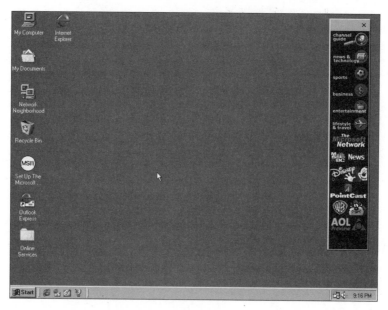

Figure 4-1. *Opening screen.*

Windows 98 dialog box, depending on whether you chose to have it auto-matically open each time you log on.) You can do many things to this screen and its components to make them better meet your needs.

 IP If you no longer see the Welcome to Windows 98 dialog box, you can re-start it by clicking Welcome To Windows in Programs | Accessories | System Tools.

Working with Desktop Icons

The first change you can make to the desktop is to rearrange the icons and perhaps remove or add some. If you want to change their placement on the screen, you may first need to open the desktop context menu (by right-clicking the desktop) and turn off Auto Arrange, as shown below. (Auto Arrange forces the icons into one or more columns on the left.)

With Auto Arrange off, you can drag the icons anywhere on the desktop, and they will remain there, as shown in Figure 4-2. This is particularly valuable with a large screen (19 to 21 inches) operating at higher resolutions (1024 × 768 and above), where you have lots of real estate for various windows. Remember, though, that windows can cover icons on the desktop. (However, you can use the Show Desktop button in the Quick Launch toolbar to minimize open windows and uncover icons.) For this reason, placing all the icons in the default position on the left side and leaving the remainder of the screen for windows has substantial merit. Of course, even if you leave them on the left side, you still can drag the icons into any order you choose.

You cannot easily delete or move to another folder the icons for My Computer, Network Neighborhood, My Documents, Internet Explorer, and Recycle Bin. You can create shortcuts for any of the desktop icons and place the shortcuts in any folder or disk drive you want to use. You can delete the Online Services folder, Outlook Express, and Microsoft Network (MSN); and you can move them to other folders. But, if you delete Outlook

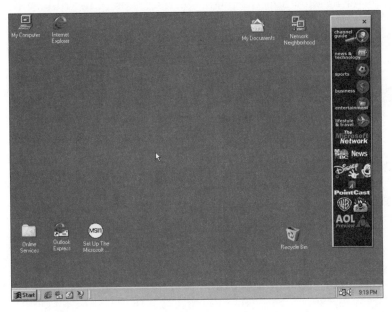

Figure 4-2.   *Drag desktop icons anywhere on the screen.*

Express or the Online Services folder, you can add them back only by selecting them in the Add/Remove Programs Properties dialog box, which you reach from Control Panel (opened from the Settings option on the Start menu). MSN, however, is only a shortcut and can be recreated from its parent in \Program Files\Online Services\MSN\Msninst.exe.

You can add as many icons to the desktop as you want or as can fit. Again, you must consider that windows can cover desktop icons and then you can access them only with Show Desktop, by reducing the size of the windows, or by minimizing the windows (either by minimizing each window individually or by right-clicking the taskbar and selecting Minimize All Windows). Two icons you might want to add are the Windows Explorer icon and a printer icon. Windows Explorer is so heavily used (at least by me) that it is natural for the desktop, and having a printer on the desktop allows you to print a document simply by dragging it to the printer icon. To add Windows Explorer to the desktop, right-drag the Explorer.exe file from the Windows folder in the Windows Explorer or My Computer window, and select Create Shortcut(s) Here from the context menu that appears, as shown next. To add a printer, open the Printers folder in Windows Explorer or My Computer, drag the printer you want to the desktop, and click Yes to create a shortcut. See Chapter 7, "Windows 98 Printing," for more information on setting up printers.

Customizing the Taskbar

You can tailor the taskbar to fit your needs. You can expand and contract it, move it to any of the four sides, have it always visible or visible only when you want it. See this for yourself by following these steps:

1. Open the Start menu, and from the Programs option, start several programs. Notice that the tasks on the taskbar get smaller as you add

more of them, until the tasks are so small that you cannot read much of the label, like this:

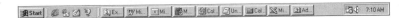

2. Move the mouse pointer to the top edge of the taskbar so that the mouse pointer becomes a two-headed arrow, and then drag the top edge up about a quarter of an inch. The taskbar doubles in size vertically, making the labels easier to read, as you can see here:

3. Point at a blank area of the taskbar, and drag the taskbar to each of the four sides of the screen. The taskbar jumps to each side as the mouse pointer approaches a side. When the taskbar is on the right side, the screen looks like Figure 4-3. When you have seen how this works, return the taskbar to the bottom of your screen.

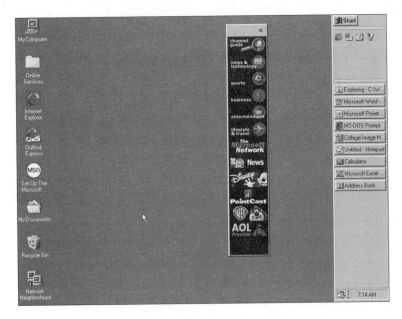

Figure 4-3.   *Taskbar moved to the right side.*

4. Right-click a blank area of the taskbar, and click Properties. The Taskbar Properties dialog box opens with the Taskbar Options tab displayed, as shown in Figure 4-4.

   ■ **Always On Top** keeps the taskbar visible regardless of how many windows you have open or the placement of those windows. If Always On Top is not checked, a maximized window will cover the taskbar, and you will be able to get to the taskbar only by closing or minimizing the window.

   ■ **Auto Hide** hides the taskbar unless the mouse pointer is moved to the edge of the screen where the taskbar is, in which case the taskbar pops up. If Always On Top is not also checked, and if you have a maximized window on your screen, you will not be able to see the taskbar when you move the mouse to the edge because the taskbar will be displayed beneath the maximized window.

NOTE   Both Always On Top and Auto Hide must be checked for Auto Hide to work properly.

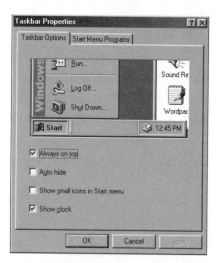

Figure 4-4.   *Taskbar options.*

■ **Show Small Icons In Start Menu** makes the icons in the Start menu small so more options can fit in an area.

■ **Show Clock** allows you to control the display of the clock.

5. Click Auto Hide, and make sure Always On Top is also checked. Then click OK to close the dialog box. If your mouse is not in the taskbar area and some other object, for example, a window, is active, the taskbar disappears.

6. Move your mouse pointer to the bottom edge of the screen, and your taskbar reappears. Now you can use the taskbar as you could before you turned on Auto Hide. If you move your mouse pointer above the taskbar without clicking it, the taskbar disappears. If you click the taskbar, it becomes the active object on the screen, and when you move the mouse pointer away, the taskbar remains on the screen until you click some other object (desktop, window, or icon).

7. Right-click a blank spot on the taskbar, and open the Properties dialog box. Click Always On Top to turn it off, and then close the dialog box by clicking OK. Now, if you start and maximize a program, you can no longer get the taskbar to appear by moving the mouse pointer to the bottom edge of the screen. If you resize the program window so you can see the bottom part of the desktop and you move the mouse pointer to the bottom edge, the taskbar appears.

8. Again open the Taskbar Properties dialog box, turn off Auto Hide, and close the dialog box. Now the taskbar is permanently on the desktop; however, if you maximize a window, the taskbar is covered, and the only way you can see it is to reduce the size of or close the program window.

9. Open the Taskbar Properties dialog box for a final time, and set the options in the manner that best suits you. The default is that Always On Top and Show Clock are selected and Auto Hide and Show Small Icons are not.

Adding and Changing Toolbars in the Taskbar

The taskbar can contain toolbars, both standard and custom ones. By default, the taskbar contains the Quick Launch toolbar with four buttons on it. You can add to this toolbar and turn it off. Look at how you do that and how you can place other toolbars in the taskbar.

1. Right-click a blank area of the taskbar, and point at Toolbars to open the list of standard toolbars (shown next) that you can place in the taskbar.

2. Select first Address and then Links. You see the standard Internet Explorer toolbars. Reopen the taskbar context menu, select Toolbars, turn off Address and Links, and turn on Desktop. This places all your desktop icons in the taskbar. Click the right arrow next to the rightmost icon to view the remainder of the icons, as you see here.

3. Again open the taskbar context menu, select Toolbars, turn off Desktop, and click New Toolbar. This allows you to select a folder to put on the taskbar. For example, if you select Control Panel, you get access from the taskbar to all the Control Panel icons, as you see here:

 OTE If you want a set of applications on the taskbar, you can put those applications in a folder and select that folder from the taskbar's New Toolbar dialog box.

---

4. If it is open, close the New Toolbar dialog box. (If you put Control Panel on your taskbar, open the taskbar's context menu, point at Toolbars, and click Control Panel to turn it off.)

5. Open Windows Explorer, and display the contents of My Computer in the right pane. Drag the Control Panel icon to the Quick Launch toolbar in the taskbar. Click Yes, you want to create a shortcut. The Control Panel icon appears in the Quick Launch toolbar, like this:

 TIP You can adjust the width of the Quick Launch toolbar by dragging the divider bar on the right of the Quick Launch toolbar, between it and the tasks on the taskbar.

---

6. Click the new Control Panel icon, and Control Panel opens. Close Control Panel.

7. In Windows Explorer, open the \Windows\Application Data\Microsoft\Internet Explorer\Quick Launch folder. As you can see in Figure 4-5, this shows all the icons on the Quick Launch toolbar. Here you can add and delete those icons.

8. Select Shortcut To Control Panel, press **SHIFT-DELETE,** and answer Yes to delete it.

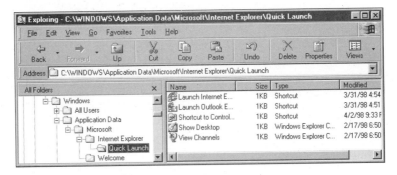

Figure 4-5.   *Locating the Quick Launch toolbar in the Windows folder.*

Starting Programs

Windows 98 has so many ways to start programs that, as you are setting up Windows 98, you need to take several minutes to consider which of the starting methods you want to use with each of your programs. Each of the following offers a different way to start a program:

- The Programs option on the Start menu
- The Start menu itself
- The desktop
- A special folder
- A taskbar toolbar
- Program Manager
- Windows Explorer or My Computer

The last option, using Windows Explorer or My Computer, is the most cumbersome and, therefore, should be used only as a fallback, for programs that you very seldom use. We will look at each of the other methods and consider how they should be used. Before doing that, though, look at how you use shortcuts to create the other methods of starting programs.

Creating and Using Shortcuts

When you use Windows Explorer or My Computer to open a folder or start a program, you go through the parent folders to find the actual program file (a file with the extension .exe, .com, or .bat) or folder that you want. Then you click it (assuming single-clicking is enabled). Windows 98 allows you to use a *shortcut* to start an application or to open a folder without finding and clicking the actual program file or folder. Shortcuts allow you to leave all the files related to a given program in a folder for that program and yet start the program or open the folder from a variety of locations. All you need in each location is a small (under 1 KB) shortcut file.

A shortcut is a link, or a pointer, to the original program file or to the original folder. When you click a shortcut, Windows 98 opens the folder or starts the program to which the shortcut points. The Programs option of the Start menu is composed of folders containing shortcuts, as you can see in Figure 4-6. Shortcuts can be virtually anywhere. You can place them on the desktop, in a folder that you create just to hold program shortcuts, and/or on the Start menu. Later in this chapter, you will see several examples of how you might set up your computer using shortcuts so that you can easily get at your programs, files, and folders.

You can create shortcuts in several ways:

- Drag a program file or a folder to the Start button and then to the position you want it on the Start menu.

 OTE In Windows 98, unlike Windows 95, the Start menu opens when you drag a program icon to it, allowing you to immediately place a new shortcut in your desired location on the menu.

- Drag a program file to the desktop or to any other folder.

- Right-click a program file or a folder to open the context menu; or select a program file or folder, and open the File menu; and in either case, choose Create Shortcut, as shown here with a context menu:

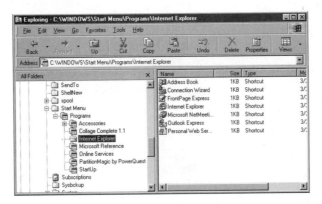

Figure 4-6.   *Folders and shortcuts that make up the Programs option of the Start menu.*

If you drag a program file or a folder to the Start button, you create a shortcut in the \Windows\Start Menu folder, and the program's name appears at the top of the Start menu. The result is that you can start the program or open the folder by opening the Start menu and clicking on the program or folder name, without using the Programs option.

If you drag a program file to the desktop or another folder, a new file is created with the words "Shortcut to" at the beginning of the name of the file. If you use a menu to create a shortcut, the new file is in the folder that contained the original file or folder, but it has "Shortcut to" at the beginning of the name. You can drag the new file anywhere.

If you right-click a shortcut and select Properties, the Properties dialog box opens. The General tab, for most files, shows the name, size, and dates that are part of the properties of all files. However, the Shortcut tab (or Program tab for shortcuts to MS-DOS programs) is unique to shortcut files and shows the original file or folder to which the shortcut is pointing, the starting folder, and any hot key that has been assigned to the shortcut, as shown in Figure 4-7. This tab also allows you to find the original file or folder (display the file or folder in its containing folder) by clicking the Find Target button and to change the icon used with the shortcut.

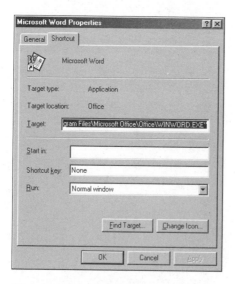

Figure 4-7.   *The Shortcut Properties tab shows the location of the original file or folder.*

IP To quickly start an application or open a folder, create a shortcut key by clicking the Shortcut Key text box in the shortcut's Properties dialog box, and then press the key strokes you want to use.

A shortcut to an MS-DOS program is the Windows 98 replacement for a PIF. (A PIF is a program information file, which was used to facilitate running MS-DOS programs under Windows 3.x.) An MS-DOS shortcut's Properties dialog box has a number of additional tabs that allow you to determine the screen font, memory handling, screen characteristics, and other facets of Windows' interaction with the program. If a Windows 3.x Pif exists for the MS-DOS program, look at that file to get the settings for a shortcut to the program. (You are not allowed to create a shortcut to a PIF, because that is like having a PIF for a PIF.) If no PIF exists, try running the program without any changes in the shortcut; it is highly likely that none are needed. If all else fails, you will need to ask the publisher of the MS-DOS program what the settings should be.

IP If you create a shortcut for an MS-DOS program or a nonprogram file, you can get additional icon choices from \Windows\System\Pifmgr.dll, \Windows\System\Shell32.dll, \Windows\Moricons.dll, and possibly, depending on what you have installed, \Windows\System\Iconlib.dll.

The Programs Submenu

If you upgraded to Windows 98 from a previous version of Windows, the Programs option of your Start menu was automatically loaded with all the programs you could start from the Programs option in Windows 95 or from Program Manager in Windows 3.x. Also, if you install a new or updated program in Windows 98, that program is added automatically to the Programs option. The Programs option of the Start menu, then, is the way that Windows 98 expects you to start your programs. Look at the steps involved in this method:

1. Click the Start button.

2. Point at the Programs option on the Start menu.

3. Point at the folder that contains the program (or just the program if it's not in a folder).

4. Click the program.

There are four steps, although Steps 2 and 3 are admittedly very simple. (If you want to use an accessory, five or more steps may be needed.) The Programs option provides reasonable access to a large number of files, and except for the programs that you use most often, it represents a good choice for the bulk of your programs.

While most programs are automatically placed in the Programs option, you can add programs on your own, and you can remove or change what is automatically placed there. If you look in the Windows folder, you find a folder labeled Start Menu, and within it the Programs folder, as you saw in Figure 4-6. The Programs folder is the basis for the Programs option in the Start menu. Any folders or files that you place in the Programs folder appear on the Programs option. If the files are shortcuts, then you can activate the shortcut by clicking it in the Programs submenu in the Start menu. To add a program to the Programs option, simply add its shortcut (see the previous section on creating shortcuts) to the Programs folder, either directly or to a new or existing folder in the Programs folder. Similarly, you can delete shortcuts and folders to remove them from the Programs option. Notice the similarity between the submenus of the Programs option in Figure 4-8 and the folder layout in Figure 4-6.

The Start Menu

In addition to using the Programs option, you can place folders and shortcuts directly on the Start menu itself so that when it opens you can immediately see them, as shown in Figure 4-9. The steps to start a program whose shortcut is directly on the Start menu are as follows:

1. Click the Start button.

2. Click the program.

This takes half as many steps as it takes to start a program in the Programs option on the Start menu. Of course, if you put a folder directly on the Start menu, you add an extra step to open the folder. The downside to the

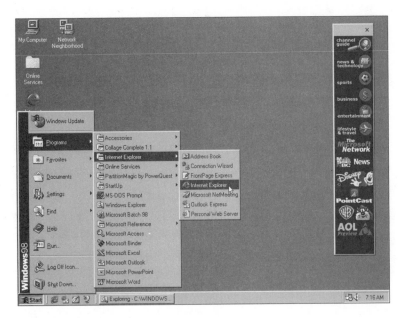

Figure 4-8.   *The resulting Programs submenus.*

Figure 4-9.   *Shortcuts and folders can be available from the Start menu.*

Start menu is that you have limited space, especially if you use large icons on the Start menu. (The Taskbar Properties dialog box allows you to select small icons.) Because of this limitation, you should use the Start menu only for your most frequently used programs.

N **OTE**   If you place more items on the Start menu than there is room for, you get up and down arrows at the top and bottom of the menu to scroll it. This adds an extra step, though, to finding some items.

You can add programs to the Start menu in several ways. The easiest is to drag a program file itself (an .exe file) from the Windows Explorer or My Computer window to the Start button on the taskbar. Windows automatically creates a shortcut and places it on the Start menu, and the original file remains in its original folder. Staying within Windows Explorer, you can create a shortcut and drag it to the Start menu folder in the Windows folder. Finally, you can open the Start menu, choose Settings | Taskbar & Start Menu, and click the Start Menu Programs tab to open the dialog box shown in Figure 4-10.

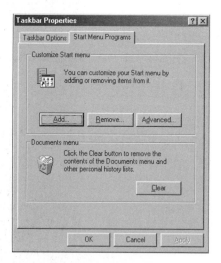

Figure 4-10.   *Start Menu Programs tab.*

If you click Add in the Start Menu Programs tab, the Create Shortcut dialog box opens. This allows you to type in the path and filename of the program you want on the Start menu. The real benefit of this method of adding to the Start menu comes from the Browse button, which allows you to search for and select a path and filename. Then, by clicking Next, you can create or select a folder, either on the desktop or within the Start menu, in which you want to place the shortcut. Clicking Next again allows you to enter or edit the name of the shortcut. In this way, the Start Menu Programs tab leads you through each of the steps used to create a shortcut and to place it on the Start menu from within Windows Explorer. As a matter of fact, the Advanced button of the Start Menu Programs tab opens Windows Explorer with the Start menu folder displayed. This allows you to directly change the Start menu folder, as if you had started out in Windows Explorer.

The Remove button in the Start Menu Programs tab displays, in detail, the entries of the Start menu, as shown in Figure 4-11. By clicking the plus sign next to each folder, you can see the shortcuts in the folder. By selecting a folder or a shortcut and clicking Remove, you can remove an entry from the Start menu. You can, of course, do this directly from Windows Explorer or My Computer.

Figure 4-11.   *Removing shortcuts and folders from the Start menu.*

The Desktop

If a program has a shortcut on the desktop, as shown in Figure 4-12, you can start it with a single step:

1. Click the icon.

This is obviously the easiest way to start a program *unless* windows cover the icon. In this case, you must first move, close, or minimize the window to reveal the icon, and the steps become the following:

1. Click Show Desktop.
2. Click the desktop icon.

While this is only two steps, if you restore the windows, you add a third step. All of a sudden the advantage is, at best, negated, and this method becomes a potential liability. If you have many windows open, you can right-click the taskbar, choose Minimize All Windows to get to the desktop, and then use Undo Minimize All to restore the windows, but that is still three steps. Except for programs that you normally start before other programs are started, using the desktop to start programs does not make a lot of sense. Other methods are more efficient.

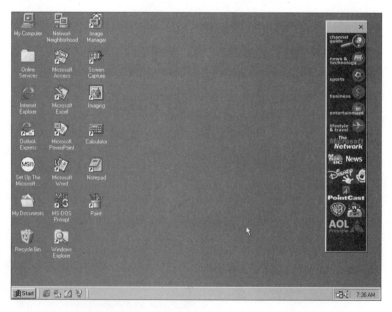

Figure 4-12.   *You can place program and folder shortcuts on the desktop.*

You can place shortcuts on the desktop by dragging them either from Windows Explorer or My Computer to the desktop or, within Windows Explorer, by dragging them from any other folder to the Desktop icon at the top of the left pane. If you just drag a program file (one with an .exe, .com, or .bat extension) to the desktop, you automatically create a shortcut without any further steps. If you right-drag any file, you are asked, among several other queries, if you want to create a shortcut. Also, of course, you can create a shortcut within Windows Explorer or My Computer and drag it to the desktop.

IP Quickly create shortcuts on the desktop by dragging a program file (one with an .exe, .com, or .bat extension) to the desktop or to the Desktop icon in Windows Explorer.

A Special Folder

Another way to set up your system for easy access to your programs is to create a special folder in which you place the shortcuts for those programs and then to leave that folder open on the desktop. Such a folder is shown in Figure 4-13. The major advantage this folder has over the desktop itself is that you can quickly get to it either by clicking the folder's task on the taskbar (the most direct way if the taskbar is visible) or by pressing **ALT-TAB** and going through the Task Switcher. The steps to start a program with a special folder are as follows:

1. Click the special folder's task on the taskbar.

2. Click the program you want to start.

These two steps are about the same as those for starting a program whose icon is on the desktop *if* you include showing the desktop to get to it, and about the same as the steps for starting a program whose icon is directly on the Start menu. The special-folder steps assume that the special folder is open on the desktop. If you leave the folder open when you shut down Windows, it is open when you restart Windows. Also, as long as you don't put an icon on the desktop *under* the special folder, you should not have any reason to close it. A negative aspect about a special folder is that it is one more thing to maintain.

Figure 4-13.   *An example of a special folder containing the shortcuts for the programs you use.*

There are several ways to create a special folder on the desktop. You can right-click the desktop and then choose New | Folder from the context menu. Alternatively, you can click the Desktop icon in the left pane of Windows Explorer and then choose New | Folder from the File menu. You can name the new folder anything you like as long as no other folder on the desktop has the same name. Examples of names you can use are Programs, Main, and Applications.

To load the special folder with program shortcuts, you need simply to drag the program files from either My Computer or Windows Explorer to the folder. The shortcuts are automatically created. If you want a shortcut to a folder to be in the special folder, you must first create the shortcut and then drag it to the special folder. Remember that placing a folder in the special folder adds another step to getting the program you want to start.

Taskbar Toolbar

You read earlier in this chapter that the taskbar can have toolbars containing icons for programs and folders that you want to start or open. For example, you could take a special folder named Programs, described in the last section, and place it on the taskbar, using the earlier instructions, and it would look like this:

The benefit of using the taskbar to start programs is that the taskbar can be always on top of any windows, always visible. The negative is that you have only so much room on the taskbar and can use it for only so many things. You will notice that in a toolbar you create in the taskbar the spacing between icons is quite large, to allow for titles. Therefore, the toolbar takes up most of the taskbar. In the Quick Launch toolbar, this is not the case; only the icons appear, so it is quite efficient.

It is also quite efficient to place icons on the Quick Launch toolbar: You simply drag them there. When you do that, a black vertical bar appears to show you where the icon will be placed. You can rearrange the Quick Launch toolbar by simply dragging the icon you want to move. Again a black vertical line will appear to show you where you are moving the icon. You can remove an icon from the Quick Launch toolbar by dragging it to the desktop and then deleting it. To edit or change the name that appears in the ToolTip, you must open \Windows\Application Data \Microsoft\Internet Explorer\Quick Launch.

Program Manager

If you are really captivated by Windows 3.x Program Manager's approach to getting the programs you want to start, you can use Program Manager in Windows 98, as shown in Figure 4-14. To start Program Manager, open the Windows folder in either My Computer or Windows Explorer, and click Progman.exe. You can place a shortcut to Program Manager on either the desktop or the Start menu to quickly get to it in the future. If you want Program Manager to be automatically started every time you start Windows 98, you can drag a shortcut to the Windows\Start Menu\Programs\ StartUp folder.

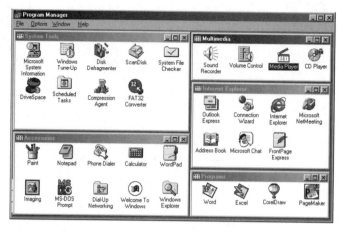

Figure 4-14.   *Windows 3.x Program Manager in Windows 98.*

Other than your personal tastes, there is no compelling reason to use Program Manager. It is at best equivalent to a special folder, and unlike a folder, you cannot just leave it on the desktop and have it open automatically the next time you start Windows 98. Program Manager was a good approach in Windows 3.x, but Windows 98 offers better approaches.

Program Starting Summary

In day-to-day usage, program icons on the Quick Launch toolbar are the easiest to use. This is definitely where you should place the program shortcuts you use most often. Because the Quick Launch toolbar's space is limited, you are going to need to use one or more of the other methods also. All things considered, it seems to me that the order of preference for starting programs is as follows:

- Program icons on Quick Launch toolbar
- Program icons on the desktop
- Program icons directly on the Start menu
- Program icons in a special folder on the desktop
- Program icons in the Programs option of the Start menu

Because the Programs option is the only source automatically built for you, you will need to build and maintain the other starting methods.

IP   You can have several shortcuts for the same program in different places. Shortcuts take less than 1 KB of disk space.

Document-Centricity

The last section described how to start programs. The historical approach to computing has been to start a program and then load a document. Windows 98 continues a trend begun in Windows 3.x to allow you to select a document to work on and have its program start and the document load automatically. This is called *document-centricity.* Its purpose is to allow you to concentrate on the documents you are creating and not worry about the programs you are using. Many documents now are created by several programs, and as this trend progresses, it will not be easy to determine, by looking at the screen, what program you are using.

Document-centricity results from associating a document file with a program; you will read more about this in Chapter 6. Once you do that, you can simply click a document (*document* is used synonymously with *document file*) or shortcut, and its associated program starts and opens the document. As a result, most of the things that you can do to quickly start programs, you also can do with documents. You can drag a document or its shortcut to the desktop (a shortcut is not automatically created for you); you can drag a document to the Start menu where a shortcut is automatically created; and you can create a special folder to hold documents or use the same special folder you created for programs. Finally, Windows 98 provides an option on the Start menu to allow you to select one of the last 15 documents that you opened by clicking the document, as shown in Figure 4-15. (Figure 4-15 also shows a document directly on the Start menu.)

Directly opening a document saves you the steps required to open a document once a program is started. This may or may not be significant to you. If it is, you should look at the previous section again and consider how you want to set up your documents to easily open the ones you use most often.

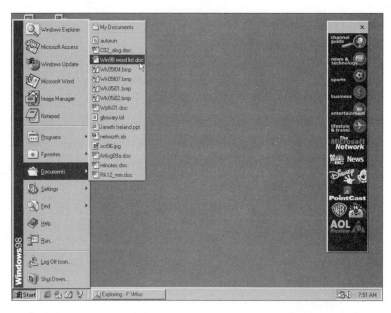

Figure 4-15. *The Documents option on the Start menu shows the last 15 documents you directly started.*

Customizing with Control Panel

Control Panel is the primary place where you set the defaults and parameters that determine how the many parts of Windows 98 will operate. It is your primary tool for customization. In the default Control Panel folder, shown in Figure 4-16, there are 20 individual control panels with settings that you can tailor to your needs. (The number of control panels in the Control Panel folder depends on what you have installed on your computer. It may be more or fewer than what is shown here.) Of these 20 control panels, 11 pertain to functions discussed in other chapters. These 11 are: Fonts, Game Controllers, Internet, Modems, Multimedia, Network, Printers, Sounds, System, Telephony, and Users. The remaining 9, plus one that is not in the Typical install, are discussed in the following sections of this chapter.

You can open Control Panel in several ways. The most common method is to open the Start menu, point at Settings, and then click Control Panel. A simpler method (although slower because of the time needed to open My

Figure 4-16. *Control Panel.*

Computer) is to open My Computer and click the Control Panel icon. You can also open Windows Explorer and click Control Panel in the left pane. Once Control Panel is open, you can open any of the control panels by clicking its icon.

 IP   If you click Control Panel in the left pane of Windows Explorer, you get a description of each of its control panels, as shown in Figure 4-17.

Accessibility Options

 OTE   The Accessibility Options control panel is not installed during a Typical installation. You can install it by using the Add/Remove Programs control panel, described later in this chapter.

The Accessibility Options control panel allows you to set up the keyboard, mouse, screen, and sound to compensate for various physical challenges you may have. When you open the Accessibility Options control panel, the Accessibility Properties dialog box appears, as shown in Figure 4-18. This dialog box has five tabs, one for each of the four areas addressed, plus a General tab for settings that relate to all areas. Each of these tabs is discussed in the following sections.

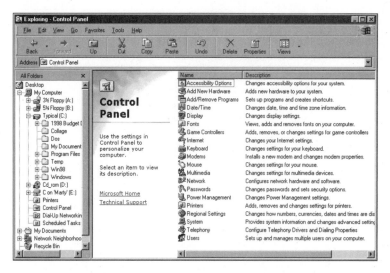

Figure 4-17. *Windows Explorer showing the descriptions of the individual control panels.*

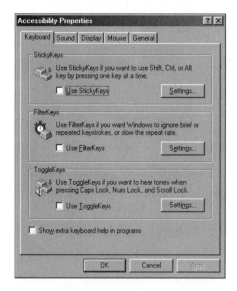

Figure 4-18. *Accessibility Properties dialog box.*

Keyboard

The Keyboard tab allows you to turn on or off three features that can make the keyboard easier to use: StickyKeys, FilterKeys, and ToggleKeys. In addition, by clicking the check box at the bottom, you can have Windows tell the programs you use to display additional help topics relating to the keyboard.

Shortcut: Press either SHIFT key five times in succession.

StickyKeys   StickyKeys allows you to press **SHIFT, CTRL,** or **ALT** plus one other key, one at a time, so you do not have to press two keys together. When StickyKeys is turned on and you press **SHIFT, CTRL,** or **ALT** (called modifier keys), the computer thinks the key is held down even though you have physically removed your finger from the key. You can turn on StickyKeys either by clicking the Use StickyKeys check box in the Accessibility Properties dialog box or by pressing the shortcut keys. If you click Settings under StickyKeys, the Settings For StickyKeys dialog box will open, as shown in Figure 4-19.

 OTE   Although you can press only one other key and have it affected by the previous **SHIFT, CTRL,** or **ALT** keys, you can press, for example **CTRL+ALT+ DELETE** one key at a time, because the **CTRL** will be "held" while you press **ALT,** and **ALT** causes **CTRL+ALT** to be "held" while you press **DELETE**. This works for any sequence of the modifier keys.

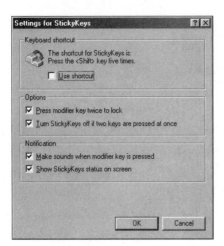

Figure 4-19.   *Settings For StickyKeys dialog box.*

The Settings For StickyKeys dialog box allows you to turn on or off the shortcut keys to enable StickyKeys and to enable several options and notification schemes. When StickyKeys is turned on, the StickyKeys icon is displayed next to the clock and indicates how many modifier keys are pressed.

Shortcut: Hold down right **SHIFT** *key for eight seconds.*

FilterKeys   FilterKeys allows you to reduce double keystrokes, slow down key repetition, and reduce the effect of accidentally hit keys. The purpose of FilterKeys is to desensitize the keyboard so that it is less likely to register unwanted keystrokes. FilterKeys does this by ignoring repeated or short-duration keystrokes, or by slowing the rate at which a keystroke can be repeated. FilterKeys is valuable for people with tremors or a tendency to "bounce" keys.

You can turn on FilterKeys either by clicking the Use FilterKeys check box in the Accessibility Properties dialog box or by pressing the shortcut key. If you click Settings under FilterKeys, the Settings For FilterKeys dialog box opens, as shown in Figure 4-20.

The Settings For FilterKeys dialog box allows you to turn on or off the shortcut key and to enable several options and notification schemes. The FilterKeys options provide the following alternatives:

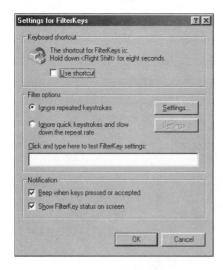

Figure 4-20.   *Settings For FilterKeys dialog box.*

- **Ignore Repeated Keystrokes** allows you to lengthen the amount of time before the start of automatic key repetition, which occurs when you hold down a key. Click Settings to set the Ignore Keystrokes Repeated Faster Than option to determine the amount of time you must hold down a key before repeated keystrokes begin. Drag the slider from 0.5 to 2 seconds. You can test the time setting from the same dialog box.

- **Ignore Quick Keystrokes And Slow Down The Repeat Rate** reduces the possibility of double keystrokes. It determines the minimum amount of time that must exist between two keystrokes (from releasing one key to pressing another) before they are considered two actual keystrokes. Another keystroke within the minimum time is ignored. Click Settings to open the Advanced Settings For FilterKeys dialog box, shown in Figure 4-21, and determine the specific characteristics of the Ignore Quick Keystrokes And Slow Down The Repeat Rate option.

- **No Keyboard Repeat** eliminates repeated keystrokes occurring when you hold a key down.

- **Slow Down Keyboard Repeat Rates** specifies both a Repeat Delay between keystrokes and a Repeat Rate. These settings reduce the possibility that an accidentally hit key will be considered a valid keystroke. Do this by adjusting the amount of time between pressing a key and accepting a valid keystroke. The slider beneath the options allows times between 0.3 and 2 seconds for both Repeat Delay and for Repeat Rate.

- **SlowKeys** sets the length of time for which keys must be held down to be recognized. The slider establishes a time from 0.0 to 2 seconds. Keystrokes that are not held down for the specified time are not recognized.

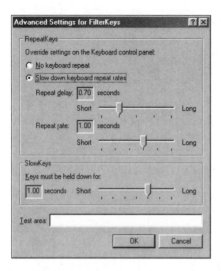

Figure 4-21.   *Advanced Settings For FilterKeys dialog box.*

    When FilterKeys is turned on, the FilterKeys icon is displayed next to the clock.

*Shortcut: Hold down **NUM LOCK** for five seconds.*

ToggleKeys   ToggleKeys allows you to hear a sound when you press **CAPS LOCK, NUM LOCK,** or **SCROLL LOCK** to turn them on or off. When ToggleKeys is turned on and you press **CAPS LOCK, NUM LOCK,** or **SCROLL LOCK,** you hear a sound to let you know you have turned on or off one of these keys. You can turn on ToggleKeys either by clicking the Use ToggleKeys check box in the Accessibility Properties dialog box or by pressing the shortcut key. If you click Settings under ToggleKeys, the Settings For ToggleKeys dialog box opens and allows you to turn on or off the shortcut key. ToggleKeys does not display an icon next to the clock when it is turned on.

Sound

The Sound tab of the Accessibility Properties dialog box, shown in Figure 4-22, allows you to enable or disable two features that help compensate for hearing impairment. These are SoundSentry, which flashes a part of the screen when making a sound, and ShowSounds, which tells applications to display sounds on the screen. You can turn on or off either of these features by clicking its check box. The SoundSentry Settings button allows you to determine the part of the screen you want to flash.

Display

*Shortcut: Press left **ALT**, left **SHIFT**, and **PRT SCREEN** together.*

The Display tab of the Accessibility Properties dialog box allows you to change into High Contrast mode, where the colors and fonts used on the screen make it easier to read for those who are visually impaired. You can turn on High Contrast mode either by pressing the shortcut keys or clicking the check box. By clicking the Settings button, the Settings For High Contrast dialog box opens, as shown in Figure 4-23. This allows you to enable the shortcut keys and to select a high-contrast color scheme.

Mouse

The Mouse tab of the Accessibility Properties dialog box allows you to turn on or off MouseKeys. This enables the numeric keypad on the right of most keyboards to perform all the functions that can be performed with a mouse. MouseKeys, which can be used at the same time you are using a

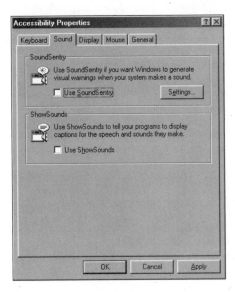

Figure 4-22. *Sound tab of the Accessibility Properties dialog box.*

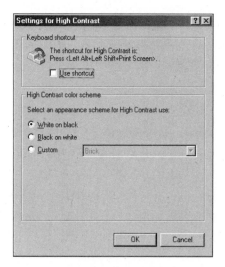

Figure 4-23.   *Settings For High Contrast dialog box.*

*Shortcut: Press
left **ALT,** left
SHIFT, and **NUM**
LOCK all together.*

mouse, is useful not only for those who have problems using the mouse,
but it is also valuable when you are trying to position the mouse very precisely. MouseKeys redefines the numeric keypad, as shown in Figure 4-24.
The specific key assignments are as follows:

- **The 5 key** acts as if you were clicking the left mouse button once,
  unless you pressed either the * key or the - key first.

- **The other number keys** move the mouse pointer in the direction
  indicated.

- **The + key** acts as if you were double-clicking the left mouse button,
  unless you pressed either the * key or the - key first.

- **The DEL key** releases the left mouse button after dragging.

- **When /, *, or – is pressed, the 5** and **+** keys function as if you were
  using the left, right, or both of the mouse buttons.

- **CTRL and a number key** except 5 causes the mouse pointer to jump
  in large increments. You can turn this off in the Settings For
  MouseKeys dialog box.

- **SHIFT and a number key** except 5 moves the mouse pointer one
  pixel at a time. You can turn this off in the Settings For MouseKeys
  dialog box.

■ **NUM LOCK** switches the numeric keypad between MouseKeys and its normal function in whatever state (numeric entry or cursor movement) is chosen in the Settings For MouseKeys dialog box. (If you keep the default of Use MouseKeys When NumLock Is On, then when NumLock is off, the numeric keypad performs its selection/insertion point-moving function.)

The Settings button opens the Settings For MouseKeys dialog box, which you see in Figure 4-25. This dialog box is where you enable or disable the use of the shortcut key, turn on or off **CTRL** and **SHIFT,** as described above, and specify how **NUM LOCK** will work and whether the MouseKeys icon appears in the notification area when MouseKeys is turned on. Additionally, the Settings For MouseKeys dialog box has two sliders that let you

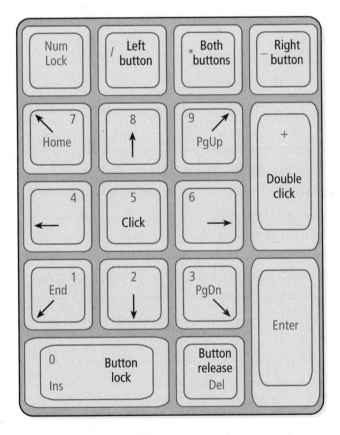

Figure 4-24. *Numeric keypad with MouseKeys.*

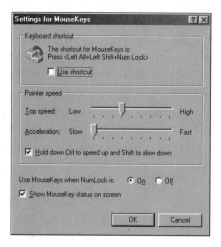

Figure 4-25. *Settings For MouseKeys dialog box.*

determine how fast the mouse pointer will move in response to your pressing the keys. Top Speed is the maximum speed that the mouse pointer will travel across the screen. Acceleration is the time delay before the pointer achieves maximum speed.

General

The General tab of the Accessibility Properties dialog box allows you to set several options that apply to all accessibility features, as shown in Figure 4-26. It also enables or disables SerialKey devices, which allow connection of an alternative input device in place of a keyboard.

Within the General tab, you can choose to have the enabled accessibility features turn off after your computer is idle for a period of time. This option allows two people with different access needs to use the same computer. The General tab also allows you to determine the kind of visual or audio notification you want when you turn a feature on or off.

SerialKey Devices allows you to connect an alternative input device using a serial port in your computer. That device can send information, which is treated as keystrokes and mouse events, to the computer. Click the SerialKey Settings button, and select the serial port (COM1 through COM4) and baud rates that you want to use (300 to 19,200).

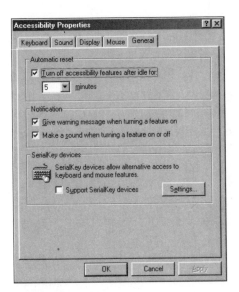

Figure 4-26. *General tab of the Accessibility Properties dialog box.*

Add New Hardware

The Add New Hardware control panel starts the Add New Hardware Wizard, which walks you through the steps to configure Windows 98 for new hardware. It is best to physically install the new hardware in your computer and then run the Add New Hardware Wizard. Use these steps:

ARNING You should not be running any other programs while you are trying to install new hardware, especially if you let Windows try to detect it. Your computer may need to be restarted, and you could lose whatever you are in the middle of in another program.

---

1. Start the Add New Hardware Wizard by clicking the Add New Hardware control panel. The first window welcomes you. Click Next.

2. The second window tells you that Plug and Play devices will be sought. Click Next.

3. If new Plug and Play devices are found, a list of them is displayed. If the device you want to install is on this list, select it and click Next. Otherwise, select No, The Device Isn't On The List; and click Next.

4. You are asked if you want Windows to try to detect new hardware that is not Plug and Play compatible. Make the choice that is correct for you. If you have not already installed the item, choose No, and click Next to select the type of hardware, as shown in Figure 4-27.

   If the hardware is installed, you can still choose No and save time by selecting the type of hardware from the list. Letting Windows detect it, though, helps answer questions that you will be asked about the item.

5. If you let Windows detect the new hardware and click Next, you are warned that the process may take a while and have problems. You must click Next again to actually start the detection process. You will see a status indicator telling you how the detection is progressing.

6. If the status indicator stops for several minutes (say more than three), you may have a problem, and you need to restart (reboot) your computer. When the detection process is complete, you are told what Windows has found and asked if you want to install that hardware. If you do, click Finish; otherwise, click Cancel.

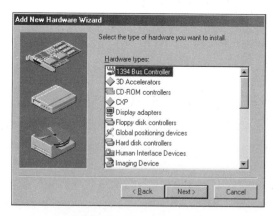

Figure 4-27.   *Selecting the type of new hardware being installed.*

If you select a specific piece of hardware and click Next, Windows tries to either detect that specific piece of hardware or present a list of manufacturers and models from which you can select your hardware. Most of the hardware lists are very extensive, and you should find your device listed. If not, each list has a Standard Types entry under Manufacturers with several models that represent varieties of each item. Select the one that is most like yours. If Windows tries to detect your hardware, it may ask you several questions concerning the device; then it will tell you what it thinks the new piece of hardware is, and you can accept it or go back and try again.

If Windows detects a conflict between a new piece of hardware and hardware you already have installed, it tells you and offers to start the online Hardware Conflict Troubleshooter. This will lead you through the process of resolving the conflict.

Add/Remove Programs

The Add/Remove Programs control panel allows you to add programs for which you have floppy disks or CDs, to remove programs that you have installed from Windows 98, to add or remove components of Windows 98, and to create a Windows 98 startup floppy disk. When you click the Add/Remove Programs control panel, the Add/Remove Programs Properties dialog box opens, as shown in Figure 4-28.

Install/Uninstall Tab

To install a new program from the Install/Uninstall tab, insert a floppy or CD in the appropriate drive, click Install, and then click Next. Windows searches your drives for an install or setup program and tells you what it finds. If it finds the correct program, click Finish. If not, click Back and then Next to have Windows search again. When you click Finish, Windows starts the setup or install program that was identified, and you can carry on with that program. This tab saves the time and effort needed for you to search for the name of the install program and to type it in the Run dialog box.

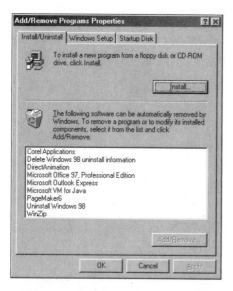

Figure 4-28.   *Add/Remove Programs Properties dialog box.*

To uninstall a program, it must have been installed through Windows 98 and, as a result, be on the list at the bottom of the Install/Uninstall tab. If the program you want is there, click it to select it, and then click Remove to begin the process.

 OTE   Some programs require that you have the CD or floppy disks you used to install the program inserted in the applicable drive to proceed with the uninstall process.

Windows Setup Tab

The Windows Setup tab, shown in Figure 4-29, allows you to add or remove the Windows 98 components displayed in the list box. Beside each component is a check box that, if it has a check mark, indicates the component is currently installed. (If the check box is shaded, it means that the component is partially installed. In the lower part of the window, you can click Details to see what parts of the component are installed, and you can remove those parts or add new ones.) If the component isn't installed and you want it to be, click the check box to add the check mark. If it is and you don't want it to be, also click the check box to remove the check mark. After you have made all the changes you want, you should see check marks in the check boxes for the programs that are either currently installed and you want to keep them, or not installed and you want to add them. When you are satisfied with the list, make sure the Windows 98 CD is in its drive, and then click OK. The Windows 98 Setup program will start and carry out your changes.

Startup Disk Tab

If something happens to your hard disk, you may not be able to start your computer. You may not be able to fix the problem because the files you need are on your hard disk. Therefore, it is very important that you have an emergency floppy disk with the files needed to start your computer, including the files needed to access your CD-ROM. When you installed Windows 98, you made a Startup Disk (which contains the same files as this startup disk). If something happened to that disk or you want a second one, you can create a new one using the Startup Disk tab in the Add/ Remove Programs Properties dialog box. Click Create Disk. You see a progress bar appear in the dialog box. Then, when you are asked, insert a disk that can be erased into the floppy drive. When the progress bar reaches the right side and disappears, the startup disk has been created. Remove the disk, and label it "Emergency Startup Disk."

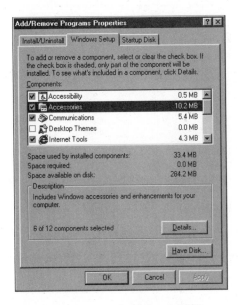

Figure 4-29.   *Windows Setup tab of the Add/Remove Programs Properties dialog box.*

Date/Time

As you might expect, the Date/Time control panel allows you to set the date and time. It also allows you to select the time zone that Windows 98 references. You open the Date/Time Properties dialog box, which you see in Figure 4-30, by either clicking the Date/Time control panel icon or double-clicking the time on the right of the taskbar. To change the time, you need to double-click the hour, minute, second, or AM/PM segment that needs adjustment and then use the spinner (up and down arrows). To change the date, you need to select the correct month and year and then click the correct day.

The Time Zone tab, shown in Figure 4-31, gives Windows 98 the ability to work in a worldwide communications environment. Knowing it is 10 A.M. where you are, you can figure out what time it is anywhere in the world (if you keep in mind daylight saving time). To set your time zone, select it from the drop-down list box.

 IP   At the left end of the drop-down list in the Time Zone tab, each time zone is defined in relationship to the hour difference (plus or minus) from Greenwich mean time (GMT). This is a handy place to determine the time differences between locations around the globe.

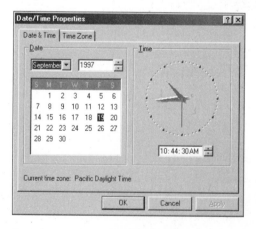

Figure 4-30.   *Date/Time Properties dialog box.*

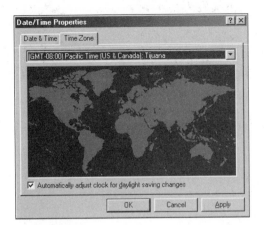

Figure 4-31.   *Time Zone tab.*

Display

You can open the Display Properties dialog box, which you see in Figure 4-32, by either clicking the Display control panel icon or right-clicking the desktop and selecting Properties. The Display Properties dialog box has

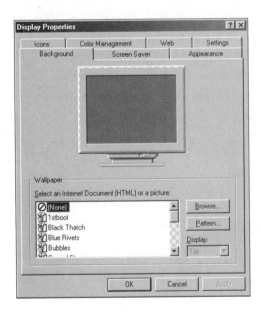

Figure 4-32.   *Display Properties dialog box.*

six tabs (the driver for your video card may add additional tabs). They allow you to do the following:

- Set the background patterns and wallpaper used on the desktop
- Select a screen saver
- Choose the colors used for various parts of a window
- Change several of the default icons used on the desktop
- Identify the objects you want on your Active Desktop
- Select a screen resolution, number of colors, and font size

Background Tab

The Background tab lets you determine how your desktop will look. You can choose from a large selection of either wallpaper or patterns that come with Windows 98, edit one of the standard patterns to create a new one, or browse through your hard disk looking for wallpaper in other programs. While you can have both a pattern and a wallpaper, if the wallpaper fills the screen (the Tile option), the wallpaper will cover the pattern. (Patterns are geometric shapes, while wallpaper is made of pictures.) To select a pattern, select None in the Wallpaper list box, and then click Pattern. The Pattern dialog box opens, as shown below. You can select a pattern by clicking it in the list box, look at it in the Preview area, edit the pattern with the Pattern Editor, and finally apply the pattern by clicking OK.

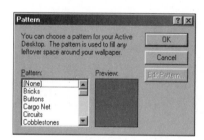

Screen Saver Tab

A screen saver places on your screen a moving pattern that replaces the normal screen contents if your computer is left idle for a set amount of time. The Screen Saver tab, shown in Figure 4-33, allows you to choose a screen saver, to see how it looks, to change its settings (speed, pattern, and so forth), to set the time your computer must be idle before the screen saver comes on, and optionally to set a password that must be entered before the screen saver is turned off.

Appearance Tab

The Appearance tab, shown in Figure 4-34, allows you to set the color and shading, as well as the font size and style, used in various parts of the screen. You can choose one of many existing schemes that come with Windows 98, or you can build one yourself by clicking the area of the screen you want to change, or by selecting a scheme from the Item drop-down list box and then choosing size, color, and font characteristics. After you select your scheme, you can save it with the Save As button.

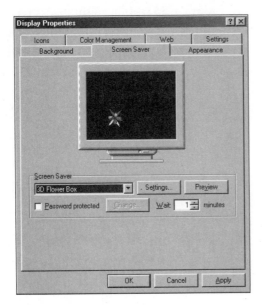

Figure 4-33. *Screen Saver tab.*

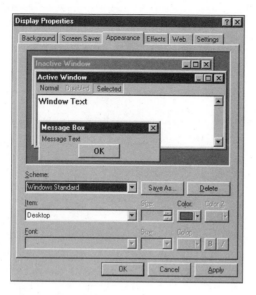

Figure 4-34.   *Appearance tab.*

Effects Tab

The Effects tab, shown in Figure 4-35, replaces the feature in Plus! that allowed you to change the look of the fixed icons on your screen. To use the Icons tab, select the icon you want to change, and click Change Icon. Select the new icon you want to use, and click OK. If you want to return an icon to its default, click Default Icon. See the tip, found early in this chapter, that lists the files containing icons you can use.

Web Tab

The Web tab allows you to add and remove and to turn on and off items, such as the Channel bar, on your Active Desktop. When you click New (assuming you first selected the View My Active Desktop As A Web Page check box), you are connected to Microsoft's Web site and its Active Desktop Gallery, where you can see the other items you can have on your desktop, as shown in Figure 4-36. Among the many items you can choose are a stock ticker, a weather map, and custom news reports. When you add an item from the gallery, it appears in the Web tab with a check box to allow you to turn it on or off without deleting it. In addition, many of the items have properties you can set.

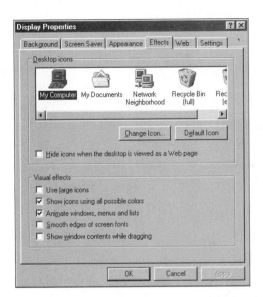

Figure 4-35. *Effects tab.*

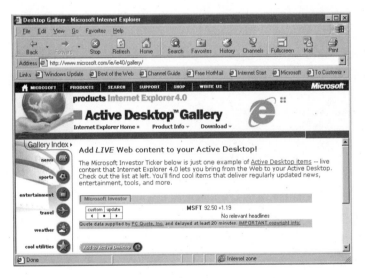

Figure 4-36. *Microsoft's Active Desktop Gallery.*

Settings Tab

The Settings tab is very dependent on the display adapter and monitor that you have. If you are running multiple monitors, this tab reflects the first, or primary, monitor. If your equipment has the capability, you can change the color palette and change the screen (pixel) area or resolution. Clicking the Advanced button opens the dialog box for your display adapter, as you can see in Figure 4-37. (If you are running multiple display adapters, you can choose the one whose properties you want to see.) Here you can select and set the properties of your display adapter and monitor, as well as set the degree of hardware acceleration, the color profile you want to use, and how you want your changes to take effect.

Keyboard

You open the Keyboard Properties dialog box, shown in Figure 4-38, by clicking the Keyboard control panel icon. This dialog box allows you to change both the speed at which repeated keys appear and your keyboard language. The character-repeat speed is set in two ways: the Repeat Delay, which determines how long the computer waits before beginning the repetition; and the Repeat Rate, which is how fast the letters appear once they have started repeating. If you frequently get repeated characters when you

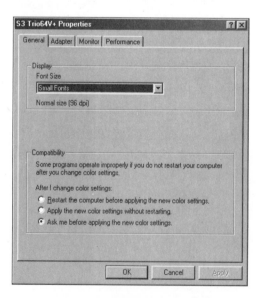

Figure 4-37. *Properties of one particular monitor and adapter.*

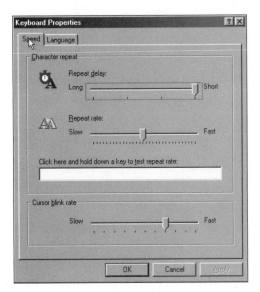

Figure 4-38. *Keyboard Properties dialog box.*

don't want them, then lengthen (drag to the left) the Repeat Delay. If you get more characters than you want when you repeat characters, then slow down (drag to the left) the Repeat Rate.

The best speed for cursor blinking is determined by what is most pleasing, or least displeasing, to your eye. Look at several settings to see the difference.

When you set up Windows 98, the normal keyboard language you use is determined. In the Language tab, you can add and remove other languages and layouts, set the shortcut keys used to switch languages, and ask to be notified of the language you are using on the right of the taskbar.

 OTE The accessibility features, described earlier in the chapter, override the keyboard speed settings if the accessibility features are enabled.

Mouse

The Mouse Properties dialog box, which you see in Figure 4-39, lets you determine how your mouse behaves. In the Buttons tab, you can switch the left and right mouse buttons so you can more easily use the mouse with your left hand, and you can change the double-click rate to one that is more comfortable for you. When you exchange the left and right mouse buttons, like all dialog-box changes, it doesn't take effect until you click

Apply or close the dialog box. The double-click speed is how quickly you must press the mouse button a second time to have it considered a double-click. You can test your double-click speed by clicking the jack-in-the-box and seeing if it opens or closes. If it doesn't open or close, you need to change the speed.

The Pointers tab lets you choose a pointer scheme from several alternatives that come with Windows 98. You may find that one of these is easier for you to see. The Motion tab allows you to set how fast the pointer image moves on the screen, to turn on or off the showing of the trail of the mouse pointer's path, and to set the length of that trail. If you set the pointer speed too fast, you may find that the pointer overshoots where you are aiming, and if it is too slow, you may get impatient. The purpose of pointer trails and their length is to make it easier to see where the mouse is moving.

TIP   If you are using an LCD screen with either your desktop or laptop computer, you may want to turn on the pointer trail to make the mouse pointer easier to see.

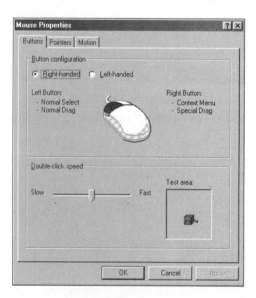

Figure 4-39.   *Mouse Properties dialog box.*

Passwords

The Passwords Properties dialog box, shown in Figure 4-40, allows you to set and change the passwords that allow you to log on to Windows, as well as other passwords to, for example, log on to a network and/or an e-mail system. To change a password, click the button for Windows or Other on the Change Passwords tab, enter the existing password (this is a null, or the absence of any password, when you install Windows), and then enter and confirm the new password. Logging on to Windows occurs when you initially start (boot) Windows or when you shut down and log on as a different user.

Also from the Passwords Properties dialog box, you can enable the remote administration of your computer and set it up so multiple users can have their own settings based on their logon password. Remote Administration allows you to use a notebook computer at home to log on and fully control your computer at work, using modems and phone lines or satellite communications. If you choose to have multiple-user settings in the User Profiles tab, you can then choose two additional items, desktop icons and Start-menu components, which can be included in each user's settings.

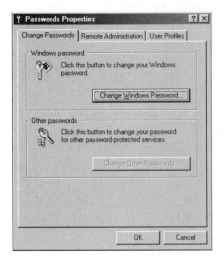

Figure 4-40.   *Passwords Properties dialog box.*

Power Management

The Power Management Properties dialog box, which you see in Figure 4-41, allows you to choose a power scheme from among desktop, laptop, and server schemes. The settings for these schemes are displayed in the lower part of the dialog box and deal with the amount of time that the computer needs to go without use before it shuts down the monitor and all hard disks. If you don't like the default settings for a given scheme, change the settings, and then save the result under the existing scheme or as a new scheme. In the Advanced tab, you can choose whether to show a power meter on the taskbar and, depending on your modem and computer, whether to turn on the computer if the modem receives a call.

Regional Settings

The Regional Settings Properties dialog box, shown in Figure 4-42, allows you to make choices that can be passed along to application programs so they use the correct formats for numbers, currency, time, and dates. Start by selecting the part of the world in which you live (or in which you want the computer set up). Based on this choice, the remaining tabs in the Regional Settings Properties dialog box are automatically set for that part of the world. You can, if you want, go into the Number, Currency, Time, and

Figure 4-41.   *Power Management Properties dialog box.*

Date tabs and further customize such things as decimal and thousands separators, currency symbol, and date format. But to use all of the standards for a given part of the world, you need only select your region in the Regional Settings tab.

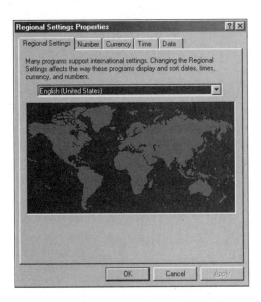

Figure 4-42. *Regional Settings Properties dialog box.*

System Management and Optimizing Windows 98

Windows 98 has an unusual, dual personality. It offers both an easy and intuitive end-user environment, and at the same time it is an excellent environment for a system or network administrator to manage. In the first five chapters of this book, you have seen the great end-user environment provided by Windows 98. In this chapter, you'll see that Windows 98 is an equally great administrative environment. The chapter is broken into two major areas: system management and optimization.

System Management

System management is one of those terms that sound great, but it has such a broad scope that it is difficult to know what it means. In this context, *system management* refers to the continuing control of who is using what on the computers in an organization and how are they doing it. Windows 98 includes many features that address system management. Among these are several layers of security measures, the use of system policies, the provision for remote administration of networked workstations, and the use of the system Registry.

Security Measures

Effective computer security protects a computer from unauthorized use or access but provides easy access and unhindered use to those that are authorized. Windows 98 has been designed to accomplish both objectives in the following ways:

- Windows 98 provides two different types of security. *Share-level* security specifies the type of access available to specific resources on the computer such as disks, printers, and folders. *User-level* security specifies the access rights of each individual using the system.

- Windows 98 provides multiple levels of security that may be used as necessary. This includes the Windows 98 logon, program access, network access, computer access, resource (printer or disk) access, and individual folder access.

- Windows 98 provides for a password list, or caching, which allows the Windows 98 logon password to open a list of passwords that are automatically used to provide access to other resources and multiple networks.

- Windows 98 provides for the use of either simple passwords or the establishment of policies that require longer alphanumeric passwords, which are harder to break.

- Windows 98 provides for the remote use of a password editor to change a user password list.

The security measures taken in a large client-server network are significantly more stringent than those on a small peer-to-peer network or on a stand-alone computer. The client-server software (either Windows NT or Novell NetWare) controls many of the security measures, and although handled well in the Windows 98 client, it is beyond the scope of this book. Here we'll focus on security measures that can be implemented on peer-to-peer and stand-alone systems.

 OTE   User-level security requires that a list of user passwords and permissions be kept on either a Windows NT or NetWare server and is not available in peer-to-peer networking.

Using Passwords

In Windows 98, passwords can be assigned to the following events or resources:

- Windows logon

- Computer (screen saver) access

- Printer and disk access

- Program access

- Individual folder access

- Remote-administration permission

Each of these passwords is applied under different circumstances and is changed in a different place, as described in the next sections. In addition to these six areas, there is another area where you can possibly run into passwords: when signing on to a network to which you are not normally connected. Since this area is outside of Windows 98, we do not discuss it further.

Windows Logon Password The password request that you see when you first start Windows 98 is the lock in the front door of Windows 98. The password that you use in response to this request is the primary logon password. If you choose, it can not only let you into Windows 98, it can also open a password list that will automatically supply the passwords that you need for network, program, and resource usage. The password list is discussed later in this chapter.

The logon password is set either during Windows 98 setup or in the Passwords control panel, shown in Figure 5-1. By clicking Change Windows Password, you open the following dialog box:

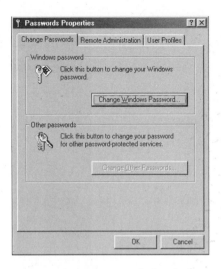

Figure 5-1.   *Passwords Properties dialog box.*

To change the Windows logon password, you must enter the existing, or old, password and then enter the new password twice to confirm it. If you have never entered a password since installing Windows 98, the default password is the absence of any password (called a *null*), and you simply press **ENTER** or click OK to use it. In the Change Windows Password dialog box, if you have not previously entered a password, you can press **ENTER** or **TAB** or click New Password to "enter" a null password. If you don't want to use a Windows logon password, you can change it to a null by pressing **ENTER** in the New Password text box and in the confirmation text box.

Computer Access Password When you step away from your computer while you are inside Windows, someone could come up, use your computer, and potentially do something you don't want done. To prevent this, you can attach a password to the screen saver. The password prevents clearing the screen and activating the keyboard, so it prevents using the computer. When you have the screen saver active, it puts an animated (and potentially energy saving if your monitor has this feature) pattern on the screen if you have not used the keyboard or mouse for a set period of time. Without the password attached, if you press a key or move the mouse, the screen saver will disappear. With password protection turned on and the screen saver active, when you press a key or move the mouse, you are asked to enter a password. If you do not enter the correct one, the screen saver continues to cover the screen, and you can't do anything with the keyboard except enter the password.

To activate the screen saver and turn on its password, follow these steps:

1. Open Control Panel, and click the Display icon.

2. When the Display Properties dialog box opens, click the Screen Saver tab to open the dialog box shown in Figure 5-2.

3. Select a screen saver other than None, and click the Password Protected check box.

4. Click Change; enter the password you want to use, first in the New Password text box and then in the confirmation text box; and click OK.

5. Set the Wait time to a time that is right for you, and then click OK again.

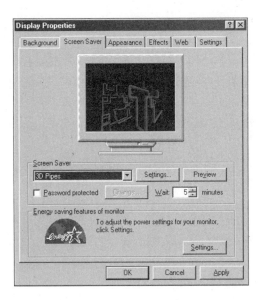

Figure 5-2.   *Screen Saver tab in the Display Properties dialog box.*

Once you have turned on the screen saver and its password, then, after waiting the set amount of time, the screen saver will appear. When you press a key or move the mouse, the password request will appear as you can see here:

When you set the time after which the screen saver will activate, you have two opposing considerations: If you set it too short, the screen saver will activate every time you take a sip of coffee; if you set it too long, you may have to wait longer than you want before leaving your desk. One way to prevent this is to make a shortcut for your preferred screen saver and place it on your desktop or even to attach a shortcut key to it. This way you can activate the screen saver by either clicking it or pressing the shortcut key. Follow these instructions to create the shortcut and the shortcut key:

1. In Windows Explorer, open the \Windows\System folder, select the Details view, and then click Type in the heading above the list of files to sort the list by type. Open Folder Options from the View menu, and in the View tab, make sure that Hide File Extensions is not checked and that Show All Files is checked. Click OK to close Folder Options.

2. Scroll down the list of files to find the screen-saver files (.scr file extension), and select the one you want to use.

3. Right-click the file, select Create Shortcut, and then drag the shortcut to the desktop.

4. Right-click the icon for the screen-saver shortcut, select Properties, and, if it isn't already selected, click the Shortcut tab.

5. Click in the Shortcut Key text box, and press a key you want to use as the shortcut key to start the screen saver. If you press a function key (**F1–F12**), you can use that key alone. If you press any alphanumeric key (**A–Z** and **0–9**), you'll get **CTRL** + **ALT** + the key you pressed. Most of the functions keys are used elsewhere, so the safest

approach is to use the **CTRL** + **ALT** + a key combination. When you have selected a key, click OK.

You now have on your desktop a screen-saver icon that you can click at any time, as well as a shortcut key you can press, to start a screen saver and protect your system when you step away from your computer.

 OTE   The screen-saver password should be used in conjunction with a logon password to protect yourself from someone rebooting your computer when the screen saver is active.

Disk and Printer Access Password   In a network environment, if you share your disks and printer, you may then want to control who has access to them. You can set a password in several different ways. Use the following steps to set a password, first for a shared disk drive, and then for a shared printer. (Chapter 16, "Using a Windows 98 Network," will discuss this further.)

1. Right-click a disk drive in either My Computer or Windows Explorer, and choose Sharing in the context menu that appears. The Sharing tab of the disk's Properties dialog box opens, as you can see in Figure 5-3.

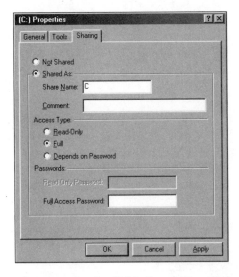

Figure 5-3.   *Sharing tab of a disk's Properties dialog box.*

2. Choose an Access Type. If you choose Read-Only or Full access, you can enter a password for that type. If you choose Depends On Password, you can enter a different password for each type. This allows you to give different people different access.

 OTE If a user is already accessing your resources when you set a password for those resources, the user will not be affected by the password change until he or she exits from and returns to Windows and tries once more to access your resources.

To set a password for a shared printer, use these steps:

1. From My Computer, Windows Explorer, or the Start menu's Settings option, open the Printers folder, and right-click the printer you want to share.

2. Choose Sharing from the context menu that appears. The Sharing tab of the printer's Properties dialog box will open, as shown in Figure 5-4.

3. Click Shared As; enter a Share Name, optionally a Comment, and a Password twice, first in the dialog box and then in the confirmation dialog box.

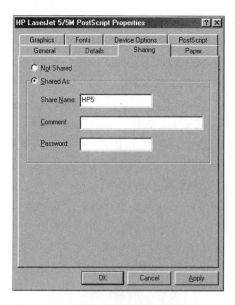

Figure 5-4.   *Sharing tab of a printer's Properties dialog box.*

If you try to use either a disk or a printer that has been password protected, you'll be asked for the password, as shown next.

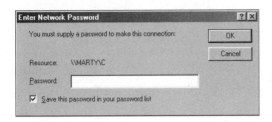

 OTE If you save the password in your password list by clicking the check box of that name, you will not have to enter the password again unless the owner changes the password.

If you have mapped another computer's drive to your computer and the password has changed, you will not be able to access the drive without remapping it with the new password. See Chapter 15 on how to map a network drive.

Program Access The use of passwords in programs is completely dependent on the program. The only program within Windows 98 with password protection is Microsoft Mail. The Microsoft Mail Postoffice administrator must set the password with the following steps:

 OTE Microsoft Mail Postoffice is not installed as part of the Typical install and is not even available in the Windows Setup tab of Add/Remove Programs Properties. You must separately install it from the \Tools\Oldwin95\Exchange folder of the Windows 98 CD.

1. Open the Microsoft Mail Postoffice from the Control Panel. The Microsoft Workgroup Postoffice Admin wizard will open and ask if you want to administer an existing postoffice or create a new one. Leave the default, Administer An Existing Workgroup Postoffice; and click Next.

2. The path to the existing postoffice will be shown. You can change it, browse for another postoffice, or leave it alone. When you are ready, click Next.

3. The administrator is then asked for her or his password. (This password is set when the postoffice is set up. It can be changed with a later step in the setup.) After entering the correct password, click Next.

4. You can then identify the postoffice user whose password you want to change. (Here is where you can identify the administrator and change his or her password.) Select the user you want to change, and click Details. The mailbox holder's information box will open, as shown in Figure 5-5.

5. After changing the password, which does not require a confirmation, click OK and then Close.

After a password has been set for Microsoft Mail, when you try to use it, you will be asked for the password, as shown next. By clicking Remember Password, you will not have to reenter the password in the future.

If you are also using the Exchange mail folders, you will also be asked for that password, which can be saved.

Folder Access Password Although you can password protect disks, you can also go one level down and password protect folders, although you must turn *off* disk sharing for folder sharing to take effect. Sharing and

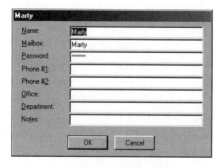

Figure 5-5.   *Changing the password for a postoffice mailbox.*

password protecting a folder requires the same steps as sharing a disk except that you right-click a folder instead of a disk. When you open the Properties dialog box, if the folder is already shared via the disk, you are told that, as you can see in Figure 5-6.

 OTE Disk sharing takes precedence over folder sharing, so if your disk is shared, all the folders are automatically shared under the disk's password.

 OTE With either Novell NetWare or Windows NT, you can assign passwords to individual files, although you cannot do that in Windows 98.

Remote Administration Permission Password In a network environment, it is sometimes desirable to have an administrator remotely (from another computer) manage all the computers in a workgroup or on the network. To do that, permission must be granted on each computer to allow the remote administration of that computer. Follow these steps to accomplish that:

1. From Control Panel, click Passwords to open the Passwords Properties dialog box.

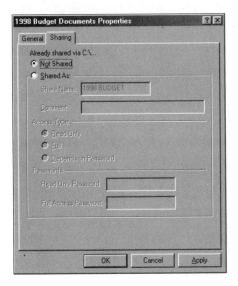

Figure 5-6. *Folder Properties dialog box showing the folder is shared via the disk's being shared.*

2. Click the Remote Administration tab to open the dialog box shown in Figure 5-7.

3. Click Enable Remote Administration Of This Server, and enter and confirm the password to be used.

Password List

If you are like me, when you have a number of passwords to remember, you tend to write them down and even to post them on the front of your computer or monitor. To solve the problem of too many passwords, Windows 98 has a password list, or cache, that stores the passwords for the following items:

- Shared disks, printers, and folders on computers running Windows 98 and accessed by the computer with the password list

- Password-protected programs

- Windows NT logon password and NetWare user IDs and passwords

When you log on, your logon password automatically opens the password list and provides the passwords as you access the resources. You can control whether a password is stored in the list by selecting, or not, the Save This Password In Your Password List check box, as you can see in Figure 5-8.

There is no way to see all the passwords in your password list, but you can see the items controlled by passwords in the list in the Password List Editor, shown in Figure 5-9 and discussed later in this chapter under *Remote Administration*. The password list can be turned off using the System Policy Editor, also described later in this chapter.

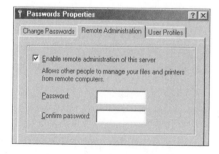

Figure 5-7.   *Remote Administration tab.*

Figure 5-8. *When you enter a network password, you can save it in your password list.*

Figure 5-9. *Password List Editor.*

User Profiles

Another way of controlling the use of a computer or computers on a network is through user profiles. User profiles are a set of specifications, which can be unique to each user who logs on to the computer, that specify how the computer will look and behave. User profiles provide for the following:

- Multiple users on a single computer, each with a different set of specifications

- A user accessing several computers with his or her own unique specifications

- A network administrator enforcing a standard set of specifications for all computers in a workgroup to better support inexperienced users

User profiles cover most of what you can customize in Windows 98, including the desktop background, the fonts used, the icons and shortcuts on the desktop, the contents of the Start menu, network connections, and program settings. The files and folders that represent the profile of a given user are stored in a folder for that user in the \Windows\Profiles folder. The files and folders include the User.dat Registry file (see also the discussion of the Registry later in this chapter) and up to seven folders that hold the contents of the desktop, the Start menu, Network Neighborhood, recent documents you have directly started, Internet history, Internet cookies, and application data. Figure 5-10 shows a Profiles folder for two users, George and Harry. In a client-server network environment, the contents of the Profiles folder are stored on the server and downloaded when a user logs on to a computer. That way, users can log on to any computer in the workgroup and get their preferences.

Enabling User Profiles User profiles are enabled through the User Profiles tab of the Passwords Properties dialog box, shown in Figure 5-11. In this tab, you can choose between all users using the same settings and each having her or his own settings. If you choose the latter, you can then choose to allow customization of two different sets of objects. If you change settings on the User Profiles tab and click OK, you will be told that you need to restart Windows for the change to take effect. Click Yes to make that happen.

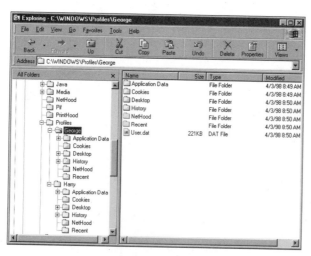

Figure 5-10.   *User profiles folder structure for two users.*

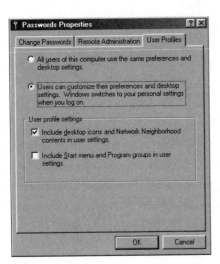

Figure 5-11. *Enabling user profiles.*

If you want to disable user profiles, simply select the All Users Of This Computer Use The Same Preferences And Desktop Settings option, and the individual profiles will be eliminated.

Using User Profiles The first time you log on to the computer after enabling user profiles, even if you have been using the computer for a long time, you will be told that

> You have not logged on at this computer before. Would you like this computer to retain your individual settings for use when you log on here in the future?

If you answer Yes, a new profile will be created for you and stored in the \Windows\Profiles folder. Otherwise, you will be logged on to the computer using the default user profile. If you have your own profile, any changes that you make to the desktop, the Start menu, or anything that is stored in the user portion of the Registry, which can include a lot of program customization, is stored in your profile and will appear when you next log on to that computer. At the same time, your changes will not affect other users, who may have their own profiles.

Managing User Profiles You can add new users to a computer by just logging on with a new user name, and each user can set up his or her own environment. Windows 98, though, gives you a better way to manage user profiles, a way that was not available in Windows 95, the Users control panel. If you haven't set up your machine for multiple users when you open this control panel, it starts the Enable Multi-User Settings wizard. This allows you to add a new user, set the user's password, and select the items that are to be personalized for the new user. Once you are set up for multiusers, then opening the control panel opens the User Settings dialog box shown in Figure 5-12. This allows you to add and delete user profiles, to make copies of an existing user profile and give each copy a new user name, and to change the password and settings of an existing user.

If you select either New User or Make A Copy, the Add User wizard appears and leads you through the process of creating a new user profile. You are asked to enter a user name and a password and to select the items, such as the desktop and the Start menu, that you want to personalize. When you use Make A Copy, the list of items that are to be personalized is copied from the previous user. Change Settings allows you to change the list of items that are personalized for the selected user, as you can see in Figure 5-13.

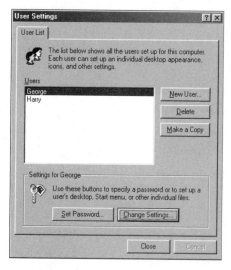

Figure 5-12.   *User Settings dialog box.*

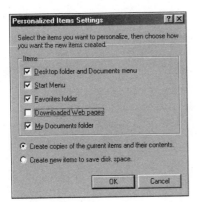

Figure 5-13.   *Changing the list of personalized items for a user.*

System Policies

System policies allow the central administration of a workgroup or network of PCs. Through system policies, the network administrator can control and easily change much of what the user sees and is able to do on his or her computer. This control extends to the look and contents of the desktop and the Start menu, the resources available on the network, the availability of Control Panel options, and many other functions that can be controlled only through system policies. System policies can also be used to establish certain password policies, such as the minimum length of passwords and whether passwords must contain both alpha and numeric information (thus making them harder to break).

System policies are established and maintained with the System Policy Editor. The System Policy Editor is a network tool and primarily used in larger networks. It creates a file named Config.pol that is stored on the network server and downloaded to individual computers where it replaces the User.dat and System.dat Registry files. Policies can be created for individual users by name, for specific computers by name, and for workgroups. Policies are also created for both default users and default computers. When a user logs on to a computer, the following steps take place:

1. The user's logon name is checked to see if it matches an individual user policy. If it does, then the policy is downloaded and applied, and

any group policies are ignored. If there is no user policy for the logon name, then the default user policy is downloaded and applied.

2. The logon name is checked for membership in a group. If one or more group memberships are found, then the applicable group policies are downloaded and applied.

3. The computer name is checked against specific computer policies, and if found, they are downloaded and applied. If no computer specific policies exist, then a default policy is used.

Setting Up the System Policy Editor

The System Policy Editor can substantially modify the look and operation of Windows 98. For that reason, it is not normally installed when installing Windows 98 and should be used with a reasonable amount of caution. The System Policy Editor is on the Windows 98 CD in the \Tools\Reskit \Netadmin\Poledit folder. Use the following steps to put the System Policy Editor on your hard disk:

1. Place the Windows 98 CD in its drive, and close the Autorun program when it appears.

2. From Windows Explorer, locate the \Tools\Reskit\Netadmin\Poledit folder on the CD, and drag it to the Program Files folder on your hard disk.

3. Open the \Program Files\Poledit folder, and create a shortcut by right-dragging the Poledit.exe file to the \Windows\Start Menu \Programs \Accessories\System Tools folder and choosing Create Shortcut Here.

 ARNING   Use of the System Policy Editor should be restricted and not installed or made available to most users.

Using the System Policy Editor

Before actually applying the System Policy Editor, it is important to lay out a plan as to how the policies will be applied across a workgroup or network. In doing this, you first need to identify what groups, computers, and individuals need policies, and then what default policies are required for everyone else. Next you need to review the many options you can set when you establish a policy. You can best do that by looking at the Standard policy sample, discussed shortly, which allows you to see all the options and what Microsoft believes should be the default settings.

When you have developed a plan for how you will implement the system policies or have decided just to study what policies you can set, start the System Policy Editor, and look at the Standard policy sample provided with Windows 98 using the following steps:

1. From the Start menu, choose Programs | Accessories | System Tools, and click Shortcut to Poledit.exe.

2. Click OK when told that the Common.adm cannot be found. Click Cancel in the Open Template File dialog box. Open the Options menu and choose Policy Template. Click Add, double-click Windows.adm, and click OK.

3. From the File menu, choose Open Policy, select the Windows 98 CD, choose \Tools\ResKit\Netadmin\Poledit, click Standard.pol, and click Open. Default User and Default Computer policies appear in the editor, as you can see in Figure 5-14.

4. Double-click the Default User policy to open it. Click several of the plus signs to open several of the entries, as shown in Figure 5-15.

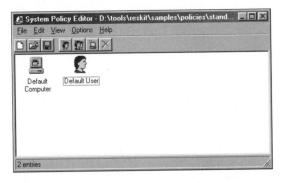

Figure 5-14.   *System Policy Editor with default policies.*

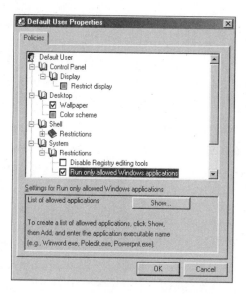

Figure 5-15. *Default User Properties dialog box.*

Notice in Figure 5-15 that there are three types of check boxes, as follows:

- **Empty** check boxes mean that the item will not be implemented. If it was previously implemented, either by a policy or in the user's Registry, it will be cleared (unimplemented) by an empty check box.

- **Checked** check boxes mean that the item will be implemented, and a group of settings will appear in the lower part of the dialog box for that item. This implementation will supersede any settings in the user's Registry.

- **Grayed** check boxes mean that the policy makes no modification to the user's settings for this item. The user can set the item any way that she or he wants.

The check boxes can be changed among the three states—empty, checked, and grayed—by repeatedly clicking the check box.

 ARNING Be sure to leave a policy item grayed if you decide not to set that item. This will allow the user's settings to remain in effect, whereas if you clear the check box, it will clear the user's settings.

Go through both the Default User and Default Computer policies in the Standard.pol sample, seeing the recommended settings and considering the impact of the settings on your organization. Decide and document the settings that you want to make for the default users (the majority of your users) and default computer. Finally, decide if you have any special user, group, or computer needing its own policies—the system and/or network administrator(s), for example, should probably have a separate set of policies.

When you get ready to prepare your policies, you can either choose New from the System Policy Editor's File menu or modify the Standard.pol, discussed above. In either case, it is important that the file be saved as Config.pol if you want it automatically downloaded at system startup. Both a new system policy and the Standard.pol sample start with default user and default computer policies. You should start with these and set the default policies for the majority of the workgroup. When you have finished with the default policies, you can add specific user, group, and computer policies by choosing those options in the Edit menu or by clicking the appropriate buttons in the toolbar as shown on the left (the fourth, fifth, and sixth buttons on the toolbar). When you open one of these policies, you will be asked to name it with a user, group, or computer name. The default and all specific policies are saved in Config.pol.

In addition to setting system policies for a workgroup or an entire network, the System Policy Editor can be used to directly edit the Registry on a particular machine, as you will see later in this chapter under *Using the System Registry*.

Remote Administration

Remote administration is the accessing of the administrative files in one computer from another—for example, the setting of passwords, profiles, and policies remotely. To use the remote administration facilities in Windows 98 you must be connected to a Windows NT or NetWare network and be using user-level security. Remote Administration must also be enabled in the Remote Administration tab of the Passwords Properties dialog boxes on each computer to be administered, as you saw previously in the discussion on passwords. Finally, you must set up the Remote Registry services, which you can do with the following steps:

1. Open the Network control panel, and click Add. The Select Network Component Type dialog box opens.

2. Double-click Service, and then, when the Select Network Service dialog box opens, click Have Disk.

3. In the Install From Disk dialog box, click Browse, and select the path to the Windows 98 CD and the \ResKit\Netadmin\Remotreg folder. Click OK four times to close all the dialog boxes, and then restart your computer.

Once you have set up remote administration, there are five tools in Windows 98 that can be used. These tools and their functions are as follows:

- **System Policy Editor,** used to create and manage system policies and to edit a Registry

- **Registry Editor,** used to edit a Registry

- **Network Neighborhood,** used to manage the file systems, including their structure and content

- **Net Watcher,** used to add and delete shared resources (printers and disks) and monitor their usage

- **System Monitor,** used to look for performance problems

To use one of the above tools, simply start the program, and then, for the System Policy Editor and System Monitor, select Connect from the File menu. For the Net Watcher, choose Select Server from the Administer menu; or for the Registry Editor, choose Connect Network Registry from the Registry menu. The Connect dialog box appears, as shown next. Enter the name of the remote computer, and click OK. You will be able to work on the remote computer.

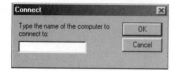

The System Policy Editor's functions for creating and managing system policies were described previously under *System Policies.*

Using the System Monitor

The System Monitor allows you to watch a number of different parameters that measure the activity and resource usage on a computer, either locally or remotely, as you can see in Figure 5-16. Start System Monitor, and observe the operation of a remote computer with the following steps:

1. Open the Start menu, and choose Programs | Accessories | System Tools | System Monitor. (System Monitor is not part of the Typical install, and so you may need to install it with the Add/Remove Programs control panel.) System Monitor opens.

2. Open the File menu, choose Connect, type the name of the computer to which you want to connect, and press **ENTER.** View the remote computer.

3. To add parameters to the display, click the Add button on the far left of the toolbar, select a Category and an Item, as shown in Figure 5-17, and click OK.

4. You can change to a different type of display by clicking the appropriate button in the toolbar. The bar chart is shown in Figure 5-18.

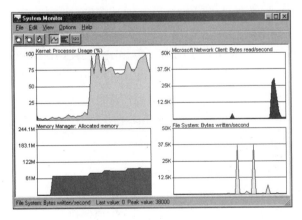

Figure 5-16.   *System Monitor.*

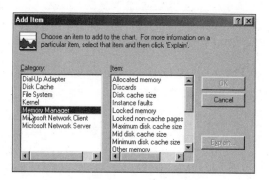

Figure 5-17. *Adding an item to System Monitor.*

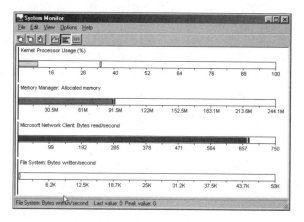

Figure 5-18. *System Monitor as a bar chart.*

5. To change the color and/or scale of a parameter, click the Edit button in the toolbar (third from the left), select the item to be edited, and click OK. The Chart Options dialog box will open, as you can see in Figure 5-19.

System Monitor provides a powerful tool for observing what is happening in your computer or another computer on your network.

Using the System Registry

The Registry is the central repository for all the configuration information in Windows 98. In earlier versions of Windows and MS-DOS, a number of different files including Config.sys, Autoexec.bat, Win.ini, and System.ini

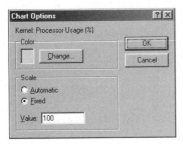

Figure 5-19.   *Chart Options dialog box.*

held similar, although much more limited, types of information. A smaller registry appeared in Windows 3.x, but the majority of the settings were still made in the .ini files. The .ini, Autoexec.bat, and Config.sys files are still in Windows 98 but only for backward compatibility with older programs and hardware. The Registry now contains all the information that Windows 98 needs to govern its operation, and all newer programs and hardware depend on only it.

The Registry is actually two different files in the Windows folder: System.dat and User.dat. (The .dat files are hidden files, and to see them you may need to select Show All Files in Windows Explorer's View menu Folder Options dialog box, View tab.) Unlike the .ini files, the .dat files are not text files and cannot be directly edited. The most common way to change the Registry is through the many settings in Control Panel. In addition, as you read above, the System Policy Editor can both change the Registry directly or through policies that are created. Finally, Windows 98 has a program, the Registry Editor, that provides a low-level form of directly editing the Registry.

 ARNING   When changing the Registry, you should first try to use Control Panel, next the System Policy Editor, and, only as a last resort, the Registry Editor. The Registry Editor allows you to directly change the Registry and does not check for syntax or semantic errors. With the Registry Editor, it is possible to change the Registry in such a way that you cannot start Windows 98.

Optimizing Windows 98

In Windows 3.x, a number of fairly complex optimization issues needed to be addressed, and it was difficult to know absolutely that you had the best configuration possible. Windows 98 significantly simplifies the optimization issues and gives reasonable assurance that you have achieved a good configuration. Windows 98 does this in three ways:

- Being a fully integrated 32-bit operating system, Windows 98 eliminates the MS-DOS versus Windows questions and the using, or not, of 32-bit file and disk access.

- Such features as preemptive multitasking, a 32-bit kernel, and 32-bit device drivers provide improved system responsiveness, smoother background processing, improved system capacity, better memory management and process scheduling, improved resource management, and better overall performance—all of which reduce the need for optimization.

- Windows 98 has a number of self-tuning features that dynamically configure the system to Windows' current needs. This reduces the need for the user to perform these same functions. Among the self-tuning features are the following:

  - Dynamic disk, CD, and network caching in memory using Vcache in which the cache can expand or contract as memory allows and needs demand. Vcache is a 32-bit protected-mode cache driver that replaces SmartDrive with a significantly improved caching algorithm for reading and writing information to and from a disk, a CD, or the network. Vcache relieves the user from having to specify the cache size and other SmartDrive settings.

  - Dynamic virtual-memory swap file that can expand and contract as memory needs demand. With a virtual-memory swap file, some of the contents of memory that aren't being used can be swapped out to disk until they are needed. This frees up memory for other purposes. In Windows 3.x, the user had to decide between a temporary or a permanent swap file and determine how much disk space to allocate for that purpose. Windows 98 now makes those decisions for you, although you can override them if you want (see the discussion later in the chapter).

■ Automatic system-configuration decisions during Windows 98 setup that tailor Windows 98 to the hardware available and relieve the user from that task. For example, in a low-memory environment, background printing is turned off to conserve memory.

With all the automation and features in Windows 98, there are still optimization issues to consider, although if you were to ignore them you would still have a reasonably optimized system.

Windows 98 Optimization Tools

Windows 98 has several tools to assist you in the job of optimization. These are as follows:

■ **System Monitor,** as discussed earlier under *Using the System Monitor,* lets you visually track system performance over time and, from that, tells you how your optimization efforts are going.

■ **Disk Defragmenter,** which is discussed in Chapter 6, optimizes your hard disk so that all the segments of a file are together on the disk, and the files that you use most often are together. This needs to be run periodically to keep the disk at its best performance.

■ **Resource Meter,** shown in Figure 5-20, shows you how you are using the three resource stacks: System Resources, User Resources, and GDI (graphic device interface) Resources. As you run more programs, these resources will get used. In Windows 3.x, it was fairly easy to use up these resources and get an out-of-memory error message as a result, even though you had a lot of regular memory free. You start the Resource Meter by opening the Start menu and choosing Programs | Accessories | System Tools | Resource Meter. You can also open Run, type **Rsrcmtr**, and press **ENTER**. Using either method, point at the Resource Meter icon in the notification area of the taskbar to display the resource use percentages, or double-click the icon to display the Resource Meter shown in Figure 5-20.

- **About Windows,** opened from the Help menu, tells you the amount of free memory that you have, as well as giving a summary of your System Resources, as you can see in Figure 5-21.

- **System control panel** provides a large amount of information about the components of your computer, as shown in Figure 5-22. It is also the primary place where you can tune your file system, graphics, and virtual memory (see Figure 5-23). The System control panel is discussed further later in this chapter.

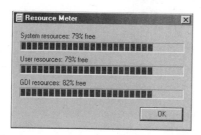

Figure 5-20. *Resource Meter.*

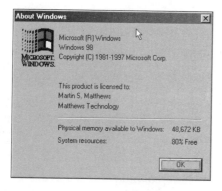

Figure 5-21. *The amount of free memory is shown in About Windows.*

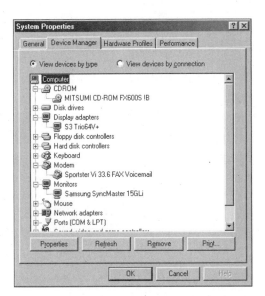

Figure 5-22. *Device Manager tab of the System control panel.*

Figure 5-23. *Performance tab of the System control panel.*

System Optimization

The task of system optimization has three components: selecting and setting up hardware, decision making, and fine tuning.

Hardware Considerations

It may sound trite, but more, newer, and faster hardware will, in fact, run Windows 98 better. That has not always been the case with earlier operating systems. Some of the areas where Windows 98 performance can be improved with hardware are as follows:

- Windows 98 will run better on a Pentium-class processor than on a 486 of the same clock speed because Windows 98 was tuned for the Pentium.

- Windows 98 gives better video and disk performance with faster CPU and bus speed because the 32-bit drivers can use the faster speeds, whereas 16-bit drivers could not.

- Windows 98 performs better with more memory than did Windows 3.x, and with dynamic caching, Windows 98 does not need to be reconfigured when you add memory.

- Windows 98 provides improved printing performance with the newer bidirectional ECP (enhanced communications port) printer ports.

Decision Pointers

Part of achieving an optimized system is making wise decisions as you set up Windows 98. Here are some pointers related to decisions you will make in setting up a system:

- Use protected-mode drivers whenever possible. Windows 98's 32-bit drivers, which have a .vxd extension, replace .386 drivers that came with Windows 3.1 and provide considerable performance improvement.

 IP Try running your system without the Autoexec.bat and Config.sys files. (Rename Autoexec.bat and Config.sys.) If it works, you know that Windows 98 is using its own 32-bit protected-mode drivers. If some piece of hardware or software requires that Config.sys or (less likely) Autoexec.bat load a driver, keep the files to a minimum, and see if you can get 32-bit protected-mode drivers for it.

■ It is not necessarily true that DOS programs will run better in MS-DOS mode than they will in Windows. In MS-DOS mode, the DOS programs will *not* get the benefit of protected-mode drivers, Vcache, and 32-bit disk access, all of which can improve the performance of the program.

■ Keep networking components to a minimum to both improve performance and reduce memory usage. Use only one networking client, either Microsoft or NetWare, but not both. Use only one network protocol: NetBEUI, IPX/SPX, or TCP/IP (see discussion in Chapter 15). Use as few network services as possible.

■ Make the fewest possible changes to Windows 98 default settings in the performance area. During setup and during startup, Windows 98 closely looks at your system, and based on that look, it determines the best settings and configuration for your system to operate at its peak.

Fine Tuning

There are four areas where you can fine tune your system performance: in the file system, in graphics acceleration, in virtual-memory usage, and in printing. It is highly likely that you do not need to do any fine tuning to get the best performance, and you may actually degrade it, but there are always exceptions. The key to fine tuning is to measure and track how you change the performance. The System Monitor is an excellent tool for observing how you are doing.

IP Near your computer, keep a notebook in which you note the hardware installed, the settings used, and the performance measures under various circumstances.

ARNING Changing the performance-related settings can not only degrade performance, but it can cause your system to not operate properly.

Tuning the file system, graphics acceleration, and virtual memory all begin by opening the System control panel and clicking the Performance tab, which you saw in Figure 5-23.

Fine Tuning the File System By clicking the File System button in the Performance tab of the System control panel, you open the File System Properties dialog box, shown in Figure 5-24. Here you can select the role of the computer from among Desktop, Mobile, and Network Server. This will be used to gauge the amount of memory to be dynamically allocated to disk caching.

Since caching is dynamic, you cannot directly set aside memory for disk caching as you could in the Windows 3.x environment. This not only saves you the trouble, but it is a far more efficient use of your memory.

The Floppy Disk tab allows you to turn on or off the startup search for a new floppy disk. If you don't initially need a floppy disk, you can turn this feature off to accelerate the startup process. The CD-ROM tab provides optimization settings that Windows 98 can use to determine the amount of cache memory to set aside for CD-ROM reading. The Removable Disk tab allows you to enable write-behind caching as a means of speeding up these devices. This allows the disk, which is generally a fairly slow device, to continue to write information on its platters while the computer goes off and gets more information.

The Troubleshooting tab allows you to turn off various aspects of the file system for use in troubleshooting, as you can see in Figure 5-25. It is strongly recommended that you fully consider the consequences of selecting any troubleshooting items and that you turn them off as soon as possible after their use.

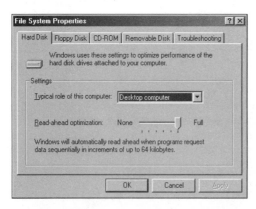

Figure 5-24.   *File System Properties dialog box.*

Figure 5-25. *Troubleshooting tab.*

 OTE You can also do a different kind of fine tuning on your disks, folders, and files with the Maintenance Wizard. You can schedule such optimization features as ScanDisk, Disk Defragmenter, and the deletion of unnecessary files. The Maintenance Wizard is discussed in Chapter 6.

Fine Tuning Graphics Acceleration The Performance tab's Advanced Graphics Settings dialog box (opened by clicking the Graphics button), shown in Figure 5-26, determines how hard Windows pushes your graphics adapter. It is a trial-and-error type of setting: increase the speed until either you begin to see errors in your display or your adapter is going as fast as possible.

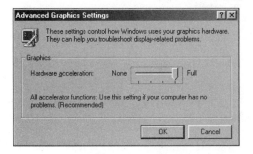

Figure 5-26. *Advanced Graphics Settings dialog box.*

Fine Tuning Virtual Memory The Virtual Memory dialog box (opened by clicking the button of the same name), shown in Figure 5-27, allows you to determine if you want to override the dynamic virtual-memory (swap file) allocation. If so, you can determine the hard disk to use and the minimum and maximum amounts of memory, in megabytes, to allocate to a swap file. If you change the disk, the best disk performance will be achieved by a fast disk with little other usage. You can also disable virtual memory altogether, although that is strongly *not* recommended.

Fine Tuning Printing In printing, you can determine several elements of the spooling that will govern how fast the spooling will take place. These are set in the Spool Settings dialog box (shown in Figure 5-28), which you reach from the Details tab of the printer's Properties dialog box. The whole purpose of spooling is to get you back to your other work faster. If you start printing only after the last page is spooled, you'll get back to your other work faster, but the overall print time will be longer than if you begin printing after the first page has been spooled.

Unless you run into some problem, you want to use EMF (enhanced metafile format) for spooling. It is much more efficient with most printers. Also, if you have a bidirectional printer port and a printer that can use it, you definitely want to enable it to speed up printing.

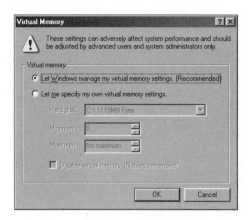

Figure 5-27. *Virtual Memory dialog box.*

The task of optimization is all but done for you in Windows 98, and unless you have unusual circumstances, there is little reason to change these automatically created settings. Your primary task is to determine if you are using 32-bit protected-mode drivers.

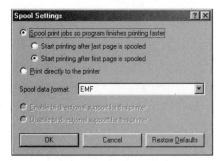

Figure 5-28.   *Spool Settings dialog box.*

Enhancing
Basic Operations

Part 3 examines the tools in Windows 98 for enhancing the day-to-day functions of an operating system. This includes the management and use of files and disks, the installation and use of printers and fonts, and exploring the Windows 98 accessories.

Working with Files and Disks

The files and folders in Windows 98 can be placed into three categories for the sake of discussion:

- Those files that are accessible from your computer and are found in My Computer

- Those files that are stored on other computers on the network to which you are connected and are found in Network Neighborhood

- Those files that are messages you send and receive over a network or a modem and are stored in special folders kept in Outlook Express

Networking and Network Neighborhood are the subjects of Part 6 of this book, beginning with Chapter 15. Messaging and Outlook Express are the subjects of Chapter 12. This chapter, then, will deal with file management as it relates to files and folders that you can access through My Computer. While this does include network drives and files, these will not be emphasized in this chapter. The purpose of this chapter is to explore both how to locate and handle files and folders and the applications they relate to and how to work with your disks.

Locating Files and Folders

In Chapter 2, you saw how you can open My Computer, select a drive, open one or more folders, and finally find the file or files you want. Each time you select a new object (drive, folder, or file), a new window opens, or the contents of the current window are replaced. This is a simple and intuitive approach, but it does not give as broad a view of your file system as you might want, and file handling is not as efficient as it might be. For this reason, Windows 98 has provided another view of your files and folders that is not only broader but also provides some efficiencies in file handling. This other view is through Windows Explorer.

Windows Explorer

Windows Explorer takes the familiar folder window and splits it vertically, as you can see in Figure 6-1. In the default view, the left pane is a hierarchical structure of computers, drives, and folders; the right pane shows the drives, folders, and files contained in the object selected on the left. This is similar to the File Manager in Windows 3.x with the major difference being that the default left pane of Windows Explorer contains all of the objects on your desktop, not just the currently selected drive, which was shown in the left pane of the File Manager. This means that Windows Explorer exposes the full continuum of everything you can access on your computer, including all of your Network Neighborhood and the Internet, as shown in Figure 6-2. Within Windows Explorer, you can drag a file from any object to any other object you can access.

 IP   A quick way to open Windows Explorer is to press **SHIFT** and double-click (even with single-click turned on) the My Computer desktop icon.

In Windows 98, the left pane of Windows Explorer is called the Explorer bar. As a default, the Explorer bar contains the All Folders view, which is the same as the left pane of the Windows 95 Explorer. Using the View menu's Explorer Bar option in Windows 98 Explorer, you can change the Explorer bar so it contains one of the Internet-related options shown here.

Figure 6-1. *Windows Explorer.*

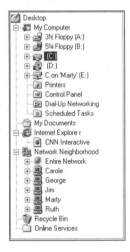

Figure 6-2. *The left pane of Windows Explorer, showing all the objects available to you.*

The toolbar and the status bar (which by default is not turned on) in Windows Explorer are exactly the same as in My Computer or a folder window, and the menu bar is the same except for the Tools menu that is shown here.

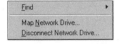

The Tools menu provides three options, one of which is similar to an option on the Start menu: Find. Find allows you to locate a file, a folder, a computer, a site on the Internet, or a person, as described later in this chapter. The Map Network Drive and Disconnect Network Drive options allow you to assign a drive letter on your computer to a drive or folder on another computer on your network or to remove that drive letter. It is not necessary to map a network drive in order to use information on a remote computer, but mapping allows you to treat the remote drive like a drive on your computer. This is especially helpful within older programs that don't otherwise recognize network drives. Chapter 15 will discuss mapping further.

Locating Files with Windows Explorer

Windows Explorer's primary function is to locate files and folders when you don't know their exact paths and filenames or simply to explore the files and folders that are available to you. You do this by selecting in the default left pane the computer, disk drive, and folders that you want to open. If a folder has a plus sign to the left of it, you can click the plus sign, and subfolders will appear. The plus sign will then change to a minus sign. You can do this for as many levels as necessary, like the hierarchy shown in Figure 6-3.

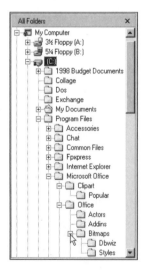

Figure 6-3.   *Folder expansion.*

Once you are in the correct folder, you can then use the scroll bars in the right pane to find the file you want, and, finally, click it to open or start it. If you then want to go to another folder that is not immediately visible in the default left pane, you can use the scroll bars in that pane to find it, or, more quickly, you can use the Address toolbar's drop-down list box to locate another drive, as shown here:

As you saw in the folder windows described in Chapter 2, the right pane of Windows Explorer can be in any one of four formats: large icons, small icons, list, and details. You can change the format with either the View button on the toolbar or with the View menu.

Find

Besides My Computer and Windows Explorer, there is a third way of locating files and folders that provides more than just the location of the objects. This is the Find option on the Start menu or on the Tools menu of Windows Explorer. When you select Find, a second set of menu options appears. These options let you choose to find files or folders, computers on the network, sites on the Internet, people, or, if it is installed, e-mail messages using Microsoft Outlook, as you see here.

The most common task is to find a file or folder. Selecting that option opens the following dialog box. This allows you to search for a file based on its name and where it is located; based on the date it was created, modified, or last accessed; or based on its file type, the text it contains, or its size.

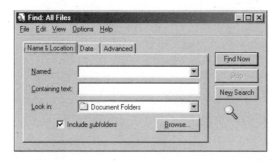

If I were to look for all the files and folders accessible from My Computer with the word *budget* in the filename, the results on my system would look like Figure 6-4.

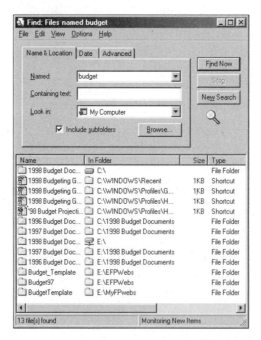

Figure 6-4.   *Results of finding a file with* budget *in the name.*

In the name field, you can enter a fragment of a name, like *bud,* and get all the files whose names contain that fragment, like *Budget, bud98,* and *Salesbud.* In this case, the fragment can be anywhere in the name. You can also use the wildcard character *, which stands for any number of characters, to select only matches where the name fragment is at the beginning or at the end of a name. For example, *bud** will return *Budget* and *bud96* but not *Salesbud,* whereas **bud* will return *1998bud* and *Salesbud* but not *Budget.*

The Options menu allows you to make the search case sensitive and to save the results. A default search is not case sensitive, meaning that if you search for files named *bud*,* you still get both *Budget* and *bud96.* On the other hand, if you select Case Sensitive, you get only *bud96.* Saving the results places on the desktop an icon that you can drag to a folder. When you open this icon, you will have the Find window with the results of the find in it. From the results of a find, you can do most file handling functions, as you will see later in this chapter.

Using Find

The Windows 98 Find option is very adaptable, allowing you to find a wide variety of files and then to manipulate what you found. The following sections provide several examples of this capability.

Group similarly named files If you have several files in different folders, all associated with a project, and each of the files has some common name fragment, for example *proj* (for *project*), you can gather all of the files into one folder using the following steps:

1. From either My Computer or Windows Explorer, select New Folder from the File menu, then type a folder name that contains the name fragment you are searching for, and press **ENTER.** This creates the folder that will hold the files. You can rename the folder after the search, if you want.

2. From the Start menu, open Find | Files Or Folders. (If Find is already open and displays the results of a search, click New Search, and answer OK to clear the current search.)

3. In the Named drop-down list box, type the name fragment being sought.

4. Open the Look In drop-down list, and make sure that the appropriate drive or computer is selected. (If you select a computer, all the drives accessible to that computer will be searched.)

5. Click Find Now.

6. When the list of found files has been returned, select the ones you want to be in the new folder (press and hold **CTRL** while clicking them), and then drag them to the folder, which should also have been found.

Finding by type and date Say you created a Microsoft Word document in the last month, but you forgot the name. To find it, you would follow these steps:

1. Open Find, or select New Search, and choose the Date tab.

2. Click Find All Files Modified, click During The Previous 1 Month, and make sure that 1 is in the numeric entry box.

3. Click the Advanced tab, open the Of Type drop-down list, and select Microsoft Word Document.

4. Click Find Now.

The Find Files dialog box will display a list of Word files you created in the last month.

Finding by content and size If you want to delete several early drafts of files that contain a phrase and you know these files are 64 KB or less in size, whereas the final files you want to keep are larger, you can use the following instructions to delete these drafts:

1. Open Find, or select New Search, and stay in the Name & Location tab.

2. In the Containing Text box, type the text you want to search for without quotation marks unless they are to be included in the search.

3. Click the Advanced tab, return the Of Type drop-down list box to All Files And Folders, and open the Size Is drop-down list box. Select At Least if you want all the files above a certain size or At Most if you want all the files below a certain size, which we do here.

4. Press **TAB** to move to the size box itself, and type the size you want to be the limit. For example, if you want to search only for files equal to or smaller than 64 KB, type **64** after selecting At Most in the drop-down list, as you can see here:

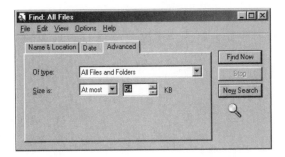

5. Click Find Now.

6. When the search is complete, select the files you want to delete, and either drag them to the Recycle Bin, or press **DELETE.**

The other Find options (Computer, On The Internet, and People) will be discussed in the applicable chapters of this book.

File Manager

As useful as Windows 98 and Windows Explorer are, you may find yourself wishing for the File Manager that you had in Windows 3.x. File Manager did have several features, such as File Move and Copy and the drive icons in the toolbar across the top, that you may long for. If so, you can still use File Manager in Windows 98. In your Windows folder is a file named Winfile.exe. Find this folder and file using Windows Explorer, and then click it. File Manager will open, as shown in Figure 6-5.

 OTE   File Manager will not display long filenames. All you will see is the 8.3 names (see *Naming and Renaming Files and Folders* later in this chapter) created by Windows 98. The "~1" tells you that a file has a long filename.

The menus and tools in Windows 98's File Manager are the same as the Windows 3.x versions except that you cannot share and unshare files in the Windows 98 version.

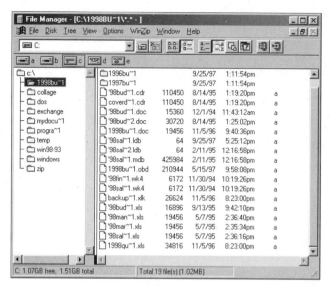

Figure 6-5.   *File Manager in Windows 98.*

 ARNING   If you delete a file in File Manager, the deleted files do NOT go into the Recycle Bin and cannot be undeleted.

Handling Files and Folders

There are many tasks that you perform on files while using your computer. These include copying, moving, naming, renaming, deleting, retrieving, and backing up files and folders. How easy and efficient these tasks are go a long way in determining how satisfied you are with your computer system. Windows 98 has many improvements in this area.

The following paragraphs will explore all of the major file-handling tasks and describe how they are performed in Windows 98.

Copying and Moving Files and Folders

There are three primary ways to copy or move files in Windows 98 and two more if you include File Manager and MS-DOS. These are, in order of their ease of use, dragging within Windows Explorer, using cut or copy and paste, dragging between folder windows or the desktop, File Manager's File Move or Copy, and MS-DOS commands.

Dragging Within Windows Explorer

By all accounts, the easiest way to copy or move a file or folder from one folder to another is to drag it from a folder that is open in the right pane of Windows Explorer to another folder or disk in the default left pane. The trick is to display the source folder in the right pane and the destination in the left. One of the great beauties of Windows Explorer is that every disk and folder that you can access from your computer can be displayed in the left pane of Windows Explorer. Therefore, any file or folder that you can display in the right pane can be dragged, and thereby copied or moved, to any disk or folder you can access.

 IP You can also open two (or more) instances of Windows Explorer and drag between them. This comes in handy when you are moving between different computers or drives. You can open the contents of each independently, similar to having two folder windows opened.

Simply dragging a file or folder from one folder to another *on the same hard disk,* as you see in Figure 6-6, will *move* that file or folder and not leave a copy in the original folder. If you press and hold **CTRL** while dragging, you will copy the file or folder, leaving the original where it was. (A copy action displays a small plus sign in a box next to the dragged item.) If you drag a file or folder from one hard disk to another, you will always make a copy of the object you drag.

 IP If you use the right mouse button to drag a file or folder from one folder to another, you will be asked if you want to copy or move it, like this:

 IP When dragging a file or folder in Windows Explorer, you can automatically scroll the default left pane by dragging the object to just below the top of the pane to scroll up, or to just above the bottom of the pane to scroll down. The alternative, which is often more straightforward, is to scroll the left pane using a scroll bar before beginning to drag.

Figure 6-6. *Moving a file to a different folder by dragging it.*

Using the Edit Menu

You can use the Edit menu options to copy and move files both in Windows Explorer and in folder windows. This is done by first selecting the file or folder to be moved or copied. Then, from the Edit menu, choose Cut if the file is to be moved (no copy left behind) or Copy if the file is to be copied. Then select the destination folder or disk, and choose Paste from the Edit menu. This technique works well when you cannot see or do not immediately know what the destination of the copy or move will be.

 IP   Independent of how you copy or move a file, you can undo the last ten copies or moves using the Undo option on the Edit menu, as shown here, or by pressing **CTRL-Z**.

Other Forms of Copying and Moving

Copying and moving files and folders between folder windows means simply that you open the receiving folder window, open the sending folder window, and then drag the file or folder from one to the other. If having two windows open at a time is a problem, you can open the sending folder, drag the file or folder to the desktop, close the sending folder, open the receiving folder, and drag the object to it.

Within File Manager, you can drag a file or folder from the right pane to the left one, but unlike Windows Explorer, the left pane contains only the folders on the selected drive. The real benefit in File Manager is the Copy and Move options on the File menu, which allow you to enter the source and destination and change the name in the process. This is useful and a major omission in Windows 98. MS-DOS also allows you to enter a Copy or Move command where you can specify the source and destination.

Naming and Renaming Files and Folders

One of the most desired features, since the earliest days of the IBM PC, has been to have filenames longer than the eight-character filename and three-character extension. This format, abbreviated as 8.3, began its life before the PC. Windows 98 provides for long filenames and does so in a manner that allows for compatibility with older systems. It gives every file two names: a long filename and an 8.3 alias.

Using Long Filenames

The long filename can have up to 255 characters and can include any combination of the following ASCII (American Standard Code for Information Interchange) character set:

- Numerals 0–9

- Capital and lowercase letters *A–Z* with case differentiation

- Blank (Spacebar, character 32)

- The special characters allowed in the 8.3 format:

    ! # $ % & ' ( ) - @ ^ _ ` { } ~

- These additional special characters, valid in a long filename but not in an 8.3 alias:

  + . = [ ] , ;

- All of the characters above character 127, which opens the full extended ASCII character set of additional special and western European characters

- But *NOT* the following characters:

  " * / : ? \ |

OTE   The length of the path that can precede a filename has been increased from 80 characters in a short name to 260 characters in a long filename.

When you name a file, Windows 98 looks at the name. If your name fits the 8.3 format *and is all uppercase,* then the filename and the alias are the same. Otherwise, Windows 98 generates an 8.3-format alias out of the long filename. This is not something you can control, and the resulting alias depends on many things. Blanks are removed, lowercase is converted to uppercase, characters not allowed in the 8.3 format are removed, and the long name is truncated at six characters and ~1 is added to the name. If this causes a duplicate filename, then the number is incremented at the end of the name. For example, if you have two Microsoft Word files, named 1998 Marketing budget.doc and 1998 Marketing plan.doc, the first will have an alias of 1998MA~1.DOC, and the second an alias of 1998MA~2.DOC.

OTE   A long filename can have multiple periods within it. When an alias is generated from a long filename with several periods, all but the rightmost period will be removed, and an extension will be created using the first three characters after the rightmost period.

Both My Computer and Windows Explorer display only the long filename. But, there are two ways you can see both the alias that Windows 98 has assigned to a file and the long filename. First, right-click the file, and choose Properties. The Properties dialog box opens, and you can see the long name at the top, next to the icon, and the short name opposite MS-DOS name, as shown in Figure 6-7.

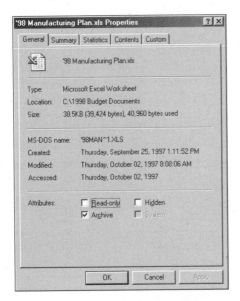

Figure 6-7. *File Properties dialog box showing both the long filename and the alias.*

The second way of seeing both the filename and the alias is from the MS-DOS prompt from *within Windows 98.* Open the Start menu, and choose Programs | MS-DOS Prompt. If you then type **DIR** in a folder that has long filenames, you will see the short aliases on the left, in the normal position of the MS-DOS filename, and the long filename on the right, as you can see in Figure 6-8. Files that do not have a long filename have the same name on both the left and the right except for capitalization.

Figure 6-8. *Typing **DIR** at the MS-DOS prompt from within Windows 98 will show both an alias and the long filename.*

When using long filenames, you should keep in mind several considerations. Most importantly, you should not use Windows 3.x or MS-DOS utilities to copy, move, back up, rename, or sort files or folders with long filenames. They will strip off the long filename. This problem will *not* occur with older file editors, such as word processors, that run under Windows 98, because of a feature called *tunneling*. With tunneling, programs that don't know about long filenames will operate on the alias, and Windows 98 will preserve the long filename in the background. However, if you do this editing outside of Windows 98 or Windows 95 (for example, on another computer or in MS-DOS), you will lose the long filename.

 ARNING   Using an older file-management utility to back up, copy, move, rename, or sort files with long filenames will strip off the long filename.

Another potential problem when using long filenames is that a file manipulation can change the alias. For example, if you copy a file from a folder with potential duplicate aliases to a folder without potential duplicates, the copy will have a different alias. This situation can also occur when you edit a file and save it to a different folder or when you restore a backup file to a different folder.

Additional Date/Time Fields

Prior to Windows 95, only one date/time was maintained for a file. This was initially the date/time that the file was created and then, as the file was changed, the last date/time the file was modified. Windows 98 now maintains three figures: the date/time that a file was created, the date/time that a file was last modified, and the date the file was last opened. All of these are displayed in the Properties dialog box for the file, as you saw in Figure 6-7, and are available to be used in new utilities, such as backup utilities.

Changing File and Folder Names

The way you change file and folder names depends on whether you are using single-click or double-click. With double-click, you click the file or folder to select it; and after a brief pause, you click the filename, or press **F2.** You can then type the new name or edit the existing name. With single-click, you point at the file to select it, but then you can only press

F2 to edit the name. This can be done in Windows Explorer, My Computer, on the desktop, or any place you see a file or folder name, like the results window of the Find option.

IP   You can also right-click the file/folder name and choose Rename from the context menu, or in Windows Explorer and folder windows you can choose Rename from the File menu.

When a name is available for editing, a vertical line, called the *insertion point,* appears in it. This tells you where the next character you type will be placed. If any characters in the name are selected (highlighted), they will be replaced by whatever you type.

Once you have the name available for editing, you can drag across the characters you want to change, and either press **DELETE** to remove the characters, or type the replacement characters. You can also use the keystrokes in Table 6-1 to edit a folder name or filename.

Associating Files

Associating, or registering, files is the process of identifying the program that is used to create and edit a type of file so that if you activate (click) that type of file, the program will start and load the file. For example, Microsoft Word is used to create and edit most files with the .doc extension. Doc files are therefore associated with Microsoft Word, and if you

Keystroke	Function Performed
ARROW keys	Move the insertion point in the direction of the key pressed
HOME/END	Move the insertion point to the left (Home) or right (End) end of the name
BACKSPACE	Deletes the character to the left of the insertion point
DEL/DELETE	Delete the character to the right of the insertion point
ENTER	Completes editing, accepting any changes made
ESC	Completes editing, ignoring any changes made

Table 6-1.   *Editing keys.*

click one of them, Microsoft Word will start and load the file so it is ready for you to edit.

Most associating is done automatically when a program is installed. You can see which file types are associated with what programs in the File Types tab of Windows Explorer's Folder Options dialog box, shown in Figure 6-9. You can open this dialog box from Windows Explorer, My Computer, or any folder View menu.

If you want to associate a file type that is not automatically registered when a program is installed, use the following steps:

1. Select a file of the type you want to register. Open the View menu from My Computer, Windows Explorer, or any folder; and choose Folder Options.

2. Click the File Types tab and then New Type. The Add New File Type dialog box opens, as shown in Figure 6-10.

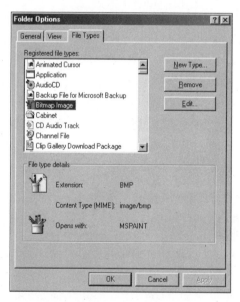

Figure 6-9.   *File associations are registered in the File Types tab of the Folder Options dialog box.*

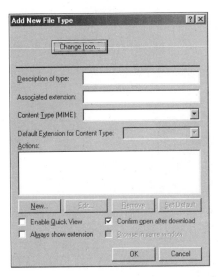

Figure 6-10.   *Dialog box to associate a new file type.*

For example, you want to create a file type for the log files that are in your root directory, and whenever you click that file type, you want Notepad to display them.

3. Type **Log file** for the description and **log** for the extension. The description will appear in the Type column in Windows Explorer's Details view and in the Properties dialog box for the files. The extension should be the extension used by all files in the file type.

4. Select Text/Plain for the Content Type and .log for the Default Extension.

5. Click New, type **Open** in the Action text box, and use Browse to locate \Windows\Notepad.exe on your computer. Double-click the filename, and click OK.

6. Back in the Add New File Type dialog box, click Change Icon, and choose an icon to be used with the file type. (See the next tip.) Click Close twice to complete the process.

 IP You can find many icons to choose from in \Windows\Moricons.dll, \Windows\System\Iconlib.dll, \Windows\System\Pifmgr.dll, and \Windows\System\Shell32.dll. (You may need to turn on Show All Files in the Folder Options View tab to see all of these files.)

There is also a quick and dirty way to associate files like this:

1. Click the file (or right-click and choose Open With) to display the Open With dialog box shown here:

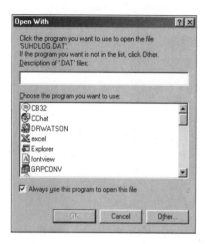

2. Use the scroll bar to find the program you want to associate with the file, and double-click that program.

This does not give you the opportunity to describe the file type and select an icon, but it does quickly associate and open the file with the program you have chosen.

Deleting Files and Folders

Deleting a file or a folder is as simple as selecting it and pressing **DELETE** or choosing Delete from the File menu, right-clicking the file or folder and choosing Delete, or dragging the object to the Recycle Bin—or is it? In Windows 98, everything you delete goes into the Recycle Bin almost independent of how you deleted it. This is a safety feature that allows you to undelete whatever you deleted until you empty the Recycle Bin. But it also means that you must take the extra step of emptying the Recycle Bin.

Using the Recycle Bin

The Recycle Bin is like a special-purpose shortcut to the Recycled folder on your primary hard disk. All files and folders that you delete by one of the above methods are automatically placed in this folder unless you take an action to prevent it. (You will see how to do that in a moment.) The contents of the Recycled folder can be viewed like those of any other folder, as you can see in Figure 6-11. This is the same view you get if you click the Recycle Bin to open it.

As in virtually all Windows 98 objects, you control the Recycle Bin by right-clicking it and opening its Properties dialog box, as shown in Figure 6-12. You can set the Recycle Bin properties either for all drives on your computer or for each drive independently. (Of course, if you have only one hard disk, that is the same thing.) In either case, you can remove files immediately upon deleting them and thus inactivate the Recycle Bin, and you can determine the amount of your disk space you want to allocate to the Recycled folder. If you remove files immediately upon deletion, you will get a warning message, shown below, every time you delete a file or a folder using any of the techniques. The same is *NOT* true if you set your disk allocation too small and then delete more files than can fit. You get no message, and the earliest-deleted files simply disappear. The default Recycle Bin is 10 percent of your hard-disk space, which, in most circumstances, should be adequate.

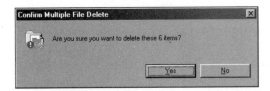

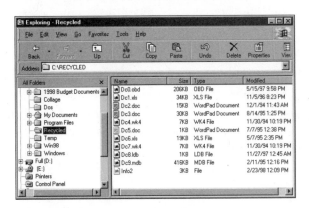

Figure 6-11.   *The Recycled folder in Windows Explorer.*

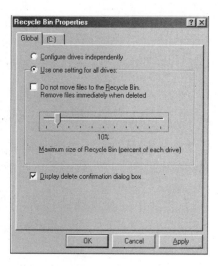

Figure 6-12. *Controls for the Recycle Bin.*

WARNING If you delete more files than can be held in the disk space allocated for the Recycle Bin, your earliest-deleted file(s) will disappear without warning.

TIP You can also permanently delete a file without placing it in the Recycle Bin by pressing **SHIFT-DELETE**.

Synchronizing Files with My Briefcase

My Briefcase provides a means to synchronize files between two computers. It is a special folder that keeps track of the change status of the files it contains. This allows you to work on the same file on two computers and to have Windows remember which is the latest file and then to update the older one so the two are the same. For example, if you use My Briefcase to take files from a computer at work and work on them on a computer at home, when you return the briefcase to the computer at work, the original files can be updated for the changes you made at home, as shown in Figure 6-13. The steps to do this are as follows:

NOTE If you do not have a Briefcase on your screen, it may not have been installed when you installed Windows 98. You can add it by using Add/Remove Programs in Control Panel.

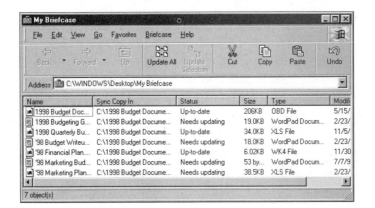

Figure 6-13. *My Briefcase showing files that need updating.*

1. Drag or copy the files you want to keep synchronized to My Briefcase.

2. Drag or copy My Briefcase to a floppy disk, and carry it to a second computer; or drag My Briefcase to another computer on your network.

3. Open My Briefcase on the second computer, and edit the files while they remain in the briefcase. Alternately or in addition, you can edit the original files on the first computer.

4. Open My Briefcase back on the original computer either while it is still on the floppy or by dragging it to the original computer's hard disk, and choose Update All or Update Selection from the Briefcase menu or the toolbar. The Update My Briefcase dialog box will open, as shown in Figure 6-14.

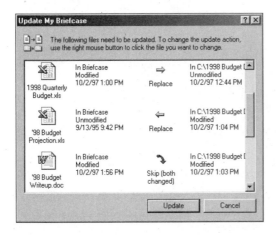

Figure 6-14. *Notification of updating to be done from My Briefcase.*

5. The Update My Briefcase dialog box shows you what Windows believes to be the direction of the updating you want done. If you want to change the way the file is to be updated, right-click the entry you want to change. In the context menu that opens, either select the opposite direction, or click Skip to not update either file.

6. After ensuring that the updating that Windows is proposing is correct or after changing it, click Update to synchronize the files between My Briefcase and the original files.

If both files have changed, Windows will suggest that you skip updating either file. You can ignore this and update either one you want, *BUT* in so doing you will lose the changes that were made in the file being updated.

Handling Disks

Disk drives provide for storing your folders and files and for transporting these objects on and off your computer. Most computers have at least one floppy-disk drive, one hard-disk drive, and probably a CD-ROM drive. The CD-ROM drive will be discussed in depth in Chapter 13, "Using Multimedia," but some of what will be said here about floppy and hard disks also applies to CD-ROM drives.

Floppy-disk and hard-disk drives can be thought of as just large folders, and some of the discussion earlier in this chapter that related to folders also pertains to disks. Most importantly, you can drag and copy files and folders to disks just as you can to other folders. But disks also have many unique features. They can be partitioned, formatted, scanned for errors, defragmented, compressed, and backed up. Those are the subjects of this section.

Using FAT32 Partitions

The File Allocation Table, or *FAT,* is the way the operating system locates files and bad sectors on a disk. When you establish a disk partition, you establish its FAT. All versions of MS-DOS and Windows through Windows for Workgroups 3.11 used the original FAT, which had a maximum disk partition of 512 MB. The original version of Windows 95 introduced VFAT (Virtual File Allocation Table), which provides for long filenames, runs in protected mode, and allows for disks or partitions of up to 2 GB while maintaining compatibility with MS-DOS. Both FAT and VFAT used 16-bit addressing. In the fall of 1996, Microsoft came out with an upgrade to Windows 95 only for new computers called OSR2 (original equipment manufacturer, or OEM, Service Release 2), which included FAT32 with 32-bit addressing for disk partitions of over 2 TB (terabytes or trillion bytes). Windows 98 allows you to continue to use VFAT or to switch to FAT32.

Besides the ability to address larger disk partitions, FAT32 also provides a much improved clustering scheme, which reduces the cluster size of large partitions, as you can see in Table 6-2. The *cluster size* is the incremental unit in which all files are written. For example, if you have a 16 KB file and a 4 KB cluster size, four clusters, or units, are written to the disk; and no space is wasted. If you have a 32 KB cluster size, one unit is written to the disk, but half of it is wasted space. The cluster size is the smallest size file that the system can use. If a lot of your files are smaller than the cluster size, you will have a lot of wasted space. If a file is larger than the cluster size, if it is even 1 byte larger than a multiple of the cluster size, it will use an additional cluster. FAT32 therefore results in a much more efficient use of disk space.

Partition Size	FAT Cluster Size	FAT32 Cluster Size
0–31 MB	512 bytes	512 bytes
32–63 MB	1 KB	512 bytes
64–127 MB	2 KB	512 bytes
128–255 MB	4 KB	512 bytes (up to 260 MB)
256–511 MB	8 KB	4 KB (over 260 MB)
512–1023 MB	16 KB	4 KB
1024–2047 MB	32 KB	4 KB
2–8 GB	Not Available (NA)	4 KB
8–16 GB	NA	8 KB
16–32 GB	NA	16 KB
Above 32 GB	NA	32 KB

Table 6-2. *FAT and FAT32 cluster sizes.*

FAT32 has two other benefits but several negatives. The benefits are that the root directory is now an ordinary cluster chain and the boot record now contains a backup for the most critical components. Being an ordinary cluster chain means that the root directory can be located anywhere and so is no longer limited to 512 entries, and with the backed-up boot-record components, the chance of boot failure is reduced. The negatives deal with compatibility with other programs. FAT32 removes your ability to easily dual boot (using the **F4** function key during boot up) with all other operating systems. If you boot from another system (other than Windows 98 or Windows 95 OSR2) startup disk, you will not be able to see a FAT32 partition. Most disk utilities and even some applications (including Microsoft's Office 95 Standard Edition) are not compatible with FAT32. Finally, no current disk-compression software, including Microsoft's DriveSpace 3, will work with FAT32.

 OTE   Most antivirus programs and third-party disk utilities written for Windows 95 are not compatible with FAT32 and should be uninstalled before installing FAT32. Check your third-party utilities before using them with FAT32, and look for upgrades.

Installing FAT32 Partitions

There are two ways to install FAT32 with Windows 98. The first is to run FDISK using a Windows 98 startup disk to partition a hard disk and to then answer Yes, you want to enable large-disk support. The second way to install FAT32 is to convert an existing Windows 98 FAT installation.

To place FAT32 on a new or "clean" hard disk, you need to run FDISK from a Windows 98 startup floppy. The easiest way to get the startup floppy is to install (or partially install) Windows 98. Early in the process, a startup floppy is created, and if you want, you can stop the install at that point and reboot using the new startup floppy. At the A:/> prompt, type **fdisk** and press **ENTER.** If the hard disk has previously been used, at the first question choose 3 to delete the existing partition, and follow through the remaining questions. (See *Preparing a New or Reformatted Hard Disk* in Chapter 3.) If the hard disk is new or after completing the previous step on a used drive, choose 1 to create a new primary DOS partition and enable large-disk support.

With an existing Windows 98 partition, you can tell if you have FAT32 installed by right-clicking a drive and choosing Properties to open the drive's Properties dialog box, as shown in Figure 6-15. If it says "FAT," then you have FAT16 installed. If it says "FAT32," that is what you have. If you have FAT and you want FAT32, you can run the FAT32 Converter by opening the Start menu and choosing Programs | Accessories | System Tools | Drive Converter (FAT32). The wizard will open, as shown in Figure 6-16. When you click Next, you are asked to choose a drive, warned about possible antivirus software and the possible incompatibility with previous operating systems, asked if you want to create a backup, and told that your computer must be restarted. ScanDisk is then run; your files are converted; and finally Disk Defragmenter is run, and you are told that the conversion was successful. If you then go back and look at the drive's Properties dialog box, you'll see that the file system now indicates FAT32, like this:

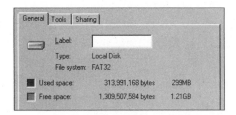

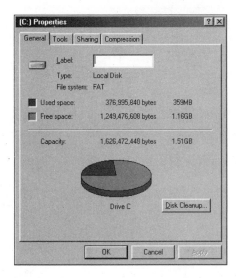

Figure 6-15. *FAT file system shown in the Properties dialog box for a drive.*

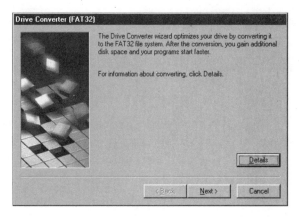

Figure 6-16. *Drive Converter (FAT32) Wizard.*

Formatting and Labeling Disks

Formatting prepares a new disk so that it can be used or erases a used disk so that it can be reused. In Windows 98, you can format a disk by right-clicking it in either My Computer or Windows Explorer and choosing Format from the context menu. The Format dialog box appears, as shown in Figure 6-17. In it, you can select the capacity of the disk you are formatting and the type of formatting you want to do. The options for format type and their purposes are as follows:

 IP Make sure the disk you are trying to format isn't currently opened in Windows Explorer. You cannot format the disk while its contents are displayed.

- **Quick** format does not check the disk for bad sectors (similar to ScanDisk discussed in a moment). It only erases the existing information and prepares the disk for use.

- **Full** format completely scans the disk for errors and, if it doesn't find any, erases the old information on the disk and prepares it to be used.

- **Copy System Files Only** does not format the disk but only writes on the disk the four system files (Command.com, Drvspace.bin, Io.sys, and Msdos.sys) that make it able to start your computer. These files take less than 390 KB of disk space.

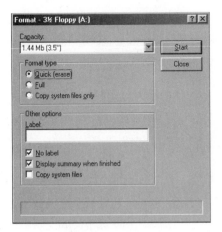

Figure 6-17. *Format dialog box.*

 ARNING Use Quick format only if you are sure you have a disk with no bad sectors. The extra time it takes to scan and let you know about bad sectors could save you problems later.

If you choose Quick or Full for the Format Type, you can optionally add a label to the disk of up to 11 characters. You can also get information about the formatted disk telling you how much space is available and how much is used by system files and bad sectors. In addition, you can add the system files so a computer can be booted with the disk. The format information looks like this:

If you add a label to a disk in formatting, you can see the label in the Properties dialog box for that disk (where you can also change the label or add one if it was not done in formatting). It also appears next to the drive letter in My Computer, Windows Explorer, and other windows and dialog boxes where drives are listed. If a used disk has a label and you want to remove it during formatting and have no label, click No Label.

Cleaning Up Disks

If you open a hard disk's Properties dialog box, as you saw previously in Figure 6-15, you find a Disk Cleanup button, which opens the Disk Cleanup dialog box, shown in Figure 6-18. This allows you to remove files that you do not want to keep in order to free up disk space. In the Disk Cleanup tab, as a default, you can choose to delete the following:

- **Temporary Internet Files** in the Windows folder of that name include Web pages and graphics files used to quickly redisplay a Web site you have previously visited. Any cookies stored in this folder are not deleted.

- **Downloaded Program Files** in the Windows folder of that name include ActiveX and Java applets that have been downloaded from the Internet.

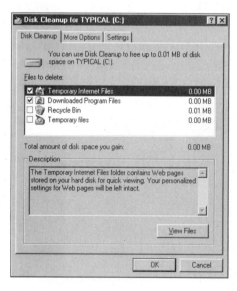

Figure 6-18. *Disk Cleanup dialog box.*

- **Recycle Bin** includes all the files you have deleted to the Recycle Bin and not removed since you last emptied it.

- **Temporary Files** in the \Windows\Temp folder include files that have been temporarily written there by various programs and then not deleted.

The More Options tab shown in Figure 6-19 gives you two more ways to free up space on your hard disk: by removing Windows components that were installed but not used and by removing programs that you installed but no longer use. Both of these options open the Add/Remove Programs dialog box. The first opens the Windows Setup tab, where you can select Windows options you want to remove; and the Second opens the Install/ Uninstall tab, where you select programs you want to remove. Finally, the More Options tab reminds you that if you haven't installed FAT32, its installation will free up disk space; you can start the Drive Converter (FAT32) wizard by clicking Convert.

The Settings tab provides a single option that allows Disk Cleanup to run automatically when your hard disk runs low on space. The option is selected by default, and it is recommended to leave it that way.

Figure 6-19. *Disk Cleanup More Options tab.*

Analyzing and Repairing Disks with ScanDisk

As disk size increases, the chance of something happening to the information you have written on the disk increases proportionally. To ease this problem with today's larger disk sizes, Windows 98 has included a general disk-diagnostic-and-repair program called ScanDisk. ScanDisk will work on hard disks, floppy disks, and RAM drives, but not on CD-ROM discs; and it will detect and fix problems in the following areas:

- Directory tree structure
- DriveSpace or DoubleSpace compression structure, volume header, volume file structure, and volume signatures
- File allocation table, or FAT
- File structure (cross-linked files and lost clusters)
- Long filenames
- Physical drive surface (bad sectors)

To load ScanDisk, open the Start menu, and choose Programs | Accessories | System Tools | ScanDisk. You can also right-click a drive in either Windows Explorer or My Computer, select Properties, and click Check Now in the Tools tab. The ScanDisk dialog box will open, as shown in Figure 6-20. This allows you to select the drive to scan and to choose between

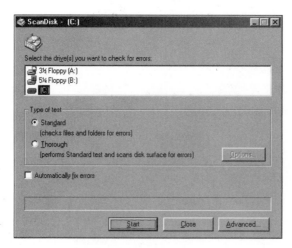

Figure 6-20. *ScanDisk dialog box.*

the Standard and the Thorough scan. The Standard scan checks for file and folder problems but not for physical damage to the disk; the Thorough scan adds the physical disk analysis. The scan for physical damage takes considerably longer than the Standard scan. Depending on the size of your drive and what is found, this can be the difference between less than a minute or more than an hour, so normally you may want to do a Standard scan.

 IP You can see how long it has been since you last ran ScanDisk on a drive by right-clicking the drive in Windows Explorer or in My Computer, choosing Properties, and opening the Tools tab.

If you encounter an error while running ScanDisk, under default settings you will be notified of the error and asked what you want to do, as shown here:

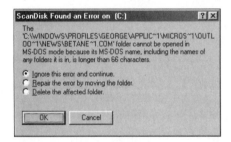

Depending on what the error is, you will be given a choice of fixing the error, deleting the offending file or folder, or doing nothing. In most instances, the dialog box will tell you what can be done with the error (repairing it is the most common) and what is recommended. Repairing works most of the time (except in the instance shown above, where ignoring it is the best solution). If you want, you can have ScanDisk fix most errors without asking you by clicking the Automatically Fix Errors check box in the ScanDisk dialog box. Unless the repairing process has a lot of repetition, it is a good idea to look at the error messages to see what is happening on your disk. A rash of problems could indicate it's time to get a new hard disk.

You can control some aspects of what ScanDisk does through the Advanced button in the ScanDisk dialog box. Clicking this button opens the ScanDisk Advanced Options dialog box, shown in Figure 6-21. The first option, Display

Summary, determines when the ScanDisk Results (shown here) are displayed. This summary provides feedback on how your disk is doing.

The second option in the ScanDisk Advanced Options dialog box determines what to do with lost file fragments. Files are stored in multiple pieces, or *fragments,* and sometimes a fragment becomes detached from the rest of the file. In most instances where the rest of the file exists, ScanDisk can reattach the fragment, and all is well. But, if the rest of the file has been deleted or if for some reason ScanDisk can't reattach it, the fragment is considered lost. There is a small chance that if the fragment can be converted to a file (difficult in and of itself), you can determine what it is and use it. In most cases, the fragments result from deleted files and are of no value. It is therefore recommended that lost file fragments be deleted and their space converted to free space.

Figure 6-21. *ScanDisk Advanced Options.*

You can keep a log file containing the results of running ScanDisk. This file, named Scandisk.log, is stored in your root directory. You can use Notepad to look at it, as shown in Figure 6-22. The default is to replace this log file each time you run Scandisk. The alternatives are to append the log to an existing file each time, or not to create a log file at all.

The fourth option in the ScanDisk Advanced Options dialog box asks you if you want to check for invalid filenames, invalid dates and times on files, and duplicate names. Invalid filenames, such as might occur on files you brought over from a Unix or Macintosh computer, might not be readable by your applications and therefore need to be fixed. Invalid dates and times can cause files to be sorted incorrectly or cause backup and setup programs to make incorrect assumptions. Duplicate filenames can safely coexist in separate folders; however, you might want to delete one or more occurrences of the same file.

Cross-linked files occur when two files share the same fragment, although the fragment is probably only correct for one file. In most instances, this corrupts both files, and they need to be deleted. The other option is to make a copy of the fragment and attach one to each file. This allows you, at least, to try to read both files and decide which file, if either, is worth keeping. The final possibility is to ignore cross-linked files. This is not a good idea because it can cause an application to crash, potentially bringing down the entire system and losing more files.

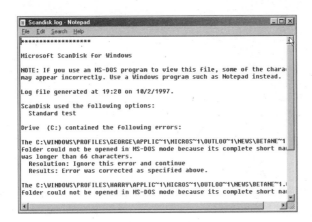

Figure 6-22.   *Scandisk.log displayed in Notepad.*

The final two options ask you if you want to check your host drive, which is your uncompressed drive if you are using DriveSpace or DoubleSpace disk compression, and whether to report on MS-DOS-mode naming errors. If the Check Host Drive First box is not checked, the host drive is ignored. If you are using disk compression, you should check your host drive before checking the compressed drive. Therefore, the box should be checked. Disk compression is discussed later in this chapter. If you want ScanDisk to inform you about name-length errors in MS-DOS mode, as shown in the error example in this section, do not change the default setting of the final check box.

Physical Surface Scan

If you choose a Thorough disk scan, ScanDisk analyzes the disk for physical defects. The Options button next to the Thorough option opens the Surface Scan Options dialog box, shown next. This allows you to determine what area of the disk you want to scan: the system area, the data area, or both. When ScanDisk finds a physical error on the disk, it flags that sector as a bad one so nothing will be written there in the future. It also writes any information found in the original sector, in another. This works well in the large data area, but the system area is small, so there is often not room to move a file. Also, some older programs look for their information in a specific location in the system area, and if it is moved, the program will not work. Often if errors occur in the system area, you will need to replace the disk.

The Surface Scan Options dialog box has one check box that allows you to disable write-testing. Another allows you to not repair bad sectors that contain hidden or system files. When ScanDisk does a surface scan, it reads a sector, then writes back the information that was in the sector, and compares the two. This fully tests the ability of the disk to be read from and written on. There is a chance that this process can corrupt data; that is the reason for the check box to turn off write-testing. The problem is that you will not know if you have a bad sector that should have been corrected. In most cases, the data is read correctly, and then if a write error is detected, the sector is flagged, and the data is correctly rewritten in a new location.

The reason you may not want to repair bad sectors containing hidden or system files has already been discussed—because of the limited size of the system area and because some older programs expect the files in a specific location. The alternative, though, is to buy a new disk, so it is recommended that you try the repair process and see whether or not you have a serious problem.

 IP While it is possible to run other programs while running either ScanDisk or Disk Defragmenter, each time you write to the disk the utilities will restart, causing the process to go slowly. This is also true with the Screen Saver. You should therefore turn off the Screen Saver and not run other programs while running either of these utilities.

Optimizing, or Defragmenting, Disks

Files are stored on a disk in pieces, or fragments. The size of the fragments depends on the size of your drive (the larger the drive, the larger the fragments) and whether you are running FAT or FAT32. (FAT32, which is discussed earlier in this chapter, provides smaller fragments on larger disks.) When you go to store a file, if there is enough room in one location on your disk to store the entire file, then the entire file is stored in one contiguous location. If there is not enough room in one spot, then the file is broken up and stored in fragments throughout the disk. In this latter case, reading the file can take much longer, and fragments can become lost, as you just read about under ScanDisk. If you add and delete a lot of files, fragmentation of your files can become a serious problem and significantly slow down your disk access. To fix this problem, Windows 98 has included Disk Defragmenter. This program goes through your disk rearranging files so that all of their fragments are contiguous, thereby speeding up disk access.

Start Disk Defragmenter by opening the Start menu and choosing Pro-
grams | Accessories | System Tools | Disk Defragmenter. You can also
right-click a drive in Windows Explorer or My Computer, choose Properties and the Tools tab, and then click Defragment Now. If you enter
through the Start menu, you will be asked to specify a drive you want to
defragment, as shown here:

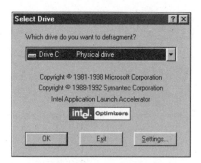

You can control some of what Disk Defragmenter does by clicking Settings
to open the Disk Defragmenter Settings dialog box, shown next. In this
dialog box, you can choose to rearrange program files to increase program
performance. This allows you to do one additional level of optimization
by looking at program usage. Based on this, Disk Defragmenter arranges
the files on your disk in such a way that the files you use most often are all
together in one area of your disk with the program that loads them. This,
of course, makes running those programs and files much faster. The other
options allow you to run ScanDisk before running Disk Defragmenter and
to choose if you want the setting to apply every time you defragment a
drive or only this time.

When the Defragmenter starts, the Defragmenting Drive dialog box opens, as shown next. This allows you to stop or pause the process and to show the details of the defragmentation. While it is fun to see the enlarged detail display, it significantly slows down the task. To get the fastest performance from Disk Defragmenter, it is best to minimize the dialog box so that you see it only in the taskbar (it still tells you the percentage complete).

 OTE Disk Defragmenter will work with DriveSpace and DoubleSpace compressed drives (the host drive should be defragmented first), but it will not work with other compression utilities, such as Stacker or SuperStor.

Compressing Disks

Compressing a disk squeezes the contents down so they fit in roughly one-half the space they took before being compressed. Thus, the storage space on the disk is roughly doubled. Disk compression is accomplished by a complex algorithm that eliminates unused space and repeated characters or patterns of characters. When a disk is compressed, it behaves and looks to you, the user, and to programs using it like any other disk; it just contains approximately twice as much data. In reality, the compressed disk is a newly created virtual drive that is given the name of the original, uncompressed drive. In addition, a new, uncompressed drive called drive H, or the *host* drive, is created. The host drive contains at least one file, the entire contents of the compressed drive. If for some reason you need other uncompressed files, they also can be placed on the host drive.

 ARNING Do not in any way change the compressed file on the host drive (called Drvspace.000), or you will risk losing all of your files on the compressed drive.

You can compress a hard disk or a floppy disk or change the compression on an existing DriveSpace or DoubleSpace disk by opening the Start menu and choosing Programs | Accessories | System Tools | DriveSpace. (DriveSpace is not installed as part of the Typical install, so you may need to open Control Panel, choose Add/Remove Programs, and from the Windows Setup tab choose System Tools | Disk Compression Tools.) You then choose what disk you want to compress in this dialog box:

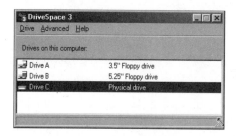

 OTE   DoubleSpace is the original Microsoft disk-compression routine, which was first available with MS-DOS 6.0. For legal reasons, it was replaced by DriveSpace in MS-DOS 6.22. Windows 98 contains DriveSpace, but it can fully utilize disks that were compressed with DoubleSpace.

 OTE   You cannot compress a drive on which you have installed FAT32. See the discussion of FAT32 earlier in this chapter.

Double-clicking a drive in the DriveSpace dialog box opens the Compression Properties dialog box, shown in Figure 6-23. This tells you if the drive is compressed, the amount of used and free space, the compression ratios, and the parent drive if the drive is compressed. The Compression Properties dialog box is just an information box, similar to the drive Properties dialog box, and the only option you have is to hide the host drive. (Only under rare circumstances, where a new user might get into trouble, should you hide a host drive. Otherwise, hiding a drive leads only to confusion.) To do anything else with a drive, you must return to the DriveSpace dialog box.

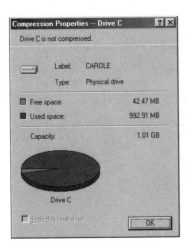

Figure 6-23. *Compression Properties dialog box.*

After selecting a drive in the DriveSpace dialog box, you can compress, uncompress, adjust the amount of free space, upgrade a previously compressed drive to DriveSpace 3, or format a compressed drive with the Drive menu. The Advanced menu allows you to mount (open) or unmount (close) a compressed drive on removable media like floppies and to create a new (empty) compressed drive using the free space on an existing drive (which may or may not be compressed). The Advanced menu also allows you to delete an existing compressed drive, to change the compression-ratio assumption used to figure free space on a compressed drive, and to change the drive letter. You can also open the Disk Compression Settings dialog box, shown in Figure 6-24.

The Disk Compression Settings dialog box allows you to choose the type of compression that you want and shows you the choices between more speed and more space. Prior to Windows 98 and DriveSpace 3, you could choose only between compression and no compression. In DriveSpace 3, you can also choose selective compression, where you compress only if you have a real shortage of disk space, and HiPack compression for the highest compression. Normally, you still want to use Standard compression.

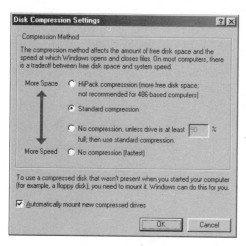

Figure 6-24.   *Choosing compression options.*

You can also start DriveSpace by right-clicking a FAT16 drive, choosing Properties, and then clicking Compression. This opens the dialog box shown in Figure 6-25. There you can see that when you start with an uncompressed drive, you can end up with either the existing drive compressed or a new, empty compressed drive created from the free space on the existing drive. (You can also create a new, empty compressed drive using the Advanced menu's Create Empty option.) For example, if you compress a 500-MB hard disk with 300 MB of files and 200 MB of free space, you would then have a 1-GB compressed drive with 300 MB of files (see note below) and 700 MB of free space plus a 500-MB host drive with little or no free space. (These are approximate numbers—in actual fact, you seldom get the full 2:1 compression ratio, and you use one or two megabytes of the host drive for system files.) On the other hand, if you create an empty compressed drive using the free space, you will have a 300-MB uncompressed drive with little free space, a 400-MB empty compressed drive, and a full host drive. In this case, it is obvious that you can get more free space by compressing the entire drive.

 OTE   The file sizes that you see reported in My Computer or Windows Explorer, after you have compressed a drive, are the uncompressed size of the files—the size the files would be if you copied them to an uncompressed drive.

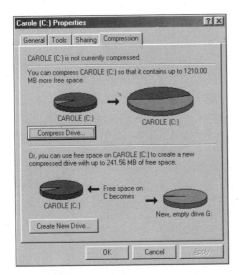

Figure 6-25. *Disk Compression Settings dialog box.*

When you choose Compress from the Drive menu to compress a drive, the dialog box shown in Figure 6-26 opens, showing you the current space on the drive and the space after compression, as well as the space to be created on the host drive. Clicking the Options button allows you to change the drive letter of the host drive, but you cannot change the allocation of space until the compression process is complete. You can also hide or expose the host drive in the Compression Options dialog box.

 N **OTE**   DriveSpace will not compress more than 1 GB of a drive if the drive is larger due to the maximum 2-GB partition size with FAT for the compressed drive. All of the space over 1 GB will be placed in the host drive, as shown in Figure 6-26.

As DriveSpace begins the process of compressing a drive, it first reminds you that you should have an updated startup disk. It then asks you if want to create one now. You are next reminded to back up the files on the drive. It then scans the disk for errors, both the files and the surface; it then defragments the files and, finally, compresses the drive. Depending on the size of the drive and the speed of your disk and processor, this can take up to several hours. It is safe, though, and can even recover from a power outage

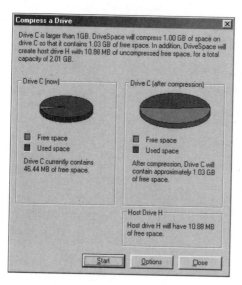

Drive C is larger than 1GB. DriveSpace will compress 1.00 GB of space on drive C so that it contains 1.03 GB of free space. In addition, DriveSpace will create host drive H with 10.88 MB of uncompressed free space, for a total capacity of 2.01 GB.

Figure 6-26. *Compress A Drive dialog box.*

in the middle of the process. You should close all open files and applications, or you will be reminded to do so once DriveSpace starts. If you are compressing the drive that contains Windows 98, DriveSpace will restart your computer with a limited version of Windows 98 to complete the compression. Upon completion, you are told how much free space was created on the disk. Then after completion, your computer will be restarted again with the full version of Windows 98.

 ARNING Always back up all data files before compressing a drive that contains them.

Compressing and using compressed floppy drives works the same as with hard disks. Under the default settings, if you insert a compressed floppy in the drive, Windows 98 will automatically see it is compressed and allow you to work with the files as if they were not compressed. This is called *automounting.* You can control whether compressed floppies are automatically mounted (opened) or not by opening the DriveSpace Advanced menu, choosing Settings, and checking Automatically Mount New Compressed drives in the Disk Compression Settings dialog box, which you saw previously. If automounting is turned off, you can manually mount the drive by choosing Mount in the DriveSpace Advanced menu.

IP If you infrequently use compressed floppy disks, turn off automounting, and save about 4 KB of memory.

You can adjust the amount of free space on the host drive and on the compressed drive by opening DriveSpace's Drive menu and choosing Adjust Free Space. This opens the dialog box you see in Figure 6-27. By dragging the slider to the left, you will increase the amount of free space on the compressed drive and decrease the amount on the host drive. Dragging the slider to the right has the opposite effect. As you drag the slider, one drive will go up as the other goes down using the compression ratio (2:1 by default) between the two. Instead of the slider, you also may type a number in one of the Free Space number boxes.

OTE You should leave at least 2 MB of free space on the host drive for your hard disk. Some DriveSpace operations require at least 1.5 MB on the host drive.

One other DriveSpace adjustment that you can make is to change the compression ratio for a compressed drive. This is done through the Advanced menu and the Compression Ratio dialog box, shown on the next page. By dragging the slider, you can change the ratio used in estimating the amount of free space. Since there is no way to know the types of files you will be

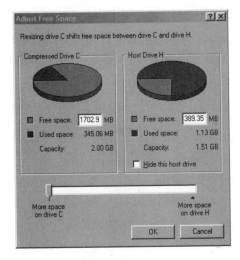

Figure 6-27. *Adjust Free Space dialog box.*

storing in the free space, and since different files compress to different degrees, you must use a rule of thumb to estimate the amount of free space on a compressed drive. By default, this ratio is 2:1. Your experience may be different. Look at the actual compression ratio, and decide how representative it is of what you might place in the free space. Also, consider the types of files you may place there. Program and word-processing files do not compress much, while drawing and bitmap files compress a lot. Then, set the compression ratio to fit your beliefs. Only the estimated amount of free space will be changed.

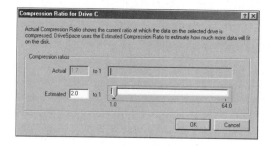

Compression Agent

Windows 98 has added a feature called Compression Agent, which gives you intelligent disk compression. This allows you to compress some of your files and not others or to use a higher compression on your least-used files and a lower compression on your more heavily used files. Since the amount of compression determines the speed of accessing the drive (more compression means slower access), the Compression Agent allows you to trade space for performance.

You can start the Compression Agent by opening the Start menu and choosing Programs | Accessories | System Tools | Compression Agent. The Compression Agent dialog box will open, as shown in Figure 6-28. By clicking Settings, you can select the rules for when you want to use UltraPack and HiPack; by clicking Exceptions, you can specify specific files and folders on which you want to use a particular type of compression.

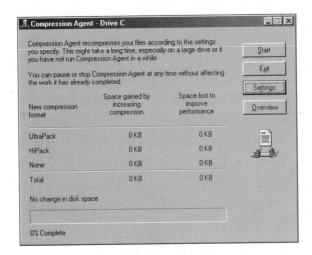

Figure 6-28. *Compression Agent dialog box.*

The Compression Agent will also keep track of the files that you use most frequently and either not compress them or use a lighter compression on those files. You can control when you don't want to do this, because of lack of disk space, by clicking Advanced in the Compression Agent Settings dialog box. This opens the Advanced Settings dialog box shown here:

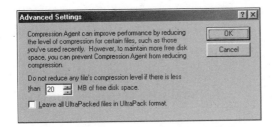

Uncompressing a Drive

Since FAT32 cannot operate with compressed drives, it may be that you will want to uncompress a drive. You can do that with the following steps:

1. Open the Start menu, and choose Programs | Accessories | System Tools | DriveSpace.

2. Open the File menu, and select Uncompress. The Uncompress A Drive dialog box will open, as shown in Figure 6-29. You can see the

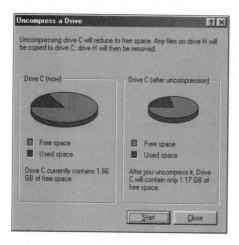

Figure 6-29.   *Uncompress A Drive dialog box.*

effects of uncompressing. If you do switch to FAT32, some of the space lost to uncompressing will be gained by the smaller sector size.

3. Click Start. The Uncompress feature suggests that you back up your files again, warns you that it will take up to several hours, and tells you that it will begin by checking your drive for errors.

4. Click Uncompress Now. When the disk checking is complete, you are asked if you want to remove the compression manager from memory. Click Yes.

5. Next you are told that Windows must restart in a special operating mode. Again click Yes. When the process is complete, you are shown the results; and when you click Close, your system will re-start with the normal Windows 98 running.

Maintenance Wizard

The Maintenance Wizard, shown in Figure 6-30, walks you through the scheduling of several processes that improve the efficiency of your computer as well as pointing out several one-time tasks that you can do to make your computer run faster. Among the tasks that the Maintenance Wizard leads you through are the following:

■   Removing one or more programs that start automatically when you start Windows

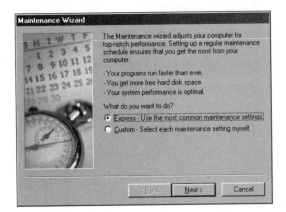

Figure 6-30. *Maintenance Wizard.*

- Running now or scheduling the conversion of your hard disk to FAT32

- Scheduling the running of Disk Defragmenter and changing its settings

- Scheduling the running of ScanDisk and changing its settings

- Scheduling the removal of unnecessary files and specifying the types of files to remove

You start the Maintenance Wizard by opening the Start menu and choosing Programs | Accessories | System Tools | Maintenance Wizard. When you are done working through the Maintenance Wizard, you are shown the results of your work in the final dialog box, such as the one shown in Figure 6-31. If you then click Finish, the tasks that you scheduled are transferred to the Task Scheduler, whose icon will appear on the right of the taskbar.

If you want to revise or delete the scheduling of the tasks you set up in the Maintenance Wizard, you can do so through the Task Scheduler. You can start the Task Scheduler by double-clicking its icon on the taskbar or by opening the Start menu and choosing Programs | Accessories | System Tools | Scheduled Tasks. When you do that, the Scheduled Tasks window opens, as you can see in Figure 6-32. Click an individual task to change its schedule, the program that is run by the task, or the settings that determine the situation in which the task will be run. If you want to delete a task

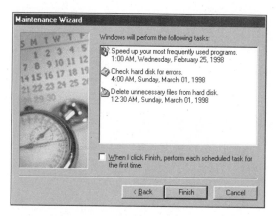

Figure 6-31. *Tasks to be scheduled.*

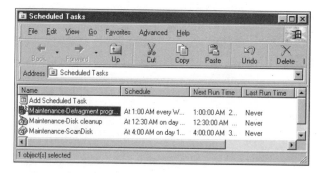

Figure 6-32. *Task scheduler.*

from the schedule, select the task, and either press **DELETE,** or choose Delete from the File menu. Independent of whether you press **SHIFT-DELETE,** the tasks go into the Recycle Bin, which you must empty to fully remove them. If you want to stop using the Task Scheduler altogether, open the Advanced menu, and choose that option.

 OTE A Scheduled Tasks folder is created in the root folder and can be opened in My Computer or Windows Explorer to view tasks or add new ones.

Backing Up Files and Folders

Backing up a hard disk or even floppies is something we are all told to do numerous times but don't do until we lose a valuable file. *Backing up* is simply copying a disk or disks to other disks or to tape. Backing up a hard disk used to require the flipping of a lot of floppies. Today, a 2-GB tape drive costs less than $200 and greatly reduces the amount of effort. Even better, Windows 98 includes a backup program that automatically recognizes these inexpensive tape drives, as well as floppies and other devices, and provides a high degree of compression and file management in backing up your files. You can keep track of the files you backed up and retrieve a single file, if you want.

You start the backup process by opening the Start menu and choosing Programs | Accessories | System Tools | Backup. (Backup is not installed as part of the Typical install; so you may need to open Control Panel, choose Add/Remove Programs, and from the Windows Setup tab choose System Tools | Backup.) The program begins by looking for backup devices, such as tape drives and removable disk drives. If none are found, you are given the option of running Add New Hardware. If you want to do that, click Yes; otherwise, click No.

The Microsoft Backup Welcome message will appear, as shown in Figure 6-33, and you are asked if you want create a new backup job, open an existing backup job, or restore backed up files. A *backup job* is a set of files and folders that you want to back up. If this is the first time you have used Backup, click Create A New Backup Job. Otherwise, you may want to choose one of the other options. In any case, click OK. Next, the Backup Wizard will open, and you can choose to back up everything on My Computer or to select the files, folders, and disks that you want backed up. After making that decision, click Next.

Figure 6-33.   *Choosing what to do in Backup.*

If you choose to select the files, folders, and disks to be backed up, a dialog box will open that allows you to select what you want by clicking it, as you can see in Figure 6-34. You do this either by selecting entire folders on the left (by clicking their check boxes), or by opening a folder (by clicking it) and then selecting files on the right (by clicking their check boxes). Once you have completed selecting the folders and files you want to back up, click Next. You then have a choice of backing up all the files you selected or just the new and changed files within that group. Again click Next.

 IP   You will speed up the backup process and reduce the size of the backup files by not backing up program files which you should already have on disk anyway, although that will mean that you may have to reinstall and set up those programs.

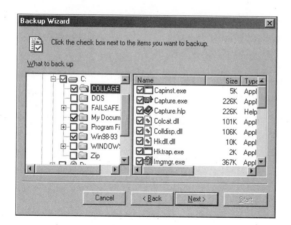

Figure 6-34.   *Selecting what to back up.*

The next step is to select where you want to place the backup—on a floppy disk drive or, if available, on a tape or another device. To do this, select the drive and possibly the folder you want to use, and click Next. Then you are asked if you want to compare the original and backup files and whether you want to compress the backup. After clicking Next, you are asked to enter a name for the backup job and are finally able to click Start to begin the process. While the backup is in progress, you are given a continuous status report of the number of files and bytes backed up, as well as the elapsed time, as shown in Figure 6-35. When the process is complete, you will be told.

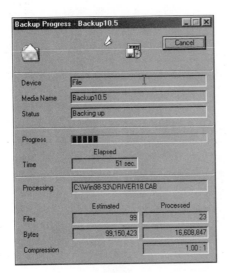

Figure 6-35. *Status of a backup.*

Once you have backed up a set of files and folders, you can restore them either to their original location or to a new location. The restore process is particularly useful because you can restore individual files and folders, as well as the entire set. To start the restore process, select Restore Backed Up Files from the original Microsoft Backup Welcome dialog box. In the Restore Wizard that opens, choose the device from which you want to restore, the backup job to use, and the specific files to be restored, as you can see in Figure 6-36. Select the folders and files as you did in the backup process. When you are done, click Next. Choose whether to restore to the original or to an alternate location; and if to an alternate, choose what that location is. Then click Next. After choosing how to replace existing files, you can click Start. You are finally asked to confirm that the media containing the backup is loaded. When you click OK, the restore will start. Again a Status dialog box is presented to tell you of the progress and elapsed time, and you are told when the operation is complete.

During the entire backup and restore process that was previously described, you did not have to use the Microsoft Backup window. At all times, you were in the Backup or Restore Wizard. If you want a more hands-on approach (to not use a wizard), simply click Close in the original Microsoft Backup Welcome dialog box. You are then presented with the Microsoft Backup window shown in Figure 6-37. If this is what you want to use in the future

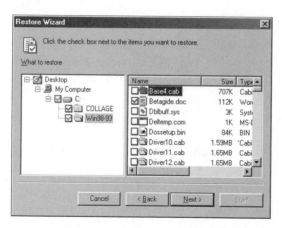

Figure 6-36. *Selecting files to restore.*

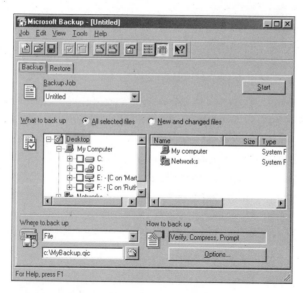

Figure 6-37. *Microsoft Backup window.*

in place of the wizards, you can turn them off by opening the Tools menu, selecting Preferences, and then unchecking Show Startup Dialog When Microsoft Backup Is Started.

Copying Disks

Copy Disk allows you to copy data from one floppy disk to another of the *same* type. For example, you can copy data from a 3.5-inch disk to another 3.5-inch disk, but you can't copy from a 3.5-inch disk to a 5.25-inch disk or vice versa. If you have two floppy drives of the same type, you can copy files directly between them. Otherwise, you will be prompted to remove the *source* disk and insert the *destination* disk in the same drive. Disk copying is activated by right-clicking any of your floppy disk drives in Windows Explorer or My Computer and choosing Copy Disk, or in My Computer by selecting the drive and choosing Copy Disk from the File menu. Using either method, the Copy Disk dialog box opens, as shown here.

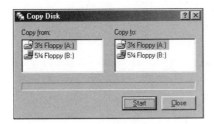

 ARNING   Any data on your destination disk will be deleted, regardless of the size of the file(s) being copied.

Select the source drive in the Copy From list box and the destination drive in the Copy To list box. Click Start to begin the process. When prompted, remove the source disk, and insert the destination disk. When complete, the process can be repeated for other disks you need to copy by clicking the Start button in the dialog box.

Windows 98 Printing

All Windows 98 printing functions are consolidated in the Printers folder, shown in Figure 7-1. Behind the Printers folder is a depth of printer functions. Central to this is a 32-bit print engine that provides the following:

■ Smooth background printing, which feeds the printer only what it requests

■ Improved printing performance, which returns to the application sooner

■ Support for over 800 printer models (versus 300 in Windows 3.x), including PostScript Level II printers

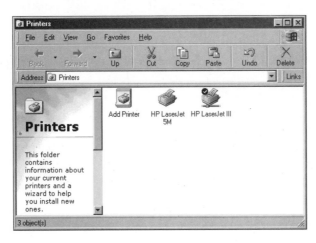

Figure 7-1.   *Printers folder.*

- Spooling for MS-DOS applications as well as for Windows applications

- Support for image color matching between your screen and your printer

- Deferred printing, which allows you to spool your printing while you are on the road and automatically print when you are connected to a printer

- Simplified printer installation and configuration through a single-user interface and full Plug and Play support

In summary, Windows 98 provides faster printing that is easier to use and truly operates in the background, allowing you to do meaningful work while your computer is printing. In this chapter, you'll learn about installing and configuring printers with Windows 98, as well as printing and managing your print queue.

What Is a Printer?

Asking "what is a printer?" may sound like a dumb question. On the surface, a printer is any device that converts digital information into a form that you can carry away with you and read. There are many forms of these electromechanical devices, including laser, ink-jet, and dot-matrix printers. To Windows 98, though, these devices are merely part of what it considers to be printers. A network address may be considered a printer, and usually a physical printer is on the other end. But, if you can "print" to a disk file, then that is considered a "printer"; and if you can "print" to a fax modem, then that also is considered a "printer." A physical printer, a network printer, a disk file, and a fax modem have three things in common: a name, a port address, and a driver program. A port address may be a hardware port address, like COM2 or LPT1, but it may also be a network path or a software port address, like FILE or FAX. A driver program is a piece of software that can take digital information and convert it in such a way that a device or another program can use it. This then makes for a broad definition of a printer. It also gives Windows 98 great flexibility in dealing with new devices and computing capabilities.

 IP   A printer is anything that has a name, has been assigned a port address, and has a driver program that can feed it information.

Installing Printers

All printer functions, including installing a new printer, begin by opening the Printers folder. You can do that in one of several ways. The easiest is to open the Start menu and select Settings | Printers. The other ways are to open My Computer, Windows Explorer, or Control Panel and click the Printers folder. In any case, the Printers folder will open and display the printers you have available as well as an icon for adding printers, as you saw in Figure 7-1.

By clicking the Add Printer icon, you start the Add Printer Wizard. This leads you through the process of installing the printer driver that is correct for your printer. Click Next to begin.

Your first decision is to determine how the printer you want to use is connected to your computer. You have two choices: Local Printer and Network Printer. A local printer has a cable that is directly connected to your computer. A network printer is connected to another computer or to just the network through its own adapter card, and you use it over the network. Determine which you want, click it, and click Next.

Local Printer Installation

If you are installing a local printer, you must next choose the manufacturer and model of your printer, as shown in Figure 7-2. First choose the manufacturer on the left and then the model on the right. If you have a recent driver disk from the manufacturer, you can use that by clicking Have Disk. After clicking Next, you are asked to identify the port you want to use with your printer, as you can see in Figure 7-3. LPT1, which is the standard parallel printer port, is the default selection.

If you choose a serial port (COM1 through COM4), you will want to configure the port by clicking the button of that name. A COMx Properties dialog box will open, similar to that shown in Figure 7-4. You may need to consult your printer manual to make the correct settings. If they are incorrect, your printer probably will not work correctly. If you are using a parallel port (LPT1 or LPT2), your configuration options are whether to spool your

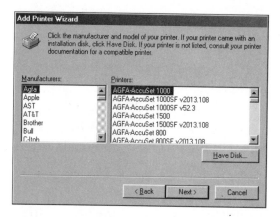

Figure 7-2.   *Choosing the printer manufacturer and model.*

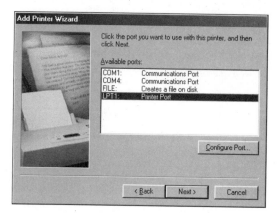

Figure 7-3.   *Choosing the printer port.*

MS-DOS print jobs and whether to check the port state before printing (the default is to do both). The other available ports do not have configurable settings. When you have chosen the port you want to use and made any necessary configuration settings, click Next.

The Add Printer Wizard then asks what name you would like to give this printer and if you would like to make it your default printer, as shown in Figure 7-5. The purpose of this is for you to give the printer a name that is meaningful to you. For example, you could name a printer "Third Floor LaserJet" or "Marketing's Printer," if those are descriptive names for you. If

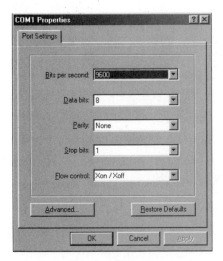

Figure 7-4. *Configuring a serial port.*

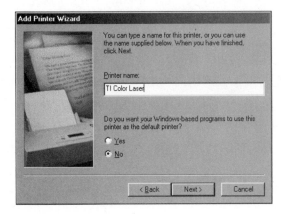

Figure 7-5. *Naming the printer.*

this printer is the primary printer that you use, then it should be your default. When you have named the printer and decided if it is your default, click Next.

 OTE   If the printer you are installing is Plug and Play compliant (there should be a sticker on it to that effect), then you will not be asked information about the printer port—Windows will have automatically gone out and gotten that information for itself.

The final Add Printer Wizard window asks if you want to print a test page to make sure the printer is working the way you set it up. This is a good idea unless you are sure of the printer setup. Many things can go wrong in connecting and setting up a printer. If you do try it and it doesn't work, see *Troubleshooting Printers* later in this chapter. After deciding on whether to test the printer, click Finish. You will see a message box that tells you the progress of installing the necessary printer drivers. If you don't see any messages to the contrary, when the Add Printer Wizard closes, the printer has been successfully installed.

Network Printer Installation

If you choose Network printer in the second Add Printer Wizard window, then your third window will look like that shown in Figure 7-6. Here you are asked to enter the network path to the printer you want to use. If you know the path, you can type it in; but in most circumstances, it is easier to click Browse. You'll be shown the computers in your workgroup. If you click the plus sign beside a computer, you'll see the shared printers on that computer, as you can see in Figure 7-7. Click the printer you want to use, and then click OK. When you return to the Add Printer Wizard, the path will be filled in for you. Decide if you want to print from MS-DOS programs on that printer, and then click Next.

As you saw with a local printer, you are next asked to enter a name for the printer and if you want to use it as your default. After doing that, click Next. Finally you are asked if you want to test the printer. When you click

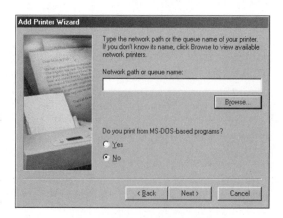

Figure 7-6. *Establishing the path to a network printer.*

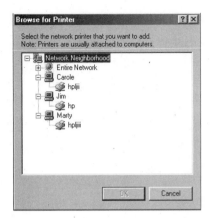

Figure 7-7. *Shared printers on your network.*

Finish, the appropriate printer-driver files will be copied to your computer, and the printer will become available for you to print on, just as if it were attached directly to your computer.

Configuring Printers

Once a printer is installed, you can change its configuration through the printer's Properties dialog box, a sample of which is shown in Figure 7-8. You can open your printer's Properties dialog box by right-clicking the printer in the Printers folder and choosing Properties. The Properties dialog box that opens for your printer may be different from the one shown in Figure 7-8, although many of the elements will be the same. In the next several sections, the HP LaserJet 5M Properties dialog box will be described. This should be instructive in making the settings for your printer. If your printer is Plug and Play compliant, much of the printer configuration will be done automatically for you.

General Tab

The General tab of the printer Properties dialog box shows you the printer's name at the top and allows you to enter a comment about the printer, identify a page to print between each print job, and print a test page. The printer's name is the one you gave it when you installed the printer. You can change this name in the Printers folder by editing the name as you would a file or folder name, or you can use the Rename option in the context menu opened by right-clicking the printer.

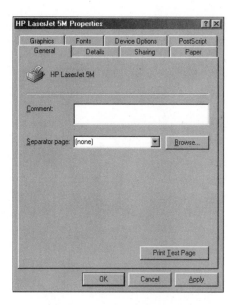

Figure 7-8. *Printer Properties dialog box.*

The Comment field is used to pass on any necessary information about the printer; for example, where the printer is physically located, what kind of paper or forms it has loaded, what the printer is to be used for, and the hours it will be turned on. The Comment field is transferred to all the users that install your printer on the network, although if you change the comments, they will not see the change unless they reinstall the printer.

 OTE Changes to a printer's Comment field are not seen by other users who have already installed the printer.

If you have multiple people using your printer or if you are printing multiple documents at the same time, then inserting a separator page between each document may help you separate the various users and documents. You have two built-in choices for a separator page in the drop-down list box: Full and Simple. The Simple option is just text that tells you the document name, the computer that printed it, and the date and time it was printed. The Full option adds the Windows 98 graphic at the top of the page and therefore takes longer to print. You can create your own separator page by using a draw program, such as CorelDRAW!, to create and then export a Windows metafile image (with the extension of .wmf). Then use the Browse button to locate this file, and identify it as the separator page you want to use. Only the computer that is directly connected to a printer may set up a separator page.

Details Tab

The Details tab shown in Figure 7-9 allows you to select the printer port and driver to use with a printer as well as define the ports and drivers that are available. The Details tab also allows you to set various port, spooling, and timing characteristics. The options available in this dialog box are grouped into printer ports, printer drivers, print spooling, and timeout settings.

Printer Ports

A printer port in Windows 98 can be a hardware port on your computer, either serial (COM1 through COM4) or parallel (LPT1 or LPT2); it can be a network path leading to a printer on another computer; or it can be a software port, like FAX for a fax modem or FILE for a disk file, which is not a

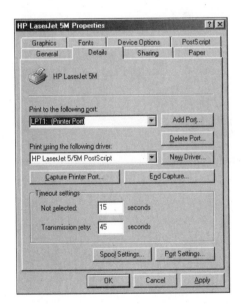

Figure 7-9.   *Printer Properties Details tab.*

printer at all. If you open the Print To The Following Port drop-down list box, you will see a list similar to this:

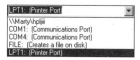

You can assign a printer to any one of these ports. If you don't find the port you want, you can add a port by clicking the Add Port button. The Add Port dialog box opens, as shown below. Here you can enter a network address, or, as you saw in *Network Printer Installation,* you can use the Browse button to locate it. Alternately, you can define a new local port, such as FILE or FAX. If you want to remove a port, you may do so by clicking Delete Port in the Details tab and selecting the port to remove.

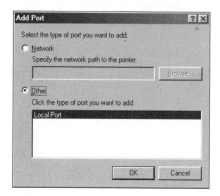

Besides entering the path to a network printer, you can define a local port address that you are not using, for example LPT3, to be a network printer address. This is similar to mapping a network disk drive to a drive letter on your local machine. For printers, though, it is called *capturing a printer port,* and the Capture Printer Port button in the Details tab opens the dialog box of the same name. Here you can choose a port from LPT1 through LPT9 and identify the network path to associate with that port, as you can see in the following illustration. If you want to continue to use this port address the next time you start Windows, then click Reconnect At Logon. If you want to disconnect the network path from the port address, click the End Capture button in the Details tab, and select the port to be released.

The Port Settings button in the Details tab (see Figure 7-9) opens the port-configuration dialog box that you saw above in *Local Printer Installation*. For a serial port, there are several significant settings, like baud rate and bit pattern. For a parallel port, you can determine if you want to spool MS-DOS printing. For other types of ports, it is not used.

Printer Drivers

Printer drivers are the programs that put the data in your computer in a form that can be printed and then control the printer while it is printing. Generally there is a printer driver for each type of printer. If you select New Driver in the Details tab, you will be told that a change to the printer driver will be saved and may change the Properties dialog box you are looking at. You are asked if you want to continue. If you answer Yes you want to continue, you will see the pair of list boxes for manufacturers and models that you saw in *Local Printer Installation* and in Figure 7-2. It is important that you use the correct driver for your printer.

Print Spooling

Print spooling quickly writes your output on disk and then allows you to go back to work while the actual printing takes place in the background. In early versions of Windows, this was a joke. Writing the output to disk took as long as printing, and you couldn't get anything done while the "background" printing took place. All you accomplished was to double your print time. In Windows 3.x, and especially Windows for Workgroups 3.11, print spooling became a real benefit. Windows 98 carries that several steps further. For non-PostScript printers, Windows 98 quickly writes the printer output on disk as *enhanced metafiles* (EMF). This is faster than the raw printer data written by Windows 3.x and allows a quicker return to your application. The background printing makes full use of the 32-bit multithreaded architecture of Windows 98 to provide smooth printing while you are working in the foreground. The net result is, if you haven't used print spooling before, you'll want to do so in Windows 98.

Print spooling is controlled in the Spool Settings dialog box, shown in Figure 7-10 and opened with the button of that name in the Details tab. Your first choice in this dialog box is whether to spool print jobs or print directly. If you spool printing, you can choose to start printing after the first or after the last page has been spooled to disk. If you start after the last page, you will get back to your application quicker, but the overall printing will take longer. Another option in this dialog box is whether to use the EMF format for spooling or to spool raw printer data. The EMF format is faster, but if you are having trouble printing, try switching to raw printer data. Since PostScript is already a printer definition language, it uses only the RAW format. Finally, with newer printers and computers, you can enable or disable a bidirectional printer port, which allows your computer to interrogate your printer and have your printer respond with information needed by the computer.

Timeout Settings

The Timeout settings in the lower half of the Details tab determine how long the computer should wait before reporting that a printer is not ready. The first of these, Not Selected, is the number of seconds to wait for a printer to be online. The second, Transmission Retry, is the number of seconds to wait for a printer to be ready. Normally whether a printer is online is up to you: have you plugged it in, turned it on, and placed it online?

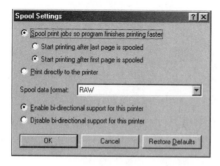

Figure 7-10.　　*Spool Settings dialog box.*

You therefore want the timeout on this to be short so the computer will tell you sooner that you need to go turn on the printer. On Transmission Retry, you are waiting for the printer to digest the last data you sent it. You therefore want Transmission Retry to be longer. If you are having problems with big print jobs being cut off, you need to make this time even longer (say 60 to 100 seconds).

Sharing Tab

The Sharing tab of the printer Properties dialog box, which is shown in Figure 7-11, allows you to determine if you want to share your printer with others on your network. If you do, you can enter a name, a comment, and a password for the shared printer. Only if you share your printer can others use it, and the name you give it will be the name they see. You cannot share a printer without giving it a name. The comment is displayed in the list of printers seen by all on the network. You might enter the physical location of the printer in the Comment field. The password starts out to be null, the absence of any password, so if you do not enter one, a password will not be used for that printer.

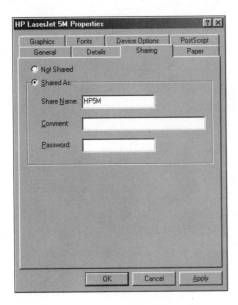

Figure 7-11.   *Printer Properties dialog box, Sharing tab.*

Paper Tab

The Paper tab, which you see in Figure 7-12, allows you to set several printer defaults that can be overridden by settings the end user may make. This is particularly important if a printer is dedicated to a certain form, for example, envelopes. Otherwise you probably will want to leave this set to the printer's defaults, and let the end user set these items. You can restore the defaults by clicking that button at the bottom of the tab.

The Paper Size list box shows the sizes your printer can handle. If your printer supports a custom size, you'll have a Custom icon you can select, along with a Custom button where you can specify the size. If you select a particular form, especially envelopes, you can see the size at the top of the list box.

Depending on your printer, you may be able to select Layout, Orientation, Paper Source, and Media Choice. If you have a media choice of Transparency, select it only when printing transparencies, or you may cause smearing and waste ink.

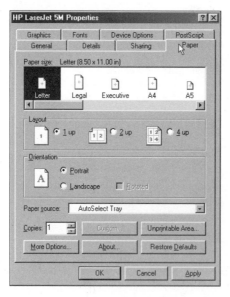

Figure 7-12.   *Printer Properties dialog box, Paper tab.*

Most laser printers can't print to the edge of the largest paper size they can handle. If you have a laser printer, you'll see an Unprintable Area button, which opens a dialog box that allows you to set the margins that can't be printed upon. It is unusual to change the defaults for this, which are set by the manufacturer.

Some printers will have a More Options button, which provides additional printer-specific settings you can change.

Device Options Tab

The Device Options tab allows you to make several settings that are directly related to your particular printer. The settings for an HP LaserJet 5M are shown in Figure 7-13. If you have a Plug and Play compliant printer and a bidirectional port, settings like printer memory will be set for you. If you have an older printer without Plug and Play, you should check such settings; otherwise you may not utilize the full capability of your printer.

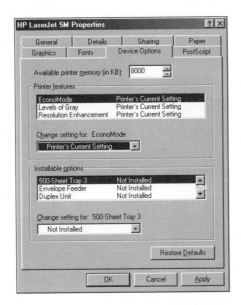

Figure 7-13. *Printer Properties dialog box, Device Options tab.*

Fonts Tab

The Fonts tab, which varies depending on the printer you use, is shown for an HP LaserJet 5M in Figure 7-14. This tab allows you to change the hardware-related font characteristics of your printer. These may, depending on your printer, include identifying any font cartridges you have installed and how you want to download TrueType fonts. Simply click the cartridges you have. If your printer can handle two cartridges, you will be allowed to select two. For TrueType fonts, if your printer can handle outlines, you'll want to download outline fonts; you'll find it faster. Bitmaps are next fastest, and graphics least fast.

Graphics Tab

The Graphics tab, which you see in Figure 7-15, allows you to determine how graphics are sent to your printer. Unless speed is more important than quality, you normally will want to print at the highest resolution you can, although settings on this tab affect only graphics.

 OTE   Text is always printed at the printer's highest resolution.

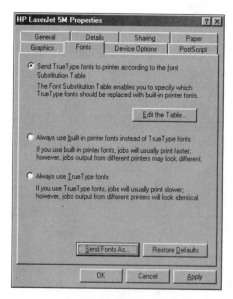

Figure 7-14.   *Printer Properties dialog box, Fonts tab.*

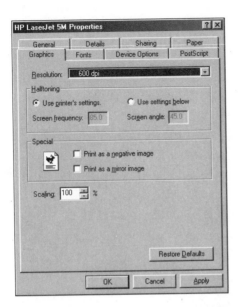

Figure 7-15. *Printer Properties dialog box, Graphics tab.*

Depending on your printer, you may have a Halftoning control, which allows you to print graphics as a series of dots with a certain screen frequency and angle. Unless you are working in a professional publishing situation where certain screen frequencies and angles are required, it is recommended that the default settings be maintained. It is possible to make a graphic look horrible with the wrong settings.

If you have a Dithering control (not shown in Figure 7-15), it is a way to give the appearance of more colors or more shades of gray than you can otherwise produce. Use the following settings under the conditions given:

- **None** if you are satisfied with your existing colors or gray scale

- **Coarse** if you are printing at a resolution of 300 dots per inch (dpi) or higher

- **Fine** if you are printing at a resolution of less than 300 dpi

- **Line Art** if you are printing drawings with well-defined borders between black and white

- **Error Diffusion** if you are printing pictures that don't have sharp, well-defined edges

TIP Do not base your Dithering setting on the example in the dialog box. Your printed result could look much different.

Again depending on your printer, you may have a number of other controls. Among these are:

- **Special,** which allows you to turn on or off special features of your printer. For example, in the HP LaserJet5M you can turn on or off printing negative (where white is black) and mirror (flipped left to right) images.

- **Intensity,** which is simply how dark or light you wish to print graphics.

- **Graphics Mode,** which determines how your printer creates a graphic. Vector graphics describe an image in terms of the position, length, width, and direction of the lines that make up the image. Raster graphics describe an image in terms of the position, size, and pattern of dots that make up the image. Vector graphics are faster and, for certain images like line art, can produce a more pleasing result. Raster graphics are simpler for the printer to produce and, for photographic-like images, can be more pleasing.

 NOTE If your image is not being printed correctly (for example, two objects are printed on top of one another when they are not supposed to be, or if you exceed your printer's memory capability, printing only a partial graphic), switch to raster graphics.

- **Scaling,** which allows you to change the size of the entire image by a set percentage.

You may have other tabs in your printer's Properties dialog box, such as the PostScript tab shown in Figure 7-16, that allow you to make settings specifically for that function or property.

Using Printers

One normally thinks of using printers from within a program—loading or creating a document and then selecting the print command. For example, in Microsoft Word 97 with a document open, you open the File menu and

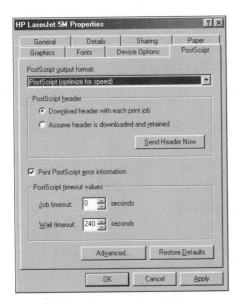

Figure 7-16. *Special PostScript printer properties tab.*

select Print, and the Print dialog box opens, as shown in Figure 7-17. Here you can select what to print within the current document, the number of copies, and so forth. Most Windows programs that produce a document have a similar function and dialog box. The settings in such a dialog box will override the settings in the printer's Properties dialog box.

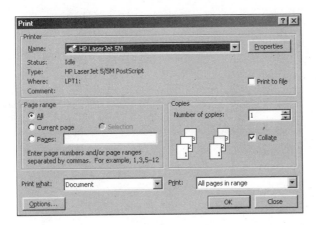

Figure 7-17. *Microsoft Word's Print dialog box.*

Drag-and-Drop Printing

Windows 98 provides another, simpler way to print. You can drag a document file to a printer icon, and the document will be printed. In some cases, the document will print directly. In other cases, the program that is associated with the document (and probably created it) will be loaded, the document printed, and then the program closed. In the process, you may or may not see a Print dialog box. As you saw in Chapter 4, you can drag a printer shortcut to the desktop and leave it there. Then from either My Computer or Windows Explorer, you can drag a document to the printer's shortcut icon and have the document printed. Of course, the document must be associated with a program, normally the one that created it, that is registered with Windows 98 to provide drag-and-drop printing. Many Windows programs are registered that way.

 OTE   In My Computer or Windows Explorer, you can also print by right-clicking a document file and choosing Print.

Managing Print Spooling

As you read earlier, if you accept the default, Windows 98 spools your print data onto your disk and then feeds the data to your printer in the background while you are doing other things. If you or others on your network are sending enough work to your printer, you will build up a print queue of jobs waiting to be printed. Windows 98 has provided a way for you to manage the print queue with the print-spooler window, similar to that shown in Figure 7-18. You open this window by clicking the printer icon, which can be a shortcut.

Document Name	Status	Owner	Progress	Started At
Untitled	Printing	GEORGE	0 bytes of 7....	1:43:22 PM 10/7/97
Untitled		GEORGE	2.33KB	1:43:30 PM 10/7/97
Untitled		GEORGE	4.75KB	1:43:32 PM 10/7/97
Untitled		GEORGE	23.8KB	1:43:36 PM 10/7/97
Untitled		GEORGE	23.7KB	1:43:40 PM 10/7/97

HP LaserJet III — Printer Document View Help — 5 jobs in queue

Figure 7-18.   *Print-spooler window.*

The body of the print-spooler window lists the print jobs in the queue with the document name, status, the name of the computer that sent the job to the printer, the job size and completion progress, and the time it arrived in the queue. You can rearrange the order in which the jobs are printed by dragging the jobs up or down in the print queue. The print-spooler window also gives you the ability to pause and restart either the printer or just one job, and to cancel a job or purge all jobs from the printer. Here's how:

■ **Pause a job** by selecting the job and choosing Pause Printing in the Document menu.

■ **Pause a printer** by choosing Pause Printing in the Printer menu.

■ **Cancel a job** by selecting the job and pressing **DELETE** or choosing Cancel Printing from the Document menu.

■ **Purge all jobs** in the queue by choosing Purge Print Documents from the Printer menu.

 IP   Drag a job to another location in the print queue to rearrange the order in which the jobs will be printed or right-click the job and you can choose Pause or Cancel.

The Printer menu also allows you to open the printer Properties dialog box, to set the printer as the default, and to close the window. If the printer is a network printer, you will also have the option to work offline. This way, if you are not currently connected to the network (for example, if you are out of the office), you can store your printing on disk and defer it until you are next connected to the network. Most of the options on the Printer menu can also be found on the context menu that opens when you right-click in the print-spooler window, as you can see here:

IP If you are using a laptop or notebook computer away from the office, you can still print by setting the printer to Use Printer Offline. This way the printing is spooled to disk and deferred until you are next connected to a printer.

Printer Context Menu

The context menu that opens when you right-click a printer has many of the same options as the Printer menu in the print-spooler window, as shown below. In addition, you can open the print-spooler window, display the Sharing tab of the Properties dialog box, create a shortcut for the printer, and delete or rename the printer.

Troubleshooting Printers

If your printer is not printing or not printing correctly when you send it information to be printed, there are three broad steps you can take to solve the problem:

- Look at the physical attributes of the printer.
- Look at the online messages you are getting.
- Look at the Printer Troubleshooter in Windows 98 Help.

Physical Attributes

The physical attributes to consider are those things that are often assumed to be OK but sometimes are not. Here is a check list for you to use:

- Is your printer plugged into a working electrical outlet?
- Is your printer connected to your computer? Is a cable securely fastened both to your printer and to your computer?

- Is your printer turned on? Is the power light lit or is there some other indication of power being on?

- Is your printer online? Does the online or Ready light show that it is enabled?

- Is your printer properly supplied with paper and ink or toner or a ribbon?

There is one other physical attribute that is important but not always easy to check: the port on your computer to which your printer is connected. First determine if the printer is connected to a parallel or serial port and then to which one. A parallel port will have a 25-pin female connector on the computer. A serial port will have either a 9-pin male connector or a 25-pin male connector on the computer. Most printers use a parallel port, and most computers have only one parallel port: LPT1. If you think your printer is using a serial port, determine what else is using a serial port. Two good candidates are your mouse and a modem. If you have a serial mouse, it is often using the 9-pin connector and is COM1. If your printer is then using the 25-pin male connector, it is probably COM2. Your mouse could be a bus mouse with a circular DIN connector and not use a serial port, and therefore your printer would be using COM1.

If you have a modem, it could be connected to any serial port. If it is working, it is easiest to open Control Panel, click the Modems icon, and click Properties. The General tab should show you the port to which the modem is connected. Unfortunately, there is no such handy place to find the port to which your mouse is connected.

Once you have a pretty good idea of the port your printer is using, then review the port assignment you made during installation, as described earlier under *Local Printer Installation*.

Online Messages

One way to find a problem is to look at the messages that you get when you try to print. Some messages are more helpful than others. Three of several possible messages you can get are shown in the following illustrations. The first is not specific and could be caused by a number of problems. Among these possible problems are:

- The printer being not physically connected to the computer

- The printer being turned off

- The printer being offline

The second message is specific about being out of paper. The third message was caused by a network problem, as it implies.

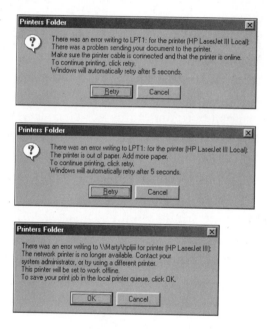

Messages give you surface facts that start you looking for the problem, and they may or may not be helpful about where specifically to look. Sometimes all you need to know is that there is a problem. For example, the first of the three messages just shown resulted because I had my printer connected to another computer; and when I saw the message, I instantly knew that I had forgotten to switch the cable. The message didn't need to specifically tell me what the problem was.

With the newer printers and bidirectional printer ports, much more information is passed to the computer and therefore displayed in messages.

Print Troubleshooter

Windows 98 has an excellent Print Troubleshooter in its Help system. To use it, click Help on the Start menu. When the Windows Help window opens, select the Contents tab, and click Troubleshooting | Windows 98 Troubleshooters | Print. This opens the Windows 98 Print Troubleshooter, as shown in Figure 7-19.

By following the instructions and answering the questions in the Print Troubleshooter, you will be able to learn a lot about what is causing your printing problem and how to fix it. There is, of course, no guarantee that you will be able to solve all possible printing problems. With the combination of looking at the physical attributes, considering the online messages, and studying the Print Troubleshooter, you have a number of tools to solve your problems.

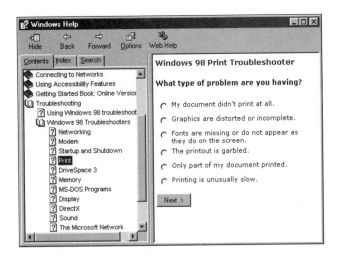

Figure 7-19.   *Opening the Print Troubleshooter.*

Handling and Using Fonts

By Dan Logan

Windows 98 comes with a variety of fonts that you can use. Well-chosen fonts enhance a reader's responses to the content you create, making your communication that much more effective. To quote *Computer Shopper* magazine, "Fonts are part of the message." This is true for both printed output and electronic displays; in fact, the Internet and the World Wide Web are placing new demands that are speeding up the development of typeface technology.

A *font* is a collection of characters with a common design. A font's appearance is characterized by its size, style, weight, width, spacing, and other features. Type families, or *typefaces,* are collections of fonts that share the same basic appearance but vary in size or some other characteristic. Windows 98 includes such typefaces as Arial, Garamond, and Times New Roman. Figure 8-1 shows the Verdana TrueType font, and Figure 8-2 shows the Wingdings font, which has a collection of characters you can use to enhance your documents.

Literally thousands of fonts are available with Windows 98. Adding and removing Microsoft TrueType fonts, which are described further in the next section, is easy in Windows 98, although managing a large variety of fonts from different vendors can be cumbersome. This chapter looks at ways to maximize the number of fonts you can use quickly and effectively.

Figure 8-1. *The Windows 98 font viewer, showing the Verdana font.*

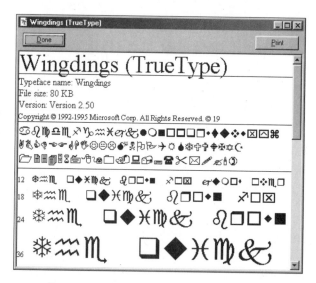

Figure 8-2. *The Wingdings font includes a variety of characters for spiffing up a document.*

 OTE Keeping lots of unused fonts on your system wastes time (because you have to work through them to find the fonts you *do* use) and takes up disk space.

Font Basics

Fonts can be categorized in many different ways, but the most basic difference between fonts is whether they're scalable or bitmapped. Windows 98 comes with both bitmapped and scalable fonts. The scalable Microsoft TrueType fonts are the most useful because scalable fonts offer more flexibility than bitmapped ones. With scalable fonts, you can change the size of the font without changing the proportions of the characters. Characters in TrueType fonts are stored as outlines, which are mathematical descriptions of the characters' curves, and a single TrueType-font file (one with a .ttf extension) has all the information the computer needs to generate the characters in a wide variety of sizes. After sizing a character, Windows runs the image through a rasterization process, which converts it to a bitmapped image intended for the particular monitor or printer you use.

Another process, called *hinting,* is also employed to minimize the jagged edges on characters when they're resized. However, you may still see jagged edges if you're using a low-resolution monitor or printer. In fact, hinting used on a low-resolution monitor or printer sometimes makes a character look worse, rather than better.

Bitmapped fonts, also called raster fonts, are a fixed size. They are designed to match the display or printer output of the devices on your system, and they produce high-quality output when used for their intended purpose. Changing the size of a bitmapped font can distort its proportions and change its look, although working in even multiples of the original size often produces an accurate image.

Windows 98 Font Installation

When you install Windows 98 for the first time, it installs several TrueType and bitmapped fonts in the Fonts folder (\Windows\Fonts), shown in Figure 8-3. Later, you can add or remove fonts, although certain fonts used to display the Windows 98 screens must remain on the system.

Windows 98 can handle about 1000 TrueType fonts, the exact number being governed by the limitations Microsoft places on the Registry key and by the file sizes of the graphics device interface.

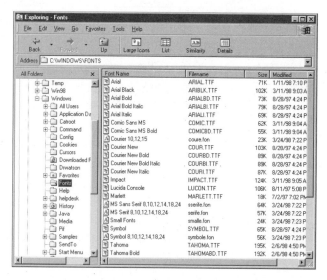

Figure 8-3.   *The Fonts folder, shown in Windows Explorer Details view.*

The Fonts That Come with Windows 98

Windows 98 typical configuration comes with 32 fonts in 16 typefaces, which it installs during setup (see Table 8-1). Five styles of the Arial typeface and several styles of most other typefaces (a font is one style of one typeface) are available. Five of the fonts (those with .fon extensions) are intended for the monitor's display, although the Modern.fon typeface is a vector font for use with such output devices as plotters.

Font Style	Font File Name	Type Sample
Arial	Arial.ttf	abcklmtwABCKLMTW12
Arial Black	Ariblk.ttf	**abcklmtwABCKLMTW12**
Arial Bold	Arialbd.ttf	**abcklmtwABCKLMTW12**
Arial Bold Italic	Arialbi.ttf	***abcklmtwABCKLMTW12***
Arial Italic	Ariali.ttf	*abcklmtwABCKLMTW12*
Comic Sans MS	comic.ttf	abcklmtwABCKLMTW12
Comic Sans MS Bold	comicbd.ttf	**abcklmtwABCKLMTW12**
Courier 10,12,15	coure.fon	abcklmtwABCKLMTW12

Table 8-1.   *Default font files installed by Windows 98 during setup.* (continued)

Table 8-1. *(continued)*

Font Style	Font File Name	Type Sample
Courier New	cour.ttf	abcklmtwABCKLMTW12
Courier New Bold	courbd.ttf	**abcklmtwABCKLMTW12**
Courier New Bold Italic	courbi.ttf	***abcklmtwABCKLMTW12***
Courier New Italic	couri.ttf	*abcklmtwABCKLMTW12*
Impact	impact.ttf	**abcklmtwABCKLMTW12**
Lucida Console	lucon.ttf	abcklmtwABCKLMTW12
Marlett	marlett.ttf	✔ ✔ ⌐ ◡⌒ ◡ ▲ ◂ □□□□□□□□□□□ □ ⊟
MS Sans Serif 8,10,12,14,18,24	sserife.fon	(system only)
MS Serif 8,10,12,14,18,24	serife.fon	(system only)
Small Fonts	smalle.fon	(system only)
Symbol	symbol.ttf	αβχκλμτωΑΒΧΚΛΜΤΩ12
Symbol 8,10,12,14,18,24	symbole.fon	αβχκλμτωΑΒΧΚΛΜΤΩ12
Tahoma	tahoma.ttf	abcklmtwABCKLMTW12
Tahoma Bold	tahomabd.ttf	**abcklmtwABCKLMTW12**
Times New Roman	times.ttf	abcklmtwABCKLMTW12
Times New Roman Bold	timesbd.ttf	**abcklmtwABCKLMTW12**
Times New Roman Bold Italic	timesbi.ttf	***abcklmtwABCKLMTW12***
Times New Roman Italic	timesi.ttf	*abcklmtwABCKLMTW12*
Verdana	verdana.ttf	abcklmtwABCKLMTW12
Verdana Bold	verdanab.ttf	**abcklmtwABCKLMTW12**
Verdana Bold Italic	verdanaz.ttf	***abcklmtwABCKLMTW12***
Verdana Italic	verdani.ttf	*abcklmtwABCKLMTW12*
Webdings	webdings.ttf	(symbol sample)
Wingdings	wingding.ttf	(symbol sample)

Windows 98 installs and uses other fonts for text on its system screens (see Table 8-2).

 OTE Several fonts have their hidden file attribute selected, such as the system screen fonts (.fon) and Marlett.

Font Description	File Name
VGA (640x480) resolution system font	Vgasys.fon
VGA (640x480) resolution terminal font	Vgaoem.fon
VGA (640x480) resolution monospaced system font	Vgafix.fon
VGA (640x480) resolution terminal font (International)	Vga850.fon
8514/a (1024x768) resolution system font	8514sys.fon
8514/a (1024x768) resolution terminal font	8514oem.fon
8514/a (1024x768) resolution monospaced system font	8514fix.fon

Table 8-2. *Fonts used for text on Windows 98 screens.*

Viewing the Available Fonts

It's easy to look at a font on your system. To view a font, open the Start menu, choose Settings | Control Panel, and click Fonts. This opens the \Windows \Fonts folder, which lists the fonts installed, as you can see in Figure 8-4. Click a font to open the dialog boxes in Figures 8-1 and 8-2, where you can see samples of the font. You can do this not only in the \Windows\Fonts folder but in any folder or disk that contains a font file. Font files are often included with such applications as Microsoft Word or WordPerfect, and you can download or buy fonts and install them in a folder of your choice.

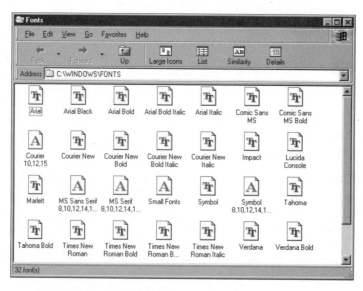

Figure 8-4. *Fonts folder, or "font manager."*

In the \Windows\Fonts folder, or "font manager," you can sort fonts according to their similarity to a font you specify, as shown in Figure 8-5. To do that, follow these steps:

1. Open the Start menu, choose Settings | Control Panel, and click Fonts.

2. Click the Similarity button or open the View menu, and click List Fonts By Similarity.

3. In the List Fonts By Similarity To drop-down list box, choose the font to which you want to compare the other fonts.

The font manager sorts and lists the fonts according to their similarity to the specified font. It categorizes the fonts as very similar, fairly similar, or not similar to the specified font.

Font-File Properties

To look at the properties of a font file, open the Fonts folder (as you did earlier), right-click a font, and click Properties. In the General tab (shown in Figure 8-6), you see the font filename, the type of file, its location, size,

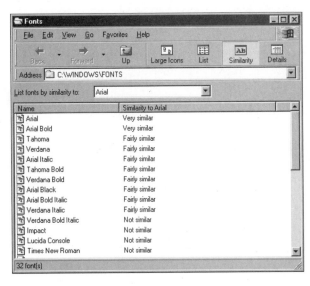

Figure 8-5.   *Fonts sorted according to their similarity to other fonts.*

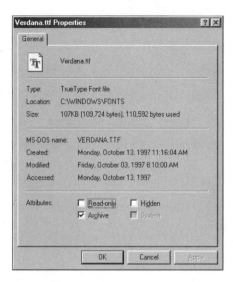

Figure 8-6.   *TrueType font Properties dialog box.*

attributes, and other information about the file. If the filename has an extension other than .ttf, you also see a Version tab with more information.

Although the font's Properties dialog box may give you all the information you need, Microsoft offers a useful, free software applet called the TrueType Font Properties Shell Extension, which gives even more information. To download this applet, open Internet Explorer, go to http://www.microsoft.com/typography/property/property.htm, and download the self-extracting file Ttftext.exe. As shown in Figure 8-7, the TrueType Font Properties Shell Extension provides tabs about embedding, hinting/font smoothing, statistics, links to Web sites concerning the font, and more.

Printing Samples of Fonts

Users of large numbers of fonts often print samples of the fonts so they can see at a glance what the font looks like. Although you may not need a binder full of printouts, occasionally you may want to print a sample of a font. To do that from the \Windows\Fonts folder, right-click the font you want to print, and choose Print on the context menu.

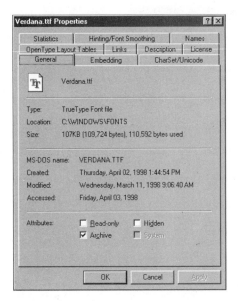

Figure 8-7.   *Microsoft's TrueType Font Properties Shell Extension supplies added details on fonts.*

Adding to Your Font Collection

If Windows 98's basic collection of fonts doesn't meet your needs, you can add fonts to your collection. Microsoft occasionally offers new TrueType fonts at the Microsoft Typography Web site at http://www.microsoft.com/ typography/free.htm (see Figure 8-8). You can download these at no charge. You can also find other free fonts on the Web, at such sites as Font You, Please Come Again; the Chankstore Freefont Archive (Crankfonts); or the Font Fairy. (You can find links to all three of these sites at The Mining Company's Desktop Publishing page, http://desktoppub.miningco.com/ msub55.htm.) You can also buy fonts either on the Web (the Desktop Publishing page just mentioned has links to a number of sites that sell fonts) or from retail outlets.

For Windows applications to recognize a new font, you can't simply copy the font file to the Fonts folder. You must install the file in the Fonts folder. For example, to install additional fonts from the Office 97 CD, follow these steps:

1. Open the \Windows\Fonts folder, open the File menu, and then click Install New Font. The Add Fonts dialog box opens.

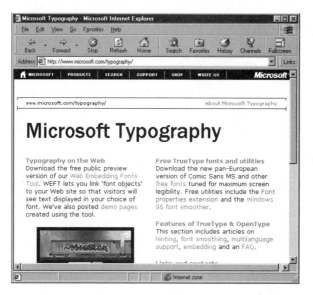

Figure 8-8.   *The Microsoft Typography Web site has lots of information about fonts.*

2. Open the Drives drop-down list box, and select your CD-ROM drive.

3. In the Folders list, select the folder containing the font you want to install. For the Office 97 CD, you want \Valupack\Msfonts. When you select a folder containing fonts, you get a message above the Drives drop-down list box that says "Retrieving Font Names." The message also shows a percentage complete. The List Of Fonts list box then displays the fonts that you can install, as you can see in Figure 8-9.

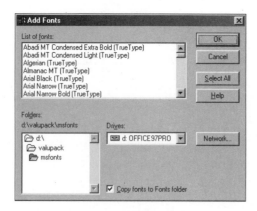

Figure 8-9.   *Add Fonts dialog box, showing the fonts on the Office 97 CD.*

4. Select the font or fonts you want to install. To select one font, double-click it. To select several contiguous fonts, click the first one, **SHIFT**-click the last font, and then click OK. To select several noncontiguous fonts, **CTRL**-click the fonts, and then click OK.

If you want to use fonts residing on a network drive (not keeping them on your hard disk), use the same steps as above, but, in the Add Fonts dialog box, clear the Copy Fonts To Fonts Folder check box. Then, when you actually go to use the fonts, they are listed in your list of fonts, but they are downloaded to the printer from the network drive.

 OTE While keeping fonts on a network drive saves disk space, it also increases the time it takes to download the fonts, so you need to choose which is more important, disk space or time. It may be worthwhile to keep seldom-used fonts on a network drive.

Accessing Fonts in Your Applications

Once you install a font, it is displayed in the Font dialog box in most Windows applications, giving you easy access to it. To access the Font dialog box from within Microsoft Word, for example, open the Format menu, and click Font. Alternately, you can open the Font drop-down list box on the Formatting toolbar, and click the font you want to use, as shown in Figure 8-10.

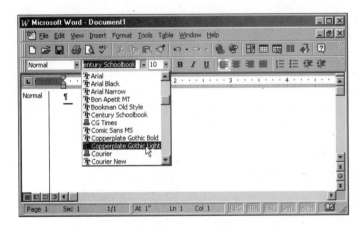

Figure 8-10. *Fonts are easily accessible in Windows applications.*

Removing Fonts

You can easily delete fonts you don't want on your system. To uninstall a font and send it to the Recycle Bin, open the \Windows\Fonts folder, right-click the font you want to delete, and then click Delete. You get a message asking if you are sure you want to delete the font(s) you have selected.

If you want to reduce the fonts shown in an application's list of fonts, but keep them on your hard disk for future use, you can do so by uninstalling a TrueType font. Open Windows Explorer, and create a backup folder, where you can store copies of the TrueType-font files you're removing from the \Windows\Fonts folder. Copy the files to the new folder; then delete the original font files, as described earlier. You can reinstall these fonts by following the steps under *Adding New Fonts* except that you need to open the backup folder you created. You can choose it in the Add Fonts dialog box, where you also want to make sure that the Copy Fonts To Fonts Folder option is checked. If you do this, you'll have two copies of the font files on your hard disk.

Managing Your Font Collection

Microsoft provides adequate font-management capability in the Windows 98 font manager, but some third-party font managers offer more power to users who spend lots of time working with different fonts. Adobe Type Manager (ATM) Deluxe version 4 from Adobe Systems is the best-known third-party font manager. In the 1980s, Adobe dominated the PC market with its PostScript technology, and, even with the spread of the TrueType technology used by Microsoft and Apple, PostScript continues to dominate the market for high-end printed output. However, when Adobe realized that its products would need to coexist with TrueType, it developed ATM.

With ATM Deluxe 4, you can manage Windows' TrueType fonts and Adobe's PostScript Type 1 scalable fonts. (Adobe has developed more than 2000 Type 1 typefaces.) ATM groups fonts in sets, and it can activate and deactivate groups of fonts on the fly. When ATM Deluxe 4 is loaded, it searches all hard disks, and even a network, to find fonts. Figure 8-11 shows some of the font management options ATM offers.

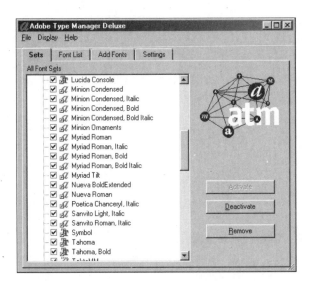

Figure 8-11.   *The Adobe Type Manager Deluxe 4 control panel.*

With ATM, Adobe supplies the Type On Call CD-ROM; you can purchase Adobe fonts on the Internet and download them from the disc with the access code you're given. If you'd like to know more, you can find information about Adobe Type Manager Deluxe 4 at http://www.adobe.com/ prodindex/atm/overview.html.

Besides Adobe Type Manager, other font managers, such as Bitstream Font Navigator (http://www.bitstream.com:80/), Agfa Font Manager (http:// www.agfahome.com/agfatype/products/afm.html), and QualiType Font Handler and Font Sentry (http://www.qualitype.com/), are available. If you're looking for more fonts, in addition to Microsoft TrueType and Adobe Type 1, you can use other font technologies, such as Bitstream TrueDoc and Adobe Type 3 fonts.

Improving the Look of Fonts on the Monitor

You can take some actions to make onscreen fonts look better. How a font displays depends on the resolution of your monitor and graphics adapter. You might see jagged edges on the characters on the monitor if the monitor doesn't have the resolution to display smooth curves.

Windows 98 has font-smoothing capability. Use the following steps to turn on font smoothing:

1. Open the Fonts control panel, click View, and then click Folder Options.

2. Choose the View tab, and select the Smooth Edges Of Screen Fonts check box, as shown in Figure 8-12.

3. Click Apply, and choose OK.

If the text still doesn't appear smooth enough for your purposes, you may need to buy a monitor and a graphics adapter that work at higher resolutions.

Display and Printer Fonts

If your printer can't print the same font shown on the monitor, it substitutes a font. However, tiny differences between fonts can be enough to alter the lines and pages of text—with disastrous results if you expect the printed output to be exactly what you see on the screen.

Windows applications using TrueType fonts don't have the problem of different screen and printer fonts. Because the PC downloads the fonts to the printer, it uses the same fonts you see on the monitor. However, depending

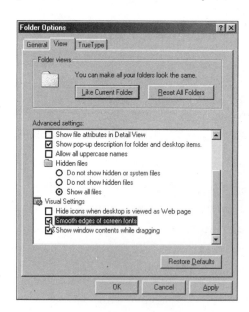

Figure 8-12.   *The Windows 98 font-smoothing option.*

on the nature of the work you're doing, you may or may not care if screen and printer fonts match. You may be sending the document to a service bureau that uses an imagesetter or printer you don't have. (However, you can install that printer's drivers on your computer to see how the document will look when printed.)

Information about your printer and how it relates to fonts is available in the printer Properties dialog box. To see this, open the Start menu, choose Settings | Printers, right-click the appropriate printer, click Properties, and finally click the Fonts tab, shown in Figure 8-13.

The content of the Fonts tab differs, depending on the printer. Many printers come with resident fonts, which are fonts stored in the printer's read-only memory. You can add more fonts by downloading soft (downloadable) fonts from the computer or by using font cartridges designed for the printer. Some printers have their own hard disks with fonts. The Fonts tab gives you options to force your system to use resident printer fonts or to always use the downloadable fonts on your computer. If you have a PostScript printer, the Fonts tab gives you the option of telling the printer to always use TrueType fonts.

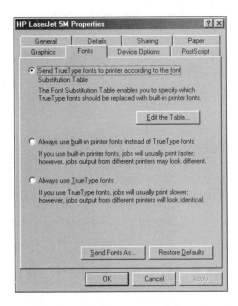

Figure 8-13.   *Printer properties Fonts tab has font information about your printer.*

Character Map

Depending on the font, more characters are available to you than appear on the keyboard. Windows 98 displays the additional characters in Character Map, which can be viewed by opening the Start menu, choosing Programs I Accessories I System Tools, and clicking Character Map.

 OTE Character Map is not installed with the Typical setup, so you may need to add it with the Add/Remove Programs control panel, Windows Setup tab.

To insert in a document a character that does not appear on the keyboard, open Character Map, double-click the character you want, then click Copy. The character is displayed in the Characters To Copy box, which shows you the characters on the Clipboard, the characters ready to be inserted. Return to your application, place the insertion point where you want to insert the character, and paste it into the document. If you cannot clearly see a particular character in Character Map, hold the mouse button down while pointing at a character; you see an enlarged view of it, as shown in Figure 8-14.

If you don't want to go repeatedly to Character Map, you can use keyboard shortcuts to insert characters into your document. First, look again at Character Map, click a character, and note the keystroke shortcut in the lower-right corner of the window, as you see in Figure 8-14. The shortcut is in the form **ALT+** a four-digit number. To use keyboard shortcuts, place the cursor where you want to insert the character, and turn on **NUM LOCK.**

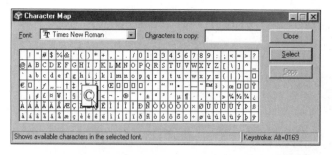

Figure 8-14. *Character Map with enlarged character and its keystroke shortcut, in the lower right.*

Then, press and hold the **ALT** key while using the numeric keypad to enter the four digits for the character you want to insert. Finally, release the **ALT** key to insert the character.

It can be difficult to recall the keyboard shortcuts for characters you use only occasionally. One solution to this is to create a "cheat sheet" file of shortcuts. For those you use most frequently, you can build macros in the application where they are used that are easier to remember.

Fonts and the World Wide Web

Font technology has been developing for hundreds of years, and text on paper can be rendered in extreme detail. The same can't be said about displaying fonts on a monitor, where it can be difficult to see screen characters composed of fine strokes. Having had less than 20 years to develop, displaying fonts on a PC is not a mature technology. Fine detail is not one of a computer monitor's strengths, and the print capabilities of service bureaus far exceed what you can display on a PC monitor.

The Internet has made the limitations of font-display technology more apparent. HyperText Markup Language (HTML) accurately shows only a limited number of fonts, but, with the rapid growth of commercial interest in the Internet, designers are chafing for an expanded collection of typefaces. Such organizations as the World Wide Web Consortium (http://www.w3.org/fonts/) are working to expand typeface options. Furthermore, the OpenType technology from Microsoft and Adobe and the TrueDoc technology from Bitstream allow Web designers to use any typeface in an electronic document, and the typeface is faithfully reproduced.

Microsoft is developing fonts that display well on the Web. Such fonts as Comic Sans, Georgia, Trebuchet, Verdana, and Webdings were designed for Web use, and they're available at no charge on the Microsoft Typography Web site at http://www.microsoft.com/typography/fontpack/default.htm.

Embedding Fonts

As a solution to the problem of substituted fonts causing formatting changes, font vendors have developed a method of embedding fonts in a document while controlling how they can be used. As you can see in Figure 8-15, four levels of font embedding are possible, as follows:

- **Restricted license** does not allow any embedding.

- **Print & Preview** embedding permits you to temporarily install fonts on the system to which they are sent, and documents are read-only.

- **Editable** embedding permits you to temporarily install fonts on the system to which they are sent; but they can be viewed, edited, and printed.

- **Installable** embedding permits you to permanently install and use fonts on the system to which they are sent.

In many Windows applications, you can save a file with embedded fonts. In the document window, choose File | Save As. Select Options, then click Embed TrueType Fonts, as shown in Figure 8-16. If you click OK, you save the file with embedded fonts.

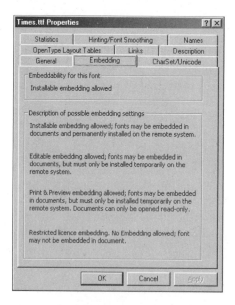

Figure 8-15.   *Font-embedding information in the print-properties extension.*

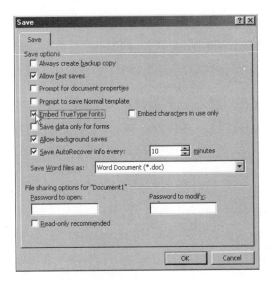

Figure 8-16. *Embedding a TrueType font in Microsoft Word.*

OpenType Fonts

Other efforts are being made to increase the range of typefaces available. Microsoft and Adobe Systems, the two leading competitors in font technology, are now working together on OpenType, a font format combining Microsoft's TrueType and Adobe's Postscript Type 1 fonts. OpenType fonts work with both monitors and printers. OpenType fonts can have TrueType outlines, Type 1 outlines, or both. Windows 98 is set up to support OpenType. The extended font Properties dialog box, using the TrueType Font Properties Shell Extension applet, has an OpenType Layout Tables tab.

For Web-page designers, OpenType fonts mean greater flexibility and the ability to deliver higher-quality documents on the Web. OpenType also addresses the basic issues of embedding fonts. If you want more information on the OpenType format, Adobe provides it at http://www.adobe.com/type/opentype.html, and Microsoft at http://www.microsoft.com/typography/faq/faq.htm.

Multilanguage Support

Windows 98 expands text capabilities even further by its support for foreign languages. Windows 98 includes fonts and character sets that allow you to read and write text not only in western European languages but also

313

in several central and eastern European languages as well. However, working with foreign-language versions of Windows 98 programs requires the appropriate language-specific versions of Windows.

To install multilanguage support, open Control Panel, and click Add/Remove Programs. Choose the Windows Setup tab, select Multilanguage Support, and then click Details (see Figure 8-17). Select the languages you want to include, choose OK, and then choose OK again to restart the computer. This allows you to display documents in the languages selected.

To write or edit documents in a foreign language, add keyboard support by selecting Keyboard in Control Panel. In the Language tab, click Add, select the desired language, and click OK. You are prompted to insert the Windows 98 CD and load the appropriate software. Finally, select the Enable Indicator On Taskbar check box. You can switch between two language scripts using left **ALT-SHIFT** or **CTRL-SHIFT,** depending on your choice in the Language tab's Switch Languages group. The taskbar shows the active language.

OTE   You can install support for multiple languages, and continuously pressing left **ALT-SHIFT** or **CTRL-SHIFT** rotates through the list of languages.

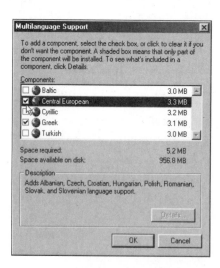

Figure 8-17.   *The Multilanguage Support Details dialog box.*

Windows 98 Accessories

Chapter 9 describes the Windows 98 accessories, or *applets,* that were not described in other chapters. You can launch many of these applets by opening the Start menu, choosing Programs | Accessories, and clicking the applet, as shown below. The following sections give you a quick overview of how to make the most of Calculator, Clipboard Viewer, Direct Cable Connection, Games, Imaging, Notepad, Paint, and WordPad.

 OTE Clipboard Viewer, Direct Cable Connection, and Games are not part of a Typical Windows 98 Install.

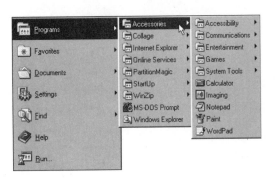

Calculator

The Windows 98 Calculator assists you with arithmetic, statistical, and scientific calculations. The Calculator window has two display modes: one for standard calculations, as shown in Figure 9-1, and one for statistical and scientific calculations. The default is the Standard view. After you've used Calculator, the view last used displays when you open Calculator.

Calculator Window

Regardless of the display mode, the Calculator window has only two menus besides the Help menu: Edit and View.

- **The Edit menu** contains the standard Copy and Paste options that allow you to copy the numbers in the Calculator display to and from the Clipboard.

- **The View menu** also contains two options: Scientific and Standard. Select Standard to display the Calculator view shown in Figure 9-1 and use it to perform normal arithmetic operations. Select Scientific to display the Calculator view shown in Figure 9-2. Use this view to perform scientific and statistical operations.

At the top of the Calculator window, you have the Calculator display area where you enter numbers and results are displayed. Below this display area in Scientific view is a row of option buttons. Click the buttons on the left to establish the number system you want to use:

Figure 9-1.   *Calculator window in Standard view.*

Figure 9-2. *Calculator window in Scientific view.*

■ **Hex** for hexadecimal numbers. When Hex is selected, the lettered buttons (A, B, C, D, E, and F) on the lower right of the Calculator become available for entering hexadecimal numbers.

■ **Dec** for decimal numbers.

■ **Oct** for octal numbers. Only 0 through 7 are available with this option.

■ **Bin** for binary numbers. Only 0 and 1 are available.

 IP Hex, Dec, Oct, and Bin are useful for converting a number in one system, or base, to another. Simply enter the number, for example, in decimal, and then click the button for the system to which you want to convert.

On the right, the option buttons set trigonometric input defaults. When the numbering system is decimal, three buttons are available:

■ The **Degrees** button has a keyboard shortcut, **F2.**

■ The **Radians** button has a keyboard shortcut, **F6.**

■ The **Gradients** button has a keyboard shortcut, **F4.**

When the numbering system is hexadecimal, octal, or binary, these are the option buttons you see:

■ **Dword,** for "double-word," displays the 32-bit representation of the number in the Calculator display area. The keyboard shortcut is **F2.**

- **Word** displays the lower 16 bits of the number in the Calculator display area. The keyboard shortcut is **F3.**

- **Byte** displays the lower 8 bits of the number in the Calculator display area. The keyboard shortcut is **F4.**

Below the number-system option buttons are check boxes that set defaults for scientific and statistical calculations:

- **Inv** sets an inverse function. It can be used with sin, cos, tan, PI, log, Ave, Sum, s, and certain other scientific functions. The keyboard shortcut is **I.** The inverse function is turned off when a calculation is complete.

- **Hyp** sets the hyperbolic function. It is used with sin, cos, and tan. The hyperbolic function is turned off when a calculation is complete. The keyboard shortcut is **H.**

In both Standard and Scientific views, you have these keys available to you on the Calculator:

- **Backspace** (same as **BACKSPACE** on the keyboard) deletes a single digit to the left.

- **Clear Entry** (same as **DELETE** on the keyboard) erases the last entry.

- **Clear All** (same as **ESC** on the keyboard) clears the calculations totally.

- **MC** clears the Calculator's memory.

- **MR** recalls a number from memory.

- **MS** stores a number in memory, overwriting any other contents.

- **M+** adds a number to the contents of memory.

- **NUMLOCK** on the keyboard allows you to use the keypad for entering numbers.

For statistical calculations, you have these buttons available:

- **Sta** displays the Statistics Box, where statistical numbers are displayed. The keyboard shortcut is **CTRL-S.**

- **Ave** calculates the average of the numbers in the Statistics Box. You can calculate the mean of the squares with Inv and then Ave. The keyboard shortcut is **CTRL-A.**

- **Sum** calculates the sum of the numbers in the Statistics Box. You can use the sum of the squares with Inv and then Sum. The keyboard shortcut is **CTRL-T.**

- **S** calculates the standard deviation where n-1 is the population parameter. Use Inv, then s, to calculate the standard deviation with population parameter as n. Click Sta first to make this button available. The keyboard shortcut is **CTRL-D.**

- **Dat** places a number in the Statistics Box. Click Sta first to make this button available. The keyboard shortcut is **INSERT.**

Many functions are available for performing scientific calculations. To see a description of any button, right-click the button and select What's This.

Performing Arithmetic Calculations

The Standard view Calculator (see Figure 9-1) performs these arithmetic functions: addition (+), subtraction (−), division (/), multiplication (*), square root (sqrt), percentages (%), and reciprocal (1/x). Follow these steps to enter an arithmetic function:

 IP To find out what a button is used for, right-click it, and then click What's This.

---

1. Enter the first number.

2. Click the operator: / to divide, * to multiply, − to subtract, + to add, sqrt for square root, % for percentages, or 1/x for reciprocals.

3. Enter the next number and click the operator. Continue entering until you have finished.

4. Click = to complete the calculation.

Using the Calculator's Memory

To store a number temporarily while you are performing other calculations, follow these steps:

1. First display the number by entering it or calculating it, and then click MS.

2. To add other numbers to the number in memory, click M+.

3. To subtract a number in the display from one in memory, click +/– to display the number as negative, and then click M+.

4. To look at the result, or to enter the result in the Calculator display area, click MR.

5. Clear the memory by clicking MC.

 OTE   Clicking MS is the same as clicking MC and then M+.

Performing Statistical Calculations

Statistical buttons, available in the Scientific view, provide average, sum, and standard deviation functions. Follow these steps to enter a statistical function:

1. If necessary, click Scientific on the View menu. The Calculator view will change to include the statistical functions.

2. Enter a number into the Calculator display area.

3. Click Sta to open the Statistics Box where data is displayed. The Statistics Box displays, as shown here.

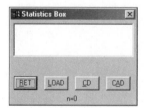

These four buttons now become available:

- **RET** returns to the Scientific Calculator view.

- **LOAD** loads the number selected in the Statistics Box into the Calculator display area.

- **CD,** Clear Digits, removes the selected number from the Statistics Box.

- **CAD,** Clear All Digits, clears all numbers in the Statistics Box.

4. Click Dat to enter data into the Statistics Box, which will then disappear.

5. Continue to enter the rest of the numbers, clicking Dat after each entry.

6. To view the contents of the Statistics Box, click Sta. To return to the regular Calculator, click RET.

7. Click one of the statistical operators to complete the function. The result appears in the Calculator display area.

8. When you are done with the Statistics Box, first click the Close button, and then click Clear All in Calculator.

Performing Scientific Calculations

Scientific calculations, such as those using logarithms, can be performed in the Scientific view. Follow these steps to perform a scientific calculation:

1. Click Scientific on the View menu to access the Scientific view.

2. If you want to change the number system, you can choose hexadecimal, decimal, octal, or binary.

3. Enter a number and click an operator.

4. Continue to enter numbers and click operators as needed.

5. Click = for the result.

Clipboard Viewer

Clipboard Viewer allows you to look at the contents of the Clipboard, as you can see below, and save the contents in a .clp file if you wish. Later you can open the .clp file in the Clipboard Viewer, which places the contents on the Clipboard where you can paste them into another document. This allows you to copy several items before pasting any of them.

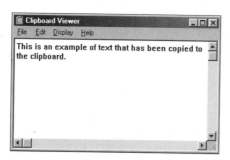

The Clipboard Viewer is not installed with a Typical Windows 98 install. If you did not install it when you installed Windows 98, you can do so by opening the Add/Remove Programs control panel, choosing Windows Setup, and selecting System Tools | Clipboard Viewer. Once it is installed, you can start Clipboard Viewer by opening the Start menu and choosing Programs | Accessories | System Tools | Clipboard Viewer.

If you have cut or copied something in any application, be it text, graphics, files, or folders, when you open the Clipboard Viewer, you will see it if it is text or a graphic, or you will see a path to it if it is a file or a folder, as shown on the next page. To save the contents, open the File menu, choose Save As, enter a path and file name, and click OK. To open a saved item, open the File menu, choose Open, identify the file, and click OK. If the Clipboard currently has something on it, you will be asked if it is OK to clear the contents of the Clipboard. You must click Yes to bring in the stored file.

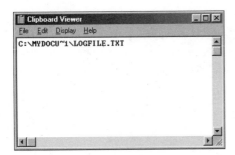

The Clipboard uses different formats to store different types of items. As a result, the Clipboard can display some items in several formats using the Display menu. For example, a bitmap graphic has the options not grayed out in the menu shown below on the left, while a text file has the options not grayed out in the menu shown below on the right. The Auto option lets the Clipboard pick the best format in which to display the item.

Direct Cable Connection

Direct Cable Connection establishes a link between you and another computer so that you can share folders, even if you are not networked. This feature is primarily used to connect portable and desktop computers. When the Direct Cable Connection is opened, a wizard of the same name is displayed, as shown in Figure 9-3.

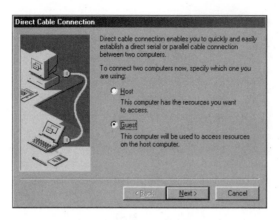

Figure 9-3. *Direct Cable Connection wizard.*

 IP You can gain access to networks if the computer with which you have a direct cable connection is connected to a network.

The Direct Cable Connection is not installed with a Typical Windows 98 install. If you did not install it when you installed Windows 98, you can do so by opening the Add/Remove Programs control panel, choosing Windows Setup, and selecting Communications | Direct Cable Connection. Once it is installed, you can follow these steps to set up your direct cable connection:

1. Open the Start menu and select Programs | Accessories | Communications | Direct Cable Connection. The Direct Cable Connection wizard will lead you through the installation.

2. Select either connecting as a Host computer, where others will access your resources, or connecting as a Guest, where you will access resources on another computer. Then click Next.

3. Select the port to be used. If you must install a new port, click Install New Ports, and follow the directions. Attach a null modem serial cable or a parallel cable with the same type of connector on each end to each computer and click Next when you are finished.

OTE   If you don't have file and printer sharing set up on your computer (it is usually done if you are connected to a LAN), then you will be asked if you want to do that. For the direct cable connection to function, you will need to enable file and printer sharing in the host.

4. To complete the installation, click Finish. (If you are installing as a host, you may also want to click Use Password Protection to protect others from casually accessing your resources.)

 IP   To successfully use the Direct Cable Connection, both the Host and Guest computers must install using Direct Cable Connection connected to the same type of port.

Games

Windows 98 comes with four games: FreeCell, Hearts, Minesweeper, and Solitaire. Here's a brief description of all but Hearts (which is discussed in Chapter 16) and how you start playing. Windows 98's games are not installed with a Typical Windows 98 install. If you did not install them when you installed Windows 98, you can do so by opening the Add/Remove Programs control panel, choosing Windows Setup, and selecting Accessories | Games.

FreeCell

FreeCell is an engaging game that can become addictive! Although similar to Solitaire, it is more a game of strategy than of chance. Follow these steps to begin playing:

1. Open the Start menu and select Programs | Accessories | Games | FreeCell. When you open FreeCell, a blank game board displays.

2. Open the Game menu and select New Game. The game board will be filled with eight columns of cards and eight empty cells along the top, as shown in Figure 9-4.

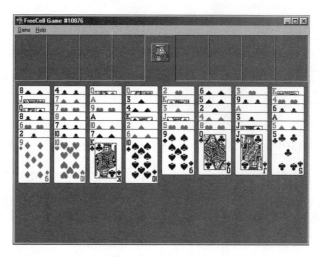

Figure 9-4. *FreeCell game board.*

The four empty cells on the left of the "king" are free cells to be used for temporarily storing cards. The cells to the right are home cells, used to hold cards of a given suit, from the ace up. The object of the game is to get all cards into the home cells. To do that, you arrange the cards at the bottom in sequence by number, colors alternating, as in Solitaire. For example, you will place a black six on a red seven, using the free cells as needed to get to the numbers you need.

3. Double-click aces to place them in the home cells, and double-click all other cards to place them in the free cells.

4. Click cards to select them, and then move the pointer to where you want to place the cards, and click there. If your move is correct, the cards will be moved.

 IP   The king icon swivels left and right to follow your mouse as it moves back and forth over the board.

Minesweeper

Minesweeper is a game of chance in which you try to accumulate points by not encountering mines. Follow these steps to start playing:

1. Open the Start menu and select Programs | Accessories | Games | Minesweeper. The game board will display, as seen in Figure 9-5.

Figure 9-5.   *Minesweeper game board.*

On the game board, you will see a mine counter on the upper left of the game board, a timer on the upper right, a reset button (smiley face) between the two, and empty squares. The object of the game is to find the mines hidden in the squares as quickly as possible without actually clicking them. When you click a square, you will see either a number or a mine. The number tells you how many mines are contained in the eight squares surrounding the clicked square. You mark the suspected mines with the right mouse button. If you actually click a mine, the game ends.

2. To restart the game, open the Game menu and select New, or click the smiley (reset) button.

 IP   You can set the difficulty of the game from the Game menu. The harder the level, the more squares are displayed.

Solitaire

Solitaire is a game of both chance and strategy. The object of the game is to end up with the deck of cards arranged sequentially in suits from the ace up to the king. Follow these steps to start playing:

1. Open the Start menu and select Programs | Accessories | Games | Solitaire. The game board will display, as seen in Figure 9-6.

   You will see a row of seven stacks of cards; all are face down except the top card. In the upper left of the board is another downturned stack of cards, which you can click. In the upper right are four

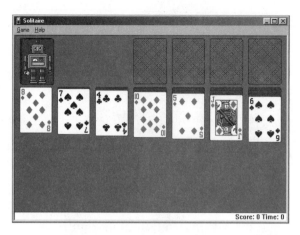

Figure 9-6.   *Solitaire game board.*

empty cells where you will place the suits, beginning with the aces. Here are some pointers:

- Double-click any aces to move them to the upper right to begin that suit's sequential stack.

- Drag any numbered cards onto the next highest number of a different color. For example, you might drag a red four onto a black five.

- When you have made all possible card sequences, click the stack of cards in the upper left of the game. If the next card fits in a card sequence, drag it to that position.

- Drag kings to any empty spaces left on the board created by dragging cards onto others to start a mixed red and black sequential run from the king to a queen of the opposite color, to a jack the same color as the king, and so on down to the 2.

- You can choose a different deck design by selecting Deck from the Game menu.

- Select Options from the Game menu to choose between drawing every third card (the default and most difficult) or drawing every card. You can also choose to score using the Vegas method or the Standard method (the default).

- When you want a new game, click Deal on the Game menu.

■ When you are finished with the game, click Exit on the Game menu, or click the Close button in the upper right corner of the window.

 IP Periodically, the graphic on the back of the card in the stack in the upper left corner displays some animation. For example, the dial and lights on the chest of the robot shown in Figure 9-6 will change.

Imaging

 Using the Imaging accessory, you can view and annotate existing images, accept scanned images, and to a limited extent, create images. Generally, Imaging is for viewing images and Paint (see a later section of this chapter) is for creating and editing images. In Imaging, you can open and look at · eight different file types.

- Bitmap image (.bmp)
- Fax document (.awd)
- GIF file (.gif)
- JPEG file (.jpg, .jpe)
- PCX file (.pcx)
- TIFF file (.tif)
- WIFF file (.wif)
- XIF file (.xif)

Five of these file types (.gif, .jpg or .jpe, .pcx, .wif, and .xif) are read-only. (You can look at them, but you cannot annotate or change them in any way, and you cannot save files in any of these formats.) The other three file types (.bmp, .awd, and .tif) can be annotated, and you can save a file in these formats. Both BMP and TIFF files provide full-color images, while the AWD format is used for black-and-white images used in faxing. In AWD and BMP files, the annotation is made a permanent part of the file and cannot be changed after you save the file. In TIFF files, you can change the annotation after saving the files.

With TIFF files, you have several choices for compressing them (so that they take up less storage space), whereas BMP files cannot be compressed in Imaging, and AWD files use a single compression scheme. Finally, with TIFF images, you can place several into separate "pages" of a single document and work with them together, as you can see in Figure 9-7. With both BMP and AWD files, you can only work with a single image at a time.

 IP   Use TIFF files for greatest flexibility in Imaging.

Viewing Images

The principal function of Imaging is to help you view images. Imaging gives you four views, as described in Table 9-1. You can either choose the views with toolbar buttons, or you can select them from the View menu.

In both the One Page view and Thumbnail and Page views, you can enlarge and reduce the view in a number of ways, as described in Table 9-2. You can select these with the toolbar buttons shown in Table 9-2 or select them from the Edit, Zoom, and Page menus.

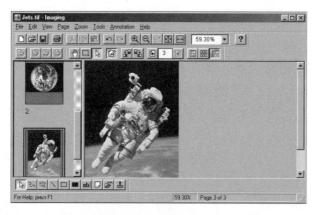

Figure 9-7.   *Viewing thumbnails with an image.*

Button	Name	Description
	One Page	Displays a single image that can fill the window.
	Thumbnail	Displays a Thumbnail view (miniature version) of each page in the document.
	Page and Thumbnails	Displays both a Thumbnail and a Page view, as shown in Figure 9-7.
CTRL-F	Full Screen	Removes the title, menu, tool, status, and task bars to allow the full screen to be used to display the current image.

Table 9-1.   *Imaging views.*

Button	Name	Description
	Zoom In	Enlarges the current view to twice its size
	Zoom Out	Reduces the current view to half its size
	Zoom To Selection	Enlarges and displays a selected area of an image
	Best Fit	Enlarges the image to fill the display area
	Fit To Width	Sizes the image to fill the width of the display area
118.60%	Zoom	Sizes the image to match the selected percentage of its actual size
	Actual Size	Displays the image at 100 percent of its actual size
	Fit To Height	Sizes the image to fill the height of the display area
	Drag	Allows dragging the image within the window
	Select Image	Allows you to select a part of an image to cut or zoom to
	Rotate Left	Rotates the image 90 degrees to the left
	Rotate Right	Rotates the image 90 degrees to the right

Table 9-2.   *Imaging view variations.*

Annotating Images

Using Imaging, you can add lines, text, and objects as annotations to either an existing image or a new image by using the annotation tools, which are described in Table 9-3. You access these tools with the buttons in the Annotations toolbar as shown in Table 9-3 or by using the Annotations menu. You can turn on the Annotations toolbar with the Annotations Toolbar button shown here.

All of the annotation tools, except the Annotation Selection tool, have an associated properties dialog box in which you can set properties. You can open the properties dialog box by right-clicking the tool and then choosing Properties on the context menu. For example, if you right-click the Text tool and choose Properties, the familiar Text Properties dialog box shown in Figure 9-8 opens.

Button	Name	Description
	Annotation Selection	Selects an annotation or one of its components
	Freehand Line	Draws freehand lines or shapes
	Highlighter	Applies transparent highlighting
	Straight Line	Draws a straight line
	Hollow Rectangle	Draws an empty rectangle
	Filled Rectangle	Draws a rectangle filled with a particular color
	Text	Applies text in a transparent background
	Attach-a-Note	Applies text in a colored, bordered background
	Text From File	Applies text from a file in a transparent background
	Rubber Stamp	Applies predetermined text in a transparent background

Table 9-3.   *Annotation tools.*

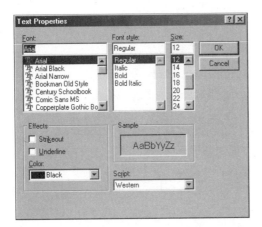

Figure 9-8. *Text Properties dialog box.*

 OTE When Table 9-3 describes text as being added in a transparent layer, it simply means that after adding text you can still see what is behind it. In other programs, this is not always the case. Often you will have an opaque rectangle containing the text and blocking out whatever is behind it.

Scanning Images

You can use Imaging to control your scanner and be the recipient of your scanned images. Select a scanner to use with the Select Scanner option on the File menu. Then set the options for scanning from the Scan Options dialog box, which you open from the Scan Options item on the Tools menu. To scan an image, you can use either the Scan New option on the File menu or one of the buttons on the Scanning toolbar, which are shown in Table 9-4.

Button	Name	Description
	Scan New	Scans a new image
	Insert Scanned Page	Scans a new image and places it before the current page
	Append Scanned Page	Scans a new image and places it at the end of the current page
	Rescan Page	Scans a new image that replaces the current page

Table 9-4. *Scanner tools.*

Notepad

Notepad is a simple editor you can use with ASCII text and program code. It contains a few special features, such as enabling you to look at the contents of the Clipboard, and to create a log of events, as explained shortly.

Notepad Window

The Notepad window, shown in Figure 9-9, contains three menus (in addition to Help) with many features common to folder windows, which were described in earlier chapters. The other features are explained here.

File Menu

The File menu contains a Page Setup option. When you select Page Setup, a dialog box opens in which you can customize your page setup, including paper size and source; orientation, either portrait (tall) or landscape (wide); top, bottom, left, and right margins; and header and footer text. As you adjust the page setup options, a miniature display of the page appears in the Preview area. By clicking Printer on the File menu, you can change the printer that will be used and its properties.

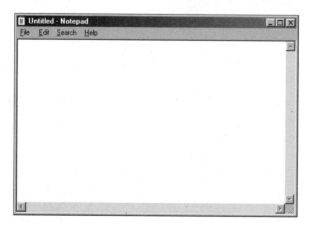

Figure 9-9.   *Notepad window.*

Edit Menu

The Edit menu contains three options that haven't been described previously:

- **Time/Date** inserts the current time and date into the document where the insertion point is located.

- **Word Wrap** is a toggle switch for turning word wrap on and off. When word wrap is turned on, as you type, the lines wrap down to the next line, so that you can see the contents without scrolling. Word Wrap does not affect the way the document will print, but it is useful for editing on the screen.

- **Set Font** opens a dialog box in which you can select the font, its style, and its size.

Search Menu

The Search menu contains two common features for finding text:

- **Find** opens a dialog box containing a text box (shown below) where you enter a string of characters for which you want to search. You can specify whether to search Up the document (backward to the beginning) or Down (forward to the end). If case is important, check Match Case.

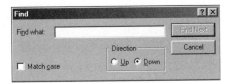

- **Find Next** repeats the previous Find. The shortcut key for this feature is **F3.**

Using Notepad

Notepad provides a handy place to view the contents of the Clipboard by simply pasting them into a Notepad document. Also, you can create a log for recording events by typing **.LOG** on the top left margin of a document and then saving it. Thereafter, each time you open the document, Notepad will append the time and date to its end to timestamp any new text, as shown below.

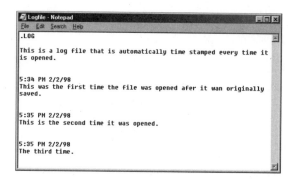

Paint

Paint is a drawing program with which you can draw colorful shapes and lines and include text and graphics. Using Paint, you can create logos, brochures, and graphics for other documents, and even backgrounds for the desktop.

The Paint window, shown in Figure 9-10, is initially labeled "untitled" in the title bar. It contains five menus (in addition to Help), a toolbox on the left of the drawing area, and a color palette beneath the drawing area.

Menus

The five menus contain options for working with your art objects: File, Edit, View, Image, and Colors.

File Menu

The File menu contains many standard options and four that are specifically intended for Paint. The four options and their descriptions are as follows:

- **Print Preview** allows you to see the image as it will be printed. When you select this option, you have additional buttons available:

  - **Print** sends the displayed image to the printer.

  - **Next Page** displays the next page of the art document.

  - **Prev Page** displays the page before the one currently displayed.

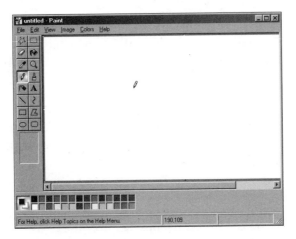

Figure 9-10. *Paint window.*

- **Two Page** displays an odd- and even-numbered page together, as you would see in a book.

- **Zoom In** enlarges the image. You can also zoom in when the pointer is a small magnifying glass (which it is by default when you open Print Preview), by clicking the part of the image you want to enlarge.

- **Zoom Out** reduces the image to its original size. You can also just click the image to reduce it.

- **Close** closes the Print Preview, returning you to the Paint drawing screen.

- **Page Setup** opens a dialog box where you can set the page specifications. You specify the Paper Size, Paper Source, orientation (portrait or landscape), and set the margins for Left, Right, Top, and Bottom. The image of the page in the top of the dialog box will reflect your changes. By clicking the Printer button, you can also change the printer or its properties.

- **Set As Wallpaper (Tiled)** creates an object that is tiled and used as a background wallpaper design. This is suitable for smaller objects that can be repeated to form a pattern. The filename, when saved in the \Windows folder, is entered into the wallpaper designs available in the Display Properties dialog box.

- **Set As Wallpaper (Centered)** creates an object that is centered on the screen as background wallpaper. This is appropriate for larger designs that are not suitable for tiled displays. The filename, when saved in the \Windows folder, is entered into the wallpaper designs available in the Display Properties dialog box.

 OTE You must save your image before it can be used as desktop wallpaper.

 IP Open the Display Properties dialog box by right-clicking an empty area of the desktop and selecting Properties from the context menu.

Edit Menu

The Edit menu presents these options for working with the drawing:

- **Clear Selection** clears a selected part of the screen. You must first use the Free-Form Select or Select tools to enclose the portion of the drawing you want to clear.

- **Copy To** allows you to copy the selected objects to a file. A dialog box will display in which you enter the path and filename.

- **Paste From** allows you to insert a file. In the dialog box, you can enter the path and filename of the file you want to insert.

View Menu

The View menu has options for determining whether you see the toolbox, color box, and status bar. It also has controls for the size of the image, and if text is being used, whether the text toolbar is displayed. The Zoom option has five suboptions for viewing the image (described next), and View Bitmap displays a full screen view of the image. Click the screen to return to the normal view.

- **Normal Size** displays the image at its original size. Choose this option after viewing the image at an enlarged size.

■ **Large Size** enlarges the image.

■ **Custom** allows you to define the view you want. You can Zoom to 100 percent, 200 percent, 400 percent, 600 percent, or 800 percent of the image's normal size.

■ **Show Grid,** available in enlarged view, displays a grid over the image, so that you can work more accurately and precisely.

■ **Show Thumbnail,** available in enlarged view, displays a small thumbnail display of the image on the screen. You can see the results on the whole image as you manipulate a small part of it.

Image Menu

The Image Menu provides features that enable you to produce some dramatic enhancements of your artwork. You can flip or rotate selected objects, stretch or skew them, invert colors, or change the attributes of your overall drawing, such as its width. Here are the options:

■ **Flip/Rotate** opens the Flip or Rotate dialog box, allowing you to flip or rotate a selected part of your image. In it you can choose to flip horizontally or vertically, or to rotate by a preset angle (which can be 90, 180, or 270 degrees).

■ **Stretch/Skew** displays a Stretch and Skew dialog box shown in Figure 9-11, in which you can stretch a selected object vertically or horizontally. You can also skew a selected object vertically or horizontally.

■ **Invert Colors** causes colors to be displayed in their complements. For example, black becomes white and blue becomes yellow.

■ **Attributes** shows you the date the file was last saved and its size on your disk. The Attributes dialog box also allows you to change the drawing's width and height, units of measurements (inches, centimeters, or pixels), whether it is in black and white or color, and its transparency. Click the Default button to return the attributes to their default settings, shown in Figure 9-12.

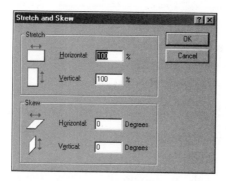

Figure 9-11.   *Stretch and Skew dialog box.*

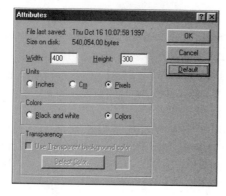

Figure 9-12.   *Attributes dialog box.*

- **Clear Image** clears the current image from the screen. You can undo Clear Image, but if you previously performed three other actions without saving the drawing, it will be lost.

- **Draw Opaque** switches your drawings from opaque to transparent. An opaque drawing hides any underlying drawing objects such as text, while transparent drawings allow the underlying objects to show through.

Colors Menu

The Colors menu allows you to edit colors to get the exact combinations you want. The Edit Colors menu option displays a dialog box where you can see the colors available and create custom colors if none meet your requirements. To create a custom color, click a basic color that seems close to the color you want, and then click Define Custom Colors. The dialog box expands to include a color matrix and alternative ways of controlling the color (see Figure 9-13). You can specify a color by setting its hue, saturation, or luminosity; by setting the amount of red, green, or blue; or by clicking the color in the color matrix. Here's how these options work:

- **Hue** is a numeric value associated with colors where 0 is red, 60 is yellow, 120 is green, 180 is cyan, 200 is magenta, and 240 is blue. By changing the hue, you change the reds, greens, and blues.

- **Sat** measures the amount of saturation of the color, up to a maximum of 240.

- **Lum** measures the brightness of the color.

- **Red** indicates the amount of red in the color.

- **Green** indicates the amount of green in the color.

- **Blue** indicates the amount of blue in the color.

 IP Drag the mouse across the color matrix to see the resulting color along with its numerical factors displayed below the matrix.

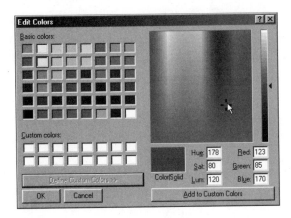

Figure 9-13. *Edit Colors dialog box expanded for defining custom colors.*

Toolbox

The Paint toolbox on the left of the Paint window displays the 16 tools you can use for creating and changing your drawings, by inserting and manipulating lines, shapes, text, and colors. By placing the mouse pointer over a toolbox button, you can see a description of the tool in the status bar below the color box.

Just under the toolbox, a blank rectangular area contains optional choices for some of the buttons. For example, if you choose Magnifier, you can specify a magnifying strength from those displayed. If you choose the Rounded Rectangle, you can vary the border and transparency of the rectangle.

You may choose these tools from the toolbox:

- **Free-Form Select** allows you to select an area by drawing a line around an irregularly shaped area. Click the Free-Form Select button, and drag the pointer around the area to select it. A selection box will replace your Free-Form Select line.

- **Select** allows you to create a rectangular selection box. Click the Select button, and then drag the pointer diagonally across the area to be selected.

- **Eraser/Color Eraser** allows you to delete part of a drawing, both color and lines, as you move the Eraser tool over it. Click the Eraser button, choose an eraser size from the area beneath the toolbox, and drag the Eraser tool over the part of the drawing you want to change.

IP   The area cleared by Eraser can be filled with color.

- **Fill With Color** allows you to fill an enclosed area with color. Click the Fill With Color button, place the end of the Fill With Color tool in the area to be filled, and click.

ARNING   If there is a break in the enclosed area, the color will leak outside the lines.

■ **Pick Color** lets you select a color in one area and transfer it to another. Click the Pick Color button, click the object in the drawing whose color you want to duplicate (the tool changes to the last tool you used or Fill With Color), and then click the object or area where you want the color transferred.

IP To check whether you have selected the right color to copy, look beneath the toolbox. The color you chose flashes as you click the Pick Color tool on an object. If you want another color, repeat the procedure.

■ **Magnifier** allows you to enlarge a defined area. Click the Magnifier button. The pointer will become a rectangular box, which you use to define the area to be enlarged. Click the area you want and it will be enlarged by the currently selected magnification shown beneath the toolbox. To change the magnification, click the Magnifier button, then click another magnification. To return to normal size, either select 1X from the power choices or click the Magnifier tool on the drawing again.

IP Use the scroll bars to see any part of the drawing that is hidden because it is too large for the screen.

■ **Pencil** lets you draw a freehand line. Click the Pencil button, click a color from the color box, and draw the shape you want.

■ **Brush** allows you to draw lines of varying shapes and widths. Click the Brush button, select the shape and width from beneath the toolbox, click the color you want the line to be, and draw the shape.

■ **Airbrush** lets you draw groupings of dots, or splotches, which make a single spot on the drawing. Click the Airbrush button, select the size of spot you want from beneath the toolbox, click the color of the spot, and drag the pointer or click the drawing to achieve the airbrushed look.

■ **Text** lets you place text on a drawing. Click the Text button, select the color for the text, and create a text frame by dragging the pointer over the area where you want to insert the text. In the Fonts toolbox that appears (see Figure 9-14), click the font, size, and style (bold, italic, underline). Click within the text box and type your text.

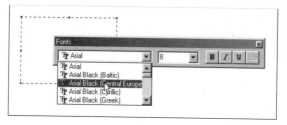

Figure 9-14.   *Text frame with Fonts toolbox.*

> **NOTE**   If you don't want the text box to show any objects or colors behind it (to be in an opaque box), click the top choice beneath the toolbox. If you want to see a color or an object behind the type (to be in a transparent box), select the bottom choice.

■ **Line** is used to draw a straight line. Click the Line button, and choose a line width. Click the color for the line, and then select the beginning point of the line. Drag the pointer to an end point, and then click once to anchor the line before continuing to draw, or release your mouse button to end the line altogether.

■ **Curve** is used to draw a curved line between two points. Click the Curve button, and choose a line width. Click a color, and then select the beginning point of the curve. Drag the line to the end point, and click once to anchor the line before continuing. To create a curve, click anywhere alongside the line and drag. Click twice to end the line.

> **TIP**   To create a teardrop, click the Curve button, and select a beginning point. Click a point twice the size of the teardrop away from and below the beginning point to form a straight line, and click a point in the direction the bulge in the teardrop is to form. The line bends in two to form the teardrop.

■ **Rectangle** lets you draw a box. Click the Rectangle button, and then click a color. Below the toolbox, choose from a transparent rectangle with border, a rectangle with border and fill, or a rectangle with fill but no border. Place the pointer at the upper left corner of the rectangle and drag it diagonally down to the lower right.

- **Polygon** is used to draw straight lines that connect in various shapes and angles. Click the Polygon button, and select a color. Beneath the toolbox, choose from a transparent shape with border, a shape with border and fill, and a shape with no border and fill. Place the pointer at the beginning point of the shape, and draw the first line segment by dragging the pointer. Release the mouse button, place the pointer where the second line segment is to end, click the mouse button, and continue clicking for each of the line segments until the drawing is complete. Click twice to end the drawing.

- **Ellipse** lets you create an elliptical shape. Click the Ellipse button and select a color. From the toolbox choose between a transparent shape with a border, a shape with a border and fill, and a shape with no border and fill. Place the pointer in the upper left of the ellipse, and drag the pointer diagonally to the lower right.

 IP To draw a perfect circle, press SHIFT while you drag the pointer.

- **Rounded Rectangle** operates like Rectangle, but the corners of the rectangular shape are curved rather than squared.

Color Box

The color box, located at the bottom of the drawing area, displays the available colors. Select a color by clicking it. The foreground color displays in the top square on the left. The background color displays on the square beneath the foreground one. Select the foreground color with the left mouse button, and the background color with the right mouse button. To use the color box, first select the tool, then the tool shape, if applicable, and finally the color. The line or shape will be drawn in the color selected.

To create your own colors, double-click the color box or select Edit Colors from the Colors menu. The dialog box displayed is explained earlier in *Colors Menu*.

WordPad

WordPad is a simple but capable word processor that can directly read both Microsoft Word and Windows Write files as well as Rich Text Format (RTF) and ASCII files.

WordPad Window

When you open WordPad, the window shown in Figure 9-15 appears. This window contains five menus plus Help. These menus contain some special items along with the common folder window options. Below the menus are a toolbar and format bar containing buttons for many commands, an optional ruler, and finally, the word-processing area. Beneath the text area is the status bar, where messages and command descriptions are displayed.

File Menu

Most of the File menu commands are common to many File menus. However, this File menu also contains these special options:

- **Print Preview** displays the document as it will be printed (see Figure 9-16). You can check the pagination, margins, page breaks, and other specifics before the pages are printed. When you select Print Preview, you'll see a different set of buttons on the toolbar:

  - **Print** sends the document to the printer.

  - **Next Page** and **Prev Page** display the next and previous pages.

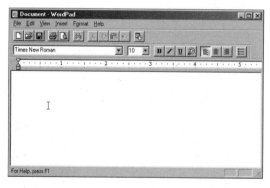

Figure 9-15.   *WordPad window with its menus and toolbars.*

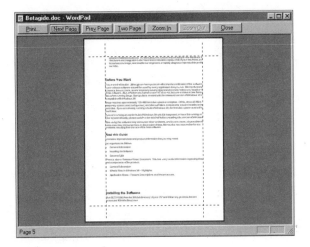

Figure 9-16. *Print Preview screen.*

> ■ **Two Page** displays two consecutive pages so that you can see pages as in a book.

> ■ **Zoom In** enlarges the part of the document where the pointer is clicked.

> ■ **Zoom Out** reduces the size.

> ■ **Close** returns you to the normal word-processing screen.

■ **Page Setup** displays a dialog box for setting paper size and source, orientation (portrait or landscape), and margins. You can also change the printer from this dialog box.

Edit Menu

The Edit menu contains the following options, which allow you to manipulate the text in word-processing documents:

■ **Paste Special** lets you copy *linked* or *embedded* information from the Clipboard into a document. (Linked or embedded information is tied to the application that created it, so you can use that application to edit the information.) When you select Paste Special, a dialog box gives you the option to link or embed the information.

- **Find** is used to search for a character string. To find whole words, select Match Whole Word Only; otherwise, you will find all embedded occurrences of the string as well. If capitalization is important, click Match Case.

- **Find Next** repeats the previous Find command.

- **Replace** allows you to replace one sequence of characters with another. You specify the search criteria in the Find What text box. You specify the new text in Replace With. As in Find, you can choose to Match Whole Word Only and Match Case. When a match is made, you can choose Replace to replace that one occurrence, Replace All to replace all occurrences, or Find Next to ignore the item and continue searching for the next occurrence.

- **Links** makes it possible to automatically or manually update any linked objects in WordPad and allows you to open the program that created the linked object, so you can edit the original. The changes are then reflected in the linked object.

- **Object Properties,** when clicked, displays the attributes of a linked or embedded object. The General tab provides the type of object, file size, and location. The View tab allows you to choose between seeing the object itself or an icon representing it. You can change the icon, and depending on the object, you may be able to scale it. The Link tab, which is present if you selected a linked object, has options similar to those of the Links option.

- **Object** allows you to edit an embedded or linked object. When you select an object, this option changes to be more explicit, for example, Bitmap Image Object. You can then either edit or open the object. If you select Edit, the menus, toolbars, and toolboxes of the creating application will open in WordPad, as shown at the top of the next page. However, if you select Open, the creating application will open in its own window. For example, if you have selected a sound file to edit, Object changes to Media Clip Object and the Media Player menus and toolbars appear in WordPad, as you can see at the top of the next page:

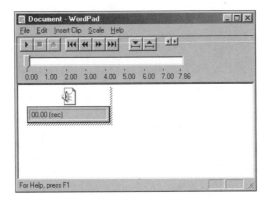

 IP   To return to WordPad when you are done editing the object, click outside the object. To return to WordPad if you clicked any option other than Edit, select Exit and Return to Filename from the File menu.

View Menu

The View menu contains five options for varying the screen display:

- **Toolbar,** when selected, displays the top toolbar.

- **Format Bar,** when selected, displays the format bar beneath the toolbar.

- **Ruler,** when selected, displays the ruler. To set tabs and margins on the ruler, click it to indicate where you want to place a tab. You can drag margin settings and tabs to different locations on the ruler.

- **Status Bar,** when selected, displays the status bar, which shows status messages and option descriptions.

- **Options** displays a dialog box, shown in Figure 9-17, in which you establish defaults for a document you are editing. The Options dialog box has six tabs, although four of them have the same contents:

  - **Options**   allows you to set the units of measurement for the document in inches, points, centimeters, or picas. If you check Automatic Word Selection, you can select one word at a time as you begin to drag the pointer over a word. If you leave this option unchecked, dragging the pointer will select character by character.

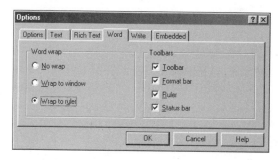

Figure 9-17.   *Options dialog box.*

■ **Text, Rich Text, Word,** and **Write** tabs allow you to set Word Wrap options and toolbar displays for each type of text. You can choose between No Wrap; Wrap To Window, which means that the screen width determines when the line wraps to the next line; and Wrap To Ruler, whereby the margins determine when the line wraps. As on the View menu, you can also set the defaults for displaying the toolbar, format bar, ruler, and status bar for each type of text (Word, Rich Text, Text, or Write).

 OTE   WordPad can save documents in Word for Windows 6 format, but it can open Word files up through Word 97.

■ **Embedded** contains the same options as the other text tabs, except that it contains no option for displaying the status bar. This is because you will be editing in the embedded object's creating application.

Insert Menu

The Insert menu offers these options for inserting the time and date or another object:

■ **Date and Time** lets you insert the time and date in the current document where the insertion point is located. You can choose from various date formats when you click the option.

■ **Object,** when chosen, displays an Insert Object dialog box. In it, you can choose whether the object to be inserted will be created from a selected application or accessed from an existing file. Click Display As Icon to display the inserted object as an icon rather than what it is, as an image, for example.

After you click Create New and an object type, the WordPad window will change to the application needed to create that type of object. For example, if you insert a sound file, the Media Player application launches. If you insert a bitmap image, Paint will load, as shown in Figure 9-18. You create the object using the tools available in the new application window. When you are finished, click outside the box containing the object to return to WordPad.

If you select Create From File, you can enter the path and filename of the file to be inserted. Browse is available if you need it. To create a linked file, click Link. This will create an address reference only in the document so that modifications are done in the original and reflected in the document. If you don't select Link, the object will be embedded within the document. In this case, it exists as a separate object that can be modified independently of the original file. Click Display As Icon to display an inserted drawing as an icon rather than as an image.

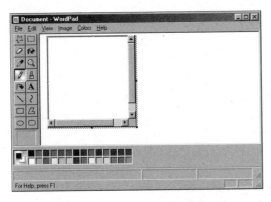

Figure 9-18. *Creating a bitmap image in WordPad loads Paint.*

351

Format Menu

The Format menu provides options that allow you to vary the format style of the text:

■ **Font** displays a dialog box where you can select the font, style, size, and effects (strikethrough, underline, and color) you want to use.

■ **Bullet Style** adds a bullet on the left side of the current paragraph and indents the paragraph. When you press **ENTER,** another bulleted paragraph appears until you turn off Bullet Style.

■ **Paragraph** allows you to set left, right, and first-line indentations, and an alignment of left, right, or center, as shown here:

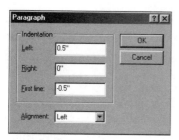

■ **Tabs,** when chosen, opens a dialog box for setting and clearing tabs. Click Clear All to remove all existing tabs. Set new tabs by typing the position of a tab stop in the Tab Stop Position text box and then clicking Set. You can clear individual tabs by selecting them and clicking Clear.

Toolbars

WordPad has two toolbars to help you work more easily and efficiently. Table 9-5 describes the buttons in the toolbar at the top, and Table 9-6 shows the buttons in the format bar. Most of these buttons duplicate options in the menus.

The accessories discussed in this chapter may not get a lot of respect, but they can do quite a bit of work for you in a pinch. It's worthwhile to know how to use them. In the next part of this book, we'll discuss communications and the Internet.

Button	Name	Description
	New, Open, Save	Creates a new document, retrieves an existing document, and saves the active document
	Print, Print Preview	Sends the current document to the printer or displays the current document as it will be printed
	Find	Searches for characters matching the criteria you specify
	Cut, Copy, Paste	Removes or duplicates text onto the Clipboard, or inserts text from the Clipboard
	Undo	Cancels the last action taken
	Date/Time	Inserts the current date and time into the document

Table 9-5. *Toolbar buttons.*

Control/Button	Name	Description
Times New Roman — 10	Font, Font Size	Changes the font and sets font size for selected text
B / U	Bold, Italics, Underline	Makes selected text bold, italic, or underlined
	Color	Changes the color of selected text
	Align Left, Center, Align Right	Aligns selected text on the left, center, or right of the document
	Bullets	Places bullets on the left and indents selected paragraphs

Table 9-6. *Format bar controls and buttons.*

Using Communications and the Internet

In line with the current demands on computers, Windows 98 offers extensive communications capabilities and all the tools necessary to make full use of the Internet. Part 4 explores the core communications features and then looks at how you can use those features to access the Internet. Part 4 concludes with a discussion of e-mail over both the Internet and intranet.

Windows 98 Communications

Windows 98 provides a 32-bit communications system that can reliably transfer data at high speeds over several types of communications links. In support of this communications system, Windows 98 uses its preemptive multitasking to handle fast data throughput and ensure that data transfers in 32-bit programs are not affected by other tasks running at the same time. Windows 98 has built-in capability to handle a broad range of communications devices, both individually and by linking two or more devices together for higher-speed communications. Additionally, Windows 98 has many features that will allow third-party developers to create state-of-the-art communications applications beyond what is available today.

Windows 98 offers four applications and three control panels relating to communications. The control panels are as follows:

- The **Modems control panel** provides for the installation and control of one or more modems that can be shared across all communications applications.

- The **Telephony control panel** allows you to set up dialing instructions, including the use of calling cards for multiple locations.

- The **Infrared control panel** provides for the installation and control of an infrared device that can be used between a computer and printer or between two computers, which in turn can be used to connect a remote computer to a network.

The communications applications included with Windows 98 are the following:

- **Dial-Up Networking** allows you to set up one computer as a client and another computer as a server. You can then connect the two computers and do standard networking functions using modems and telephone connections. When you connect to the Internet using a modem, you use Dial-Up Networking with your computer as the client. This application is discussed in Chapters 11 and 16.

- **Direct Cable Connection** allows you to connect two computers using a cable between either the serial or parallel ports. You can then transfer files between the computers, and if one of the computers is connected to a network, the other computer can access the network through the direct cable connection. This and the next two applications are discussed in this chapter.

- **HyperTerminal** allows you to connect to a remote computer using phone lines. The remote computer can be running a bulletin board or another program similar to HyperTerminal, or it could be an information service. After you've connected, you can read information or transfer files to and from the other computer.

- **Phone Dialer** allows you to use your computer and modem to dial telephone numbers with speed dialing, calling-card capabilities, and other telephoning conveniences. After you've connected, you can use your regular telephone to talk, or use other telephony applications for audio and video conferencing.

Setting Up a Modem

Windows 98 includes a modem wizard that assists you in setting up your modem. The modem wizard uses Plug and Play technology to make setting up a modem as easy as possible. If your modem is Plug and Play-compliant, it will respond to queries during setup and provide information that you would otherwise have to enter. Even if you don't own a Plug and Play device, Windows 98 can determine much about your modem and how it is connected to your computer.

You can initiate the setup of a modem in several different ways. All routes, though, lead to the same destination, the starting of the modem wizard.

- If you have a modem installed prior to setting up Windows 98, you will be prompted during setup to configure your modem using the modem wizard.

- If you add a modem after installing Windows 98, you can open the modem wizard by clicking either the Modems control panel or the Add New Hardware control panel.

- If you try to run an Internet or communications program, such as Internet Explorer or HyperTerminal, without first configuring your modem, the modem wizard will open.

Whichever path you take displays the Install New Modem dialog box, shown in Figure 10-1.

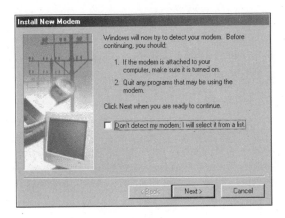

Figure 10-1.   *Install New Modem dialog box.*

Modem Wizard

The Install New Modem dialog box, which is the first step of the modem wizard, gives you the option of having Windows 98 try to detect your modem, or letting you pick your model from an extensive list. Your best bet is to let Windows 98 begin the configuration process on its own. If it doesn't detect your model, you can always search the list and select the closest match to your modem. The documentation that came with your modem might offer some alternate choices if your particular model is not detected or listed. Selecting a modem from the list is described in more detail after step 1 below.

TIP If you have an external modem, make sure it is turned on before you try to set it up.

To install and configure a modem using the modem wizard, follow these steps:

1. Click the Next button.

   Windows 98 begins by checking your communications ports to locate a modem. If you have an internal modem but you haven't set the communications port (COM1, COM2, COM3, or COM4) that you want the modem to use, you may need to do this. Usually, you do this by setting a jumper or DIP (dual-inline-package) switch on the modem circuit card. An external modem is connected by cable to a serial port that is already designated as COM1, COM2, COM3, or COM4.

WARNING COM1 and COM3 typically share the same interrupt request line (IRQ4) and COM2 and COM4 share IRQ3. If two devices are concurrently trying to use the same interrupt, you will experience significant problems. The most common conflict occurs when a serial mouse on COM1 and a modem on COM3 share an interrupt.

After a short time, the modem wizard will recognize the presence of your modem and ask you to verify the model, as you see in Figure 10-2. If the wizard fails to recognize your modem, it asks you to choose a model from its list of manufacturers and models, which is shown in Figure 10-3.

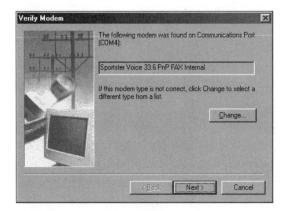

Figure 10-2. *Verify Modem dialog box.*

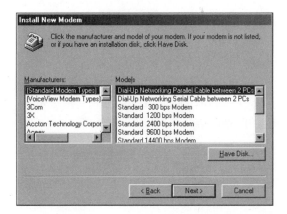

Figure 10-3. *List of modems by manufacturer and model.*

2. If the modem wizard recognized your modem correctly, click Next to finish the configuration process. If you need to select a modem or change the modem wizard's selection, click Change, select the modem manufacturer and model that you want to use, and then click OK or Next depending on how you got to the selection dialog box. If that brings you back to the Verify Modem dialog box, click Next again to go on to the final dialog box.

 IP If you cannot find a manufacturer and model that match your modem, try using the most generic driver by selecting the first manufacturer listed (Standard Modem Types) and the speed of your modem in the Models list box.

3. The next dialog box informs you of a successful installation. Click Finish and skip to step 6 or Next to complete this stage.

4. If you are using a voice modem (one that can answer the phone for you and handle voice mail), you are told that the Add New Hardware Wizard will search for a driver for a Wave Device For Voice Modem. Click Next. You can then choose Search For The Best Driver For Your Device (the recommended default) or Display A List Of All The Drivers. Accept the default and click Next. The wizard next asks where you want Windows to search (floppy disk, CD-ROM, Microsoft Windows Update, or a location on your hard or other disk). Make that choice and click Next. You are shown the driver or drivers found (if more than one, choose one). Click Next. If a driver is not found, you can click Back and try a different source, or if you do not want to install a driver at this time, click Next and then click Finish.

N OTE   One of your choices when searching for a new driver is Microsoft Windows Update. This will connect you over the Internet to a server at Microsoft on which the most recent drivers reside. Your computer is analyzed for its driver needs (an ActiveX program is downloaded to your computer to do this), and then your current drivers are compared to a database of the most recent drivers on the server. If a driver that you need is more recent in the database than the one you have installed, you will be asked if you want to download and install it.

---

5. If this is your first modem installation, you chose Next in step 3, and the Location Information dialog box opens and asks you questions that pertain to your dialing location. Select or enter the information that pertains to your most common dialing location. You can set up multiple locations in a moment if you choose. When you are done, click Next. You are returned to the Install New Modem dialog box. Click Finish, and you are back in the Modems Properties dialog box. Click Dialing Properties.

6. If you have set up a modem previously, you have already defined a dialing location and you chose Finish in step 3. You are returned to the Modems Properties dialog box. Click Dialing Properties.

Dialing Properties

You can open the Dialing Properties dialog box, shown in Figure 10-4, by clicking Telephony in Control Panel, or by clicking Dialing Properties in the Modems Properties dialog box. Dialing Properties is a utility used by Windows 98 to support several telecommunications programs, including Internet Explorer, discussed in the next chapter, and Dial-Up Networking and HyperTerminal, discussed later in this chapter.

The I Am Dialing From section displays some of the data you provided in the Location Information dialog box and lets you change the name of what Windows 98 calls your New Location. For example, you could highlight New Location and type **Office** to specifically label your office computer's location. You can add more locations by clicking the New button. You will see a message that a new location has been created. You can then change its name from New Location to whatever you want by typing a new name. To switch locations, select the one you want from the drop-down list.

The option for multiple locations was designed for the laptop or notebook user, so if you are using a desktop computer, you probably won't have much need to add multiple locations.

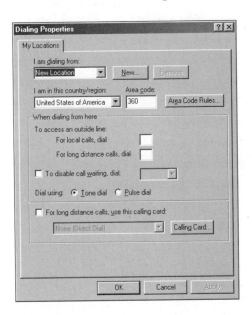

Figure 10-4.   *The Dialing Properties dialog box.*

IP If you are dialing from a location outside the United States, use the Area Code text box for the city code. Omit any leading zeros.

The When Dialing From Here section further defines the dialing parameters of a particular location. The first option provides the numbers used to access an outside line. The remaining two options in the section let you turn call waiting on or off with an appropriate local code, like *70, and select whether your phone is tone- or pulse-dialed.

Using a Calling Card

If you want to use a calling card to pay for your long distance calls, click that check box and then click Calling Card. The Calling Card dialog box opens, as you can see in Figure 10-5. Click the drop-down arrow at the top of the dialog box to open the list of services, and choose the one you want, as you can see here:

After you have selected a service, click Calling Card Sequence For Long Distance Calls. The Calling Card Sequence dialog box opens. Here you can specify up to six steps in the calling card sequence. In each step you can

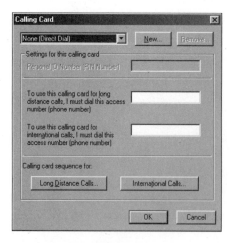

Figure 10-5. *Calling Card dialog box.*

specify one of eight actions explained in Table 10-1 and have the system wait for a tone or a specified period of time. Figure 10-6 shows an example of a possible sequence. The purpose of breaking out the series of steps is that you need to wait in between them; you can't just pour out a series of numbers. All of the actual numbers (except for the Specified Digits action) are specified elsewhere, either in the Calling Card dialog box, or when you are initiating the call.

When you are satisfied with your Calling Card Sequence, click OK to return to the Calling Card dialog box. If you specified that one of the steps was to enter your PIN, a dialog box for that purpose is now available. If you want, you can enter a second calling card by selecting a different service from the list and entering the necessary information. You can then choose which calling card you want to use in the Dialing Properties dialog box. If you want to enter a service that's not on the list, click New and then enter the appropriate information including the required phone numbers. When you are done, click OK twice to return to the Modems Properties dialog box. You are now ready to alter settings that directly affect your modem, if necessary.

Action	Description
Calling Card phone number	Dials the number you must dial to reach the calling card company to place your call
Destination Number (without area code)	Dials the number you want to dial, but without its area code
Destination Number (including area code)	Dials the number you want to dial with its area code
Destination Country/Region	Dials the country or city codes you want to dial
PIN	Dials your calling card number
Specified digits	Opens a dialog box allowing you to enter a series of numbers
Done	Completes the sequence
Do Tone Dialing Hereafter	Switches to tone dialing

Table 10-1.   *Calling Card Actions.*

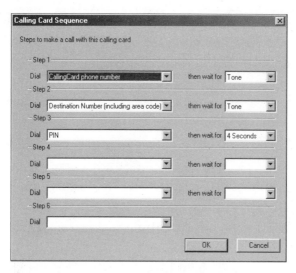

Figure 10-6.   *Calling Card Sequence dialog box.*

Setting Your Modem Properties

You can open the Modems Properties dialog box, which you see in Figure 10-7, by clicking the Modems control panel. The list box and its associated three buttons display the modem(s) you have installed and let you add additional units, remove those currently installed, or change their properties. If you click the Add button, the modem wizard, described earlier in this chapter, opens. Removing a modem uninstalls it from Windows 98. To change a modem's properties, first highlight the name of the modem, and then click the Properties button. A four-tab Properties dialog box for that particular modem displays, as shown in Figure 10-8.

General Tab

The Port drop-down list box lists the communications (or serial) ports that are available for use. Make sure that the port displayed is the port that is being used by the modem (either plugged into or selected by Plug and Play or by setting the jumpers or switches on your modem). If the ports are not the same, you will receive an error message from Windows indicating that it cannot find a modem on the listed COM port.

The Speaker Volume slider adjusts the volume of your dialing and other telecommunication sounds. With an internal modem, the sounds are sometimes the only way to monitor the status of a connection. (I keep my volume

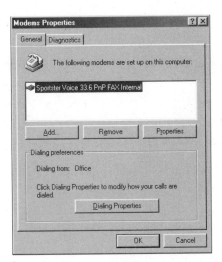

Figure 10-7. *Modems Properties dialog box.*

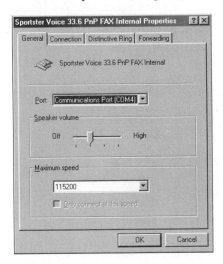

Figure 10-8. *Properties dialog box for a particular modem.*

louder so I can hear the connection being made and any error messages from the phone company.) External modems usually have a bank of LEDs (light-emitting diodes) that let you monitor the progress of your transmit-and-receive signals.

The Maximum Speed drop-down list box lets you choose the fastest data-transfer speed you want your modem to try. The numbers listed are in bits per second (bps) and are sometimes referred to as the baud rate of the modem.

When describing a newer modem's speed, the terms "baud rate" and "bps transfer rate" are not the same. Newer modems use various compression schemes to increase the actual number of bits that are transmitted per second. For example, a 28,800-baud (often abbreviated 28.8) modem, through compression, can transmit up to 115,200 bps. You should select the fastest listed speed that your modem supports. If you find that you are having transmission errors, decrease the speed to the next lower setting.

Modem speeds generally coincide with enhanced international standards that make telecommunication more reliable and faster. These standards can be quite confusing to keep track of because there is nothing in the standard number that relates to its corresponding modem speed. To make this even worse, the telecommunications standards-setting body changed its name in 1993 from CCITT (Comité Consultatif International Télégraphique et Téléphonique, or International Telegraph and Telephone Consultative Committee) to ITU-T (International Telecommunications Union). Modem standards and associated speeds are listed in Table 10-2.

CCITT/ITU-T Standard for dial-up, full-duplex modems	Speed (bps uncompressed)
V.21 (similar to Bell103)	300
V.22 (similar to Bell212A)	1,200
V.22 bis*	1,200 and 2,400
V.32	4,800 through 9,600
V.32 bis	4,800 through 14,400
V.34**	All speeds through 33,600
V.90***	All speeds through 56,000

* The term *bis* (French for the second) after the number indicates that the standard is a revision to a previously established standard.

** A number of 28.8 Kbps modems were manufactured prior to the V.34 standard being set. It is not wise to use these modems.

*** This standard was set as this was written and settles a battle between the Rockwell/Lucent K56Flex standard and the U.S. Robotics/3Com/TI x2 standard.

Table 10-2. *Modem standards.*

ARNING Before buying a 56 Kbps modem, make sure it conforms to the new V.90 standard. Also check with the organization you plan to connect with, such as an Internet service provider (ISP) or online service (MSN, AOL, or CompuServe), and make sure it is also using the new V.90 standard.

Compounding the confusion that surrounds modem nomenclature is that compression and error control standards are named with a similar format. For example, the U.S. Robotics Sportster Voice 33.6 PnP FAX modem, shown in the figures in this section on modems, has a V.34 transmission standard, V.42 and MNP2-4 error control standards, and V.42 bis and MNP5 data compression standards. Fortunately, newer standards are backward-compatible with older ones. A modem tries to establish a connection using its highest standards. If the transmission line or modem on the other end doesn't support those standards, the sending modem will try the next lower set of standards, unless you have selected the Only Connect At This Speed check box. This option forces a connection retry only at the specified speed.

Connection Tab

The Connection tab, shown in Figure 10-9, allows you to set the defaults that are used when Windows telecommunications programs try to make a connection with another computer. You can modify each connection to meet specific needs of the remote modem. The defaults in this tab establish a good overall baseline for most connections.

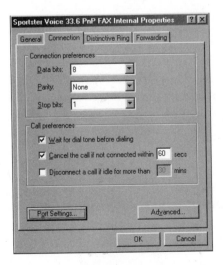

Figure 10-9. *Connection tab for a specific modem.*

The Connection Preferences section contains the three main parameters involved in making a connection: number of data bits, the type of parity used, and the number of stop bits. The most common configuration is 8-N-1, or 8 data bits, no parity, and 1 stop bit. This topic is explored in more detail in *HyperTerminal* later in this chapter.

The Call Preferences section further customizes the nature of your outgoing calls. The Windows default settings should work fine and need not be changed unless you have a specific reason.

The Port Settings button opens the Advanced Port Settings dialog box shown below. Most modern modems use a 16550-compatible UART (universal asynchronous receiver-transmitter—an integrated circuit chip), so you can adjust how full you want the buffer to be before you pause transmission. Generally you want to leave the default settings. This setting is hard to optimize. The higher the setting, the fewer the pauses during transmission, and therefore the faster the transmission, *unless* you overrun the buffer and then need to retransmit the block of information, which, of course, slows down the transmission.

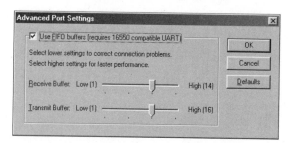

Clicking the Advanced button in the Connection tab displays the Advanced Connection Settings dialog box, which you see in Figure 10-10.

 WARNING If you are not having modem problems, you probably don't need to alter these settings. If you do change any of these settings, have your modem documentation available to verify your changes.

The Use Error Control section provides options that tell Windows 98 whether you want error control to be used for each connection, whether data compression is used, and, for cellular phone users, whether a cellular protocol is used.

Figure 10-10. *Advanced Connection Settings dialog box.*

The Use Flow Control section determines whether flow control is used and whether it is hardware- or software-controlled. Flow control determines the type of connection that is established between the telecommunications program and the modem. Check with your ISP or online service to determine whether flow control should be used, and if so, which type. Hardware control is generally preferable if the two modems that are communicating support it.

The Modulation Type drop-down list allows a choice between Standard and Non-Standard modulation. Only in a special, non-public connection, such as in an organization with unique equipment, would you want to change the modulation.

If you need to send any additional initialization data to your modem, you can type the data in the Extra Settings text box. Be aware that any change to the initialization string is made to all connections you attempt. Changes are best made to a specific connection within a telecommunications program, such as a dial-up network connection. The Append To Log check box, when checked, creates a Modemlog.txt file in your Windows directory that maintains an audit trail of connection data. This log comes in handy if you are having connection difficulties.

Other Tabs

Depending on your modem, you may have other tabs in your modem's Properties dialog box. The U.S. Robotics Sportster Voice PnP FAX modem shown in this chapter has Distinctive Ring and Forwarding tabs. You may have others. In the Distinctive Ring tab, you have a choice in assigning different rings to data, fax, or voice use. In the Forwarding tab, you can enter codes that activate and deactivate call forwarding that you have programmed into your phone.

Testing Your Modem

The Modems Properties dialog box contains a Diagnostics tab, which looks like Figure 10-11. If you click the port to which your modem is connected, and then click More Info, you will get a message that your computer is communicating with the modem and that it may take a few minutes. When this is done, if your modem is working correctly, your More Info dialog box will look something like Figure 10-12, providing port information and a series of responses from the modem to a list of commands. If your modem is not operating correctly, you will get a message to that effect or you will get "Error" in response to the first several commands (on some modems you may legitimately get "Error" in response to several of the later commands).

Installing Multiple Modems

Installing two or more modems is really no more difficult than installing one modem multiple times, except that you may need to install additional communications ports and juggle your IRQs to make sure that no two devices

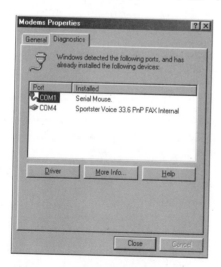

Figure 10-11. *Modems Properties Diagnostics tab.*

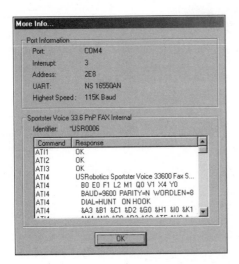

Figure 10-12. *Results of testing a modem.*

share one. A modem typically uses a serial communications port. Most computers contain four serial communications ports labeled COM1 through COM4. Often your mouse uses COM1, leaving COM2 through COM4 for modems. The problem comes from the fact that typically COM1 and COM3 share IRQ 4 and COM2 and COM4 share IRQ 3. That means that if you have a mouse on COM1 and your first modem on COM2, you still have two COM ports, but you have used all of the IRQs that are usually assigned to COM ports.

Looking at IRQ Usage

Since you can't use the IRQs usually assigned to COM ports, you must find another IRQ that is both available on your system and can be used with your modem. To look at how your system has distributed IRQs, use these steps:

1. Open the Start menu, choose Settings | Control Panel, and then click System.

2. Click the Device Manager tab, scroll down the list of devices until you see Ports (COM & LPT), and click the plus sign to see the details of the port assignments. Figure 10-13 shows what mine look like. Yours may be different.

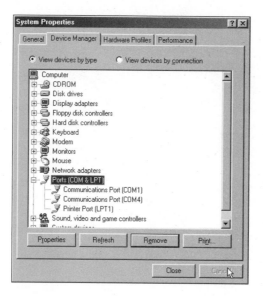

Figure 10-13. *Typical port usage.*

3. Double-click one of the COM ports, and click the Resources tab. Here you can see the IRQ (Interrupt Request) assignment, like this:

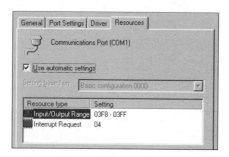

4. Close the Communications Port Properties dialog box, and click Print. In the Print dialog box, click System Summary, and then click OK. The report that you get has several sections, but one entitled IRQ Usage Summary lists how all your IRQs are used. Mine looks like this:

```
IRQ Usage Summary:
    00 - System timer
    01 - Standard 101/102-Key Keyboard
    02 - Programmable interrupt controller
    03 - Communications Port (COM4)
    04 - Communications Port (COM1)
```

```
05 - Sound Blaster 16 or AWE-32 or compatible
06 - Standard Floppy Disk Controller
07 - Printer Port (LPT1)
08 - System CMOS/real time clock
09 - Bt848A Video Capture Card
10 - NE2000 Compatible Network adapter
11 - S3 Trio64V+ Display adapter
13 - Numeric data processor
14 - Intel 82371SB PCI Bus Master Primary IDE Controller
15 - Intel 82371SB PCI Bus Master Secondary IDE Controller
```

You can see that the only unused IRQ on my system is 12. The next step is to look at your modem card and see what options you have. For this exercise I am using a pair of U.S. Robotics 28.8 Vi FAX Voicemail modems that can use IRQs 2, 3, 4, 5, 6, and 7. One of these modems is on COM4 using IRQ 3. I want to put the other modem on COM3, but I can't use IRQ 4 because my mouse on COM1 is using that. My only obvious choice is to move my sound board from IRQ 5 to 12 and use IRQ 5 for my second modem. In my case, I am doing most of my printing on a network printer, so I don't often use LPT1 and IRQ 7. Since using IRQ 7 would mean that I don't have to make any other changes, that is my choice.

Installing a COM Port

You'll notice in Figure 10-13 that I only have COM1 and COM4 installed on my computer, so the next task for me and probably for you is to install COM3 so I can then use it when I install the second modem. Use the following steps to install a COM port.

1. Open the Start menu, choose Settings | Control Panel, and click Add New Hardware. The Add New Hardware Wizard starts. Click Next twice to begin the search for new Plug and Play hardware.

2. The Plug and Play hardware search will not find another COM port, so click No, The Device Isn't In The List, and click Next.

3. In the next dialog box click No, I Want To Select The Hardware From A List, and click Next.

4. Scroll down the list, and select Ports (COM & LPT) like this:

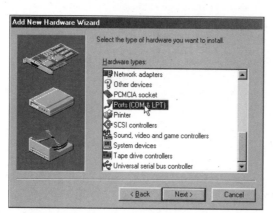

5. Click Next. In the dialog box that opens, Standard Port Types and Communications Port should already be selected. If not, select them, and then in any case, click Next.

6. The next dialog box, shown in Figure 10-14, says that Windows can install your hardware (what you selected in the previous dialog box) with the settings shown. It does not tell you which COM port was installed, although you can get a clue by the IRQ used. Click Next, then Finish, and finally Yes to restart your system. You can then check which COM port was installed.

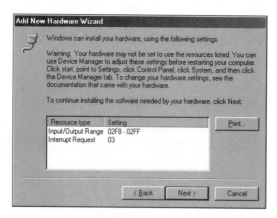

Figure 10-14. *Settings chosen by Windows for your new COM port.*

7. Reopen Control Panel, click System, and then the Device Manager tab. In the Device Manager, click the plus sign to the left of Ports to expand the list of that device. In my case, shown below, COM2 was installed, but I wanted COM3.

8. If, like me, you did not get the correct port, repeat steps 1 through 7. When you get back to the Device Manager list of ports, you should see the port you want if you didn't in step 7.

9. Double-click the new port you want to use, and then click the Resources tab of its Properties dialog box.

10. In the Setting Based On drop-down list, select Basic Configuration 5. (Clear the Use Automatic Settings check box if necessary.) Then click Interrupt Request and the Change Setting button. In the Edit Interrupt Request dialog box, change the Value to the one you need to use. In my case, I needed to change it to 7. Click OK. I picked a value that had already been assigned to my printer port, so I got an error message saying that the value I picked conflicts with another device. Since I don't use this printer port, I clicked Yes to go ahead. The Resources tab of the port's Properties dialog box continues to show this conflict, as you can see in Figure 10-15.

11. Click OK to close the Properties dialog box. You are told that you have made changes to your hardware settings and that you need to shut down your system and change your hardware to reflect the change in settings. What you have actually done is change the setting to reflect your hardware setup. Click Yes anyway to reboot your system and make sure that all changes take effect. You will have to restart your computer manually.

You should now have a second COM port and unused IRQ to use to install your second modem.

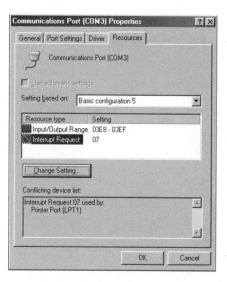

Figure 10-15. *Conflict with the Printer port clearly spelled out.*

Installing the Second Modem

Since you have already installed a modem, the following steps to install another are abbreviated.

1. In Control Panel, click Modems and then click Add. The Install New Modem dialog box opens.

2. Click Next. Your COM ports are queried for a modem. Two will be found, your current one and the new one. You can tell the new one by the COM port to which it is assigned. If necessary, correct the type of modem by clicking Change.

3. When you have the correct modem on the new COM port, click Next twice. You are returned to the Modems Properties dialog box, where you see your two modems, similar to Figure 10-16.

4. Click the Diagnostics tab, click the port that is assigned to your new modem, and click More Info. The results should show that your modem is operating and that it is on the port and IRQ that you wanted. In Figure 10-17, you can see that mine is on COM3 and IRQ 7.

In Chapter 11, you will see how to use both modems at the same time with Dial-Up Networking to connect to the Internet.

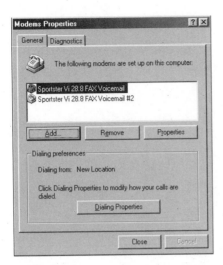

Figure 10-16. *Completed installation of a second modem.*

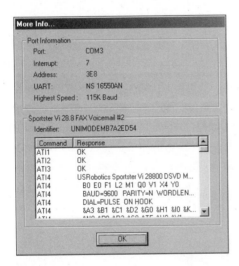

Figure 10-17. *New modem operating on the port and IRQ chosen.*

Using HyperTerminal

HyperTerminal, as the "Hyper" prefix implies, is a supercharging of Terminal, the program integral to Windows 3.x. More than just an upgraded Terminal with a few added whistles and bells, HyperTerminal takes full advantage of the Windows 98 32-bit architecture to provide more flexible and robust communication.

If you have been using programs designed for MS-DOS or Windows 3.x, you will appreciate the improved performance of your modems and better multitasking.

Getting Started

You access HyperTerminal by opening the Start menu, selecting Programs | Accessories | Communications, and then clicking HyperTerminal. The folder that opens contains the HyperTerminal icon as well as icons for several mail and online services and each connection that you have established. If you haven't created a connection yet, the window should look similar to Figure 10-18.

Setting Up a New Connection

Clicking the HyperTerminal icon allows you to create a new connection through the Connection Description dialog box, as shown in Figure 10-19. This dialog box allows you to establish the parameters you need to create a connection. HyperTerminal saves each connection as a file that can be displayed in a folder window like any other file, either as an icon or in a list.

You can make a connection to any computer connected with a modem to a phone line. That computer can be across town or around the world, and it can be to another PC like yours, to one that contains a BBS (or Bulletin Board Service), or to a computer that's part of an online service such as CompuServe, Prodigy, or a stock market quotation service.

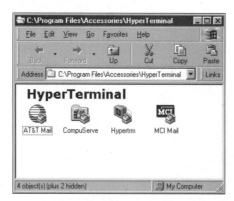

Figure 10-18. *HyperTerminal folder.*

Figure 10-19. *Connection Description dialog box.*

For the purposes of learning about HyperTerminal, it is not necessary to have a connection that actually links with another computer, although it will certainly help illustrate HyperTerminal's capabilities. You can find many public (and free) BBS phone numbers in computer magazines and newspapers that service your local area. Also, many online services have free trial memberships you can log on to through an 800 number. Using whatever information you have available, set up a new connection with the following instructions:

1. Type the name of the service or BBS to which you want to connect in the Name text box. This name appears with the icon you choose in the HyperTerminal folder and in the title bar of HyperTerminal whenever the connection is active.

2. HyperTerminal provides a number of icon choices including many from well-known online services. Use the horizontal scroll bar to find one you like, click it, and then choose OK. The Connect To dialog box opens.

3. Use the Country Code drop-down list box to establish the country you are calling, and type the area code of the number in the Area Code text box.

4. In the Phone Number text box, type the phone number of your connection without area code or special dialing prefixes, as shown in Figure 10-20.

Figure 10-20. *The Connect To dialog box.*

5. Select the device (modem) you want to use from the Connect Using drop-down list box. If your modem doesn't appear on the list, you should return to the previous sections on modem setup to ensure your modem is properly installed. Your completed dialog box should look similar to Figure 10-20 with the phone number of the service you are connecting to and your modem. Click OK when you are satisfied with your settings.

At this point the Connect dialog box appears, as you can see in Figure 10-21, and you are ready to dial. If you need to change the phone number or add any special dialing instructions, you can use the Modify and Dialing Properties buttons to access dialog boxes to make the changes. The Dialing Properties dialog box, which you saw in Figure 10-4 and was discussed earlier in this chapter, lets you change your location to another location you have set up and change the dialing parameters associated with that location. If you are dialing outside your area code, HyperTerminal will automatically

Figure 10-21. *HyperTerminal Connect dialog box.*

provide the modem with the number 1 and the dialing area code you typed in the Connect To dialog box. If you are dialing within your own area code and it's considered long distance, click the Dial As A Long Distance Call check box at the bottom of the Dialing Properties dialog box.

Before you actually dial and make a connection, spend a few more minutes reading the remainder of this section on HyperTerminal to see all that Hyper-Terminal can do for you. Cancel out of the dialog box(es) you may have on your screen until your screen looks like Figure 10-22. This is the standard HyperTerminal window. Notice the name of your connection in the title bar. You will be prompted to save the connection before you exit HyperTerminal.

Looking Around HyperTerminal
The HyperTerminal window contains the standard elements including a title bar, menu bar, toolbar, and status bar. In the center is the terminal window where the actual telecommunication displays. It will contain such things as the AT commands used to establish modem synchronization or the latest stock quotes from a retrieval service.

Menus
Four of the six menus—File, Edit, View, and Help—contain mainly standard Windows options. The remaining two menus—Call and Transfer—are unique to HyperTerminal and provide the gateways to the key HyperTerminal operating features.

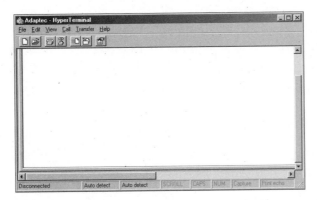

Figure 10-22.   *The HyperTerminal window.*

The options on the Call menu allow you to start, wait for, and end connections. The Call option opens the Connection dialog box you've already seen. The Wait For A Call option tells HyperTerminal it should prepare to receive an incoming call. The Disconnect option breaks the modem-to-modem link, or in more familiar telephone terms, simply hangs up.

In the Transfer menu, two options, Send File and Receive File, allow you to upload and download files from and to your computer. The Capture Text option creates a file of any incoming ASCII text. Send Text File transfers the text of an ASCII file to the remote computer. In this transfer, the file is not transferred; the text of the file appears on the remote computer's screen. Finally, Capture To Printer directly prints out any received ASCII text as it arrives on your computer.

Toolbar

The toolbar provides quick access to the most commonly used menu options. Shown below, starting from the left, are the New and Open buttons, the Call and Disconnect buttons, the Send and Receive File buttons, and the Properties button. All of these buttons perform the same functions as their menu counterparts.

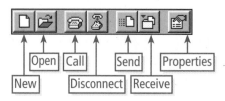

Status Bar

The status bar, located at the bottom of the window, provides useful information on many of HyperTerminal's features and settings. The status bar is divided into eight areas, as shown here:

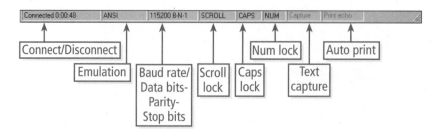

> **TIP** Maximize the HyperTerminal window to view all of the status bar areas.

The first area on the left tells you whether you are connected or disconnected. The first area also can extend the full length of the status bar and provide a short description of the menu option you are pointing at. The second area in the status bar can display the type of terminal you are emulating. Normally, HyperTerminal will emulate the type of terminal the other computer is expecting. The third area gives useful data on the parameters set up to connect with another computer. The first number shown is the transfer speed in bits per second. The second component is a three-part term that identifies the number of data bits (4 through 8), whether parity is used (none, odd, even, mark, or space), and the number of stop bits (1, 1.5, or 2). For example, you might see 9600 8-N-1 in this area. Eight data bits, with no parity, and one stop bit is the most common configuration. The next three areas let you know if your **SCROLLLOCK, CAPSLOCK,** and **NUMLOCK** keys are on or off. The final two areas, Capture and Print Echo, become activated when you are capturing text to a file or to your printer.

Terminal Window

The terminal window is where you see what is happening while you are connected. As more new data appears in the terminal window, previous data is still available, but it is scrolled up and out of the terminal window. You can access the unseen region by using the vertical scroll bar. When working with data in the terminal window, you can click the right mouse button anywhere in the window, and a context menu appears, as shown here:

The first six options are the same as the typical menu options. The Snap option lets you expand the size of the terminal window to its maximum height and width.

Calling Another Computer

Now that you've taken a tour of HyperTerminal, it's time to try it out. First you'll connect with a BBS and then with another PC.

Connecting to a BBS

Many bulletin board services are available, especially in the computer industry. Their primary function is to provide information and software updates that you can download. Although most of these companies also have Internet sites, sometimes it is faster to use a BBS if you know what you want. Try that now using the next series of steps.

1. If it is not already running, open the Start menu | Programs | Accessories | Communications options and click HyperTerminal.

2. Click the Hypertrm.exe icon to open the Connection Description dialog box, or if you are already in HyperTerminal, open the File menu and click New Connection.

3. Type a name for the connection you want to make (three examples are Adaptec, the SCSI adapter manufacturer; U.S. Robotics, the modem manufacturer; and Symantec, publishers of Norton AntiVirus and other products). Choose an icon (any icon is fine), and then click OK.

4. In the Connect To dialog box that appears, enter the area code and seven-digit phone number (as of this writing, Adaptec is 408-945-7727, USR is 847-982-5092, and Symantec is 541-484-6669), and verify that your modem appears in the Connect Using drop-down list box. Click OK.

5. You can now dial out in the Connect dialog box that displays, but you might want to check the Modify and Dialing Properties settings before you dial to make sure they are the way you want them. When you are ready, click OK to return to the Connect dialog box.

6. Click Dial to begin the calling sequence. You should hear a series of tones as the number is being dialed by the modem, the distinctive "whoosh" sound of a successful link, followed by silence. Often you will then see some sort of introductory message appearing in the terminal window. For example, Figure 10-23 shows the Symantec

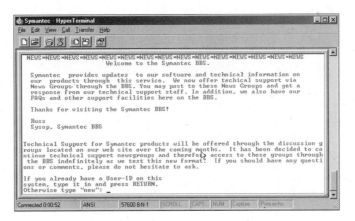

Figure 10-23. *Symantec's logon screen.*

opening message. If these actions don't occur, double-check your settings and try again. A second failed attempt probably means your modem isn't properly installed.

Most BBSs require a user identification number, or UserID, and password combination to log on. When you log on for the first time, the BBS generally prompts you for some personal data and then provides a temporary UserID and password for limited access. After you provide the requested information, you are presented with a menu structure that allows you to navigate the particular service. Adaptec's main menu is shown in Figure 10-24.

From the main menu, you are free to roam the offerings of the service. When you have completed your investigation of the service, sign off. You should see an acknowledgment of your leaving the service in the terminal window, and the status bar Connect area changes to Disconnected. If you remain connected, manually disconnect by clicking the Disconnect button (fourth from the left on the toolbar), or by opening the Call menu and choosing Disconnect.

Besides tapping into repositories of information as just demonstrated, the other key capability of HyperTerminal is the sending and receiving of files and text. The next few sections cover the steps involved in these procedures. You will create a new connection identifying another desktop computer and see how easy it is to exchange information.

Figure 10-24. *Adaptec's main menu.*

Preparing for PC-to-PC Communications

Begin by asking a friend who has a modem-equipped computer and tele-communications software to set aside a few minutes to do some telecommunication with you. The ideal situation is for each of you to have two phone lines, one to send data and one to talk through any problems. If you are limited to one phone line, it's not an insurmountable problem; you just have to communicate verbally what's going to happen before you begin the modem connection. Information that should be available to both parties includes the following:

- Each computer's phone number

- Each voice line phone number

- Protocol to be used (see Table 10-3)

- Modem speed (baud or bits per second)

- Number of data bits, parity mode, and number of stop bits (for example, 8-N-1)

- Path and name of the file(s) to be sent or received

The protocol used in data communications is a common set of instructions each modem uses to control the flow of transmitted and received data. HyperTerminal supports the seven protocols listed in Table 10-3.

Protocol	Description
Xmodem	Xmodem sends small blocks of data and uses a simple method of error correction. Xmodem is slower than most other protocols.
1K Xmodem	Derived from the Xmodem protocol, 1K Xmodem uses 1 KB data blocks in place of Xmodem's 128-byte data blocks.
Ymodem	Another name for 1K Xmodem.
Ymodem G	Derived from the Ymodem/1K Xmodem protocol, Ymodem G adds hardware error control. Modems that do not support hardware error control should use Ymodem.
Zmodem	A very fast and reliable protocol. The Zmodem protocol can send multiple files and automatically start file downloads (receiving) after the remote computer starts sending a file.
Zmodem with Crash Recovery	Essentially the Zmodem protocol with an added feature to recover file transfers that have been interrupted by system problems.
Kermit	A rather slow, though flexible, protocol generally used by mini-computers and mainframes. Use faster protocols when the remote computer has them available.

Table 10-3.   *Telecommunication protocols supported by HyperTerminal*

Sending Files

The first step in sending or receiving information is to make a connection. Use the following steps:

1. Create a new connection using the procedures previously covered.

2. In the Connect dialog box, click Dial to call the remote computer. After you hear the typical modem sounds, an acknowledgment of a successful connection appears in the status bar. You and the other computer can now send messages back and forth, as shown in Figure 10-25.

3. Click the Send button (fifth from the left), or open the Transfer menu and choose Send File to open the Send File dialog box shown here:

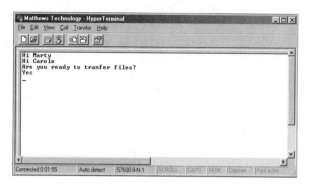

Figure 10-25. *Desktop-to-desktop computer communications.*

4. Supply the path and name of the file you want to send in the Filename text box, or use the Browse button to locate the file.

5. Choose a protocol for your transfer. Zmodem, the default, is generally your best choice unless the receiving party can't support it.

6. Click the Send button to start the transfer process. A dialog box that shows the progress of your file transfer is displayed, as in Figure 10-26.

When the file has been transferred, the progress dialog box closes, and you can disconnect by clicking the Disconnect button.

Receiving Files

If you are using HyperTerminal to answer an incoming call, you must first set it up as if you are going to make a call, but you don't make the call. Procedurally, it is almost identical to sending a file, as shown in these steps:

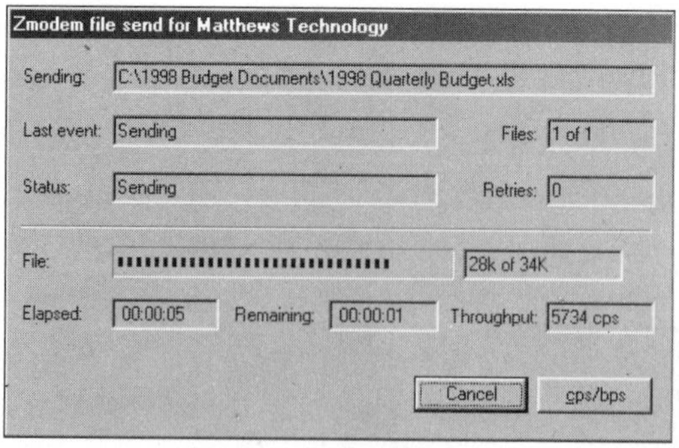

Figure 10-26. *A sample progress dialog box for sending a file.*

1. Use the same connection that you used to send a file, create a new one, or open another existing connection.

2. In the Connect dialog box, click Cancel to *not* place the call. The terminal window appears.

3. Open the Call menu and click Wait For A Call. "Waiting For Calls" appears in the status bar. When the sending party attempts to make a connection, you will hear the phone ring, see "Connecting" in the status bar, and finally see "Connected."

4. After you make a successful connection, type any communication you need with the sending party.

5. Click the Receive button (sixth from the left), or open the Transfer menu and choose Receive File to open the Receive File dialog box, shown here:

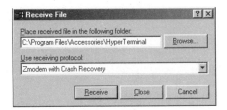

6. Supply the path where you want the received file to be located. Choose a protocol for your transfer. Timing is somewhat crucial here. The sending party should send the file just before you start the receive process. It's helpful to have two phone lines at this point.

7. When you think the sending party has initiated the transfer process, click the Receive button. A dialog box that shows the progress of your file transfer is displayed, as in Figure 10-27.

8. When the file has been completely transferred, the progress dialog box closes, and you can disconnect by clicking the Disconnect button.

Zmodem with Crash Recovery file receive for Matthews Technology

Receiving: 1998 QUARTERLY BUDGET.XLS

Storing as: C:\Program Files\Accessories\HyperTermi   Files: 1 of 1

Last event: Receiving   Retries:

Status: Receiving

File: ■■■■■■■■■■■■■■■■■■■■■■■■■■   25k of 34K

Elapsed: 00:00:05   Remaining: 00:00:01   Throughput: 5120 cps

Cancel   Skip file   cps/bps

Figure 10-27. *A sample progress dialog box for receiving files.*

Capturing Text

It is often handy to have a copy of online data that usually just flashes by on your screen. Using HyperTerminal's text capture feature, you can save the text that appears on your screen from a remote computer in ASCII (.txt) format. You can then open the file in a text editor (such as Notepad) and view, edit, or print it at your convenience. Follow the next few steps to see how easy this feature is to use.

Captured text is appended to the end of any existing .txt file. HyperTerminal has a default file called Capture.txt. If you don't want to use the default file, create one now using WordPad, and then capture some text.

1. From the Start menu, click Programs | Accessories | WordPad.

2. From the File menu, choose Save As, enter the path and filename you want to use, and choose Text Document in the Save As Type drop-down list box. Click Save, and then click Yes to confirm that you want to save the file as a text-only file and remove all formatting. Close WordPad.

3. Make your connection with the remote computer.

4. From the Transfer menu, click Capture Text. The Capture Text dialog box opens, as shown here:

5. If you do not want to use the default file, either type a path and filename in the File text box, or use the Browse button to locate the file you created in steps 1 and 2. Click Start.

You can control when to stop, pause, or resume capturing text once you start. The Capture Text option on the Transfer menu changes to produce a submenu when text capturing is activated, as shown here:

To see the results of text capturing, you should be able to click the Capture.txt icon in the HyperTerminal folder if you used the default file for capturing. If you used some other filename with a .txt extension, you can also click it to see it.

 OTE   The Capture.txt icon doesn't appear until the first capture is made.

Sending a Text File

Just as sending a file is the opposite of receiving a file, sending a text file is the reverse of capturing text to a file. You send a text (.txt) file from your computer, and the text appears on the receiving party's screen, as if it were being typed very fast. This is what appears on your own screen when you access an online service or BBS. The remote computer opens a file that contains the logon and introductory information and sends it to your computer. As with any HyperTerminal data transfer, you first must set up a connection with the remote computer. After you establish a connection, you can send a text file by following these steps:

1. Click the Send Text File option on the Transfer menu. The Send Text File dialog box appears, as you can see in Figure 10-28.

2. Locate the file you want to send, using the Look In drop-down list box to locate the correct folder. Click the file, and its name appears

in the File Name text box. Click Open. The text in the file will appear simultaneously in your terminal window and on the receiving party's screen.

3. When the end of the file appears in the terminal window, hang up by clicking the Disconnect button.

Printing

You can take three different routes to print data that comes to your computer:

- For a file that was transferred to your computer or a file that was created by capturing ASCII text, use an appropriate program such as WordPad or Notepad.

- For information that is in your terminal window, use the Print Setup and Print options on the File menu to format and print it.

- For ASCII text as it is being received, use the Capture to Printer option on the Transfer menu.

To format data that is in the terminal window, use the Page Setup option on the File menu to change the size, orientation, margins, and paper source of your printed information, as shown in Figure 10-29. As you change a setting, the sample document dynamically adjusts to show the effect of your action. The Printer button, located at the bottom of the dialog box, opens a secondary dialog box where you can change printers and adjust printer properties.

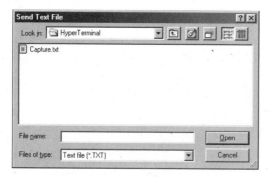

Figure 10-28. *Send Text File dialog box.*

If you know in advance that you want to print everything that will eventually appear in the terminal window, you can use the Capture to Printer option on the Transfer menu. This option is a toggle, meaning it will remain on or off until you click it again. A check mark appears to the left of the option when it is turned on. When this option is active, all data coming to your computer is sent to your printer as it arrives. You need to set up two things before this option can work properly. First, make sure your Page Setup specifications from the File menu are correct, and second, ensure your printer is turned on and is online.

Using Phone Dialer

The Phone Dialer applet is a feature of Windows 98 that combines the capabilities of a computer and a telephone. Although a phone dialer is nothing new, this applet has a number of advanced features (including conference calling, logging, speed dialing, and handling call waiting) that haven't been commonly available. To see how Phone Dialer can make your computer a complete communications center, click Phone Dialer located in Start menu, Programs | Accessories | Communications.

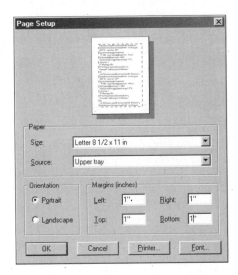

Figure 10-29. *Page Setup dialog box.*

Phone Dialer closely resembles the dialing face of many desktop telephones, as you can see in Figure 10-30. You can use Phone Dialer to dial a local, long distance, or international phone number in one of the following ways:

■ With Phone Dialer as the active window, type the number on your keyboard. The number appears in the Number To Dial drop-down list box, and you need only click Dial to initiate the call.

■ Open the Number To Dial drop-down list box, select a recently dialed number, and then click Dial.

■ Click the applicable letters or numerals on the alphanumeric keypad. The results of each mouse click appear in the Number To Dial text box. Click Dial to initiate the call.

■ Click a Speed Dial button. The number you assigned to a particular button appears in the Number To Dial text box, and then Phone Dialer initiates the call.

The Speed Dial buttons are set up by choosing Speed Dial from the Edit menu. The Edit Speed Dial dialog box opens, as shown in Figure 10-31. You can also double-click a blank button to open the Program Speed Dial dialog box, which limits editing to a single button and provides the same text boxes as the Edit Speed Dial dialog box for naming the button and assigning a number to be dialed.

Figure 10-30. *The Phone Dialer window.*

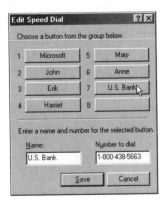

Figure 10-31. *The Edit Speed Dial dialog box.*

You can assign your most frequently used phone numbers to the Speed Dial buttons by simply clicking a button and typing in a name for the button and then the number to be dialed. Click Save after entering all the numbers you want to enter.

Menus

Three of the four Phone Dialer menus—File, Edit, and Help—contain mainly options with which you are familiar. The first option in the Tools menu, Connect Using, opens a dialog box of the same name, as shown here:

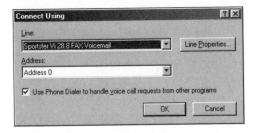

Windows 98 provides the capability to handle multiple connections that are voice and/or data lines. A listing of all the lines you have set up is provided by the Line drop-down list box. This listing corresponds to the number of devices you have installed. For the majority of users who have a single modem and one line, the default line and its associated address need not be changed. If you have more than one modem installed in your computer, you can choose on which line to make your call. Click the Line

Properties button to open your modem's Properties dialog box for the modem that is selected in the Line drop-down list box. This is the same dialog box that you use to change the properties of an installed modem.

The Dialing Properties option on the Tools menu opens the same Dialing Properties dialog box used in modem setup. The final option, Show Log, opens the Call Log window, which keeps a record of your incoming and outgoing calls from Phone Dialer. You can choose to log incoming, outgoing, both, or neither category of calls, using Options from the Log menu.

Finally, the Call Log dialog box gives you a dialing option; you can select a call in the log and choose Dial from the Log menu.

Though this chapter has covered a lot of material in the world of telecommunications, it has just scratched the surface of what Windows 98 is capable of handling. The next chapter, "Getting Connected and Using the Internet," explores how communications has merged with the Internet to become a pivotal focus of computing.

Using the Internet
with Internet Explorer and MSN

The *Internet* is a network of thousands of independent organizations (companies, universities, governmental units, other organizations, and individuals) linked by high-speed communications lines. Each organization owns one or more computers with associated communications equipment, and each decides what services and information it is going to offer on the Internet and how it will offer it. The Internet is also a collection of computer networks (a network of networks) that spans the globe for the purpose of sharing information and communicating. The Internet is, finally, a huge collection of information that is the sum of what is available from all the sources that are connected to it. This information includes a number of international libraries; encyclopedias; extensive databases of reference material for finance, law, literature, medicine, and science; and online access to many publications, journals, and newspapers.

With a connection through either your modem or your local area network (LAN) to the Internet, you get access to not only a phenomenal amount of information, but also many communications functions such as mail exchange, chatting with others, shopping, trading stock, and making travel reservations. You will see in Chapter 12 how you can use the Internet as a post office through which you can send and receive mail to transfer both messages and files. Equally important are the many specialized *newsgroups* where you can send and receive messages and files on a particular topic. You can also read and *download* (copy from the Internet to your computer) those messages and files placed in the newsgroup by others. Good examples of newsgroups are those that provide customer support for computer hardware and software. Finally you can establish your own or your company's presence on the Internet by building a Web site for others to visit.

> **N OTE**   The use of the word "modem" above and in most instances in this chapter refers to any direct connection to the Internet, including a satellite connection or the use of an analog or cable modem or an ISDN adapter.

In this chapter, you'll learn how to connect to the Internet and explore it with Internet Explorer. In addition, the chapter looks at online or information services, such as The Microsoft Network (MSN), which provide access to the Internet.

Setting Up a Connection to the Internet

Within Windows 98, at least four major applications relate to the Internet: Internet Explorer, Outlook Express, TV Viewer, and The Microsoft Network. All of these applications plus most third-party Internet applications use a common means to connect to the Internet. You can set up this connection, which can use either Dial-Up Networking or your LAN, using the Internet Connection Wizard or directly.

Using the Internet Connection Wizard

Installing an Internet connection with Windows 98 is easy; you simply click the Connect To The Internet icon on the desktop and answer the questions asked by the Internet Connection Wizard. See how with these steps:

1. Click the Connect To The Internet icon on your desktop. The Internet Connection Wizard opens with a welcome message. You are presented with three options for connecting, as you can see in Figure 11-1.

   ■ The first option assumes that you want to establish an account with an Internet service provider (ISP) and then to connect to that ISP.

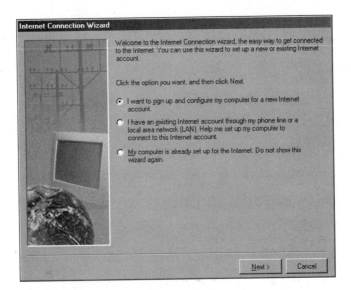

Figure 11-1. *Internet connection options.*

- The second option assumes that you have an account with an ISP and want to establish a connection to it.

- The third option assumes that you have both an account with an ISP and a connection from your computer to that ISP and all you need to do is tell Internet Explorer about this connection by selecting the third option. You can then close the Internet Connection Wizard and start using Internet Explorer. The first two options are fully described in the next two sections. There is nothing more to know about the third option.

2. Click the option that is correct for you, and then click Next.

> **NOTE** Windows 98 initially displays only the Connect To The Internet icon on the desktop and not the Internet Explorer icon. The first time you click the Connect To The Internet icon on the desktop, you get the Internet Connection Wizard. After you complete the wizard the Connect To The Internet icon will disappear from your desktop and the Internet Explorer icon will appear. If you want to restart the Internet Connection Wizard, you may do so by opening the Start menu and choosing Programs | Internet Explorer | Connection Wizard.

Establishing a New Account

If you choose to set up a new account with an ISP, you are told that the Internet Connection Wizard may need to access some programs on the Windows 98 CD-ROM.

 OTE All of the procedures in this chapter that deal with connecting to the Internet with an analog modem assume that you have already set up your modem as described in Chapter 10.

---

1. Place your Windows 98 CD-ROM in the appropriate drive, and click Next.

2. If you don't have a LAN connection to the Internet and haven't installed your modem, the Install New Modem wizard will start, which you saw in Chapter 10. Click Next and follow the instructions both on the screen and in Chapter 10 to install a modem. When the installation is complete, you will be asked if it is OK to restart your system. Click Yes, your system will restart, and the Internet Connection Wizard will resume. Click Next.

3. If you have more than one modem or have both a modem and a LAN connection, you are asked which you want to use to connect to the Internet. Choose one and click OK.

4. Enter your country (in the U.S. this will be entered for you), area or city code, and the first three digits of your phone number. When you are done, click Next. You are connected to the Microsoft Internet Referral Server over a toll-free number, and a list of ISPs for your location, language, and operating system will be downloaded to your computer. When the download is complete, the Microsoft Internet Referral Service screen lists ISPs that it found for you. Figure 11-2 shows what it found for me. Click More Info to learn more about the services of the ISPs you are interested in.

What to Look For in an ISP The criteria that you use in choosing an ISP somewhat depend on what you want to do on the Internet. For example, do you want to use the Internet primarily for mail, for browsing, or for a

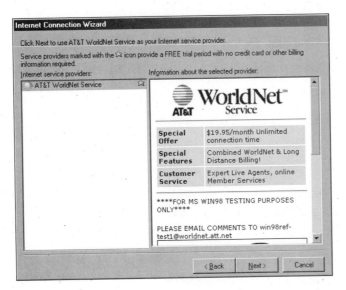

Figure 11-2. *You can get a list of ISPs for your location from the Microsoft Internet Referral Server.*

Web site? Here are some questions to ask yourself; your answers will help you determine the ISP to use. The importance you place on each question, though, depends on what you primarily want to do on the Internet.

- Is there a toll-free phone number to connect to the ISP?

- Are there toll-free phone numbers to connect to the ISP from the cities to which you frequently travel?

- Do they support the modem speed (28.8, 33.6, or 56 Kbps) you want to use without additional charge? (If 56 Kbps, is it the new V.90 standard or one of the older standards?)

- If you want to use ISDN, how much extra will that cost?

- Are there limits to your connect time (hours per month)?

- Is there a toll-free number to call for technical and customer support? Is it available 24 hours a day seven days a week, and do you get to talk to a person?

- Is there a "busy-free" policy that guarantees you will get connected within a short time?

- What reputation does the ISP have for both Internet availability and support?

- How many mail accounts can you get for the basic fee?

- How much mail can you leave on the server, and for how long?

- Are the newsgroups that you want to access available through the ISP?

- How much storage space is available on the server for a Web site at the basic price, and what does additional space cost?

- How much bandwidth (measured in terms of total number of bytes transmitted from your Web site per month) is allowed at the basic price, and what does additional bandwidth cost?

- Are the FrontPage server extensions available so you can make full use of FrontPage Express?

 OTE Many of the answers to these questions are not in the Microsoft Internet Referral Service listings. If that is the case for one or more questions that are important to you, most ISPs have a toll-free phone number that you can call for additional information.

Signing Up with an ISP In addition to the ISPs listed in the Microsoft Internet Referral Service, a number of local and regional ISPs provide excellent services, including local phone numbers. To find a local ISP, ask your friends who use the Internet which service they use and how they like it. Ask the same question at computer stores, and/or look in the yellow pages or the business section of a local newspaper. When you have selected several ISPs as candidates, call them and get the answers to the questions in *What to Look For in an ISP* that are important to you.

IP Even if you are reasonably sure you want to use one of the ISPs in the Microsoft list, it would be a good idea to call them and make sure that they give a positive answer to the questions that are important to you.

If you decide to use an ISP shown in the Microsoft Internet Referral Service, click the name of the service. Information about the selected provider will appear in the right pane. Click Next and you are presented with an online registration form, similar to the one shown in Figure 11-3 for AT&T. When

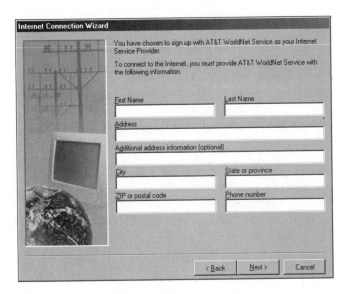

Figure 11-3. *Form used by AT&T to set up a new customer.*

you complete the registration form and click Next, the wizard dials a toll-free number for the service. The registration system for the ISP will often tell you if you have been successful and offer to set up your computer to use your selected ISP for browsing, e-mail, and newsgroups. If you choose to have your computer so configured, the configuration will complete in a second or two, after which you will immediately be able to connect to and use the Internet. If you choose to set up Internet Explorer and Outlook Express yourself, you will be given the information that you need to do that. You can use the instructions in *Connecting with an Existing Account* later in this chapter.

 OTE You will need to come up with a unique account, or user, name like the "someone" in someone@microsoft.com, as well as a password. Often your first choice for an account name will already be taken, and you will need to make a second or third choice. Also, you may have to follow rules to create a password. A common set of rules is that you must use six to ten characters that are a mixture of letters, numbers, and special characters (for example, apple#428).

NOTE   Most ISPs require that you give them a credit-card number and an expiration date as parts of the form that you fill out. In most instances, all of the form information is transmitted using a secure hypertext transfer protocol (HTTPS) that is probably a lot safer than using your credit card over the telephone.

If you decide to use an ISP that isn't shown in the Microsoft Internet Referral Service, you will have to acquire information over the telephone and then enter it as you follow the procedure described in *Connecting with an Existing Account,* later in this chapter. The information that you need to get is

- The **phone number** that you are to use for your modem speed to connect to the ISP.

- The **user name and password** to connect to the Internet.

- The **domain name** for your ISP, for example "microsoft.com."

- The type of **data link protocol** used by the ISP's Internet server, PPP (Point to Point Protocol) or SLIP (Serial Line Internet Protocol); PPP is used by most ISPs.

- Your **e-mail address,** for example "someone@microsoft.com."

- The **type and name of the mail server** you will use, POP3 (Post Office Protocol 3) or IMAP (Internet Message Access Protocol) and "microsoft.com" (the ISP's domain name and mail server name are often the same).

- Whether your ISP automatically assigns an **IP (Internet Protocol) address** each time you sign on; if not, you will need to get a permanent IP address, for example 111.22.33.444.

- Whether your ISP requires primary and secondary **DNS (Domain Name Service) server addresses** or thinks that it is a good idea for you to use them; if so, get the addresses assigned to your ISP.

- Whether your ISP requires a **terminal window** and/or a **sign-on script**; if so, have the ISP give you the appropriate sign-on script file.

- Whether your ISP allows **IP header compression.**

TIP Shop for an Internet provider as you would shop for anything else that has long-term importance for you—look in newspapers, probably the business section; ask people whose opinions you trust; call several providers and compare prices, services, and staying power.

Connecting with an Existing Account

If you have an existing account with an ISP and only need to configure your system to use it, you need the information described at the end of the previous section. You can then use these steps to get connected:

1. Choose the second option in the Internet Connection Wizard Setup Options shown in Figure 11-1, and click Next. A second set of options is displayed. Choose whether you are accessing the Internet using an ISP or LAN, or by using an online service. Click Next. The Set Up Your Internet Connection dialog box, shown in Figure 11-4, opens, giving you a choice between connecting using a phone line and a modem and connecting to your local area network (LAN).

2. If you choose to connect using a LAN, you will next be asked if your LAN uses a proxy server to connect to the Internet. (A *proxy server* is a means of protecting an intranet from Internet intrusion.)

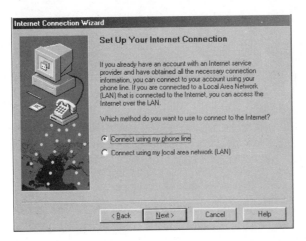

Figure 11-4. *With an existing account, you can connect using a LAN or a phone line.*

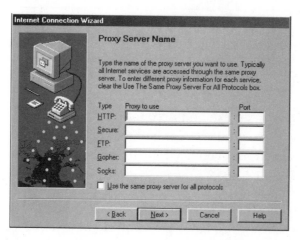

Figure 11-5.   *A proxy server on a LAN must be identified.*

If you choose Yes to using a proxy server, you will be asked to enter
the name of the proxy server, as shown in Figure 11-5. In most situations, you only need to enter a name for HTTP and then click Use
The Same Proxy Server For All Protocols (check with your network
administrator). You may also identify Internet and intranet addresses that do not use the proxy server.

3. If you choose to connect using a modem and haven't installed your
   modem, the Install New Modem wizard will start, which you saw in
   Chapter 10. Click Next and follow the instructions both on the
   screen and in Chapter 10 to install a modem. When the installation
   is complete, you will be asked if it is OK to restart your system.
   Click Yes; your system will restart, and the Internet Connection
   Wizard will resume. Click Next.

   If you have two or more modems or a modem and a LAN connection
   installed on your computer, you'll be asked which you want to use
   to connect to the Internet. Choose one and click Next. If you have an
   existing dial-up connection, you will be asked if you want to use
   that connection or create a new one. If you choose to use a new one,
   enter the phone number, dialing properties, user name, and password. Then you are asked if you need to enter any advanced settings
   (most people do not). The advanced settings allow you to

- Use SLIP in place of PPP

- Log on manually in place of automatically or with a script

- Log on using a script file in place of logging on automatically or manually

- Use a fixed IP address in place of having your ISP assign you one each time you log on to the Internet

- Set the primary and secondary, or alternate, DNS server in place of having your ISP set this each time you log on to the Internet

If you need to make any of the advanced settings, click Yes, and then work your way through them, entering the necessary changes and clicking Next. Independent of whether you go into the advanced settings, you will be asked to enter a name for your dial-up connection. Do so, and click Next.

4. For both LAN and dial-up connections, you will be asked if you want to set up an Internet mail account. If you have an account set up with an ISP, click Yes to set it up in Windows 98, and click Next. If you already have an Internet mail account set up in Windows 98, you will be asked if you want to use that or create a new one. If you create a new account, you will have to enter the name to display in the From field of your outgoing messages, your e-mail address, the type of incoming mail server you are using, and the name of both the incoming and outgoing mail servers (often these are the same). You can then choose to log on using a standard account name and password, or, if your ISP requires it, log on using SPA (Secure Password Authentication), as shown in Figure 11-6. Finally you are asked to enter a friendly name for your Internet mail account.

5. Next you can set up an Internet news account where you can read and contribute to newsgroups. If you want to set one up, click Yes and then Next. If you already have a news account set up in Windows 98, you can use that, or you can create a new one. If you create a new account, you will need to enter a name to display on your outgoing messages, your e-mail address, and the name of your news server (often this is your ISP). If your news server requires you to log

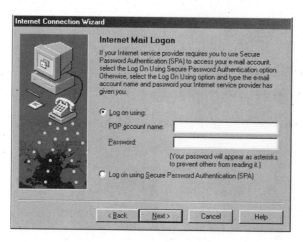

Figure 11-6. *Setting up an account name and password for Internet mail.*

on, click the appropriate check box, and then enter your account name and password or choose to log on using SPA. Finally enter a friendly name for your news account.

6. You are then asked if you want to set up an Internet directory service, or "white pages." If you want to set up an LDAP (Lightweight Directory Access Protocol) account, click Yes, and then click Next. You can choose to set up a new directory service or modify one of the services that are already set up in Windows 98. If you choose to set up a new service, you must enter the name of an LDAP server and whether that server requires you to log on. If you need to log on, enter your account name and password or choose to log on using SPA. If you want, you can have your e-mail program automatically check the addresses of your e-mail recipients against your directory service before sending your mail by checking Yes to that question. However, this verification will significantly slow down the sending of e-mail.

If you want to modify an existing directory service, click that option and select the service you want to use, as shown in Figure 11-7. You can then accept or change the settings for that service. If you change the settings, it is the same as setting up a new service. If you accept the settings, you are done setting up your Internet account.

7. When you are told you have completed setting up your Internet account, click Finish.

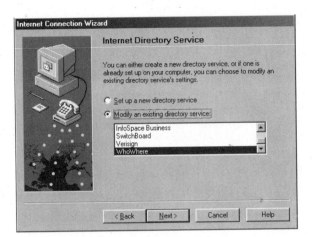

Figure 11-7.   *Selecting an Internet directory service or "white pages."*

Using an Existing Connection

If you installed Windows 98 over Windows 95, it is possible that you already have an Internet connection set up on your computer. In that case, you want to select the third option in the Internet Connection Wizard Setup Options dialog box, which you saw in Figure 11-1. If you do that and click Next and then click Finish, you are done. Internet Explorer, Outlook Express, and other Internet applications will use your existing connection.

Connecting Using ISDN

ISDN, which stands for Integrated Services Digital Network, provides a fast, all-digital means of communicating over existing phone lines. (Normal forms of telephonic data communications use an analog signal over the phone lines themselves and convert that signal to a digital one on either end using a modem.) Because ISDN is all digital, it does not use modems, but it does need an ISDN adapter to provide a hardware interface between the telephone line and the computer. On a single standard phone line (a single pair of wires), you can get three ISDN channels: two B channels and one D channel. The two B channels can be used for voice or data, and each channel can handle data up to 64 Kbps. The D channel is used only for control information and is not available for voice or data. With Multilink Channel Aggregation and Multilink PPP, the two B channels can be linked together to provide data transmission of up to 128 Kbps. With some ISDN adapters, you can handle both voice and data at the same time, automatically switching data during its transmission from two channels and 128 Kbps to one channel and 64 Kbps so the other channel can be used for voice or fax.

 NOTE Setting up Multilink Channel Aggregation to combine the two ISDN B channels is the same as setting up Multilink to combine two regular modems, as described in Chapter 10.

Windows 98 has an ISDN Configuration Wizard to assist you in setting up an ISDN link. You start the ISDN Configuration Wizard by opening the Start menu, choosing Programs | Accessories | Communications, and clicking ISDN Configuration Wizard. The wizard will open and lead you through the necessary steps. When you are done, you can treat each ISDN channel as a data connection for the sake of connecting to the Internet, and by using Multilink, you can combine the two channels to establish a 128 Kbps Internet link.

Setting Up an Internet Connection Directly

Using the Internet Connection Wizard is by far the easiest way to connect to the Internet and the method recommended by this book. You can, though, connect to the Internet by directly entering the necessary settings into the appropriate dialog boxes. To do this, besides a modem and a phone line, you need the information from your ISP that was listed in *Signing Up with an ISP* earlier in this chapter, unless you are using a LAN for your Internet connection.

 NOTE The one reason you might want to directly set up an Internet connection is to learn what is involved in one so that you can better diagnose and fix problems with your connection in the future.

Setting up an Internet account directly is one of the more complex chores in Windows 98, but you may have already done some of it. Assuming that your modem is already set up and running, you have three tasks to perform:

1. Set up Dial-Up Networking.

2. Set up TCP/IP networking protocol.

3. Set up a Dial-Up Networking connection.

Setting Up Dial-Up Networking

Dial-Up Networking allows you to remotely access a network using a modem and phone lines or other communications links. The network being accessed can be a LAN or the Internet. In Chapter 16, you'll look at using Dial-Up Networking with a LAN. Here you'll see how to set up Dial-Up Networking to connect to the Internet.

To use Dial-Up Networking to connect to the Internet, you need to set up your computer with a dial-up connection to your ISP's computer. You set up Dial-Up Networking through the Dial-Up Networking folder in My Computer or Windows Explorer. Do that now with these instructions:

1. Open My Computer, and click the Dial-Up Networking folder. If you have not set up a Dial-Up Networking connection before, the Make New Connection wizard will open. Otherwise, click Make New Connection, and the wizard will open, as shown in Figure 11-8.

2. Type in a name for the computer you are calling; make it a name that is meaningful to you.

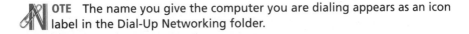

NOTE The name you give the computer you are dialing appears as an icon label in the Dial-Up Networking folder.

Figure 11-8. *Setting up a new Dial-Up Networking connection.*

3. If your modem is not displayed in the Select A Device drop-down list, you need to install your modem in Windows 98. See Chapter 10 on how to do this. The Configure button allows you to make settings pertaining to your modem. These settings are also described in Chapter 10. If you have two or more modems, choose one to use for your dial-up connection. (You'll see how to use multiple modems at the same time later in this chapter.)

4. Click Next, and enter the area code and telephone number of the computer you want to call.

5. Click Next again. You'll be told that you have successfully created a new connection. Click Finish to complete the process. The Dial-Up Networking folder will reappear with an icon for your new connection, like this.

Setting Up TCP/IP Networking Protocol

TCP/IP (Transmission Control Protocol/Internet Protocol) is the set of rules two computers use to exchange information with each other over the Internet or an intranet. Your computer must use that protocol to connect to the Internet. If you are connected to a LAN, you may already be using TCP/IP, or you could be using either NetBEUI or IPX/SPX for your networking protocol. Even if you are using TCP/IP on your LAN, it is probably not bound to your modem, or dial-up adapter. Given that you do not already have TCP/IP installed for Dial-Up Networking, the following steps will guide you through that setup. (You must have Dial-Up Networking installed first—you should see a folder by that name in My Computer.)

1. Open the Start menu, choose Settings | Control Panel, and click the Network control panel. The Network dialog box should open as you

see in Figure 11-9. At the minimum, you should have a dial-up adapter showing in the list of components. Creating the Dial-Up Networking connection placed the dial-up adapter in the list. (If you are not connected to a network, you will not see the other components shown in Figure 11-9.)

 IP If you don't see a dial-up adapter in your list of network components, restart your computer and you will see it.

2. Click Add | Protocol | Add. This will open the Select Network Protocol dialog box.

3. Click Microsoft in the left list box, click TCP/IP in the right list box, and click OK. This brings you back to the Network dialog box, where you should see TCP/IP bound to both Dial-Up Adapter and to your LAN adapter if you have one.

4. If you are going to connect to the Internet through Dial-Up Networking and not your LAN, you probably do not want TCP/IP bound to

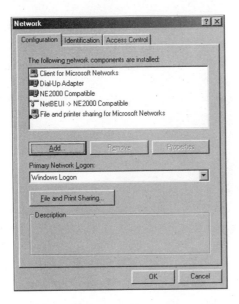

Figure 11-9. *Dial-up adapter set up as a network component.*

your LAN adapter (unless you are using the TCP/IP protocol on your LAN), and you need to make doubly sure it is bound to your dial-up adapter. Use these substeps for that purpose:

a) In the Network dialog box, click the protocol line showing TCP/IP being bound to your LAN adapter, and then click Remove, like this:

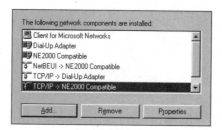

b) Click Dial-Up Adapter (not the TCP/IP protocol) in the Network dialog box, and then click Properties. The Dial-Up Adapter Properties dialog box should open.

c) Click the Bindings tab, and you should see a check mark next to TCP/IP, as shown below. If not, click the check box. There may be other protocols bound to your dial-up adapter if you use Dial-Up Networking for connecting to your LAN or to another Windows 98 computer, but for the Internet all you care about is that TCP/IP is bound to it. Click OK. You'll be returned to the Network dialog box.

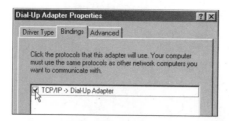

5. Click the TCP/IP protocol bound to your dial-up adapter and then click Properties. You will get a message telling you that it is advisable

to change the TCP/IP properties for each individual connection and that you do that from the Dial-Up Networking folder. Click OK. The TCP/IP Properties dialog box will open. Click OK again to close it.

6. Click OK to close the Network dialog box and select Yes in answer to the question "Do you want to restart your computer now?"

Setting Up a Dial-Up Networking Connection

The final task is to set up the properties for your new Internet connection. Use the following steps for that purpose:

1. Reopen My Computer and then the Dial-Up Networking folder. Right-click the Internet connection that you created above, and choose Properties from the context menu that appears. The connection's properties dialog box will open, as shown in Figure 11-10. The settings should be as you entered above.

2. Click the Configure button to check your modem settings. The settings should be as you set them in Chapter 10. If your provider said that you needed to use a terminal window to log on, click the Options

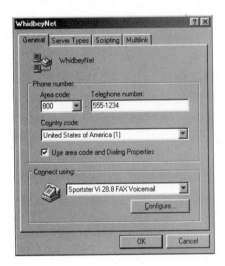

Figure 11-10. *A sample Internet connection properties dialog box.*

tab, and click Bring Up Terminal Window After Dialing, as shown
next. Then click OK to close the modem's Properties dialog box.

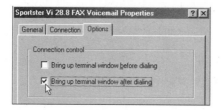

3. Click the Server Types tab. The settings should be as shown in Figure 11-11, except that the Type of Dial-Up Server should be as your ISP specified (normally PPP).

4. Click TCP/IP Settings. This opens the TCP/IP Settings dialog box. The default TCP/IP Settings dialog box looks like Figure 11-12. If your provider gave you your own IP address, click Specify An IP Address, and enter that address, typing a period between each number segment. In most cases, the server automatically assigns the IP address.

5. If your ISP requires or recommends that you use a primary and secondary DNS address, click Specify Name Server Addresses, and enter your provider's addresses.

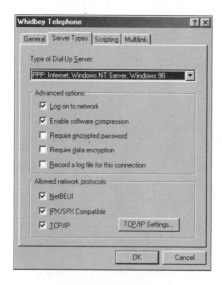

Figure 11-11. *Server Types tab of the dial-up connection's properties dialog box.*

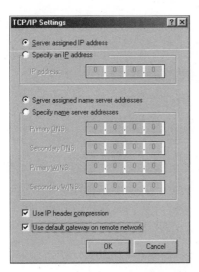

Figure 11-12. *Dial-up connection's TCP/IP settings.*

6. If your ISP cannot handle IP header compression, click Use IP
   Header Compression to turn it off. Use Default Gateway On Remote
   Network should be turned on.

 IP   Using IP header compression can cause your Internet connection not to
work even if you get connected.

---

7. When your TCP/IP Settings dialog box is the way you want it, click
   OK to return to the Server Types tab of your dial-up connection's
   properties dialog box.

   The default TCP/IP Settings dialog box works with the majority of ISPs.

8. If your ISP indicated that you need to use a script file to log on to
   the Internet, click the Scripting tab and enter or browse for the path
   and filename of the file. If the ISP and/or the script require that a
   terminal screen be open on your computer, click Start Terminal
   Screen Minimized.

9. If you want to use more than one modem or other device in a
   Multilink-PPP connection, click the Multilink tab, click Use Additional Devices, and then click Add. In the Edit Extra Device dialog
   box, open the drop-down list of device names and choose the device

you want to use. Then enter the phone number you want to use to access your ISP, like this:

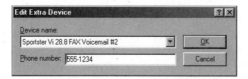

10. Click OK to close the Edit Extra Device dialog box. The additional device will appear in the list on the Multilink tab. You can add as many devices as you have, and you can remove and edit the devices on the list.

11. When you are done with the settings that you want to make in the dial-up connection's properties dialog box, click OK.

Trying Out Your Internet Connection

Try out your new dial-up Internet connection with these steps:

1. In the Dial-Up Networking window, click the icon for your new connection. The Connect To dialog box should appear with your user name and the provider's phone number filled in, as you can see in Figure 11-13. Type your password, and if you don't want to type it each time, click Save Password. Then click Connect.

Figure 11-13. *Starting a connection to the Internet.*

2. You should hear some sounds from your modem and see a Connecting dialog box appear. If you specified a terminal window to open, one will. Either your script will run or you will see a request to enter your user ID, password, and type **PPP.** Click Continue or press 7, and the terminal window will disappear. In any case, the Connection Established message box will appear, as shown in Figure 11-14. You should also see the dial-up connection icon in the taskbar next to the clock.

If you have file and printer sharing set up for your LAN, it will automatically be set up for Dial-Up Networking. As a result, you will get a message, shown below, that says you should turn it off for access to the Internet. Click Yes to do that. You will also need to restart your computer.

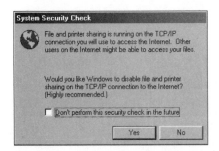

Figure 11-14. *Proof that you have established a connection.*

ARNING If you leave file and printer sharing enabled for your LAN, it will automatically be set up for your dial-up networking. With it, there is a slight chance that someone could get into your computer while you are connected to the Internet. Since there is no reason to bind this service to TCP/IP if you are using it only for the Internet, it is best not to have it available for that protocol.

If you set up two or more modems with multilink PPP, you should hear the additional modems dial and go through the connection process. When the connection is established, you will receive a message to that effect.

Now that you are connected, you can use any Windows-based Internet application, such as Internet Explorer or Outlook Express, to communicate across town or around the globe.

Using Internet Explorer

In Chapter 1, you had a brief introduction to Internet Explorer. In this chapter, you'll look at it in more detail and see how to get the most out of it. Begin by clicking the Internet Explorer icon (either on your desktop or on the Quick Launch toolbar) to start it. If you are still connected to the Internet from the previous procedure, Internet Explorer will open without more dialog boxes. If you are not connected to the Internet, Internet Explorer will open the Dial-Up Connection dialog box, shown below, and make that connection before opening itself, as shown in Figure 11-15.

Figure 11-15. *Internet Explorer displaying the Microsoft home page.*

Exploring the Internet

With Internet Explorer open, you can find what you want on the Internet in many ways. Among them are the following:

- Type an Internet address or URL (Uniform Resource Locator) in the Address toolbar, or select a site you previously typed from its drop-down list.

- Click a pre-established link on the Links toolbar to open the Web site pointed to by the link.

- Click a link on a Web page to open the Web site pointed to by the link.

- Use Search to open one of the Internet search engines to search for a particular Web site.

- Use the Open dialog box to type, select, or browse to an Internet address.

- Return to a Web page you visited during the current session by using the Back and Forward buttons on the Standard toolbar or their drop-down lists.

■ Return to a Web site you previously visited and stored in your Favorites folder by clicking the icon of the site in the folder.

■ Return to a Web site you previously visited by opening your History folder and selecting the site.

Entering a URL for a Web Site

The most obvious way to get to a Web site is through its address or URL, for example http://www.microsoft.com. Although you can type this entire address in the Address toolbar box as shown below, there are several ways of simplifying the process:

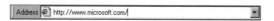

■ You don't have to type the "http://" and often you don't have to type the "www." or the ".com" to visit a Web site. You can just type **microsoft** to get the Microsoft site.

■ If you have previously entered a URL, you only need to type enough characters to identify a unique URL. Depending on what you have recently entered, this could even be just one character, as you can see here (the shaded portion was automatically added by Internet Explorer):

■ You can see recent Web sites you have typed in the Address toolbar by clicking the arrow on the right of the Address toolbar. This will open a list of your recent sites, like this:

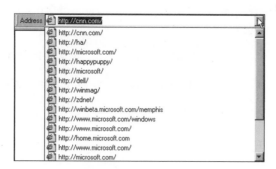

The first two methods just described are part of the Address toolbar's AutoComplete feature. It uses your history of recent site visits to predict the site you want to open. It also adds prefixes and suffixes and identifies syntax errors such as putting only one slash after http:. When a portion of a URL is automatically filled in for you, AutoComplete gives you a set of options to manipulate the resulting URL, as follows (these options do not work until *after* AutoComplete has filled in what it thinks you want for a URL):

- Press **UP** or **DOWN ARROW** to have AutoComplete fill in other recently visited sites in your history list that begin with the characters you typed.

- Right-click the automatically filled-in portion, select Completions from the context menu, and get a list of the URLs that you have recently visited that start with the characters you have typed. An example of this is shown in Figure 11-16.

- Press **CTRL-ENTER** to have AutoComplete add the prefix http:// www. and the suffix .com, so if you type **cnn** and press **CTRL-ENTER,** AutoComplete will change it to http://www.cnn.com.

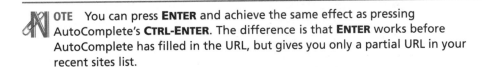 OTE   You can press **ENTER** and achieve the same effect as pressing AutoComplete's **CTRL-ENTER**. The difference is that **ENTER** works before AutoComplete has filled in the URL, but gives you only a partial URL in your recent sites list.

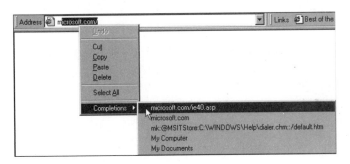

Figure 11-16. *Selecting options for a URL.*

- Press **CTRL-RIGHT ARROW** or **CTRL-LEFT ARROW** to move to the next separator character (// / . , ? +) in the URL being typed. (You do not have to be in a URL filled in by AutoComplete.)

Following a Link to a Web Site

Internet Explorer comes with a Links toolbar that is all but buried in the default Internet Explorer window where you only see the word "Links" to the right of the Address toolbar. You must drag the Links toolbar to the left to see its contents, which, in the Internet Explorer window, looks like this:

You can reduce, expand, and rearrange the default set of links on the Links toolbar. Each link on the toolbar is an Internet shortcut, a shortcut to a Web page. If you right-click the Links toolbar, you get the context menu shown below. This allows you to open, print, edit (with FrontPage Express), and subscribe (see *Using Webcasting* later in this chapter) to the Web page pointed to by the selected link.

The Links toolbar context menu also allows you to

- Cut and copy the selected link to the Clipboard

- Delete the selected link and place it in the Recycle Bin

- Open the Properties dialog box for the selected link

- Send the selected link to a floppy drive, the desktop, a mail recipient, My Briefcase, the My Documents folder, or other locations depending on what applications you have installed

You can add a link to the Links toolbar by dragging an Internet shortcut from any other source, such as the Address toolbar. Do this by pointing at the Internet Explorer icon in the Address toolbar and dragging it to the place you want it in the Links toolbar. In a similar manner, you can rear-range the Links toolbar by dragging an existing link to a different position on the toolbar, like this:

With these techniques, you can customize the Links toolbar so that it be-comes the tool you use for your most frequently visited sites.

 IP You can also access the links shortcuts on the Links toolbar in Windows Explorer by opening the \Windows\Favorites\Links\ folder.

Searching for a Web Site

Often you do not know the specific Web site that you want, but rather you have a subject for which you want to find a Web site. This is the purpose of the Search button on the Standard toolbar. When you click the Search button, the Search bar opens, as you can see on the left in Figure 11-17. As a default, the Search bar displays a search engine Provider-Of-The-Day, which is Yahoo in Figure 11-17. You can select another search engine by clicking the Choose A Search Engine link at the top of the Search bar. Each search engine provider allows you to enter a word or phrase for which you want a list of related Web sites. Each provider also has a list of categories that you can browse to find the specific topic on which to search. If the Provicer-Of-The-Day is not sufficient, clicking Choose A Search Engine opens a page in the right pane with many more search engine providers, some in specialized areas, as shown in Figure 11-18. Using the Search bar to do a search provides a big benefit over searching using a full Web page be-cause the Search bar keeps the search results in front of you while you are looking at Web pages in the browser area. This means that you can quickly get back to the search results no matter how many pages deep you are in a Web site.

Figure 11-17.   *Search bar in the left pane of the Internet Explorer window.*

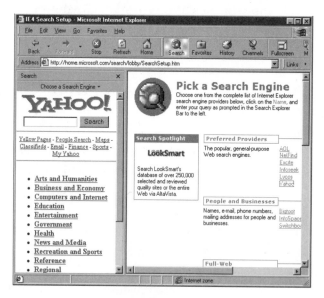

Figure 11-18.   *Microsoft's Search Web site.*

> **TIP** It is worthwhile to search using several of the search engines because they often produce different results.

Look at an example of a search and see how it proceeds. In this case, search for information on Windows 98.

1. Click the Search button on the Standard toolbar. The Search bar will open.

2. Type **Windows 98** in the search field, and click the button that carries out the search (it is named differently by the various providers). Click Yes to continue when told that you are about to send information over the Internet. A list of sites will appear in the Search bar.

3. Click one of the sites in the Search bar, and the site will open in the right pane of Internet Explorer, as you can see in Figure 11-19.

4. Scroll to the bottom of the Search bar and, if there are more sites than can fit in a single bar, you will be able to display the next set of sites.

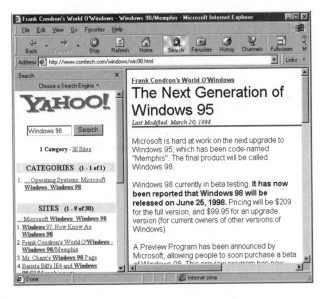

Figure 11-19. *Displaying a Web site found in a search.*

IP   If you want to search on an exact phrase, place double quotation marks
("") around the phrase. If you want just a subset of the sites that contain the
exact phrase, add a word that describes the subset outside the quotation
marks. For example, to find books that deal with Windows 98, enter
"Windows 98" +books. If you want to find all the sites except those that involve a subset, add a word that describes the subset preceded by a hyphen (-).
For example, to find Windows 98 sites that do not involve books, enter
"Windows 98" -books.

Returning to a Web Site

After you have found an interesting site, you probably will want to return
to it. Internet Explorer provides several ways to do that, including

- History bar that automatically captures all of the sites that you visit.

- Favorites bar and menu where you can add sites that are of particular interest to you.

- The drop-down lists available from the File menu and the Back and
  Forward buttons, which identify the last several pages you have visited
  during the current session (since you last started Internet Explorer).

History Bar   The History bar, which you open by clicking the History button on the Standard toolbar, groups the pages you visit first by Web site,
then by days of the current week, and finally by weeks, as shown in Figure
11-20. When the History bar is open, you can return to a given page by
clicking the week or day of the week in which you previously visited the
page, clicking the parent site, and finally clicking the page. The History
bar is a good source of recent pages when you can still remember the related day and site, but if you visit many pages over a short period of time,
it may be difficult to find the page you want.

Favorites Bar   The Favorites bar, shown in Figure 11-21, stores the Web
sites that you place there (the same sites that are on the Favorites menu).
You can place a Web site on the Favorites bar and menu in several ways.
For example, if a Web site you want to add to your Favorites bar is open in
the browser, you can drag the URL from the Address toolbar to either the
Favorites bar or the Favorites menu. You can right-click the Web site and
choose Add To Favorites from the context menu, or you can choose Add To
Favorites from the Favorites menu. When you drag a URL to the Favorites

bar or menu, you have the added benefit of being able to position it where you want on the list. When you drag a URL to the Favorites menu, the menu automatically opens, allowing you to position it, as you can see in Figure 11-22.

Figure 11-20.   *Using the History bar to return to a Web page.*

Figure 11-21.   *The Favorites bar lets you return to a Web page you have selected.*

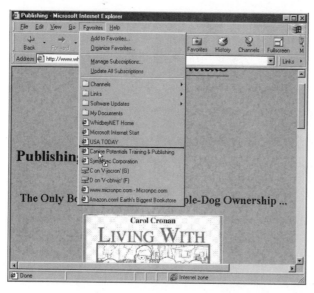

Figure 11-22. *You can position a URL when dragging it to the Favorites menu.*

If you use the Add To Favorites options, the Add Favorite dialog box will open, as shown below, asking if you want to subscribe to the page. (Web page subscription is discussed later in the chapter under *Using Webcasting*.) If you choose either of the Yes options, you will be notified if the page is updated by a "gleam" (a small red dot) on the upper left of the Web site's icon on the Favorites menu (see the second illustration below). Also, when you move the mouse pointer over a subscription that has been updated, you will get a ToolTip that tells you the last time you visited the site and the last time it was updated.

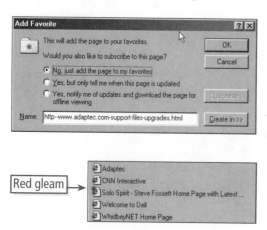

In the Add Favorite dialog box, you can click Create In to expand the dialog box to show the folders that are in Favorites. This allows you to choose one of those folders in which to place the new Web page. You can also click New Folder to create a new folder within whichever folder is selected. A Create New Folder dialog box will open, allowing you to enter a name for the new folder. You can then use the new folder to contain the Web page you are adding to Favorites.

The Favorites menu also has an option to Organize Favorites. This opens the Organize Favorites dialog box, shown in Figure 11-23. Here you can drag the Favorites shortcuts to one of the folders, delete or rename either the folders or shortcuts, or create new folders. If you want to move a shortcut to a folder within one of the folders shown, select the shortcut, and click Move. This will open a hierarchical view of the folders within Favorites. If you click one of the folders and then click OK, the selected shortcut will be moved there.

Back and Forward Buttons If you have been browsing the Internet for any length of time during the current session and you want to return to a page you viewed early in the session, you can quickly get there in Internet Explorer. You do that by clicking the down arrow to the right of the Back button to open its drop-down list, and then clicking the page you want, as you can see on the next page. The Forward button has a similar down arrow and

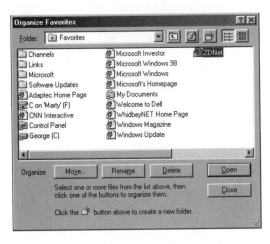

Figure 11-23. *Organizing Favorites shortcuts in folders.*

drop-down list, and you can get the same lists by right-clicking either button. Also, you can get the Back button's list on the File menu with the addition of the current page.

Printing Web Pages

Internet Explorer 4 has solved several common problems with printing Web pages. Most frustrating of these was the need to display a page in order to print it. This meant that if a document had 20 pages, you would have to display all 20 pages to print the entire document. Printing frames on Web pages is another problem that has been solved. The Print dialog box, which you can open by clicking the Print button on the Standard toolbar, or choosing Print from the File menu, or choosing Print from a context menu, implements the solutions (see Figure 11-24). In the Print Frames section, you can choose to print

- An entire Web page as it appears on the screen independent of frames

- Just the frame you last selected by clicking it

- All the frames individually, one per page

At the bottom left of the Print dialog box is an option to Print All Linked Documents. When you select this, Internet Explorer will cache all the hyperlinks on the current page and then follow those links, printing each. You can start by printing a table of the links to see what will print.

 IP   Unless you already know the number of links on a page, it is worthwhile printing the table of links to get that information before printing a page with all of its links.

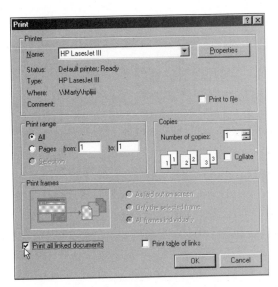

Figure 11-24. *Internet Explorer printing allows you to print linked documents.*

If a Web page uses cascading style sheets, Internet Explorer will use them to define many page-formatting features. This allows the printed Web page to look as good as it does on the screen.

> **OTE** A cascading style sheet allows a Web author to apply a consistent set of text-formatting styles across all pages on the site and store the styles separately.

You can determine how a page will be printed by opening the File menu and choosing Page Setup. The Page Setup dialog box will open, as shown in Figure 11-25. Here you can set the paper size, source, and orientation (portrait or landscape); the margins on all four sides; and the contents of the header and footer. You can use a series of codes to place various pieces of variable information in the header and footer, in addition to entering static text. The codes and their meaning are shown in Table 11-1.

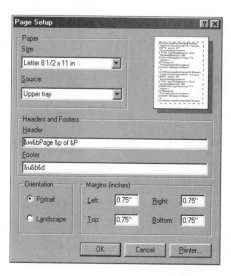

Figure 11-25. *Determine how a Web page will print from the Page Setup option on the File menu.*

Code	Effect on or text that will be added to a header or footer
&b	If at the left of all codes, the following text will be centered; otherwise, following text will be right-aligned
&b&b	Text following the first &b will be centered, and text following the second &b will be right-aligned
&d	Current date in short date format as specified in the Regional Settings control panel
&D	Current date in long date format as specified in the Regional Settings control panel
&p	Current page number
&P	Total number of pages
&t	Current time in the format specified in the Regional Settings control panel
&T	Current time in 24-hour format
&u	URL or address of the Web page being printed
&w	The title of the Web page being printed
&&	Adds a single ampersand to the header or footer

Table 11-1. *Codes used in the header and footer of a printed Web page.*

Customizing Internet Explorer

You can do a number of things to make Internet Explorer look and act the way you want. The View menu provides access to Internet Explorer's customizing features. Here you can

- Turn the toolbars, status bar, and Explorer bars (Search, Favorites, History, and Channels) on and off

- Choose to display text labels on the toolbars

- Set the font size and choose the alphabet to use

- Expand the Internet Explorer window to full screen covering the taskbar and displaying only a minimal toolbar, as shown in Figure 11-26

TIP In full-screen view, you can recover the taskbar by moving the mouse pointer off the bottom edge of the screen.

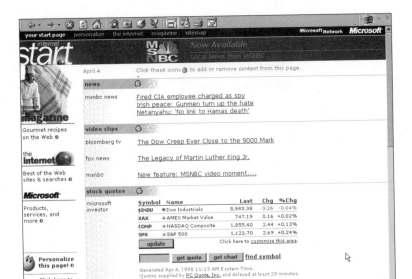

Figure 11-26. *Using the entire screen to display a Web page.*

The Internet Options item at the bottom of the View menu opens the dialog box of that name, shown in Figure 11-27, where you can choose many other ways to customize Internet Explorer. It is worthwhile spending time looking at what you can do in this dialog box. Among the features are

■ Setting the Web page, called "home page," that comes up when you start Internet Explorer. The default is http://home.microsoft.com. When you find another page that you would like to use as the home page, open that page in Internet Explorer, open the Internet Options dialog box, and click Use Current.

■ Determining the amount of disk space that is used to store temporary Internet files and allowing you to delete those files. Click Settings to open the dialog box shown at the top of the next page. Besides determining the amount of disk space, you can look at the files and objects (Internet applications) that are stored, and you can move the folder that is used to store the items.

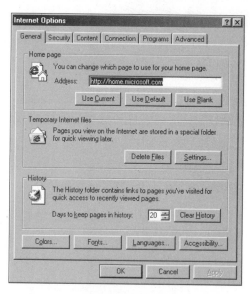

Figure 11-27. *The Internet Options dialog box gives you many ways to customize Internet Explorer.*

- Deciding on the number of days to automatically keep the history of the Web sites you have visited and allowing you to delete that history.

- Setting colors, fonts, font styles and sizes, and languages to make Web pages you view both more pleasing and accessible to you.

- Determining the level of security that you want to use, whether you want to control the Web content that can be viewed, and how you want to use certificates to identify yourself and material you are downloading.

- Setting up or changing your Internet connection using the Internet Connection Wizard, identifying a proxy server to use, or identifying a configuration file to automatically set up Internet Explorer.

- Selecting the programs that you want to use for e-mail, newsgroups, audio and video communication over the Internet, scheduling, and your list of contacts.

Additionally the Advanced tab offers a number of detail options in many areas, as you can see in Figure 11-28.

Using Webcasting

Webcasting is automating the receipt of Web information. It allows you to be notified or to automatically receive Web pages that you have requested. This can be done on either a scheduled basis or when the pages have been updated. Any existing Web site can be webcast by subscribing to it when

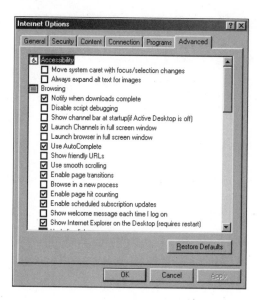

Figure 11-28. *The Advanced tab of the Internet Options dialog box offers many detail options.*

you add it to your Favorites. This is referred to as *pull technology,* which allows you to determine what you get, how you get it, and when you get it. Additionally Internet Explorer provides for webcasting through channels using *push technology* where the webcaster determines how and when you get what information. Although you must also subscribe to a channel, we will use *subscriptions* to refer to the webcasting of otherwise standard Web sites, while *channels* refer to the webcasting of automated Web sites. A third form of webcasting is called "true webcasting" or *multicasting,* which is supported by Internet Explorer.

Subscriptions

Many users go back to the same Web site time after time looking for what is new. Subscriptions handle that for you. When you add a Web site to your Favorites, the Add Favorite dialog box appears, as shown at the top of the next page. This dialog box gives you two ways to subscribe to a site. The first simply notifies you when the site is updated. The second both notifies you and downloads the page so you can look at it offline. In both cases, you don't have to do anything further to be reminded of any changes to the site.

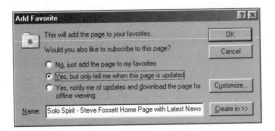

 OTE Subscribing to a Web site does not obligate you to pay anything. It simply means that you are signed up to be notified and possibly receive a Web page when it is updated.

When you select one of the subscription options, the Customize button becomes available. When you click this button, the Subscription Wizard opens, as shown in Figure 11-29. The initial dialog box tells you that when the Web page is updated, a red gleam will appear on the upper left of the pages icon in the Favorites menu. You can choose whether you also want an e-mail notification. If you do want an e-mail notification, you can change the address to which it will be sent. In the second dialog box, you can indicate whether the site requires a password and what it and the user name are.

Figure 11-29. *Customizing a subscription.*

You can subscribe to an existing Favorites site by right-clicking the entry in the Favorites menu or bar and choosing Subscribe from the context menu. When you do that, you can choose to be notified and download the page, or only to be notified. In either case, you can customize the subscription as discussed previously. The Subscribe option on the context menu changes to Unsubscribe once you have subscribed to a site.

You can schedule, edit, and delete subscriptions in the Subscriptions window, which you open from the Favorites menu Manage Subscriptions option. In the Subscriptions window, by opening the View menu and choosing Custom Schedules, you open the Custom Schedule dialog box, as shown in Figure 11-30. Here you set the schedule that is used by default to update your subscriptions. You can also create or change additional named schedules that may be used by some of your subscriptions. To set a unique schedule for a particular subscription or to edit its other properties including unsubscribing, right-click the subscription and choose Properties. The subscription's Properties dialog box will open, like the one in Figure 11-31. In addition to changing the subscription settings, the Properties dialog box allows you to set some limits on what is downloaded.

If you have chosen to automatically download a Web site, the Receiving tab of the Properties dialog box has an Advanced button that opens the

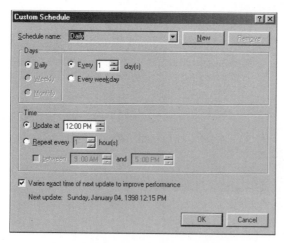

Figure 11-30.   *Setting the default schedule.*

Advanced Download Options dialog box, shown in Figure 11-32. Here you specify the depth in links, if the page has links, that you want to download, the type of items to download, and whether you want to set a size limit for a given download.

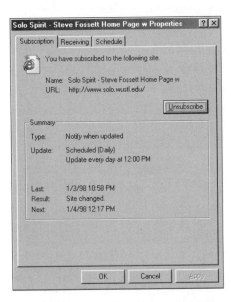

Figure 11-31. *Editing the properties and schedule of a particular subscription.*

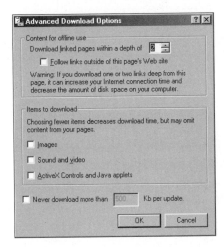

Figure 11-32. *Setting limits for automatic downloading of files.*

Channels

A channel is like a magazine that is delivered to your door, except that on most channels, you can custom tailor the content you want to receive. Channels are periodically updated by their publishers and delivered on either their schedules or on one that you establish. The primary difference between a Web site and a channel is that a channel is a complete package of pages, images, and active elements that is downloaded all at one time and then viewed, normally offline. A Web site is viewed one page at a time and requires that you stay connected to view additional pages. Another difference is that since channels are aimed at only the newest browser applications, most take advantage of the latest technology such as Dynamic HTML, ActiveX, and Java to give users an interactive, truly multimedia experience. Standard Web pages, on the other hand, are generally aimed at a broader browser population that cannot use the latest technology.

On the surface, it might seem that a channel and a Web site to which you have subscribed are equivalent. They are not, because in downloading a subscribed Web site, you don't know

- Whether the value of the linked pages you are picking up are of any value to you, since the links are simply those that are on the pages

- Which images and pages have been updated, forcing you to download them all

- If your download schedule matches the Web site's update schedule

Using CDF Files The component that sets channels apart from standard Web pages is a Channel Definition Format (CDF) file that defines the pages and images that make up the channel. This is what allows the downloading of an entire channel and gets around the limitations of subscribing to a standard Web site. Windows 98 comes with a set of CDF files for the initial set of channels on the Channel bar, but these files simply point to the Web page that is used to subscribe to the channel. After you have subscribed, each time the channel is accessed, a new CDF file is downloaded with all of the URLs for the pages and images *that have changed* since the last time the channel was downloaded. This allows rapid updating of a channel while maintaining a complete site on your hard disk. Figure 11-33 shows a

CDF file for MSNBC. A CDF file is created with a scripting programming language that defines how objects such as pages, graphics, and programming controls relate to one another and appear in the browser. In addition, CDF files contain

- Information that personalizes a channel to you, so only the information you are interested in is downloaded

- A site map or index of the channel, which groups similar information, such as business or weather, and provides a hierarchical structure of the site

- Information to identify pages that can be used for screen savers and "tickers," like stock market tickers, as well as special headlines and ToolTips

Initiating and Managing a Channel Subscription The Channel bar that comes with Windows 98 appears either on the desktop or in the Internet Explorer window and offers a broad range of channels to which you can subscribe. To do so, you need only click the channel you want and then follow the instructions on the screen. For the most current selection and many more channels to which you can subscribe, select the Channel Guide in the Channel bar. This opens the Microsoft Active Channel Guide Web site shown in Figure 11-34. Here you can select a category and review the many options within it. Again, to subscribe you need only click the

Figure 11-33. *A CDF file defines how to download a channel Web site.*

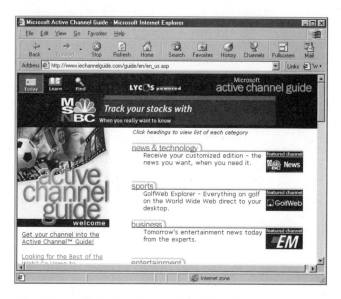

Figure 11-34. *The Microsoft Active Channel Guide offers a large and current list of channels.*

channel you want. As an example, here are the steps to subscribe to the CMPnet channel from within Internet Explorer (except for opening the Channel bar, the steps are the same from the desktop Channel bar):

1. Click the Channels button in the Standard toolbar to open the Channel bar.

2. In the Channel bar, click News and Technology, and then click CMPnet.

3. Click Add Active Channel. When asked, click the subscription option you want.

4. If you want, click Customize to be notified of updates by e-mail or to set your own download schedule.

5. Click OK. Your subscription is complete and the channel will be downloaded, as you can see in Figure 11-35.

Some channels require more information, such as your agreement to a license and your name and e-mail address. Also, some channels may charge for a subscription and request a credit card number. If the channel includes content for a screen saver, you will be asked if you want to replace your current screen saver with this new content.

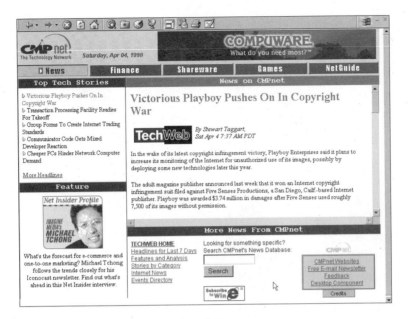

Figure 11-35. *The CMPnet channel opened in full screen.*

Channels are managed in two ways. As with subscribed Web sites, you can open the Favorites menu, choose Manage Subscriptions, right-click the channel, and choose Properties. In the Properties dialog box that opens, you can change the type of subscription, how you want to be notified, and the download schedule, as you saw earlier. The second way to manage a channel is within the channel itself, and how you accomplish that depends on the channel. PointCast, for example, provides several forms to personalize the information you receive, as shown in Figure 11-36.

Multicasting

Multicasting, which uses multicast protocols, is similar to radio and TV broadcasting: a Web site sends out its pages and images, and those clients who are online at the same time with software enabled to receive the broadcast will do so. Multicasting is particularly applicable to organizational intranets where the clients (those receiving the broadcasts) are always online and can be easily made aware of the webcast. Multicasting can also work well in sending out information to proxy servers, which cache the information and disseminate it on demand one client at a time like standard Web pages. Multicasting makes efficient use of the network

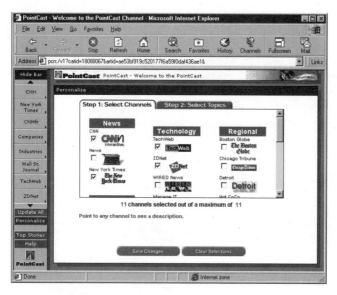

Figure 11-36. *PointCast personalization form.*

bandwidth. In standard Web page dissemination and the other forms of webcasting, each client separately requests and separately receives each Web page and image. In multicasting, no individual request occurs, and only one transmission is received by all clients at the same time.

Multicasting is currently available through Microsoft's NetShow multimedia software, which is discussed in Chapter 14. Third parties, such as Starburst Communications, are creating software that integrates with NetShow to provide a full-featured, one-to-many Multicast File Transfer Protocol (MFTP) transmission Also, Microsoft's Broadcast Architecture is being designed into products to provide multicasting through direct broadcast satellites and cable TV channels.

Although multicasting is in its infancy, its efficiency and ability to deliver high-bandwidth content promise multicasting a significant role in the future.

Internet Explorer Security

As the Internet is more commonly and heavily used, the need for improved security increases. Internet Explorer addresses that in a number of ways. Among these are the following:

- **Improved privacy,** which allows you to safely transmit documents, credit cards, and passwords without fear that someone can intercept and misuse them.

- **Comprehensive authentication,** which allows you to connect to a server, download files, and communicate with an individual and be assured that the other parties or objects are who or what they said they were.

- **Security zones,** which allow you to segregate Web sites that you trust from those that you do not.

- **Content control,** which allows you to specify content that you do not want viewed on your computer.

Privacy

The Internet provides transmission privacy through security protocols that encrypt and appropriately decrypt information being transmitted. The security protocols commonly in use and supported by Internet Explorer are Secure Sockets Layer (SSL) 2 and 3 and Personal Communications Technology (PCT) 1. These protocols are implemented by using HTTPS (secure HTTP). From the user or client viewpoint, the use of HTTPS is almost transparent. All you see is a message that says that you are about to begin viewing pages over a secure connection. From that point until you see a message that you are returning to an unsecure connection, all transmissions between you and the server are automatically encrypted on sending and decrypted on receipt. All you have to do is click Yes that you want to continue over a secure connection. The Web site author is the one who has established that a particular Web page will use HTTPS, and the server administrator has selected which protocol to use. The net result is that you can be reasonably sure that your credit card number or password is safe—a lot safer than telling it to someone over the telephone.

If you send information over a link that is not secure, you will be warned with a message like the one at the top of the next page. In Internet Explorer, these messages are based on the security zone you are in (see *Security Zones* later in this chapter), and you can turn them off for a particular zone.

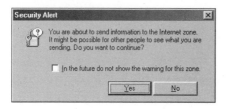

Private Key and Public Key Encryption The actual means of encryption in the security protocols is a combination of public and private key encryption. (A "key," as it is used here, is a mathematical algorithm that facilitates the encryption and decryption of a piece of information.) Private key encryption is the oldest and depends on a single key that is used by both the sender and receiver and that must be kept secure from everyone else. Private key encryption is up to a thousand times faster than public key encryption, but it requires a secure way for the key to be transmitted. The most common scheme for private key encryption on the Internet is RC4 from RSA Laboratories.

Public key encryption, which is about 20 years old, actually uses a pair of keys, a private key and a public key. The prospective recipient of information sends the prospective sender a public key to encrypt information to be sent. Anyone can have this key because only the recipient who has the matching private key can decrypt it. This provides a safe means of sending a key, but it is much slower than a private key scheme. Most public key encryption schemes are based on the RSA Public Key Cryptosystem from RSA Laboratories.

The Internet security protocols combine private and public key schemes by using a public key scheme to send a private key and some authentication information. It then uses the much faster private key to send the information to be transmitted.

Authentication

The problem of authentication is complex and requires a multistage solution. Complete authentication has these components:

- The recipient wants to verify the identity of the sender and prevent the sender from being able to deny having sent the information. This is *client authentication.*

- The sender wants to verify the identity of the recipient and prevent the recipient from being able to deny having received the information. This is *server authentication.*

- Both the recipient and the sender want to verify that the information being sent has not been modified before it is received. This is *data authentication.*

The SSL 3 security protocol provides most of this process with these steps:

1. As the sender is preparing to transmit secure information, a *message digest* of the data is generated, similar to a checksum for a number. This message digest is extremely sensitive to any change in the data.

2. A public key scheme is used with the sender's private key to encrypt the message digest to create a digital signature, which is sent along with a public key to the recipient.

3. The digital signature is decrypted with the sender's public key. If this is successful, the sender is authenticated to be whoever sent the initial public key.

4. The recipient then sends a public key to the sender, who uses it to encrypt and send a private key to the recipient. The main body of information to be transmitted is then encrypted with the private key and is sent. The recipient uses the public key to decrypt the private key, which in turn is used to decrypt the information.

5. As the recipient is receiving the information, a new message digest is generated and compared to the original message digest. If the two message digests are the same, the data is authenticated to the recipient.

6. The recipient then uses a public key scheme with his private key to encrypt the message digest to create a new digital signature, which is sent back to the original sender.

7. The second digital signature is finally decrypted by the original recipient's public key. If it works, the recipient is authenticated to be whoever sent the final public key. The initial and final message digests are then compared, and if they are the same, the receipt of the original data is authenticated.

This entire process is handled automatically by the security protocols on the Internet. You only know about it if there is a problem. The only problem is how senders and recipients identify each other.

Certificates and Authenticode The identity problem is handled by having a third party verify the identities of senders and recipients. This third party, a *certifying authority,* issues a certificate protected by a public key that proves the identity of the person, organization, or data. The certificate is sent along with the original message digest and becomes strong proof of the identity of the sender.

Internet Explorer takes the certification process two steps further with Authenticode technology in conjunction with VeriSign, a certifying authority. Authenticode will automatically time-stamp any certificate that it receives. Internet Explorer will then check, prior to downloading any further information, whether the certificate's time stamp is within its valid and limited lifetime and the certificate has not been revoked. Given these two assurances, the recipient can feel reasonably comfortable about the information or applications he or she receives.

When you are shown a certificate and asked if you want to accept it, you are also asked if you want to accept all certificates from that publisher. If you click Yes, that publisher is added to your file of accepted publishers, and all future certificates from that publisher are automatically accepted. You can edit the list of publishers whose certificates you want to automatically accept, as well as the certifying authorities and your personal certificates, in the Internet Options dialog box Content tab, which is shown in Figure 11-37.

Security Zones

All of the checking and cross-checking that was described above to ensure the security of information transfer can take a lot of time, and until everybody is fully certified, numerous holes can exist in the protection. For that reason, Internet Explorer has security zones in which you can segregate Web sites with which you deal into various levels of trust. There are four zones that you can use:

Figure 11-37. *Manage your certificates and those of others in Internet Options.*

- **Local Intranet Zone** includes all sites on your intranet, all sites that bypass your proxy server, and all network paths (UNCs), plus specific sites you add.

- **Trusted Sites Zone** includes all the sites that you put there in which you have a lot of trust.

- **Internet Zone** is the default for all the sites you haven't placed in some other zone.

- **Restricted Sites Zone** includes all the sites you put there in which you have little trust.

The Internet Options dialog box Security tab, shown in Figure 11-38, allows you to assign one of three levels of security to each of the zones, or assign a custom level in which you can supply detailed specifications of what you will accept or not. This allows you to have the best of two worlds: to have little or no interruption when working with sites you trust, while getting the maximum protection in sites you question.

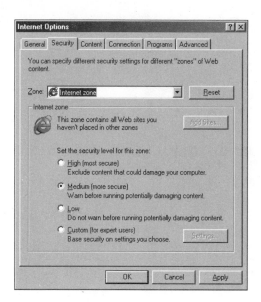

Figure 11-38. *Setting security levels for various Internet or intranet zones.*

Content Control

In both organizational and home use, situations may arise in which you want to place limits on the types of content that can be viewed in the Internet Explorer. You can do this in the Internet Options Content tab, shown in Figure 11-37. In the Content Advisor, clicking Enable allows you to set and confirm a password that must then be used to change or bypass the Content Advisor settings. After you have established a password, the Content Advisor dialog box will open. There, four categories of potentially offensive material are presented. If you click one of the categories, a slider appears beneath the categories. If you drag the slider, a description of the various settings will appear beneath the slider, as you can see in Figure 11-39.

In the General tab, you can determine how to handle sites without ratings and whether to allow the use of the password to enter restricted sites. In the Advanced tab, you can set the rating systems and rating bureaus you want to use. When you close the dialog box, you will be informed that your rating system is set up and be warned to close and restart Internet Explorer to prevent returning to any open pages. When a site is found that

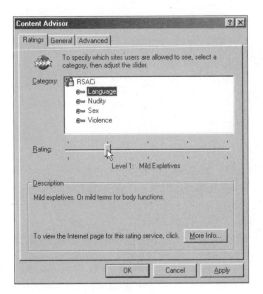

Figure 11-39. *Settings limits on potentially offensive content.*

either does not meet your rating criteria or is unrated, and you have said that you don't want to allow opening unrated pages, the Content Advisor dialog box will open, as shown below. If you have allowed a password override, you can enter the password and then view the site. Also, the original Enable button becomes a Disable button. When you click the Disable button, you can use the password to discontinue using the rating system.

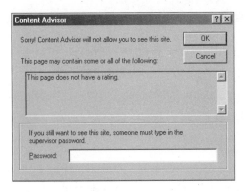

Using The Microsoft Network

The Microsoft Network (MSN) is an online service with full access to the Internet. As an online service, it provides its own proprietary content in addition to serving as an ISP. MSN also makes full use of the Windows 98 graphical user interface and takes advantage of the multitasking and multithreaded design provided in Windows 98. This allows MSN to carry out several tasks at the same time and to have a look and feel similar to other parts of Windows 98. MSN's proprietary offerings, though, are similar to those of CompuServe, AOL, and other online services, including the following:

- **Bulletin board systems,** where you can exchange messages and files on a particular subject

- **Chat rooms,** where you can interact with other people signed on to MSN by typing messages to them or just monitoring the conversation of others

- **Directories, encyclopedias, and reference volumes,** where you can look up information on many subjects

- **Electronic mail,** which you can exchange with other MSN members and anyone connected to the Internet

- **File libraries,** where you can download articles, graphics, programs, and product support information to your own computer

- **Forums,** which group bulletin boards, chat rooms, file libraries, guest books, and suggestion boxes for a particular subject

- **Guest books,** where you can introduce yourself in a particular forum

- **Information services,** where you can get news, sports, weather, and product information

- **Internet access,** where you can send and receive e-mail, participate in newsgroups, and browse the World Wide Web

- **Suggestion boxes,** where you can leave your comments to MSN on how a particular area might be improved or changed

MSN offers worldwide access with local phone numbers in many countries covering a large part of the population. In the United States, almost everyone can connect using a local phone number. If you already have an Internet connection and want to access MSN's proprietary content, you can use your Internet connection to access MSN. Payment for MSN services in the United States is by means of credit cards whose number you enter when you sign up for MSN.

Signing Up for MSN

In order to use MSN, you must sign up by giving Microsoft your name, address, phone number, and a credit-card number to pay for the service. Also, you need to find out what phone number your computer will call to connect to the service. (Initially you use an 800 number, but after you've signed up for MSN, you must use a phone number in your local area.) If you choose to install MSN, you can sign up by clicking the MSN icon on your desktop.

With your credit-card number, its expiration date, and a user name and password that you want to use ready, follow these instructions to sign up for MSN:

1. Click the Microsoft Network desktop icon. If you did not install MSN when you installed Windows 98, you will be told that you need to insert your Windows 98 CD-ROM. When MSN Setup is found, the opening window will appear. Click Next and follow the on-screen instructions. MSN will need to restart your computer.

2. If you don't have an Internet connection, the Internet Connection Wizard discussed early in this chapter will be used with an 800 number to contact MSN initially.

3. Enter all of the information requested, and then click Next. Select the credit card that you want to use to pay for your MSN services, enter the necessary information, and click Next. You will again be connected to MSN. When you return, you will be shown the Membership Agreement. Read this membership agreement. If you want to proceed, click I Agree; if not, click I Don't Agree. In either case, click Next. If you don't agree, you will exit MSN Setup.

4. Enter the user name you want to use and then enter a password between 8 and 16 digits long. When you are done, click Sign Me Up;
otherwise, click Cancel. Once more, you will connect to MSN, and
your user name and password will be checked for uniqueness. If it
is not unique, you will be asked to change it. With a unique user
name and password, you will be told that you have successfully
signed up to use MSN, and the setup program will finish.

5. To actually use MSN, click its desktop icon again. Enter your user
name and password and, if you want, click Remember Password.
Click Settings to select the phone number to use to connect to MSN.
For both the phone number and backup phone number, click Phone
Book, and select your state, city, and the phone number you want to
use. When you are done, click OK. Your Sign-In dialog box should
look like Figure 11-40.

6. Click Connect, and MSN will then use the primary phone number to
connect you to the service. Several more setup screens will appear
after you connect. Follow the instructions on the screen.

7. When you are finished, the MSN opening screen will appear, as you
can see in Figure 11-41.

Figure 11-40. *MSN Sign-In dialog box.*

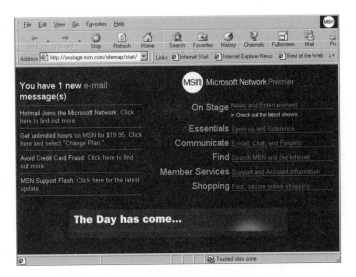

Figure 11-41. *MSN opening screen.*

The Microsoft Network Environment

The Microsoft Network has many features. The purpose of this section is to get you started with MSN. Begin by seeing how you will usually sign on.

Signing On to MSN

When you click the MSN desktop icon, you will be asked if you are connected to the Internet, as shown at the top of the next page. You can use either a LAN or modem connection to do that. Otherwise, click No, Dial Using MSN. (If it is never possible for you to connect other than through MSN, click Don't Ask Me Again.) Click OK. If you are connecting through MSN, you will see the Sign-In dialog box you saw in Figure 11-40. The user name stays in the dialog box from one session to another. You can enter the password each time you sign on or, if you want, you can click Remember My Password, and you will not have to reenter it (see the Warning in this section). If you have selected Remember My Password, all you need to do is click Connect. Otherwise, enter your password, and click Connect.

 ARNING If others use your computer and might possibly sign on to MSN when you don't want them to, do not activate Remember My Password.

The Settings button in the Sign-In dialog box opens the Connection Settings dialog box, where you can change the MSN phone numbers. Also, you can change the modem used and several options related to timing and use of dial-up access.

When you have successfully connected, you will see the MSN opening screen, shown in Figure 11-41. You are also reminded that the MSN Quick View icon in the notification area of the taskbar provides quick access to much of MSN. If you click the MSN Quick View icon, a menu will pop up that repeats all of the options on the opening screen, as you can see here:

If you have mail waiting for you, you will also see a message telling you so. To look at your mail, simply click where indicated on either the opening screen or the context menu, and Microsoft Outlook Express will open showing your mail. See Chapter 12 for a discussion of how to use Outlook Express.

Using MSN

The MSN opening window and the MSN Quick View context menu provide a central transfer point to go from one area of MSN to another. The context menu has ten options that allow you to quickly get to the major areas of MSN. These options open the following areas:

- **Favorites** opens the Internet Explorer's Favorites list with the same choices as in Internet Explorer.

- **On Stage** gives you a choice of its home page or six channels covering news and entertainment. The home page gives you a brief preview of what is available on the six channels and has a bulletin area. Channel 1 is MSNBC, a news magazine, as shown in Figure 11-42. Channels 2 through 6 offer a wide variety of other material.

- **Essentials** provides ten sites plus one you can customize that offer information on such subjects as personal finance, travel, computers, and automobiles.

- **Communicate** allows you to participate in forums and chat rooms, send and receive e-mail, and access the Internet.

Figure 11-42. *MSNBC reached from MSN.*

- **Search** allows you to search MSN by word, phrase, or subject or to search the Internet using one of four search engines.

- **Member Services** provides help using MSN, allows you to check and change your MSN account, and give MSN feedback.

- **Set Up Friends Online** allows you to establish a list of friends and check to see if they are online. You can also put out a Do Not Disturb sign so you won't be bothered.

- **You Have x New Messages** opens Outlook Express, which allows you to receive, read, create, send, and store Internet mail messages.

- **MSN Options** allows you to change many settings relating to Internet Explorer, your Internet connection, and use of multicast, in addition to MSN.

- **Disconnect from MSN** or **Connect to MSN** allows you to establish or discontinue your connection with MSN.

 OTE   Some of the above features, such as MSNBC, while reached from MSN, are actually on the Internet and not part of MSN.

The content of these areas varies so greatly that it is worth your while to open up and explore each of them. When you explore the Communicate option, look at the bulletin boards and chat rooms to see how they work. Finally see how MSN provides access to the Internet through Internet Center in the Communicate option.

Windows 98 provides a comprehensive set of tools to connect to and utilize the Internet. Central to that is Internet Explorer, which provides its own complete set of features.

Using Outlook Express
for E-Mail and Newsgroups

Of all the current uses of a PC, none have faster growth and few have more widespread use than e-mail. The reasons are simple: it is easy to use, it is fast, and it is inexpensive. E-mail alone has been the reason for many PC sales. To satisfy this demand, Windows 98 includes Outlook Express.

Outlook Express is a mail and news client that lets you create, send, receive, forward, and store messages to and from several messaging sources, in addition to reading and submitting newsgroup articles on the Internet. The messaging sources with which Outlook Express can work include the Internet, MSN, LAN-based messaging, online services, and fax, although all but the Internet require that you install additional software to implement the particular form of messaging.

Windows Messaging and Outlook Express

Messaging services within Windows 98 are handled with the *Windows messaging system,* or MAPI (Messaging Application Programming Interface). MAPI provides the low-level services and acts as the interface between Outlook Express and the internal file system on one side and between Outlook Express and external messaging systems on the other side. Figure 12-1 shows a simplified representation of the MAPI interface. In Windows 98, the principal components of MAPI are as follows:

- **Internet mail drivers** use the Transport Control Protocol/Internet Protocol (TCP/IP) and Point-to-Point Protocol (PPP) built into Windows 98 to give Outlook Express the ability to send and receive Internet mail.

- **Other MAPI drivers,** available separately from Microsoft and third parties, give Outlook Express the ability to send and receive messages on a LAN, through an online service, with other dedicated mail systems, and with fax.

- **Personal Address Book** provides Outlook Express and other MAPI messaging applications with comprehensive contact information including name, address, e-mail address, phone number, fax number, and other information for multiple e-mail systems.

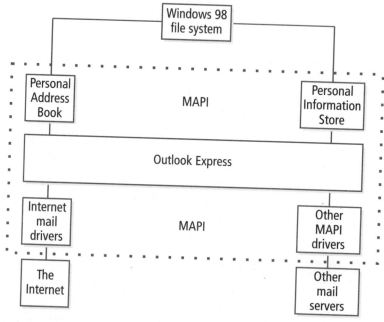

Figure 12-1. *MAPI components and interfaces.*

- **Personal Information Store** provides Outlook Express and other MAPI messaging applications with a full-featured file system that works with the Windows 98 file system to store messages, forms, and other documents in a common place using long filenames and predefined and user-defined folders.

MAPI includes the set of applications and drivers that make up Windows messaging, and the way that set interfaces both with the rest of Windows and with other messaging systems. In Windows 98, Outlook Express is included in that definition, as it is included within the dotted line representing MAPI in Figure 12-1. In fact, Outlook Express is a major component of MAPI, serving as its "universal inbox" and mail creation application.

Advances in Outlook Express

Outlook Express includes a number of new or enhanced features that make it far from a simple mail handler. Among these are the following:

- **A rich-text editor** combined with OLE allows you to create and read documents with extensive formatting and embedded objects. Figure 12-2 is an example of such a message. The rich-text elements of the message, such as bolding and underlining, are compressed and along with the plain text are sent to the receiving mail system. If that system can handle the rich text, it is uncompressed, combined with the plain text, and the rich-text message is displayed. If the message is received by a message system that does not handle rich text, the plain text is displayed without the formatting. Any embedded objects are sent as attachments and, if received by a mail system that can display them, are displayed in the message. In other systems, they are simply attachments. You can set as a default whether you want to use plain text or rich text, and you can specify in your address book that a user is to receive only plain text. Also, when replying to a message, Outlook Express automatically uses the same level of formatting as the original message to ensure its readability.

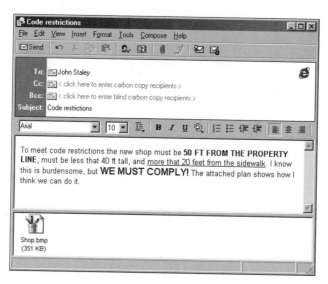

Figure 12-2.   *You can add formatting and attached files.*

- **Enhanced security** allows you to encrypt and digitally sign your e-mail and attached documents so that it is virtually impossible for others to read the documents if they were able to intercept them. This security is provided through S/MIME (Secure Multipurpose Internet Mail Extensions), which in turn relies on a public key encryption system and certificates as described in Chapter 11. The message is encrypted using the public key of the recipient, so the recipient with his matching private key is the only one who can open and read it. Digitally signing a document reverses the process; the sender uses his private key to encrypt a message and then sends the matching public key to the recipient with a certificate of its authenticity. If the public key works, the recipient can be sure the message is from the stated sender.

- **Sending and receiving Web content** allows you to include all or part of an actual Web page within a mail message, as well as an active hyperlink to a Web page. This capability uses MIME HTML (MIME Hypertext Markup Language), which gives recipients three possible ways to receive the message depending on their level of MIME HTML implementation:

- If the recipient has MIME HTML, the mail reader will display the Web page.

- If the recipient has only MIME, the HTML will be in an attachment that can be displayed by a Web browser.

- If the recipient does not have MIME, the raw text HTML will appear in the message.

- **Remote access to mail** allows you to receive your messages from any computer connected to the server if the server is using IMAP4 (Internet Message Access Protocol 4) and the computers have Outlook Express.

- **Multiple protocol support** lets Outlook Express not only support IMAP4, but also POP3 (Post Office Protocol 3), which is commonly used by ISPs instead of IMAP, as well as SMTP (Simple Mail Transfer Protocol). Either IMAP or POP is used on a mail server to transfer messages from the server to the mail client, while SMTP is used to transfer messages from the client to the server and route them on the Internet.

- **Interchangeability between news messages and e-mail** allows you to take a news message, which comes from an NNTP (Network News Transfer Protocol) server, and send it out as an SMTP e-mail message or store it in your mail folders, or take an e-mail message and post it to a newsgroup.

- **Integrated directory support** allows Outlook Express to search a local address book, corporate directories on a LAN, and virtual Internet white pages to find people's e-mail or street addresses and phone numbers. This is accomplished through LDAP (Lightweight Directory Access Protocol) directory services, with which you can search on a full name, a partial name, or an e-mail address. This capability is also available in Windows 98 itself through the Start menu | Find | People.

- **Handling multiple e-mail and news accounts** means that you can have several e-mail and news accounts and work with them either together or individually all within a single copy of Outlook Express. With multiple e-mail accounts, you can receive your mail from all accounts at once or from individual accounts by opening the Tools menu and choosing Send and Receive. A list of your e-mail accounts will appear on a submenu along with All Accounts, as shown below. In the Compose window, you can choose which account you want to use to send a particular message by opening the File menu and choosing Send Message Using. Again a submenu will give you a choice of the accounts you can use. Using either the Connect button on the toolbar or the Connect option on the File menu, you can choose one of several news or mail services to which you can connect. You manage your multiple accounts by choosing Accounts from the Tools menu, which opens the Internet Accounts dialog box, as shown in Figure 12-3.

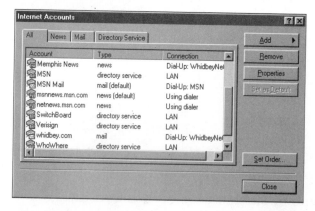

Figure 12-3.   *Managing multiple news, mail, and white pages accounts.*

■ **Automatic handling of incoming e-mail** is set up in Outlook Express using the Inbox Assistant, which you activate from the Tools menu. The Inbox Assistant allows you to define a set of rules that govern your incoming e-mail and result in actions that you establish, as you can see in Figure 12-4. Two actions you can take are to avoid downloading certain messages or to delete certain messages at the server. If you can identify spammers (people sending you junk e-mail), you can automatically delete all their messages before they are downloaded.

■ **Multiple user support** allows several people to use a single copy of Outlook Express, each with their own e-mail and news accounts, address book, and rules for handling mail. You can accomplish this by setting up Windows 98 for multiple users and having a user sign off from Outlook Express, with the File menu Log Off option.

■ **Personalized stationery** allows you to create backgrounds, use your choice of fonts, and include a personal signature block that you append to your outgoing messages. Outlook Express comes with a number of backgrounds ("stationery") that you can use (shown at the top of the next page), or you can create your own with FrontPage Express.

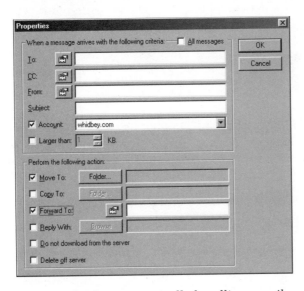

Figure 12-4.   *Setting rules for automatically handling e-mail.*

You can also use this process to create a form that you use for messages with repetitive information. The Stationery option on the Tools menu provides this capability.

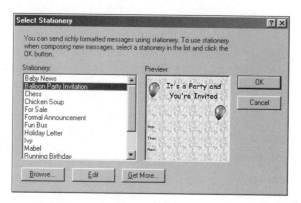

■ **Attach virtual business cards** to your e-mail by creating a *vCard*. vCards use the information in a contact card you select, which you can create like any other entry in your address book, to create this attachment. When it is in use, you will see it on the right of the address block of a message, as you can see below. Recipients can drag it to their address book and immediately have a complete contact entry. You can add a business card to an e-mail message by clicking Business Card on the Insert menu.

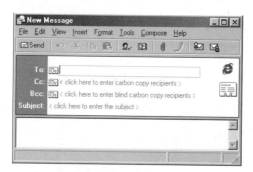

Setting Up Outlook Express

Before you can use Outlook Express, you must have an Internet mail account with several pieces of related information from your Internet Service Provider (ISP), and you must ensure that Outlook Express is installed on your system. The information that you must have for e-mail and news accounts includes the following:

- The ISP's phone number that will connect you to a modem that will handle your modem speed and whether you need to include the area code and/or country code.

- The user ID or account name and password that you are to use when logging on to the Internet.

- Whether you have to open a terminal window and/or use a script to log on. If so, have your ISP tell you how to do this and give you the script to use.

- Your e-mail address (such as someone@microsoft.com), whether the incoming mail server is POP3 or IMAP type, and the names of the incoming and outgoing mail servers (for example, microsoft.com).

- Whether you have to use Secure Password Authorization (SPA) to log on to the mail server and the mail account name and password that you are to use.

- The name of your Internet news server, whether you are required to log on, and the account name and password that you are to use if you have to log on.

Outlook Express is added to your system by Windows Setup as part of a Typical install. Its connection to the Internet is handled by the Internet Connection Wizard using the Connect To The Internet icon on your desktop, as described in Chapter 11. (This icon, and the Internet connection it creates, are used by both Internet Explorer and Outlook Express.) If your desktop has an icon for Outlook Express, it has been set up and an Internet connection has been established. If not, install it with the steps that follow:

1. Click the Connect To The Internet icon on the desktop. The Internet Connection Wizard will open with a Welcome message, and you will be offered three setup options: setting up a new account and connection, setting up a new connection to an existing account, and using an existing connection and account, as you can see in Figure 12-5. These were discussed in detail in Chapter 11, so here we'll take the middle option.

2. Click I Have An Existing Internet Account Through My Phone Line Or..., and click Next. You are then asked if you are accessing the Internet using an ISP or LAN, or an online service provder such as MSN or AOL. Make the choice that is correct for you and click Next. If you chose ISP or LAN you are asked to choose between using your phone line and your local area network (LAN). This was also discussed in Chapter 11, so just the phone line will be covered here.

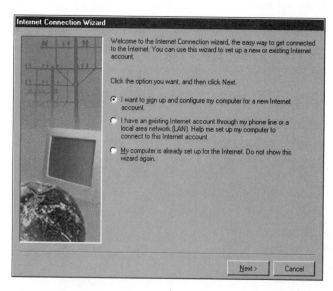

Figure 12-5.   *Choosing the type of setup.*

3. Click Connect Using My Phone Line, and click Next. If you have more than one, choose the modem you want to use, or install one if necessary, and again click Next.

4. Enter the phone number that you need to dial to connect to your ISP. Indicate whether you need to dial the area code and country code, entering and/or changing those as necessary, and then click Next.

5. Enter the user name and password that you need to use to log on to the Internet, and click Next. Unless your ISP has given you some special instructions that you need to use to log on, such as using a script or opening a terminal window, keep the default No under Advanced Settings, and click Next again.

6. Enter a name that you want to use for this connection (maybe the name of the ISP), and click Next. Finally you are asked if you want to set up an Internet Mail account; accept the default Yes, and click Next.

7. Enter your name as you would like it to appear in the From field of outgoing mail (this can be a nickname or "handle"), and click Next. Enter your e-mail address that was given to you by your ISP, for example someone@microsoft.com, and click Next.

8. Choose between POP3 and IMAP for the server type, and then enter the name of both the incoming and outgoing mail servers (they may have the same name), for example adomain.com (see Figure 12-6), and click Next.

9. Choose between a typical (POP) mail logon and an SPA logon. If the former, enter the account name and password you need to use (this may or may not be the same as the account name and password you use to log on to the Internet). Click Next. Enter a friendly name for this mail account, and once more click Next.

10. Choose whether you want to set up an Internet news account, and click Next. To set up an account, enter the name you want to use when submitting news articles, click Next, enter your e-mail address, and again click Next.

11. Enter the name of your news server as shown in Figure 12-7, indicate whether you are required to log on, and click Next. If you are required to log on, enter your account name and password, and click Next. Enter a friendly name for your news account, and click Next.

12. Choose whether you want to set up an Internet Directory service, and click Next. To set up a service, enter the name of the directory server, whether you are required to log on, and click Next. If you are required to log on, enter your account name and password, and click Next.

13. Choose whether you want to check the addresses of your outgoing e-mail against a directory service (unless you have a fast directory service, it is generally not advisable), and click Next. Enter a friendly name for your directory service, click Next, and click Finish. The Internet Connection Wizard will close, and Outlook Express will start.

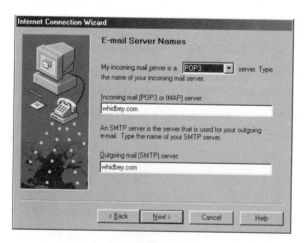

Figure 12-6. *Choosing the type and naming your mail server.*

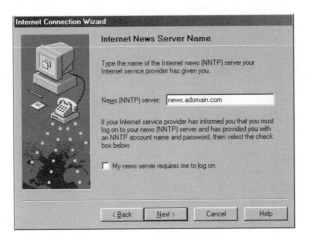

Figure 12-7. *Entering the name of your news server.*

14. You will be asked where you want to place your e-mail and news messages with the suggestion that you place them in a folder in C:\Windows\Application Data\Microsoft\Outlook Express.

15. If that location is acceptable, click OK. Otherwise, click the folder in which you want your messages stored, and then click OK. Outlook Express will open and ask to dial your ISP, like this:

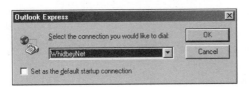

16. Click OK. You should hear your modem dialing and see progress messages on the screen. When you are connected, the connection icon will appear on the taskbar next to the clock, and Outlook Express will appear without any dialog or message boxes in front of it, as you can see in Figure 12-8.

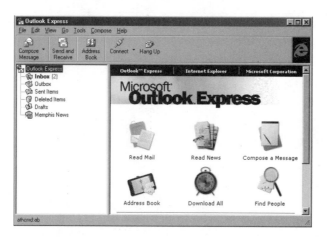

Figure 12-8. *First full view of Outlook Express.*

T IP If you don't hear your modem dialing, open the Modems control panel, open the Properties dialog box for the modem being used, and increase the Speaker Volume.

---

17. Outlook Express will automatically check for any new messages that you have received, but you can also click the Send and Receive button on the toolbar to do that.

18. To disconnect from the Internet, right-click the connection icon on the taskbar and then click Disconnect, or choose Hang Up from the File menu.

Using Outlook Express

This section uses Internet mail to demonstrate the capabilities of Outlook Express to send, receive, and organize messages. If you use a messaging service other than Internet mail, some features might work differently and appear different from those in this section, but the underlying principles are the same.

You open Outlook Express by clicking its icon on the desktop (the same one you may have clicked to set it up), or opening the Start menu and choosing Programs | Internet Explorer | Outlook Express. Depending on how you set up your messaging service to connect when Outlook Express opens, you might have a delay while Outlook Express dials a connection or goes out on the LAN to retrieve messages. When a connection is completed, the Outlook Express window opens, as you saw earlier in Figure 12-8. If you click the Inbox in the left pane, or folder view, Outlook Express will show three panes, similar to Figure 12-9. The left pane displays the folders that are available within Outlook Express. The top-right pane shows the contents of the active, open folder, and the bottom-right pane shows the content of the selected message above it.

Outgoing Mail

You can send a message in several ways. You can compose a new message, reply to a received message, or forward to new recipients either received or self-composed messages. Outlook Express provides a multiuse form for creating messages that offers a wide variety of options for sending mail. To see that form, click the Compose Message button on the toolbar, or choose New Message from the Compose menu, or click an existing message and then click one of the Reply or Forward buttons that are described later in this chapter. The New Message window appears, as shown in Figure 12-10.

As you can see from the array of menu and toolbar choices, creating a message in Outlook Express is not limited by a shortage of features or formatting possibilities. To give you a feel for all the features that are available, the next several sections describe the unique menu options and their uses. Many of these options are also available from the toolbar and perform the same function.

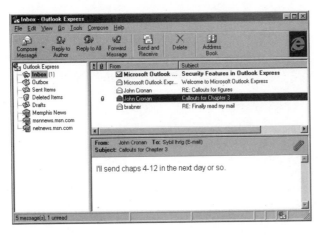

Figure 12-9. *Outlook Express window in its three-pane view.*

Figure 12-10. *Outlook Express New Message window.*

File Menu

The File menu options allow you to perform the following tasks:

■ **Send Message Using** allows you to choose a messaging service that you want to use to transmit the message, as you can see on the next page. If you have only one messaging service, this option is just Send Message. The effect of this option, or the effect of the Send button in the toolbar, which uses your default messaging service, is to move the message to the Outbox folder and attempt to immediately transmit it. If you are connected to the messaging service, this will happen. If not, Outlook Express will attempt to connect, although you can change this default in the Outlook Express window by opening the Tools menu and choosing Options | Send.

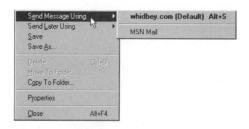

- **Send Later Using** (or Send Later if you have only one messaging service) moves the message to the Outbox but does not attempt to transmit it. This allows you to work offline and send the messages later when you are connected to your messaging service, by clicking the Send and Receive button on the Outlook Express toolbar.

- **Save** stores a copy of the message in the Drafts folder, but leaves the message open. You can either close the message without sending it, or continue working on it. When a draft message is sent, it is removed from the Drafts folder and placed in the Sent Items folder.

- **Save As** lets you save a message in formats that e-mail programs and text editors support: .eml and .txt. The .eml format is preferred because it retains formatting, embedded objects, and even attached objects. Unfortunately not many programs other than Outlook Express and Microsoft Outlook, a full-featured personal information manager, can read an .eml file. The .txt file picks up only the plain text part of a message, but can be read by a large number of programs.

- **Move To Folder** and **Copy to Folder** let you transfer a message to other folders within Outlook Express, which is discussed in the *Organizing Messages* section later in this chapter.

Edit Menu

The Edit menu, shown below, has only one unique option: Remove Hyperlink. Outlook Express, like Microsoft Word, senses when you type a text string that looks like a URL and automatically makes it a hyperlink that you can click to open that Web page in your browser. If you select the hyperlink and click Remove Hyperlink, it will be returned to normal text.

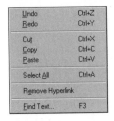

View Menu

The View menu allows you to display or hide the toolbar, the Formatting toolbar, and the status bar.

Insert Menu

The Insert menu, shown below, allows you to attach separate files or insert text from files; add a stored signature or a selected business card; or insert a horizontal line, pictures, or hyperlinks.

- **File Attachment** is the same as the Insert File button on the toolbar. Both open the Insert Attachment dialog box, where you can select the file.

- **Text From File** inserts the entire contents of a text file into the message. You can then edit it as necessary.

- **Signature** and **Business Card** depend on these options being set up in Outlook Express. Do this by opening the Outlook Express Tools menu, choosing Stationery, and clicking Signature. That opens the Signature dialog box, shown in Figure 12-11. For the signature, which can be automatically placed at the end of all messages, you can either type what you want to insert or specify a file that has the information. After you have the signature, you can add it to a message with the Insert Signature button on the toolbar. For the business card, or vCard, you must specify a contact in the address book that will be used for the data on the card. In essence, what you are doing with a vCard is sending an address-book entry that can be added to the recipient's address book.

- **Horizontal Line** inserts a separator line across the message. This line works on both plain text messages as well as those with rich text.

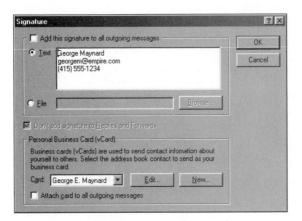

Figure 12-11. *Signature dialog box.*

- **Picture** allows you to specify a graphic that you want to include on the message, as shown below. You can also specify text that displays if the receiving mail client can't display pictures.

- **Hyperlink** confirms that text that looks like a hyperlink is in fact one. After you have typed the text and Outlook Express has converted it to a hyperlink, you can select the link and this option to have its status confirmed.

Format Menu

The Format menu, shown on the next page, allows you to apply various formatting styles, as well as specific font and paragraph formatting. Additionally you can

- **Insert a picture** to be used as a background or apply a solid color for that purpose

- **Select the alphabet** that the message is to use
- **Choose between rich text and plain text**
- **Select a stationery**

 The Formatting toolbar, shown below, allows you to directly apply all of the formatting options, including styles. Styles are applied with the Style Tag button, which is the third object from the left.

Tools Menu

The Tools menu, shown below, gives you three ways to utilize your address book:

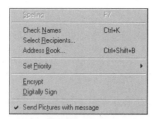

- **Check Names** compares the names in the address block with the local address book, then an organization's directories, if on a LAN or intranet, and finally Internet white pages. If the name is found, an underscore will appear under the name. If the name was not found, you will receive a message to that effect.

- **Select Recipients** opens the Select Recipients dialog box, shown in Figure 12-12, where you select names from your address book to use in a particular message.

- **Address Book** opens your address book so you can look up a name, delete an entry, or otherwise make changes.

In addition to the options related to the address book, the Tools menu allows you to check spelling, set the priority of the message, encrypt or digitally sign the message (which can also be done from the toolbar), and allow pictures to be sent with the message.

OTE The Spelling option uses the spell-checking engine provided by Microsoft Office or Microsoft Works; if you don't have Office or Works installed, the option is unavailable.

Within the Address Book dialog box, you can quickly find names by typing them in the text box under the toolbar, adding and deleting names, and editing the names already there. Additionally you can create groups of people if you commonly send the same messages to all members of the group. After

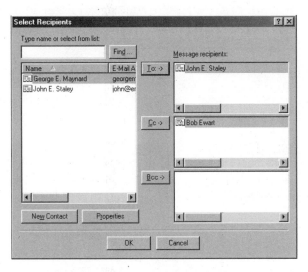

Figure 12-12. *Selecting names from the address book.*

a group is established, the single selection of the group selects everyone in the group. To edit a name in the address book, double-click the name, and the Properties dialog box for that name will open, as shown in Figure 12-13. If all you want is to see the information associated with a name, simply move the mouse pointer over the name, and the ToolTip for that name will appear with all the information, as you can see in Figure 12-14.

Compose Menu

The Compose menu, shown here, allows you to create a new message:

- Without special stationery or a particular person

- Using special stationery

- In reply to the sender or all parties on a message you received

- To forward a message you received to recipients who were not on the original distribution, as a standard message or as an attached .eml file

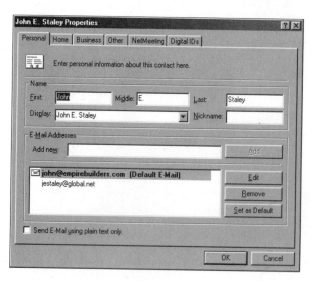

Figure 12-13. *Address book properties for a given name.*

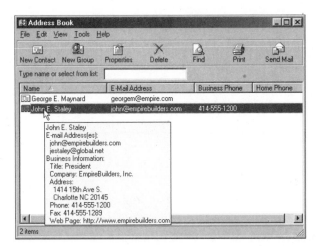

Figure 12-14. *Address book information shown in a ToolTip.*

Sending, Replying to, and Forwarding Mail

To illustrate Outlook Express, look at a typical mailing scenario where a message is sent, replied to, and then forwarded. Refer to the foregoing section on menu options if you need to review the specifics of a particular option or dialog box.

Sending a Message

If you don't have Outlook Express open, open it now from either its desktop icon or the Start menu, and then follow these steps to create and send a message:

1. Open the New Message window by clicking the Compose Message button on the toolbar.

2. Type in the To, Cc, and Bcc recipients, or open the Select Recipients dialog box by clicking the card to the right of the To, Cc, or Bcc buttons and double-click entries you want. Entries taken from an address book or checked in the address book show up underlined.

IP Separate multiple recipients in the To, Cc, and Bcc boxes with a semicolon. This is automatically added when you add recipients from the address book.

3. Enter a subject, add any text to the message, and then insert a file, message, or object from the Insert menu or by clicking the Insert File button (the paper clip) and selecting the file. If the recipient is using Outlook or Outlook Express, that program will display a small paper clip in the message header whenever there is an attachment.

 TIP Using a clear, succinct subject is important. It may be the only thing that the recipient reads, and it can be used to find the message at a later time.

---

4. Notify the recipient(s) that this is a high-priority message by opening the Tools menu and choosing Set Priority | High. A red exclamation point will appear in your message and in the message header of the recipient's mail program.

Your message should look similar to Figure 12-15. The attachment is shown at the bottom of the message. When you are satisfied with your own message, click the Send button.

 NOTE You can drag attachments from Windows Explorer or other applications to your message. Also, if you get a message with an attachment, you can drag the attachment to Windows Explorer or another folder.

Opening and Replying to Messages

 Messages arrive in your Inbox folder when you open Outlook Express (and possibly connect to your message service, such as your ISP, if you are not connected full-time), and periodically thereafter as long as Outlook Express is active on your computer and you are connected to a message service. You are notified of new arrivals by an envelope icon appearing next to the taskbar's clock.

Unread (or unopened) messages appear with a closed envelope icon and a bold header in the Inbox, as you can see in Figure 12-16. After you have read (or opened) a message, the icon becomes an open envelope, and the header returns to a normal style. You can change the marking of a message

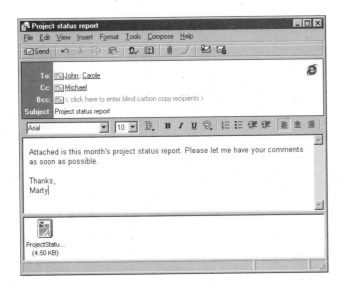

Figure 12-15.   *Outgoing message example.*

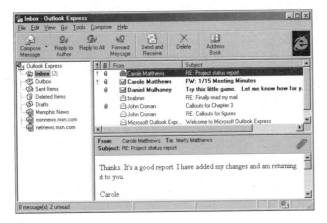

Figure 12-16.   *Outlook Express with unopened messages.*

(its icon and whether it is bold) by opening the Edit menu or the context menu and choosing the appropriate Mark As option. Open a message using one of the following methods:

■ Double-click a message header.

■ Select the header, and choose Open from the File menu.

- Right-click the header to open a context menu, shown here, and select Open.

 OTE The context menu, opened by right-clicking a message header, combined with the bottom pane of the Outlook Express window, allows you to do most of what you can do by opening the message.

The message opens in a window similar to the Message window. An example message is shown in Figure 12-17. This window offers a set of buttons that accommodates tasks you can perform with messages, such as saving, printing, forwarding, and opening any previous or following messages in the current folder.

Double-clicking an attached-file icon opens a dialog box that asks if you want to open the file in its associated program such as Microsoft Word, or save it to disk. You can also right-click an attached file to open a context menu that allows you to open the file, print the file, save the file on your disk, or quickly display the file.

 If you want to send a reply to the person who sent you the message, click the Reply To Author button on the toolbar. Alternately, you can send a message to all the people who sent or received the original message by clicking the Reply All toolbar button. In either case, the reply window opens, looking similar to Figure 12-18.

 IP You can reply to messages directly from the Inbox by right-clicking the message header and choosing the reply option you want from the context menu.

The original message is repeated with space above it for your reply message. You can also add To, Cc, and Bcc recipients. Click the Send button when your message and any attached documents or objects are ready to be sent.

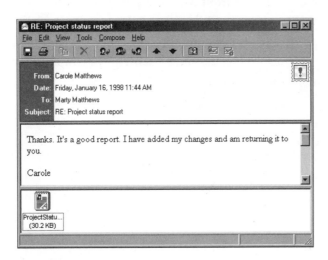

Figure 12-17. *An open message.*

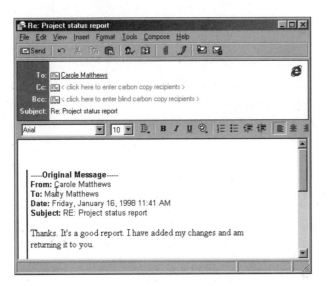

Figure 12-18. *A reply window showing the top of the original message and leaving room for a reply.*

Forwarding Messages

Forwarding is similar to replying except that you send messages to recipients who were not on the original distribution. Any composed or received message in a messaging folder can be forwarded. Selected messages can be forwarded directly from the Inbox by clicking the Forward Message toolbar button or from an opened message window in the same manner. The forwarding message is displayed with space above it for any forwarding comments, as shown in a reply message. The toolbars appear as they do for new messages.

Managing Messages

The real power of Outlook Express lies in its organizational features. You can store messages and faxes in cascading folders, sort messages by their message header categories, change which columns of header information to see, and list only specific messages through a find command.

Storing Messages

Outlook Express folders and messages within those folders are saved in a folder that you identified when you first started Outlook Express. By default, this is in the \Windows\Application Data\Microsoft\Outlook Express folder. If you open this folder or the one that you choose to use, you will see, as shown in Figure 12-19, a content file (.mbx) and an index file (.idx) for each of Outlook Express's folders. This compares to the single .pst file used with both the Exchange's Inbox in Windows 95 and Outlook 97 or 98, or to the .mmf file used in Windows for Workgroups. Upon upgrading to Windows 98, you are given the choice of maintaining your existing mail system or converting your .pst or .mmf files to the set of files used by Outlook Express.

 IP   When backing up critical files, include your Outlook Express Mail and News folders. To quickly locate these folders, open the Start menu, choose Find, then Files or Folders, and search for the file named Inbox.mbx.

Initially Outlook Express creates five mail folders: Inbox, Outbox, Sent Items, Deleted Items, and Drafts, plus one or more news folders. These serve most immediate needs. However, as your inventory of messages grows and your usage matures, you may want to clear out the Inbox and move the messages into more meaningful locations. You create new folders by selecting the folder one level above the level of the new folder. You then open the File menu, and choose Folder | New Folder, and name the new folder. You can also right-click the parent folder and select New folder from the context menu. You can create sublevels of folders just as you do in Windows Explorer. Figure 12-20 shows an added level of folders.

You can easily move messages from one folder to another by dragging them from one pane of the Inbox to the other. Pressing the **CTRL** key as you drag them copies the message. You can also use the Move and Copy options on the File menu or the context menu opened by right-clicking a message.

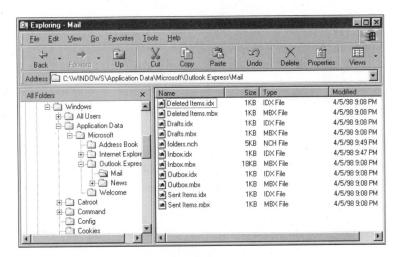

Figure 12-19. *Locating Outlook Express files.*

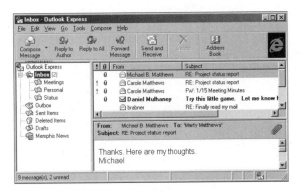

Figure 12-20. *An additional level of Inbox folders.*

Using the Inbox Assistant

The Inbox Assistant automates message management within Outlook Express. You establish rules for how you want to handle the messages that you receive, and the Inbox Assistant will move, copy, forward, reply, or delete the messages based on those rules without your ever having to see the messages. Here is an example of how to select messages that talk about the fall planning meeting and forward those messages to a colleague.

1. From Outlook Express, open the Tools menu, choose Inbox Assistant, and click Add. The Properties dialog box that you saw in Figure 12-4 opens.

2. Click the Subject text box, and type **fall planning meeting.**

3. Click the Forward To check box, click the address card to its right, and select the colleague to whom you want to send the messages. Your Properties dialog box should look like Figure 12-21.

4. Click OK to complete the rule.

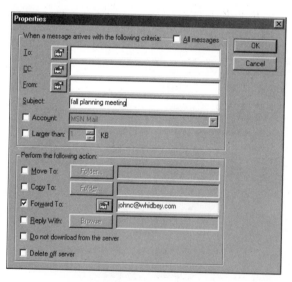

Figure 12-21. *Setting rules for handling e-mail.*

You can establish several rules in a similar manner. When you have the rules you want, you can see them in the Inbox Assistant dialog box, shown in Figure 12-22. Here you can turn the rules on or off, rearrange the rules (the top rules are executed first), remove them, and edit them.

Viewing Messages

You can view messages in a number of different arrangements: according to column headings, several layers of more specific categories or groups, and ascending and descending order. Finally, you can find messages that fit a set of parameters you choose. The View and Tools menus contain options that allow you to customize how you view your messages and faxes.

Organizing Columns The View menu Columns option lets you choose the header columns that appear on the right pane of the Inbox. Figure 12-23 shows the Columns dialog box with lists of available and shown columns. To display additional columns, select them from the Available Columns list box, and click Add. To remove a displayed column, select it and click Remove. While a displayed column is selected, you can use the Move Up and Move Down buttons to change its placement in the header.

 IP   Change the width of a column by pointing at the divider to the right of a column header, waiting for the mouse pointer to change into a cross, and then dragging left to decrease or drag right to increase the column size.

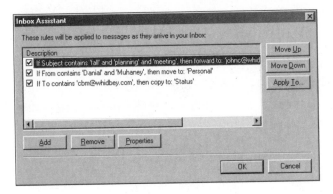

Figure 12-22.   *Managing rules in the Inbox Assistant.*

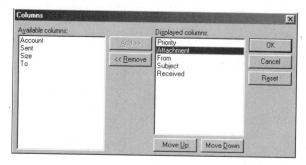

Figure 12-23. *Customizing the columns displayed in Outlook Express folders.*

Sorting Messages You can sort on any of the columns by clicking the column heading. The first time you click the heading, the list will be sorted in ascending order, and the second time you click the same heading, it will be sorted in descending order. The View menu Sort By option provides the same capability by allowing you to select the column to be sorted and then selecting whether to sort it ascending (if you don't select Ascending, the column is sorted descending).

Finding Messages Finding messages with the Edit menu Find Message option offers the most precise manner to locate a specific message. Much like a query in database terminology, Find Message lists those items that meet the criteria you establish. The Find Message dialog box, shown in Figure 12-24, provides text and check boxes to enter your search parameters. When you have entered the criteria, click Find Now, and the matching entries will be listed.

Customizing Outlook Express

You can customize Outlook Express to meet your preferences in a number of ways. Many of these are set in the Window Layout Properties dialog box (shown in Figure 12-25), which you open by selecting Layout from the View menu. In the Window Layout Properties dialog box, you can display or hide window elements, customize the toolbar, and manipulate the preview pane. Within Outlook Express itself, you can resize the panes and the columns by dragging the dividers between them, as described earlier.

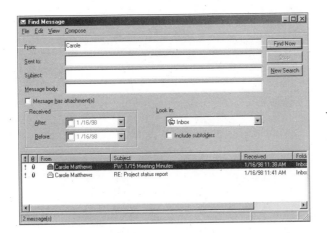

Figure 12-24. *Finding messages.*

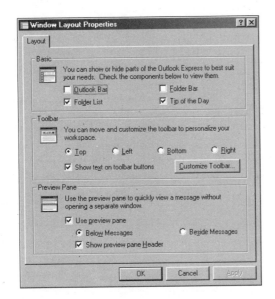

Figure 12-25. *Changing the Outlook Express layout.*

Multimedia on
and off the Internet

Part 5 explores the multimedia world available with Windows 98, where the role of multimedia on the Internet or intranet is important, as it is on the desktop or laptop. Part 5 is therefore broken into two chapters. Chapter 13 looks at how to use Windows 98 multimedia tools on your computer, and Chapter 14 focuses on what you can do with multimedia on the Internet or an intranet.

Using Multimedia

Multimedia is the frosting on the Windows 98 cake! Anyone who has used a computer-based encyclopedia with multimedia, played a computer game with multimedia, or spent a day in front of a computer with an audio CD playing will agree. You can use a computer without multimedia and perform the majority of tasks you need to accomplish, but multimedia makes these tasks much more pleasant and fun. Multimedia is CD-quality digital audio and full-motion video integrated into the programs on your desktop (or laptop) computer. The pleasure is found in looking up *Louis Armstrong* in a computerized encyclopedia and seeing a film clip with sound of him playing his trumpet, as shown in Figure 13-1. (Sorry you can't also hear it.) It is found seeing a film clip with sound of a tax expert giving you advice in the middle of your tax-preparation package (Figure 13-2). It is found in greatly enhanced audio and video in such games as Riven (Figure 13-3).

Windows 98 provides built-in support and many enhancements for multimedia. These include the ability to record and play back high-quality digital audio; to play back digital video more smoothly in a larger viewing area; to compress and decompress audio and video files with several built-in choices of compression schemes (codecs); and to support other applications in capturing and recording full-motion video. The 32-bit, multitasking, multithreaded architecture of Windows 98 lends itself to providing higher-quality, more smoothly running, more realistic multimedia sequences.

In this chapter, you'll review what hardware and software are necessary for multimedia and see how to install them. You will then examine the multimedia accessories that are available in Windows 98. Finally you will learn how to use codecs with multimedia files and how to assign sound clips to events on your computer.

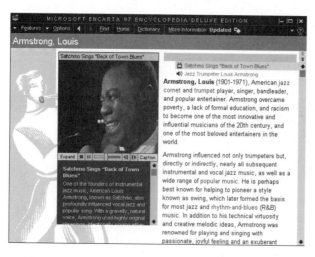

Figure 13-1.   *Louis Armstrong playing his trumpet from Microsoft Encarta.*

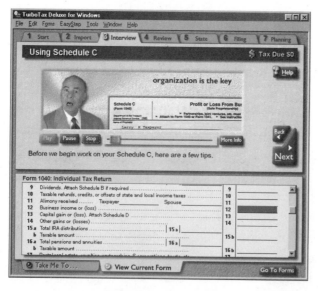

Figure 13-2.   *Marshall Loeb giving tax advice in Turbo Tax Deluxe.*

Figure 13-3. *Riven, the game.*

What Do You Need for Multimedia?

You can implement multimedia to many different degrees. A basic computer for multimedia would have a Pentium 100 processor, a floppy-disk drive, 1 GB of hard-disk space, a keyboard, a VGA monitor (640 × 480 pixels), a video adapter, 16 MB of RAM, a sound card, speakers, and a CD-ROM drive. With such a system, you will be able to read a multimedia CD-ROM and play digital audio and video clips. However, the video image will be small and may be jerky, there will be pauses as new segments are loaded off the disk, and the audio will be of lower quality.

To improve on the minimum system, you do not have to go to the opposite extreme on any component. Rather, upgrade all components evenly. The following components represent a reasonably balanced system:

- Pentium processor, 166 MHz MMX
- 32 MB of memory
- 3 GB hard disk
- PCI bus hard disk controllers
- PCI bus video adapter with 2 MB video RAM
- 15" SVGA (800 × 600) monitor running with at least 16,000 colors
- 12x CD-ROM drive
- 16-bit sound card with MIDI support

Of the foregoing components, the PCI-bus video controller probably gives you the greatest benefit; PCI-bus performance is approximately ten times that of an ISA-bus system. A faster processor will probably not buy you much improvement in multimedia. On the other hand, going to a 17" monitor using 1024 × 768 and 24-bit video with more than 64,000 colors will significantly improve the playback of video sequences. After PCI-bus and improved video, the next thing to improve is memory, followed by a higher speed (16×–24×) CD-ROM drive.

You can add many additional pieces of equipment to your system from this rapidly growing area of computer technology, including:

■ Still and full-motion digital video cameras

■ Video capture cards

■ Television and radio tuners

■ Microphones and headsets

■ High-fidelity stereo speaker systems

■ Large screen, high-quality monitors

■ Recording and rewritable CDs

■ DVDs, including players, recorders, and rewritable recorders

Your only limitation to making these additions (besides budget, time, and interest) is the ability of your base system to handle them. The "reasonably balanced system" described above is probably the realistic minimum if you want to experience multimedia as it is intended. And you should have a 230- to 250-watt power supply. As you add these items, you may want to upgrade your system, especially if you get into full-motion video work where the fastest processors and lots of memory, both RAM (128 MB) and hard disk (8 GB), are common.

Installing Multimedia Cards

Multimedia cards, unless they are Plug and Play (PnP), require you to make several settings on the cards, so that they communicate properly and work in harmony with the rest of your computer. For example, 16-bit sound cards typically have the following settings:

- I/O port addresses for

  - Game port (fixed at 200h–207h)

  - Audio interface (variable; 220h–22Fh is typical)

  - MIDI interface (variable; 300h–301h is typical)

  - FM music synthesizer (fixed at 388h–38Bh)

- Interrupt request line (IRQ) (variable with 5 typical)

- Direct memory address (DMA) channel for

  - 8-bit data (variable; channel 1 is typical)

  - 16-bit data (variable; channel 5 is typical)

If your sound card also has a CD-ROM controller on it, there may be additional settings. If your CD-ROM uses its own controller, that controller may have settings. These settings must be made so they do not conflict with other devices in your computer. Of particular concern are SCSI-disk controllers (possibly used for a CD-ROM drive), which, by default, tend to use the same I/O port address as a sound card's MIDI interface and the same high (upper) DMA channel. To determine which resources are currently used and which are currently available, open the System control panel, and click the Device Manager tab. Here, as shown in Figure 13-4, you can select a device, click Properties, and then click the Resources tab to see the settings for that device, similar to those shown in Figure 13-5. Back in the System Properties Device Manager, you can click Print to print the System Summary report. This report lists the resources used by every device in your computer. From this you can determine what resources are available for a multimedia card.

 IP A quick way to open the System control panel is to right-click My Computer and select Properties.

As you saw for a sound card, the normal resources used by a multimedia device are interrupt request lines (IRQs), I/O port addresses, and direct memory access (DMA) channels. If a card is Plug and Play, these settings are set for you automatically, and you do not have to worry about them. On all other devices, you have to manually make the settings on the card.

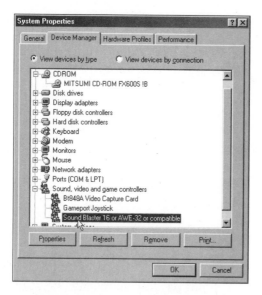

Figure 13-4. *Selecting a device in the Device Manager.*

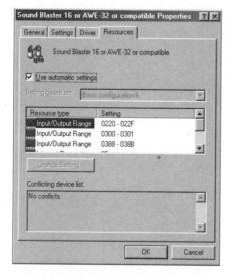

Figure 13-5. *Looking at the resources for a device.*

 ARNING Before handling a sound card or any other electronic circuit card, be sure to ground yourself by touching some grounded object to make sure that static electricity does not damage some component on the circuit card. An even better idea is to get, connect, and wear a grounding wrist strap while working with the circuit card.

Cards that are not PnP use different methods of changing the settings. Some have a small set of pins sticking up, called a *DIP header,* with little plastic or metal blocks, called *jumpers,* connecting some of the pins. Others have tiny banks of numbered switches, called *DIP switches.* If you need to set up a card with either jumpers or switches, you'll need to study the manual that came with the card to determine the purpose of each jumper or switch. Then with your list of what other devices are using, read the following sections to determine how to set up your card.

With a DIP header, you need to lift off the jumpers (you may need to use a small screwdriver to pry it up or needle-nose pliers to grasp it) and then place the jumper back on the correct pins. With a DIP switch, note which side is *ON,* and then press down or slide across (depending on the type) the appropriate switches so they are set correctly to be on or off.

Interrupt Request Line or IRQ

The *IRQ* determines which interrupt line on your computer the adapter card uses to request service. On all the computers on which Windows 98 will run, there are 16 interrupt request lines numbered 0 through 15. Table 13-1 shows default assignments and some possible uses of the lines that are typically available for added devices. Some possible choices for the multimedia cards are IRQs 5, 10, and 11. Look at what your other devices are using, and then decide what you want to use for this card. Next look at your card's manual, and decide how your choice translates into pins or switches on your card.

 OTE Tables 13-1 through 13-3 show *typical* assignments. Your device may have a different assignment.

I/O Port Address

The *I/O port address* is the address through which the computer, the card, and the driver software for the card all communicate. It is actually a range of numbers that are expressed in hexadecimal notation (base 16), so you often see them with a small *h* after the number. Table 13-2 shows default assignments and some possible uses of the addresses that are typically available for added devices. For multimedia, there are two fixed settings, for the game port joystick and the FM music synthesizer, and two variable

IRQ	Default or Typical Use
0	System timer
1	Keyboard
2	Programmable interrupt controller (implements IRQs 9–15)
3	Serial communications ports COM2 and COM4
4	Serial communications ports COM1 and COM3
5	Available, but possibly used by a bus mouse or a sound card
6	Floppy disk controller
7	Parallel communications port LPT1
8	System CMOS and real-time clock
9	Available, but possibly used by a PCI device like video or network adapters
10	Available, but possibly used by a PCI device like video or network adapters
11	Available, but possibly used by a PCI device like video or network adapters
12	Available, but possibly used by a SCSI disk controller
13	Numeric data processor or math coprocessor
14	Primary IDE disk controller
15	Secondary IDE disk controller

Table 13-1. *Interrupt request lines (IRQs) and their typical uses.*

settings for the audio and MIDI music interfaces. You need to worry only about the latter. Some possible choices for audio are 220h–22Fh and 230h–23Fh. For MIDI, 300h–31Fh and 330h–34Fh are often used. Look at what your other devices are using, and then decide what you want to use for this card. Next look at your card's manual, and decide how your choice translates to pins or switches on your card.

 OTE Hexadecimal (hex) numbers go from 0 to 15 instead of 0 to 9 for decimal numbers. Alphabetical letters A–F are used to represent the hexadecimal numbers beyond 9. The range of hexadecimal numbers is 0, 1, 2, 3, 4, 5, 6, 7, 8, 9, A, B, C, D, E, and F. The I/O port address range 300h–31Fh represents 32 decimal (20 hex) addresses: 300–309 is 10, 30A–30F is 6, 310–31F is 16 (310 follows 30F).

> **OTE** Many adapter cards and their manuals identify only the base I/O port address. This is the number on the left in the address range shown in Table 13-2. For example, for the range 300h–31Fh, 300h is the base I/O port address.

Port Address	Default or Typical Use
000h–0DFh	System components like system timer, keyboard, speaker
0F0h–0FFh	Numeric coprocessor
170h–177h	Secondary IDE hard disk controller
1F0h–1F7h	Primary IDE hard disk controller
200h–20Fh	Game port joystick
220h–22Fh	Generally used by sound card
230h–23Fh	Available, may be used by bus mouse, Sony CD-ROM, or sound card
278h–27Fh	LPT2 parallel port (LPT3 if present)
2E8h–2Efh	COM4 serial port
2F8h–2FFh	COM2 serial port
300h–31Fh	Available, may be used by a sound card
320h–33Fh	Available, may be used by a SCSI controller or a sound card
340h–35Fh	Available, may be used by a SCSI controller or a sound card
376h–376h	Secondary IDE hard disk controller
378h–37Fh	LPT1 parallel printer port (LPT2 if LPT3 present)
388h–38Fh	FM music synthesizer
3B0h–3BBh	Display adapter monochrome area
3BCh–3BFh	(LPT1 parallel printer port if LPT3 present)
3C0h–3DFh	Display adapter color area
3E8h–3Efh	COM3 serial port
3F2h–3F5h	Floppy disk controller
3F6h–3F6h	Primary IDE hard disk controller
3F8h–3FFh	COM1 serial port

Table 13-2.   *I/O port addresses and their typical uses.*

DMA Channel

A DMA channel allows your multimedia card to read and write directly to memory without going through the CPU. This significantly speeds up whatever process is under way and is very important to handling audio and video. Table 13-3 shows some possible uses of DMA channels and some that can be used for multimedia adapters. For a 16-bit card, you will need two DMA channels. Some common choices are channels 1 and 5 or channels 3 and 7.

 ARNING Watch out for I/O port address and DMA channel conflicts between SCSI-disk controllers and 16-bit sound cards.

Completing Installation

Based on the System Summary report and on the table here, you will be able to make the appropriate settings on your card(s). When that is done, install the card in your computer, being careful of static electricity, and run the Add New Hardware Wizard in the Control Panel folder. With the hardware configured and installed, install the multimedia components of Windows 98 with the following steps:

1. Restart Windows 98. Windows will often detect the new card during startup and ask if you want to install it. Click Yes and follow the on-screen instructions. Otherwise, click Add New Hardware in Control Panel, and follow the on-screen instructions.

DMA Channel	Default or Typical Use
0	May be available
1	May be available, may be used by a sound card
2	Standard floppy-disk controller
3	May be available
4	Direct memory access controller
5	May be used by a SCSI controller or a sound card
6	May be available
7	May be available

Table 13-3. *DMA channels and their typical uses.*

2. Click Add/Remove Programs in Control Panel to open the Add/Remove Programs Properties dialog box.

3. Click the Windows Setup tab, and scroll the list until you see Multimedia.

4. Double-click Multimedia to open the list of multimedia components, as you can see in Figure 13-6.

5. Select (make sure the check box has a mark in it) the multimedia components you need or want.

   The Windows multimedia components include three types of objects: software multimedia tools, including CD Player, DVD Player, Media Player, Sound Recorder, and Volume Control; audio and video compression techniques; and various schemes for assigning sounds to computer events, such as opening a window or getting a warning message. The sound schemes vary significantly in size, so if you have limited disk space, you'll want to consider these carefully. On the other hand, you will probably want all of the software devices.

6. When you have selected the components you want, click OK twice to install them.

With your hardware installed, you are ready to set up and try some of the multimedia accessories included with Windows 98.

Figure 13-6.   *Adding the multimedia components of Windows 98.*

Using Windows 98 Multimedia Accessories

The Windows 98 multimedia accessories include CD Player, DVD Player, Media Player, ActiveMovie Control, Sound Recorder, and Volume Control. These represent some good, if basic, means to explore audio and video multimedia. You can start any of these accessories by opening the Start menu and choosing Programs | Accessories | Entertainment, as you can see in Figure 13-7. The following discussion looks at each of the multimedia accessories.

Using the CD Player

The CD Player allows you to control and play audio CDs. Unless you are in the music business, this is something that you will do purely for pleasure. For those of us who spend most of our lives in front of a computer, though, it is a great enhancement to our lives!

Although you can use the Start menu as described above, the easiest way to start the CD Player is to simply insert an audio CD in your CD-ROM drive. After a brief time, the CD Player will start automatically and play the audio CD. When started, the CD Player task will appear in the taskbar. As usual, you can click the task to open the dialog box, as you can see in Figure 13-8.

Figure 13-7. *Opening the Windows 98 multimedia accessories.*

Figure 13-8. *CD Player dialog box.*

 IP If you do not want to play a CD automatically when you insert it in the drive, hold down **SHIFT** when you insert the audio CD.

The CD Player has a primary set of controls, described in Table 13-4, that are much like a mechanical CD or tape player. The toolbar buttons, which you can turn on from the View menu, are described in Table 13-5. The menus add functionality not found in many mechanical CD players.

Button	Name	Description
▶	Play	Starts playing the audio CD in the drive
▋▋	Pause	Pauses playing the audio CD in the drive
■	Stop	Stops playing the audio CD in the drive
▏◀◀	Previous Track	Goes back to the beginning of the current track, or if already there, to the beginning of the previous track
◀◀	Skip Backwards	Goes back one second on current track
▶▶	Skip Forwards	Goes forward one second on current track
▶▶▏	Next Track	Goes to the beginning of the next track
▲	Eject	Ejects the CD from the drive

Table 13-4. *CD Player controls.*

Button	Name	Description
	Edit Play List	Opens the list of tracks for editing (see Figure 13-9)
	Track Time Elapsed	Displays in the digital panel below the toolbar the time elapsed playing the current track
	Track Time Remaining	Displays in the digital panel the remaining time to complete playing the current track
	Disc Time Remaining	Displays in the digital panel the remaining time to complete playing the entire disc
	Random Track Order	At the end of a track, the next track to play is randomly selected
	Continuous Play	At the end of the last track, the player starts over at the beginning of the first track
	Intro Play	Plays the first ten seconds of each track

Table 13-5. *CD Player toolbar buttons.*

One of the best features of the CD Player is the Play List, shown in Figure 13-9, where you can select the tracks you want to play and the order in which you want to play them. You can also enter the artist, title, and description of each track, and this information will be stored for you and appear the next time you insert that particular CD. Use the following instructions to select specific tracks in the order you want them played:

1. Open the Play List either by clicking the Edit Play List button on the left of the toolbar or by choosing Edit Play List on the Disc menu.

2. Click Clear All to clear the Play List.

3. If you want, you can enter the name of the artist, the title of the CD, and the description of each track.

 IP When you are entering the track descriptions, if you press **ENTER** at the end of each entry, you will both set the name and be ready to enter a new name. If you click Set Name, you will have to separately highlight the next old name to replace it.

Figure 13-9.   *List of tracks to be played.*

4. Double-click the tracks in the right column in the order you want them played. You may click the same track multiple times if you want that track repeated.

5. When the Play List is the way you want it, click OK to close the dialog box, and then click Play to begin playing your list of tracks.

If you do take the time to enter your CD titles and track descriptions, you will get a very informative display of what you are currently playing, as you can see in Figure 13-10.

The digital display shows the track currently being played and one of three times: the elapsed time in the current track, the time remaining in the current track, or the time remaining on the disc (which does not show the current track number). In both cases in which the remaining time is displayed, the figure has angle brackets on either end of it, as shown to the left. When you minimize the CD Player, the taskbar entry, if it is large enough, will still show the track and time, also shown to the left. You can control which time is displayed from both the View menu and the toolbar.

> **IP**   If the taskbar area is too small to see the digital display, move the mouse pointer to the task. You will see a ToolTip with the track and time.

Figure 13-10. *CD Player with artist, title, and track information.*

The Preferences option on the Options menu opens the Preferences dialog box, shown below. Most of the entries are self-explanatory, except possibly the Intro Play Length, which is the length of time that the beginning of each track is played when you click the Intro Play button. This can be from 5 to 15 seconds; the default is 10 seconds.

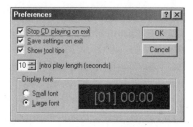

Using the DVD Player

"DVD" is a trademark of the DVD Consortium and does not stand for anything. In this book, though, and in many other sources, DVD is synonymous with "digital video disc." DVD uses a disc the size of a CD and on it stores over two hours of very high-quality full-motion, full-screen video (better than a laser disc) along with multiple tracks of very high-quality audio (better than a CD). Alternatively, a DVD can hold from 4.7 to 17 GB of data depending on whether the disc is single-sided, double-sided, or double-sided and double-layered. While any DVD can contain video, audio, data, or a combination of the three, DVDs can come in the following "flavors":

■ **DVD-ROM** is an extension of CD-ROM and holds 4.7 to 17 GB of read-only computer data, which can include video and audio segments.

- **DVD-R** or **DVD-WO** is an extension of CD-R and provides for writing data once on blank media (4.7 to 17 GB).

- **DVD-RAM** is an extension of CD-RW and provides writing and re-writing on blank media (4.7 to 17 GB).

- **DVD-Video** or **DVD-Movie** is an extension of audio CDs and holds a full-length feature motion picture with surround-sound audio in eight languages, with 32 subtitle tracks, and support for interactive branching.

The home-entertainment DVD players will play DVD-video discs and CD-audio discs. The DVD-ROM drives available for personal computers will handle DVD-video, DVD-ROM, CD-ROM, and CD-audio. At the time of this writing, early models of DVD-R and DVD-RAM are being shown and will be on the market before long. By 1999, most computers will be sold with DVD-ROM drives. DVD represents a significant increase in large-capacity, portable storage media as well as a potential for many applications yet to be developed.

Using DVDs in a computer requires both a DVD-ROM drive and a decoder card, which is used to provide real-time hardware decompression of the MPEG-2 video and the Dolby AC-3 audio. Due to the need to handle large amounts of video information, the decoder card needs to be directly connected to the video adapter card. This may mean that a new video adapter is required, possibly with more memory. In addition to the audio and video streams, DVDs provide a subpicture stream that can contain subtitles, a director's comments, or other data that is displayed while a movie is being displayed. To adequately handle DVD, the computer should be at least a Pentium 166 MMX with 32 MB and a 4 MB video card capable of 1024 × 768 and 2-D/3-D acceleration.

You can start the DVD Player included with Windows 98 from the Start menu or by inserting a DVD-video disc. If you have a DVD-ROM drive, the basic controller for the DVD Player will appear on your screen. This provides controls for selecting the channel, using on-screen menu navigation, and controlling playback. If you select Advanced User, you will be able to select an audio channel, choose a language, and control other features. If you drag the DVD Player controller to the edge of the screen, it will change to a narrow vertical controller similar to a TV or VCR remote control.

Displaying Video Files

Windows 98 gives you two ways of displaying video files on your computer: ActiveMovie and Media Player. Both allow you to display a wide range of video files as well as some audio files. The file types that you can play on either device include

■ ActiveMovie files in the .au, .aif, .aiff, and .aifc formats

■ QuickTime movies with .qt extension

■ Video for Windows format (.avi extension)

■ Moving Pictures Expert Group (MPEG) format (.mpg extension)

■ Waveform audio clips in the waveform format (.wav extension)

■ MIDI sound clips in either .mid or .rmi formats

■ Audio CDs

Using ActiveMovie Control

ActiveMovie is new to Windows 98 and uses the DirectShow technology. ActiveMovie is designed to use Internet Explorer to display video files that you have downloaded. Independent of Internet Explorer, ActiveMovie is the Windows 98 default video player, and unless you have reassigned the file types, it is what opens and plays video files when you click them. If you look in the \Windows\Media folder on your hard disk (depending on your installation choice), or in the \Cdsample\Videos and Sounds folders on the Windows 98 CD-ROM, you will find a number of these files to try out. For example, the Msnbc.mpg video clip is shown being played in Figure 13-11. The Active Movie Control provides a wide sampling of multimedia capabilities. Try out several of the files in the mentioned folders to see this for yourself.

You can start the ActiveMovie Control by using the Start menu or by clicking a media file. The controls in ActiveMovie are extremely simple, as described in Table 13-6, and there are no menus.

Figure 13-11. *Video file being played with the ActiveMovie Control.*

Button	Name	Description
▶	Run	Starts the playing of the current media clip
■	Stop	Stops the playing of the current media clip
❚❚	Pause	Pauses the playing of the current media clip

Table 13-6. *ActiveMovie controls.*

 NOTE The ActiveMovie Run button becomes a Pause button after you have started playing a clip.

If you want additional controls, want to change the picture size, or want another way to adjust volume, right-click the ActiveMovie window and choose Properties. The ActiveMovie Control Properties dialog box will open, as you can see at the top of the next page. Within the Movie Size tab, you can adjust the movie size from the original size at which it is stored, through a number of intermediate sizes to full screen. Within the Controls tab, you can add additional controls so ActiveMovie is closer to Media Player, which is described next, or you can remove all controls so the movie will almost fill your screen.

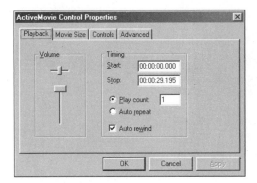

Using the Media Player

The Media Player allows you to play the same audio and video files as the ActiveMovie Control, but it provides a more comprehensive set of controls, and it gives you an analog scale instead of a digital readout on where you are in the file, as shown in Figure 13-12. You can start the Media Player from the Start menu. The controls in the Media Player are similar to the CD Player controls, as described in Table 13-7. The Options item on the Edit menu provides further controls, as shown in Figure 13-13. Several of the settings in the Options dialog box determine how media clips that are embedded in a document are handled. The Play In Client Document check box allows you to double-click an audio or video file in, say, a

Figure 13-12.   *Video file being played with the Media Player.*

Microsoft Word document, and have it played. The Selection option on the Edit menu allows you to define a specific selection of a media clip. The Device menu allows you to select a type of device and open a folder containing files for that device.

Button	Name	Description
▶	Start	Starts the playing of the current media clip
■	Stop	Stops the playing of the current media clip
▲	Eject	Ejects the CD in the drive
⏮	Previous Mark	Backs up and begins playing at the previous mark, either set by you or naturally occurring, like a track on a CD
◀◀	Rewind	Backs up a small increment and begins playing
▶▶	Fast Forward	Jumps forward a small increment and begins playing
▶▶▮	Next Mark	Jumps forward and begins playing at the next mark, either set by you or naturally occurring
▼	Start Selection	Sets a mark to begin a selection you want to define
▲	End Selection	Sets a mark to end a selection you are defining

Table 13-7. *Media Player controls.*

Figure 13-13. *Media Player Options dialog box.*

OTE The Media Player Start button becomes a Pause button after you have started playing a clip.

Using the Sound Recorder

The Sound Recorder allows you to digitally record sounds from a number of sources including microphones, CDs, MIDI devices (keyboards and synthesizers), and other audio devices like tape drives. The recordings are saved as waveform files (with a .wav extension), which can be attached to computer events and embedded in other documents (see related sections at the end of this chapter).

 You start the Sound Recorder from the Start menu as described earlier in the chapter. The Sound Recorder is a simple device with controls similar to a mechanical tape recorder, as you can see in Figure 13-14, and as described in Table 13-8. You can use Insert File and Mix With File from the Edit menu to replace existing .wav files or blend them into the recording. One interesting result of this is that you can mix several .wav files in the \Windows\Media folder or place them one after the other to create a unique sound recording. You can also create some interesting special effects by increasing or decreasing the volume and/or speed of, or adding an echo to, the playback of a sound clip.

Using the Volume Controls

The volume controls, shown in Figure 13-15, allow you to set the volume and balance and, thereby, to mix four or five different audio inputs and an overall audio output. The volume controls are used in conjunction with the other Windows 98 multimedia tools, especially the Sound Recorder.

Figure 13-14. *Sound Recorder.*

Button	Name	Description
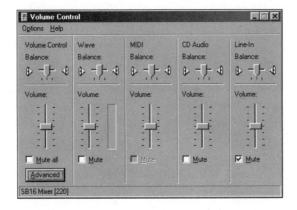	Seek To Start	Returns to the beginning of the clip
	Seek To End	Goes to the end of the clip
	Play	Plays the current clip (either what was recorded or what has been opened)
	Stop	Stops playing or recording
	Record	Starts recording.

Table 13-8. *Sound Recorder controls.*

Figure 13-15. *Volume controls.*

> **NOTE** Depending on your system, sometimes the Volume Control dialog box is titled "Speaker," and you may have slightly different options.

You open the volume controls from the Start menu, or if you have a Volume icon on the taskbar, you can double-click it. You can adjust the volume of a particular device by dragging the volume slider up to increase the volume or down to reduce the volume. From the Properties option on the Options menu, you can determine if the volume controls are for recording, playback, or the mixing device you are using, and the volume controls you want to have available, as you can see in Figure 13-16. If you have turned on Advanced Controls on the Options menu, an Advanced button will appear in the Volume Control dialog box, as shown in Figure 13-15. When you click the Advanced button, a set of tone controls appear like this:

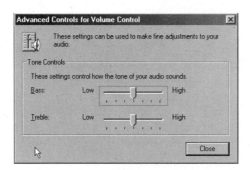

The Volume icon on the right of the taskbar not only opens the Volume Control dialog box when you double-click it, but when you click the icon, a pop-up volume control opens, as you can see below. The pop-up volume control allows you to raise or lower the volume as well as mute it (turn it off altogether) and is the same as the far left control in the Volume Control dialog box in playback mode.

Figure 13-16. *Volume Control Properties dialog box.*

Multimedia Control Panel

 The Multimedia control panel, which is shown in Figure 13-17, provides the central point for all multimedia settings. The Audio tab allows you to choose the devices you will use for audio recording and playback, what the volume level for each will be (by clicking the large volume-control button on the left), your speaker setup, and the recording quality you want to use. The Audio tab is also where you can turn the Volume icon on the right of the taskbar on or off. When this icon is turned on, a small speaker appears next to the clock, as shown on the left and discussed in the previous section.

The Video tab allows you to adjust the size of the video image. The MIDI tab allows you to configure the MIDI output and start the MIDI Instrument Installation Wizard. The CD Music tab allows you to specify the drive letter of the CD-ROM drive that you use for playing music CDs if you have more than one CD-ROM drive, the volume for the headphone jack, and whether to use digital instead of analog playback. The Devices tab lets you change the properties of your installed multimedia devices, described next.

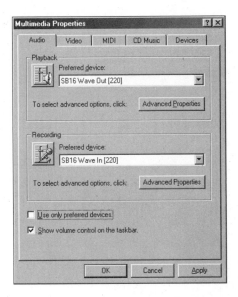

Figure 13-17. *Multimedia control panel.*

Multimedia Device Drivers

The Multimedia Properties Devices tab, shown in Figure 13-18, provides access to the multimedia device drivers that you have installed. This tab lists all the available categories of multimedia devices. The categories that have one or more drivers installed show a plus sign to the left. If you click the plus sign, the category will open and provide a description of the driver that is installed for that category. If you click a driver or select it and click Properties, you will get the Properties dialog box for the driver, such as that shown in Figure 13-19. For the most part, these dialog boxes simply allow you to turn the drivers on or off, and the Settings button tells you only the copyright and version information. Two of the entries in the Multimedia Properties Devices tab are for audio and video compression. This subject will be covered in detail in *Audio and Video Compression.*

The Media Control Devices entry in the Devices tab represents a special class of device drivers that implement the Media Control Interface (MCI) for specific devices. MCI provides a common set of commands, such as Play, Pause, and Stop, that can be applied to a wide variety of devices such

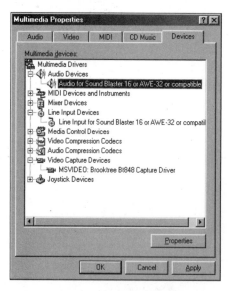

Figure 13-18. *Devices tab of the Multimedia control panel.*

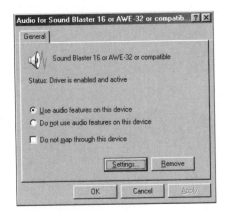

Figure 13-19. *Properties dialog box for a device driver.*

as VCRs, CD and DVD players, and laser-disc players. The detail entries under Media Control Devices, as shown next, represent all those that are available in Windows 98 and not necessarily those for installed devices.

Using Audio and Video Compression

When you digitize audio and video material, a very large amount of disk space is needed. For example, a little more than an hour's worth of music can fit on a CD-ROM that is equivalent to about 640 MB, and the same amount of space will hold only a little more than two minutes of uncompressed video. Also, color video requires a data stream of more than 5 MB per second, and 6x CD-ROM drives provide only 900 KB per second. For these reasons, audio and video compression have become important to computer multimedia and a major asset of Windows 98, which includes alternative schemes, called *codecs,* for compressing and decompressing digital audio and video. The default audio and video codecs in Windows 98 are shown in Figure 13-20, and the more popular codecs are described in Tables 13-9 and 13-10.

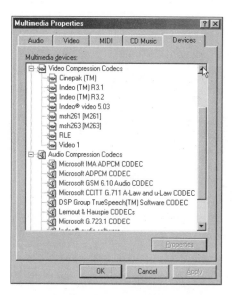

Figure 13-20. *Windows 98 audio and video codecs.*

Codecs are selected and applied at the time an audio or video clip is saved on a disk. You can see that by looking at the Sound Recorder, choosing Save As from the File menu, and then clicking the Change button at the bottom of the dialog box. This opens the Sound Selection dialog box. If you open the Format drop-down list box, you'll see the list of audio codecs, as you can see here:

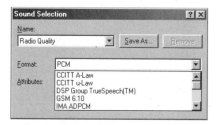

The video codecs in Windows 98 are for decompressing and playing video clips. To compress a video image, you must have a video capture board, which in most cases includes hardware capability or software for compression. Intel, for example, sells a video capture board with Indeo compression built into the board. If you get a video capture card that uses a codec not included with Windows 98, for example, either Motion JPEG or MPEG (MPEG is superior for motion pictures), use the Add New Hardware Wizard to install the card. You will be asked to select the codec you want to install, or the manufacturer will tell you to install software with the codec.

Codec	Description
DSP Group TrueSpeech	High-quality voice compression, although it should not be used for other than voice. Cannot be compressed in real time, so you must temporarily store the uncompressed audio. Can be decompressed in real time. Good for audio notes in a text document, and for voice mail.
Microsoft ADPCM	An early codec originally used with most .wav files and now generally replaced by either TrueSpeech for voice or IMA ADPCM for music.
Microsoft CCITT G.711	Consultative Committee for International Telephone and Telegraph standards for compressing and decompressing telephone conversations in North America. Provides a 2-to-1 compression ratio.
Microsoft GSM 6.10 Audio	European Telecommunications Standards Institute—Groupe Special Mobile recommendation. Uses real-time compression with good voice quality. Developed for cellular phones.
Microsoft IMA ADPCM	Interactive Multimedia Association's standard for 4-to-1 compression of 16-bit .wav files. Provides real-time compression, primarily of music, without much loss in fidelity. (ADPCM stands for adaptive delta pulse code modulation, a form of compression.)
Microsoft PCM Converter	Used to convert 16-bit .wav files so they can be played with 8-bit sound cards. Used whenever a sound clip is beyond your card's capabilities.

Table 13-9.   *Audio codecs in Windows 98.*

Codec	Description
Cinepak	Provides high-quality playback but at an extreme cost of more than 12 hours of compression time for ten minutes of finished video. Normally used in high-quality CD titles.
Indeo R3.1–R5.03	Intel-developed video codec that provides almost the quality of Cinepak but with real-time compression. Release 3.2 offers a common codec between the Apple Macintosh and Windows.
RLE	Meant for use with simple bitmapped images and will not work well with detailed photographs and motion pictures. (RLE stands for run length encoding.)
Video 1	Microsoft-developed codec that provides very efficient (low CPU usage) moderate-quality compression of full-motion video and higher-quality detailed photographs.

Table 13-10. *Video codecs in Windows 98.*

When you play back a media clip, the codec used to store the clip will be identified and correctly applied as the clip is playing. Besides video codecs included with Windows 98, Apple's QuickTime for Windows provides good performance and a good balance between the resources required and the resulting quality.

Assigning Sound Clips to Events

Windows 98 includes the capability to assign sounds to various computer events, such as starting Windows, opening a menu, maximizing a window, exiting Windows, the appearance of a message, and the arrival of e-mail. You can access this capability through the Sounds control panel, which opens the Sounds Properties dialog box, shown in Figure 13-21. You can use this dialog box in two ways. First, you can use the Schemes drop-down list box in the bottom of the dialog box to select a prefabricated scheme that assigns sounds to events. Secondly, you can select an event in the top list. If the event has a loudspeaker next to it, a sound has been assigned to it. You can hear that sound by pressing the right-pointing arrow in the Preview area of the dialog box. If you want to assign a different sound, you can open the Name drop-down list box and select a different

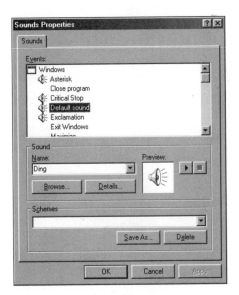

Figure 13-21. *Sounds Properties dialog box.*

sound, or you can use the Browse button and look for other sounds on
your hard disk or Windows 98 CD-ROM. When you have created a new
scheme, you may save it by clicking Save As.

 OTE Windows 98 comes with several sound assignment schemes that you
can use. These schemes, though, are not part of the Typical install, and you
must separately select them at installation time or add them through Add/
Remove Programs | Windows Setup | Multimedia | Multimedia Sound Schemes.

Using Audio and Video over the Internet and Intranets

By Dan Logan

Windows 98 allows you to use the Internet to make telephone calls. You can also videoconference and collaborate with others over the Internet with audio, video, and data sharing. You can receive and even broadcast audio and video programming. The Internet's potential for delivering audio and video content is only just beginning to be exploited, but Windows 98 will help you take advantage of new audio/video technologies as they appear.

Windows 98 with Internet Explorer makes it easy for you to take advantage of Internet telephony, video conferencing, and broadcasting. To do that, Internet Explorer includes

- **Microsoft NetMeeting,** which is a powerful multipoint audio and video conferencing and collaboration tool, as well as a tool for Internet telephony

- **NetShow Player,** which allows you to access Internet and intranet audio and video broadcasts, both streaming and downloaded (streaming allows the user to see or hear content without first having to download an entire file)

- **Third-party support,** which allows you to install and use third-party Internet telephony, video conferencing, and streaming audio and video products

Internet Multimedia Climate

The inclusion of Internet Explorer's audio and video tools and the emergence of the technologies behind them result from several factors coming together at the same time.

- Personal computers, on average, are becoming powerful enough to handle audio and video content over the Internet. Faster processors, more RAM, and more capable multimedia equipment provide the power you need to experience real-time audio and video, even over standard telephone lines. Most new computers now come equipped with the modems, sound cards, microphones, and speakers needed for audio and video. As a result, you can apply those capabilities with the Internet and intranets to which you are connected.

- Protocols (such as the International Telecommunications Union's T.120, H.323, and H.324 protocols) are in place to encourage telephony development over LANs (intranet) and the public telephone network (Internet). Also, organizations such as the Enterprise Computer Telephony Forum (ECTF) and the Internet Telephony Interoperability Consortium (ITC) are formalizing standards that allow vendors to quickly move the necessary systems to market.

- Audio and video conferencing and collaboration software on both the server and client sides have advanced so much that their use is compelling. With software such as NetMeeting, the Internet becomes a place for real-time collaboration, having a major impact on the way you conduct business, not to mention your personal life.

- Video conferencing is moving into the mainstream and is no longer limited to expensive equipment set up in a dedicated room. You can videoconference from your desktop over dial-up connections. Video conferencing now typically includes six components that contribute to collaboration: audio, video, chat, file transfer, application sharing, and Whiteboard.

The only factor slowing this forward momentum is that real-time audio and video are extremely demanding when it comes to *bandwidth*—the amount of information that must be exchanged for them to work. While audio and video delivered over narrow-bandwidth Internet connections, such as standard phone lines, are advancing in speed and quality, several technological problems remain unsolved. The principal problem is the inability of standard phone lines and current analog modems to move data quickly enough. On a standard phone line with 33.6 Kbps modems, video can be choppy or even stall, audio can cut in and out, or not be in synch with the video. How much of an impact these problems have depends on what you use the system for. If the present state of Internet audio and video isn't adequate for your needs, wait a minute—it's changing rapidly.

 OTE 56 Kbps modems with the new V.90 standard only partially help Internet telephony and video conferencing because both use two-way communication, and V.90 56 Kbps modems gain their speed only in downloading from the server to the client. When uploading from the client to the server, V.90 modems have speeds up to 33.6 Kbps.

If various audio and video technologies will enhance content delivery on the Internet, they're showing even greater promise for intranets, where the added bandwidth is generally available. An intranet is built on the same TCP/IP protocols as the Internet, thereby reducing network costs. Because they're less expensive to establish and maintain than private networks built on proprietary protocols, intranets are rapidly coming into wide use. Because intranet bandwidth allocations can be controlled by network managers, audio and video on intranets can be distributed more efficiently than on the Internet. Voice calls using TCP/IP can be made to take priority over non-critical data traffic, providing more bandwidth for calls. Using intranets with Microsoft NetMeeting and NetShow is an easy way for a company's employees to share information internally.

The rest of this chapter looks at how to use the tools within Windows 98 to utilize the Internet's audio and video capability.

Internet Telephony

Internet telephony refers to the software that allows your computer, modem, sound card, microphone, and speakers to work together to perform the functions of a telephone. At this stage of development, Internet telephony doesn't threaten AT&T. The Internet was designed for moving packets of data, not for transmitting voice continuously in real time. As a result, producing high-quality voice transmission is a tall order in technological terms.

 OTE   When we say "Internet telephony" or "Internet videoconferencing" we really mean "Internet and intranet telephony" or "Internet and intranet videoconferencing." If there are differences between the two we'll point that out. These technologies may actually be more important on an intranet than on the Internet because generally there is more bandwidth available.

Internet telephony doesn't yet deliver the quality of a standard phone call over regular phone lines, but it is improving. Even though narrow-bandwidth audio content delivery still hasn't completely matched standard phone service, people who try it quickly recognize its usefulness. Internet telephony is going to make a big impact on the telephone system over the long term. Telephone calls, faxing, and video conferencing over the Internet have one big advantage: they're inexpensive for long-distance calls, particularly international calls. Internet telephony is the cost-conscious alternative to the public switched telephone network (PSTN). Gateways that facilitate the mixing of Internet and PSTN are being put in place. These gateways enable phone calls to travel over the Internet for much of the way to their destination, thereby cutting the cost of long-distance calls by 50 percent or more. The big phone companies are already showing signs of nervousness because the competition from Internet telephony is eventually going to force them to cut rates.

The cost advantage for Internet-based phone systems will largely disappear over time, as standard long-distance charges come down and the Internet moves to higher-bandwidth, more expensive connections. Using the computer network for both voice and data, though, could also reduce equipment costs since companies could move away from having separate phone and data networks. Also, more voice (and fax) calls can be crammed into the Internet's packet-switched bandwidth than on the circuit-switched PSTN.

For the time being at least, the federal government is letting Internet telephony grow without interference, despite complaints from the phone companies that it should be regulated. Also, the phone companies want to be allowed to impose new fees on Internet service providers. In the background, the phone companies themselves are exploring the opportunities in Internet telephony services.

NetMeeting and Internet Telephony

Microsoft NetMeeting is the Windows 98 tool you use to make Internet phone calls (as well as videoconference and collaborate with several people). NetMeeting was designed for a corporate environment, but individuals and small businesses can also put its capabilities to good use.

The minimum system required for NetMeeting is a 486–66 MHz processor with 16 MB of RAM, and that will be adequate only for NetMeeting sessions not using audio or video. To make voice calls over the Internet, you'll want a Pentium 133 or faster, 16 MB or more of memory, a 28.8 Kbps or faster modem, a sound card, and a head set (earphones and a boom microphone) or speakers and a microphone.

Can you call anyone you want to on the Internet? Not yet. To do that, you and the person you're calling would both have to be connected to gateways that connect the Internet to the PSTN. The technology for these gateways is new and not yet widely used. For information about finding gateways you can use for long-distance calls, visit Web sites such as the following:

- **Voice on the Net** (http://www.von.com)
- **Free World Dialup** (http://www.pulver.com)
- **Delta Three** (http://www.deltathree.com)
- **NetWorks Telephony** (http://www.networkstelephony.com/)

So who *can* you call? For starters, you can call anyone with compatible equipment who's on a directory server. Another way is to go to Four11 (http://www.four11.com), a popular site for finding people on the Internet. (You can find more about directory servers and Four11 in the section *Placing Calls Using a Directory Server.*) You can also directly call someone with a computer if you know that person's IP (Internet Protocol) address. (See the section *Placing Direct NetMeeting Calls.*) The problem is that in most instances the IP address is dynamically assigned each time you log on to the Internet, so you cannot give it to someone to use to call you.

The steps to using the Internet to make a phone call include

1. Setting up the software

2. Setting up the Internet connection

3. Dialing the call

4. Talking

5. Disconnecting

Later in this chapter, you'll see how to use NetMeeting to make phone calls. You can choose to take advantage of NetMeeting's video and collaboration capabilities at the same time—it's all part of the same process.

Even though we use NetMeeting in this chapter to illustrate how to use the Internet for making telephone calls, other software vendors have products that run on Windows 98 with which you can do the same thing.

Quality of Internet Telephony

As we've already discussed, the Internet wasn't designed to handle heavy voice traffic, and its limitations in that regard are still being overcome. The two characteristics that most affect the quality of an Internet phone call are latency and distortion. *Latency* is the time between when someone speaks and when the listener hears the words. This lag time destroys the familiar conversational rhythm that's second nature on a telephone. If you've ever used a walkie-talkie, you know how annoying a conversation can be until you adapt to the instrument's rhythms.

Distortion occurs when some packets carrying the speaker's words over the Internet are lost. Internet telephony software is designed to make a best guess about the information contained in the lost packets. As you might expect, the software's guesses range from accurate to terrible, producing distortion in varying degrees. You don't notice this problem when the Internet is sending you data because the software waits until all the packets are received, even if a number of packets have to be resent, before telling you the data transmission is complete. In a real-time voice call, however, wayward packets can't catch up, leaving the gaps to be filled in by the software.

Many people are willing to put up with a bit of latency and distortion in order to save a lot of money on a call. And new technologies are being introduced that promise to improve the quality of Internet calls. Latency and distortion problems won't disappear quickly, but eventually they'll be overcome.

Many variables influence the quality of an Internet telephony connection. As you can see from the following list, some of these variables are harder to control than others.

- **Connection speed.** Narrow bandwidth connections at 28.8–56 Kbps are prone to distortion. Faster connections are often available in corporate environments, but the cost of such a connection is often too high for a home or a small office.

- **Equipment quality.** Higher-quality sound cards, microphone, speakers, and other components help enhance call quality.

- **Number of people on the Internet when you're making the call.** The more people online, the more likely the call quality will suffer.

- **Number of people on the telephony server when you're making the call.** The more people using the server, the greater the chance of a poor connection.

If the quality of your Internet phone calls sometimes falls below what you consider acceptable, here are a few tricks that might help you improve call quality:

- If you are using a full-duplex sound card and full-duplex audio, try setting the card to half-duplex.

- Your connection may be the culprit. If changing settings doesn't improve call quality, try these suggestions:

  - Disconnect from the call, and call again.

  - Disconnect from the Internet, reconnect, and try the call again.

Internet Video Conferencing

Internet video conferencing takes Internet telephony several steps further. In video conferencing, you have a powerful collaboration tool for sending and receiving audio, video, and data in something close to real time, even on a dial-up connection. In video conferencing, you'll not only see the person at the other end, but you can exchange information and work on the same telephone line as you speak.

For lifelike motion, video must be delivered at about 30 frames per second (fps), which is the speed at which a standard video camera operates. In contrast, video conferencing over a modem delivers only 1 to 10 fps. This is too huge a gap for showing a basketball game. However, if you're sitting at a desk or table and you aren't moving too much, the throughput is usually adequate. More important may be the quality of the audio connection, which is likely to be the dominant factor in your perception of the quality of your videoconferencing connection. If the audio comes through loud and clear, many people accept lower-quality video.

While bandwidth problems are even more pronounced in video conferencing than in moving data, other factors encourage wider use of desktop video conferencing:

- Standards, such as the recent International Telecommunications Union's H.323 protocol, prompt vendors to develop interoperable products instead of proprietary systems. This means H.323-compliant software will usually work with similar software from other vendors. The H.324 standard, which targets narrow-bandwidth video conferencing over standard telephone lines, also aims at encouraging interoperability among H.324-compatible clients.

- Full-featured videoconferencing software, such as Microsoft NetMeeting, is available for download at no charge over the Internet.

- Improved compression techniques are improving the quality of the connection.

- Internet videoconferencing systems can be installed for $100 to $500 per desktop.

- Companies making frequent overseas calls see Internet connections as a way to cut phone costs drastically, even if it means sacrificing call quality.

- Businesses of all sizes see video conferencing as a way to cut travel costs, because there are many situations in which video conferencing provides an adequate level of interaction.

As videoconferencing capability becomes more widespread, more uses are being found for it, and these are helping to spread the videoconferencing gospel. The following areas are just a few that can benefit from video conferencing.

- **Customer service** allows customers to look at and share information while talking with a company representative.

- **Direct sales** allow a prospective customer and a sales person to talk, see a product (maybe even in use), and share information about it.

- **Distance learning** allows students to interact with their teachers, including listening to or talking with them.

- **Job recruiting interviews** allow an applicant and an interviewer to talk, see each other, and share information.

- **Multimedia presentations** allow a presenter to give a full audio and video presentation complete with handouts to a number of people in remote locations.

- **Technical support** allows you to share information and talk to a tech support person. You may be able to solve a problem solved during a session by sharing an application or operating system component.

- **Telecommuting** allows a remote worker to participate in meetings, talk to coworkers, and share information without coming into the office.

- **Telemedicine** allows a doctor to see and talk to a patient and share information with them.

NetMeeting and Internet Video Conferencing

Microsoft NetMeeting is a full-featured videoconferencing and multipoint data communication program. It was designed to enable real-time collaboration with participants at several different sites over the Internet or a corporate intranet. NetMeeting offers the following tools for Internet/intranet conferencing and collaboration:

- **Audio** allows real-time voice communication among several people.

- **Video** allows the sharing of a video image among several people.

- **Chat** enables you to type messages to one or more individuals in the meeting. With it, you can pass private notes to specific participants or all participants in a meeting.

- **Shared Clipboard** allows you to copy and paste information from one of your documents to a document being shared in a meeting.

- **Application and document sharing** allows you to share most Windows-based applications with the other participants in the conference, even if the others don't have the application on their systems. This means, for example, that you can open a document in Microsoft Word, and all participants in the meeting can edit the document.

- **File transfer** allows you to send files in the background to one or all of the participants in the meeting.

- **Whiteboard** allows you to collaboratively create and share images, add text, or drop in images from the Clipboard.

You can use any of these tools individually or in any combination. With NetMeeting, you don't have to have a microphone or camera to take advantage of the other tools, such as Chat, file transfer, and Whiteboard.

Equipment Needed
to Use NetMeeting for Video Conferencing

You can do video conferencing with the same system you use for Internet telephony; the only additional equipment you need is a video camera with either a video capture card or a parallel port connection and a Video for Windows capture driver. The faster the processor and the more RAM you have, the better. You also need a 28.8 Kbps or faster modem, a sound card, speakers, and a microphone. NetMeeting needs about 15 MB of hard disk space to set itself up and about 5 MB of hard disk space after installation.

 IP A headset (earphones with a boom microphone) is superior to speakers and a microphone because you do not get feedback interference, which gives you an echo for everything coming out of the speakers. Additionally, the microphone volume remains constant as you turn your head.

An example of a popular video camera for narrow-bandwidth video conferencing is the Connectix QuickCam (http://www.connectix.com), which uses a parallel port to transfer its information to the computer. The golfball-sized QuickCam was originally available only in a black-and-white version, but now it is also offered in two color models, including the inexpensive QuickCam VC, which retails for approximately $100. The even less expensive black-and-white version may be the best choice for narrow-bandwidth video conferencing, because each image contains less information and can thus be sent more quickly than its color equivalent.

Many other vendors are marketing cameras. For example, the Panasonic EggCam (under $200) uses a PCI-bus video capture board to connect to a PC, rather than a parallel port. Because much of the processing takes place on the video capture board, the frame rate and image quality are better than that of the parallel port models, which make greater demands on the computer's CPU. However, the parallel port models are a bit less expensive than those cameras like the EggCam that use video capture boards. More information about the EggCam is available from Panasonic at 1-800-742-8086, or at http://www.panasonic.com/pcsc/pcpc/.

Configuring NetMeeting

NetMeeting is typically installed when you install Windows 98. If you did not install NetMeeting when you installed Windows 98, you can install it by opening Control Panel and choosing Add/Remove Programs | Windows Setup | Communications | Details | Microsoft NetMeeting, as you can see in Figure 14-1.

To start NetMeeting, open the Start menu and choose Programs | Internet Explorer | Microsoft NetMeeting. The first time you do that, the Microsoft NetMeeting configuration wizard opens, as shown in Figure 14-2. Follow the configuration wizard with these steps:

1. Click Next. You are asked if you want to log on to a directory server. The suggested default is that you do, using Microsoft's server. For now, accept that and click Next.

2. Enter your name, e-mail address, city, and state, and click Next.

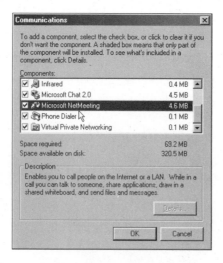

Figure 14-1.   *Installing NetMeeting as one of the Windows 98 Communications applets.*

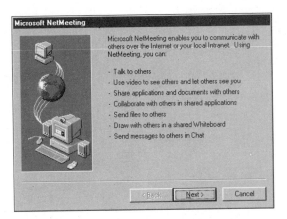

Figure 14-2. *NetMeeting configuration wizard leads you through its setup.*

3. Select the category that you want to be associated with, click Next, choose your modem speed, click Next, and then click Next again to begin tuning your audio settings with the Audio Tuning Wizard, shown in Figure 14-3.

4. First you set the playback volume for your speakers or headphones. Click Test, and drag the Volume slider until the volume is comfortable to you. Then click Next.

5. You set the volume of your microphone. To do this, you must read a short paragraph aloud in your normal speaking voice and watch a volume indicator in form of a thermometer bar (see Figure 14-4). If

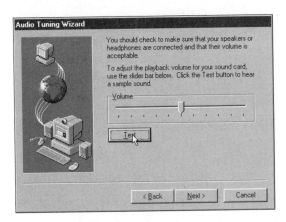

Figure 14-3. *You adjust the volume of your speakers and then your microphone with Audio Tuning Wizard.*

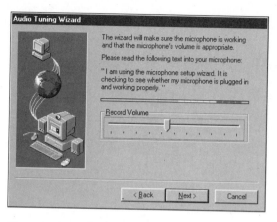

Figure 14-4.   *If your microphone volume is too high, the Audio Tuning Wizard will auto-matically lower it.*

you see any yellow or red in the bar, you should reduce the volume until you see only green. Then raise the volume a small amount so you are at the loudest comfortable volume. You should infrequently see a bit of yellow, but never any red. If you are consistently running the volume too high, the wizard will automatically reduce the volume.

6. When you are satisfied with your microphone volume, click Next, and then click Finish. You are done with audio tuning. The Microsoft NetMeeting window opens and connects you to the Microsoft directory service, as shown in Figure 14-5.

 OTE   You can rerun the Audio Tuning Wizard at any time except during a conference session. To do that from within NetMeeting, open the Tools menu, and select Audio Tuning Wizard.

NetMeeting has a number of other configuration options that you can change. To do this from within NetMeeting, open the Tools menu and click Options to open the Options dialog box shown in Figure 14-6. The function of each of the tabs is as follows:

■ **General** sets your preferences for how you want to work.

■ **My Information** provides information to callers.

■ **Calling** speeds the calling process, adding names to your personal directory.

Figure 14-5. *Microsoft NetMeeting window.*

Figure 14-6. *NetMeeting Options dialog box.*

■ **Audio** tunes your audio for best performance.

■ **Video** tunes your video for best performance.

■ **Protocols** lets you choose among the protocols available to your system.

General Tab

The General tab allows you to set preferences that will make NetMeeting match your work style. The function of each of the options is as follows:

- **Show Microsoft NetMeeting Icon On The Taskbar** puts a NetMeeting icon on the taskbar alongside the clock.

- **Run When Windows Starts And Notify Me Of Incoming Calls** causes NetMeeting to run in the background. When someone tries to call you, NetMeeting shows a message.

- **Automatically Accept Incoming Calls** causes NetMeeting to automatically accept all incoming calls and automatically allow callers to join meetings in progress. Otherwise, NetMeeting will ask you if you want to accept each incoming call.

- **Show The SpeedDial Tab When NetMeeting Starts** brings up the SpeedDial tab rather than the Directory tab when you launch NetMeeting. This gives you immediate access to the people that you call most often.

- **Show Intel Connection Advisor Icon On The Taskbar** gives you information about system performance during a call. This option allows you to place the Intel Connection Advisor icon on the taskbar. Right-clicking the icon and choosing Open brings up the Connection Advisor shown below. By clicking Options, you can choose to keep the Connection Advisor on top of other windows, or to open it automatically if a problem occurs.

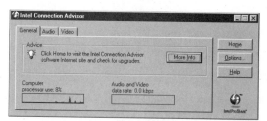

The Intel Connection Advisor dialog box has three tabs. The General tab shows a graph of computer processor use and the audio and video data rate. The Audio tab shows audio loss, audio delay, and the audio data rate. The Video tab shows video loss, video delay, and video data rate.

- **Network Bandwidth** allows you to choose the connection that matches your system. Choices include 14,400 bps modem, 28,800 bps or faster modem, ISDN, or local area network.

- **File Transfer** allows you to choose the folder in which you want to save the files you receive when you are in a meeting. The default folder is C:\Program Files\NetMeeting\Received Files, but you can click Change Folder and choose another folder. You can click View Files to see a list of the files you have received.

My Information Tab

On the My Information tab, shown in Figure 14-7, you enter information about yourself that is listed when you connect to a directory server. This is the same as the information that you initially entered when setting up NetMeeting. There are text boxes for your first and last names; e-mail address; and the city, state, and country where you live. The Comments box is useful if you're using an Internet Locator Server (ILS) and want to open

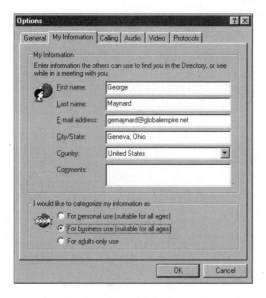

Figure 14-7. *NetMeeting Options My Information tab.*

the door to conversations with strangers—a good way to learn to use NetMeeting. For example, you might include "Testing NetMeeting" or "NetMeeting Newbie" in the Comments box. You'll soon get calls from people at the same stage or from people willing to help beginners. As you become more proficient, you can change your comments to attract or ward off different categories of users. As you'll quickly discover, a wide range of interests are expressed on an ILS. Some will interest you; others you won't want any part of.

The required fields include the first name, last name, and e-mail address, but you can alter the required information to maintain a degree of privacy about where you live. The e-mail address is needed to connect to the directory server.

Below the text boxes you can choose how you want to categorize your use of NetMeeting, as you did when you set it up. When you are connected to an ILS, the category you have chosen as most appropriate for your interests will cause the Directory pane and directory filters to list other users who have chosen this category.

Calling Tab

The Calling tab, shown in Figure 14-8, allows you to set directory options for the current call, as well as SpeedDial options for future calls. The use of each function is as follows:

- **Log On To The Directory Server When NetMeeting Starts.** If this is not checked, you must manually log on through the Call menu.

- **Server Name.** Choose this option to open a list of directory servers to which you can log on. You can choose a server from the list, or type in another directory server of your choice. If you are connected to a server as you choose a different one, you will be disconnected from the original server and connected to the new one.

- **Do Not List My Name In The Directory.** Normally when you are connected, you are listed on the directory server. When you aren't listed, only people who know your e-mail address will still be able to reach you with the SpeedDial or New Call options.

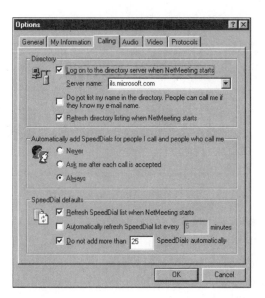

Figure 14-8. *NetMeeting Options Calling tab.*

- **Refresh Directory Listing When NetMeeting Starts.** If you choose this option, NetMeeting builds a list of connected users when you launch the program. Otherwise, you won't see the directory of users even if you're logged on. Choosing this option also allows you to see the list of connected users even if you're not logged on to a server.

- **Automatically Add SpeedDials For People I Call And People Who Call Me.** If you choose Never, you must manually add callers to your SpeedDial list. Otherwise, NetMeeting asks you if you want the caller added to your SpeedDial list or do it automatically depending on the option you choose.

- **Refresh SpeedDial List When NetMeeting Starts.** Check this option to update your SpeedDial list when you launch the program.

- **Automatically Refresh SpeedDial List Every X Minutes.** If checked, NetMeeting updates your SpeedDial list at a specified interval.

- **Do Not Add More Than X SpeedDials Automatically.** Check this option to set a maximum number of entries that can be added automatically to your SpeedDial list.

Audio Tab

The Audio tab, which you can see in Figure 14-9, helps you to tune your audio performance.

■ **Enable Full Duplex Audio So I Can Speak While Receiving Audio** allows you to use a full-duplex sound card that will send and receive audio at the same time, like a telephone. If the option is grayed out, your sound card supports only half-duplex audio, which means you cannot send and receive audio simultaneously.

■ **Enable Auto-Gain Control** allows NetMeeting to automatically maintain a steady microphone volume when your voice changes volume, if your sound card supports auto-gain control.

 OTE With auto-gain control enabled, NetMeeting will also adjust the gain if there's loud background noise.

■ **Tuning Wizard** button starts the Audio Tuning Wizard that you saw when you set up NetMeeting. You can bypass setting up your microphone's record volume by pressing **CTRL+TAB.**

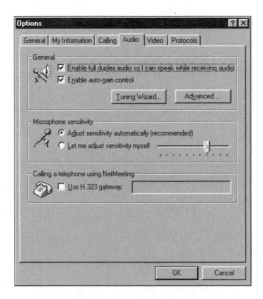

Figure 14-9.   *NetMeeting Options Audio tab.*

■ **Advanced** button opens the Advanced Compression Settings dialog box, shown below, where you can choose to manually set the order of audio compression codecs that will be used from a list of available codecs. (See Chapter 13 for further discussion on codecs.) The default primary codec for Pentium computers is Microsoft G.723.1 (5 Kbps). For non-Pentium computers, the defaults are Lernout & Hauspie SBC (8 Kbps) for 14,400-baud modem and Lernout & Hauspie SBC (16 Kbps) for all other connections.

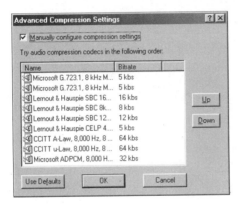

■ **Adjust Sensitivity Automatically** tells NetMeeting to automatically adjust your microphone's sensitivity to maintain a steady volume while eliminating some of the background noise.

■ **Let Me Adjust Sensitivity Myself** allows you to use the slider to increase or decrease the microphone's sensitivity.

■ **Use H.323 Gateway** allows you to enter an H.323 gateway where you can dial a standard telephone number while using NetMeeting.

Video Tab

The Video tab, shown in Figure 14-10, helps you set up your video the way you want to use it. The following options are available:

■ **Automatically Send Video At The Start Of Each Call** automatically transmits video images to another meeting participant. The My Video window appears when you start a call and displays the images that you transmit for the duration of the call. NetMeeting transmits video only when the My Video window is open.

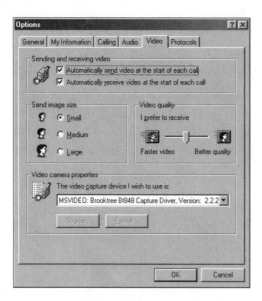

Figure 14-10. *NetMeeting Options Video tab.*

- **Automatically Receive Video At The Start Of Each Call** automatically receives video images from another meeting participant. The Remote Video window appears when you start a call and displays the images that you receive for the duration of the call. Even if you don't have a camera, you can receive video sent by another user with a camera.

- **Send Image Size** gives you the option to send a small, medium, or large video image. Obviously, the larger the image, the more bandwidth required. Set the desired image size before starting the meeting; otherwise, if you want to resize the video image during a meeting, you will have to leave and then rejoin the meeting for the resized image to take effect.

- **Video Quality** provides a slider that goes from Faster Video to Better Quality. Better-quality images are less compressed, so fewer frames are sent each second, making the action choppy and less fluid. Choosing the Faster Video option increases compression and increases the frame rate. The action is smoother, but the images are poorer in quality.

- **Video Camera Properties** allows you to choose the driver for your video capture device. Depending on your equipment, the two buttons may be available or grayed out.

- **Source** button, if available, allows you to change your camera's settings for brightness, hue, and saturation.

- **Format,** if available, allows you to change the format of the video image from among such formats as 24-bit RGB, 15-bit RGB, YUY2, and BTYUV.

Protocols Tab

The Protocols tab, shown in Figure 14-11, lets you choose the protocol you want to use. To add or remove a protocol, click its check box. To set the properties of a protocol, select the protocol, and click Properties. You might have any of the following protocols:

- **Modem** allows you to connect directly with another NetMeeting user by directly connecting to each other's modem. The Modem protocol, though, does not support NetMeeting audio and video.

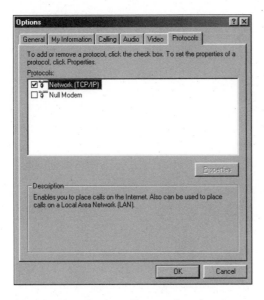

Figure 14-11. *NetMeeting Options Protocols tab.*

Clicking Properties brings up the Modem Protocol Properties dialog box. If you want your computer to answer modem calls, click Use Modem To Answer Incoming Calls, but there might be a conflict if you are using other call-answering applications, such as a fax application.

- **Network (IPX)** supports calls on a local area network, but NetMeeting's audio and video aren't supported with this protocol.

- **Network (TCP/IP)** is the default protocol. This allows you to place calls on the Internet or on a LAN that supports TCP/IP.

- **Null Modem** enables one NetMeeting user to connect to another using a direct cable connection between serial or parallel ports, but doesn't support NetMeeting's audio and video.

Placing and Receiving Calls with NetMeeting

With NetMeeting, you can place calls directly if you know the other party's IP address. The more common approach is to connect using a directory server such as Microsoft's Internet Locator Server.

Placing Calls Using a Directory Server

As described earlier in the section *Calling Tab,* you could choose to log on to a directory server automatically when NetMeeting starts. If you start NetMeeting without logging on, you can log on by opening the Call menu and choosing Log On To (the listed server). If you want to change servers after you are logged on, choose Options from the Tools menu, and then click the Calling tab, and in the Directory section, choose the new server you want to log on to. NetMeeting will log you off the original server and on to the new one.

The default directory server is the Microsoft Internet Locator Server. At this writing, Microsoft is actually running six directory servers (ILS plus ILS1-ILS5). In addition, the list of servers also includes three Four11

directory servers. Four11 (http://www.four11.com) is a leader in the business of Internet phone directories. If you visit the Four11 Web site, you can fill in a form of contact information, making it easy for other Internet users to find you.

When you log on to a directory server, the NetMeeting software ties your user information (your name, address, and so forth) to the IP address given you automatically (and generally unknown to you) by your ISP or LAN server when you connected to the Internet for the current session. After logging on to one of the directory servers, which lists the users online, you can choose the person you want to call by double-clicking the entry in the NetMeeting Directory listing, as is being done in Figure 14-12.

The point of NetMeeting is to have someone at the other end of the line with whom you want to communicate. If you don't have a friend available for a practice session, you can log on to an ILS and find someone willing to work with you. Participants can enter and leave a session, so you can ask to join an existing one. NetMeeting asks if the participants want to accept or ignore your attempt to join the session.

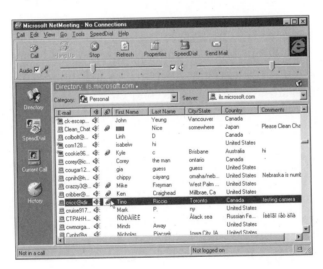

Figure 14-12. *Selecting an entry from the NetMeeting Directory.*

OTE If you want to create your own directory server for your company or organization, you can download ILS from the Microsoft NetMeeting Web site (http://www.microsoft.com/netmeeting/ils/main.htm#FAQ). There is currently no charge. An ILS can support up to 10,000 connections. This is useful if you want to run NetMeeting on an intranet.

Filtering Directory Entries NetMeeting has a number of options for filtering the directories of NetMeeting users. These filters help you narrow your search for users with your interests. As you saw earlier in the section *My Information Tab,* you can categorize your information in one of three broad categories: personal, business, or adults-only, which filters out users not in your category. With the NetMeeting Directory open, you can open the Category drop-down list, shown below, and set filters for people who live in the same country as you, in a call, not in a call, or who are using video cameras.

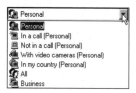

As with other Windows 98 columns, you can sort and rearranage the Directory columns by clicking or dragging the column headings. If you click the column heading with the audio and video icons, you will select just those people with either audio or video capability, and the second time you click, it will be just those who don't have the capability.

Using SpeedDial SpeedDial is a list of frequent contacts, as shown in Figure 14-13. After you have logged on, your SpeedDial list is refreshed so you can tell if a person is logged on. If so, you can simply click that person's name to call him or her. If you clicked the option for automatic saving in the Options Calling tab, NetMeeting will save in SpeedDial the contact information for each of the people you call. In the Calling tab, you can also specify whether you want to be asked before a contact is placed automatically in SpeedDial or you never want a contact to be placed there automatically. You can delete an entry from SpeedDial by selecting the entry and clicking **DELETE.**

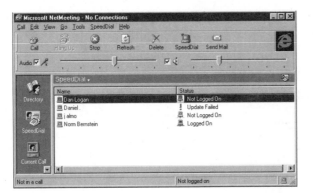

Figure 14-13. *SpeedDial allows you to quickly connect to people you frequently call.*

If you right-click a SpeedDial entry and choose Properties, you can see the address of the person, as you can see below. Note that this address includes the directory server he or she was using when you last contacted him or her. If the person changes the directory server, the SpeedDial entry will not work.

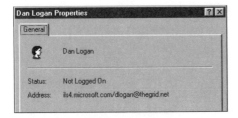

Using History NetMeeting keeps a list of all the calls in which you participate in the History list, shown in Figure 14-14. You can repeat a previous call, whether or not you initiated it, by double-clicking the appropriate entry. You must first be online, but you don't have to be connected to the correct directory server.

Placing Direct NetMeeting Calls

Using a directory server can slow down a NetMeeting session, sometimes to the point of making it not worthwhile. One way around that is to place a direct call, bypassing the directory server. The problem is that one person's IP address must be known by the other parties and they must call him or her. Sometimes an ISP does assign a fixed IP address, but in most cases

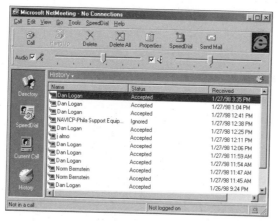

Figure 14-14. *You can use the History list to repeat a call.*

your IP address is dynamically and automatically assigned each time you log on to the Internet. You therefore must get the IP address of the person being called *after* he or she has logged on.

You can determine your IP address using a little-known utility that comes with Windows 98 called WinIPCfg. If you open the Start menu, click Run, type **winipcfg,** and press **ENTER,** you will get a dialog box that looks the one shown here:

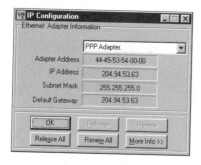

The IP address in this dialog box must then be transmitted to the other parties in the conference. You can do this with e-mail or a standard telephone call. If you have this address, you can place the call by clicking the Call button on the toolbar or opening the Call menu and choosing New Call. In either case, the New Call dialog box will open, as shown below. In the Address box, type the IP address that you were given, and click Call. You will see "Finding IP address" in the status bar, and eventually you should connect.

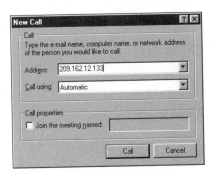

 OTE   If your IP address is assigned by the server each time you log on the Internet, it is good for a single session only, and as soon as you log off, it will cease to be your address. The next time you log on, you will probably be assigned a different address.

Other Ways to Make NetMeeting Calls

Within Windows 98, you can make NetMeeting calls from Windows Explorer, Internet Explorer, Outlook Express, and Outlook by opening the Go menu and choosing Internet Call. That will open NetMeeting and connect you to the Internet if you are not already connected.

In Windows 98 itself, if you have the e-mail address of the person you want to call and you are both logged on to the same directory server, you can open the Start menu, click Run, and in the Run dialog box, type **callto:** and the person's e-mail address. For example:

   callto:dlogan@thegrid.net

If the person you are calling is logged on to a different server, you have to add the name of the server, followed by the person's e-mail address. For example:

   callto:ils5.microsoft.com/dlogan@thegrid.net

If you are creating a Web page, you can place a NetMeeting hyperlink on your page, and people can call you by clicking the link. The HTML code for such a link would be in the following form:

```
<A
HREF="callto:ils5.microsoft.com/
dlogan@thegrid.net">ils5.microsoft.com/dlogan@thegrid.net</A>
```

If you use Outlook Express or Outlook, you can make calls using the NetMeeting entries in the Address Book if you are both logged on to the same directory server. Open the Address Book, select the person to call, open the Tools menu, and choose Internet Call.

If you place a call but it doesn't go through, NetMeeting will ask you if you want to send an e-mail message to the other person. If you respond Yes, NetMeeting will open your e-mail client, create a new message addressed to the person you were calling, and automatically add a SpeedDial shortcut to that message. The person you were calling can then return your NetMeeting call by clicking the SpeedDial shortcut.

Accepting and Handling a Call

To accept an Internet call, you must be connected to the Internet (or an intranet for intranet calls), and NetMeeting must be loaded. When a call comes in to you, you will hear the sound of a telephone ringing (with the default sounds), and you will see the dialog box shown below. If you click Accept, the Current Call pane will appear, as you can see in Figure 14-15. The Current Call pane shows everyone taking part in the call, whether they're using audio and/or video, and whether or not they're sharing or collaborating. In the Current Call pane, you have many options for handling both one-on-one calls and multipoint conferences with several people.

Docking and Undocking the Video Windows

Within the Current Call pane, there can be up to two video windows during a call. One is My Video, which shows the video image you are sending out, and the other is the video image you are receiving. You can detach either or both of the video windows and place them where you want either

Figure 14-15. *Starting a call in the Current Call pane.*

within or outside the Current Call pane; see Figure 14-16. You can do this by simply dragging the windows, or you can open the View menu and select Detach My Video or Detach Remote Video. When the video windows are undocked, they stay on top of other applications, so you can always see them, no matter what else you are doing. If you want to return the video windows to the Current Call pane, you can drag them into position, or you can use the options in the View menu.

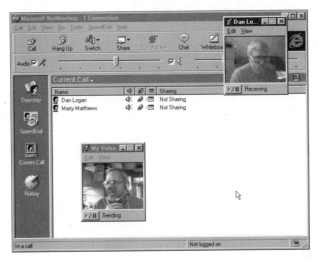

Figure 14-16. *You can undock and drag the video windows where you want them.*

You can pause both the sending and receiving of video images to allocate more bandwidth to other functions. To do that, click the double-bar icon under the image. After they are paused, you can restart the sending and receiving of video by clicking the triangle icon under the image.

Switching Audio and Video

If you are in a multipoint conference call with several people, you will be able to talk to (audio) and see (video) only one person at a time, although the other collaboration tools (Whiteboard, Chat, and file and application sharing or collaboration) may be available with others in the session. However, you can switch your audio and video from person to person in the session. On the Current Call pane, click the Switch button on the toolbar, and select the person you want to switch to in the menu that appears. Another limitation is that only three participants can share an application at the same time.

Using the Go Menu

The Go menu on the NetMeeting menu bar allows you to open other Internet Explorer products, plus it provides a way to reach white pages directory information on the Web. The Go menu options include

- **Web Directory.** Takes you to Four11's Directory Web page (http://www.four11.com/py/npSearch.py) to search for someone online.

- **Home Page.** Opens Internet Explorer with your default home page.

- **Search The Web.** Opens Internet Explorer with one of the commercial search sites.

- **Best Of The Web.** Opens Internet Explorer with a Microsoft Web page that lists interesting Web sites.

- **Mail.** Opens your Internet e-mail client, Outlook Express by default.

- **News.** Opens your newsgroups client, Outlook Express by default.

Leaving a Call

To exit a call, click Hang Up in the NetMeeting toolbar. Any party in a meeting can leave the session this way without disturbing the rest of the meeting.

Using Do Not Disturb

If you don't want a conference interrupted, you can choose Do Not Disturb from the Call menu. You will be asked if you really don't want to receive calls, as shown below. When you select Do Not Disturb, anyone trying to contact you will receive a message that you are not accepting calls. NetMeeting will ask if the caller wants to send you a message.

Conferencing and Sharing Information

Although the hottest components of NetMeeting are audio and video conferencing, they often provide less than satisfactory performance because of limited bandwidth. To supplement audio and video conferencing and because of their own innate value, NetMeeting includes the additional means of conferencing and sharing information described in the following sections.

Sharing the Clipboard

In a NetMeeting session where you are sharing an application, session participants share the Clipboard. Anything that you copy or cut during the session goes onto the shared Clipboard and can be pasted by anyone in the conference onto a document in either a shared or local application. You can copy the video image you are receiving or sending to another application by right-clicking either video window, choosing Copy to copy the video image to the Clipboard, and then pasting the image into a document in an application.

Sharing Applications, Folders, and Operating System Windows

NetMeeting allows meeting participants to share applications, folders, and operating system windows across the Internet or an intranet. A meeting participant can open a document in an application, and that application will be available to all the session participants, even if they don't have the application on their computers. For example, Figure 14-17 shows an early version of this chapter being collaboratively worked on between Dan Logan (who wrote this chapter) and myself.

There are two aspects to sharing applications. First, participants can simply share the application, whereby only the participant opening the application will control what is being done in the application. Second, you can use the Collaborate option, which allows the other participants to take control of the shared application.

To share an application:

1. Open a Windows application on a computer participating in a NetMeeting session.

2. Click the Share button on the toolbar, or open the NetMeeting Tools menu, and choose Share Application.

3. Click the shared application window for the other conference participants to see the window.

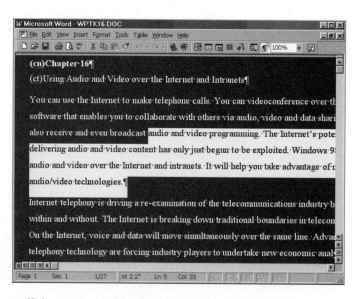

Figure 14-17. *Collaborating on this chapter in Microsoft Word using NetMeeting.*

Collaborating Using NetMeeting

After an application and document have been shared, multiple participants can work together on the document using the Collaborate option, as follows:

1. The sharer of the application must click the Collaborate button on the toolbar or open the NetMeeting Tools menu and choose Start Collaborating.

2. The other participants click the Collaborate icon on the toolbar. They can then gain control of the application by double-clicking it. The mouse pointer becomes theirs to use and appears on all participants' screens as a remote pointer with the user's initials. The person in control can manipulate the application and the document it contains.

3. Pressing **ESC** cancels the collaboration.

It takes time to acclimatize to collaboration. Each participant collaborating in the session can take control of the remote pointer at any time by double-clicking the mouse. This is easy, but at first it can be annoying because the participants tend to fight for the pointer. We're used to having total control of the mouse, so to see it running around the screen seemingly at random can be frustrating. A participant might get momentary control by double-clicking, only to have it immediately snatched away by another participant double-clicking a moment later. It's a lot like interrupting when someone else is talking.

IP   When you have control of a collaboration, moving the mouse pointer off an edge of the screen will scroll the screen in the opposite direction. For example, moving the mouse off the bottom edge will scroll the screen up.

It can also be a bit confusing at first as to who is in control of the remote pointer at the moment. Because NetMeeting supports audio and video between only two of the session's participants at a time, you can't quickly ask everyone to let you have control. However, the pointer shows the initials of the person who is in control of it, and the Current Call pane also indicates which user is in control.

Participants have to develop a rhythm or response pattern when involved in a collaboration session. For example, you might do a round robin. Or, the person in control could stop moving the pointer—or move it to a certain spot on the screen—to indicate he or she is ready to relinquish control.

Using the Whiteboard

The Whiteboard, which looks and feels like Microsoft Paint, as you can see in Figure 14-18, is a way to collaborate with visual information. Unlike a shared application, though, the Whiteboard allows all the participants in a conference to work simultaneously. You might use the Whiteboard to sketch ideas or drop in an image from another program for other participants to comment on or rework. You can paste content from other applications to the Whiteboard, or cut and copy information from the Web.

 Launch the Whiteboard by clicking the Whiteboard icon on the toolbar or choosing Whiteboard from the Tools menu. Any conference participant can launch the Whiteboard, and then it will be available to all participants.

Using Multiple Whiteboard Pages The Whiteboard is not limited to one screen or page. You can add more pages to your Whiteboard and easily move from one to the next. In the lower right corner of the Whiteboard window, as shown below, you can click the + sign button to add a blank page. Clicking the symbols on either side of the page number lets you move forward or backward through the Whiteboard's pages. Clicking the buttons on either side of the symbols moves you to the first and last pages.

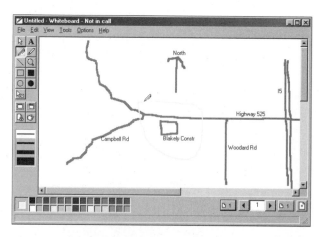

Figure 14-18. *Collaboratively sketching a map on the Whiteboard.*

Saving a Whiteboard Session When you exit the Whiteboard, the program will ask you if you want to save the contents of the session. It will save the Whiteboard session with the name you assign it, giving it the .wht extension.

Using Chat

Before audio and video conferencing, people could talk in real time over the Internet or a LAN using Chat. It allows participants in a meeting to type messages to each other, as you can see in Figure 14-19. Unlike e-mail, Chat is almost instantaneous.

Chat is also handy during Internet video conferencing, as a way to keep the conversation moving ahead if the audio becomes choppy. If one person remembers to try Chat and starts it, a Chat window will automatically pop up on everybody's screen. You can keep two different conversations going, one where you're speaking to each other, and the other using Chat. Chat turns out to be a good way to make use of conversational lapses.

  Starting Chat and Sending Text Messages After you have established a connection with another user, click the Chat icon on the toolbar to bring up the Chat window. The Chat window provides an area for typing in your comments and a drop-down list where you can select who you are going to send them to, everyone in the session or only to one individual. When you press **ENTER** or click the Enter button (to the right of the Message box),

Figure 14-19. *Using Chat to try to establish communications when voice isn't working.*

the comment is uploaded to the participants. All Chat comments, whether you have sent them or received them, are visible in your Chat window, identified by the name of the person making the comments.

Using Whisper Mode NetMeeting has a whisper option that allows you to carry on a private communication with another user while you're in a chat session with several others. To use whisper while in the Chat window, click the user's name in the Send To list, and then press **ENTER** or click the Enter button to send your private message. Only the two of you will see the message, and the Chat window shows it is a private message.

Saving a Chat Session When you exit Chat, the program asks if you want to save the contents of the Chat session. It will save the Chat session as a file with the .txt extension.

Transferring Files

In NetMeeting, you can transfer a file in the background to other participants in the session. To send a file, right-click a participant and choose Send File. A dialog box opens to allow you to choose the file to send. An alternative is to drag the file into the Microsoft NetMeeting window, which will automatically send it to all the participants. Each participant can accept or immediately delete the file, as shown in Figure 14-20.

Figure 14-20.   *You can keep or delete a file transferred to you.*

Playing Audio and Video on Web Pages

Originally, receiving audio and video on a Web page required you to download a file before you could hear or view it. Often these files are several to many megabytes, and the download time is long. Streaming audio or video allows you to hear or view the content as it is being downloaded. With Microsoft NetShow, you can listen to streaming audio and view streaming video in Microsoft's Active Streaming Format (ASF). NetShow also supports RealAudio 4.0 content. NetShow also allows you to view real-time live audio and video.

NetShow can receive both unicast and multicast Internet and intranet broadcasts. *Unicast* is the standard on-demand information transfer that is commonly used on the Internet. *Multicast* is an Internet or intranet broadcast that is similar to a typical radio or television broadcast. It happens at a certain time, and if you tune into it at the time it is broadcast, you'll receive it. It is most useful for live events, and in many cases, it is recorded and also sent out as a unicast.

NetShow is available in two forms: it is an ActiveX control that comes with Internet Explorer, and as NetShow Player, it is a stand-alone applet that can be installed with Windows 98. (It is not part of the Typical installation.) In other words, if you use Internet Explorer, you will automatically use NetShow to hear and/or view compatible streaming content. In addition, if you separately install it, you can use NetShow Player to play ASF and other files.

You can insert NetShow ASF files in e-mail messages. When the recipient double-clicks the file, the content will begin to stream, NetShow Player will open and begin to play the file using only a few of the application's resources. The user doesn't have to have a Web browser installed to stream the NetShow file.

If NetShow Player was not installed with Windows 98, you can install it by opening the Control Panel folder, clicking Add/Remove Programs and the Windows Setup tab, selecting Multimedia, clicking Details, clicking Microsoft NetShow Player, and clicking OK twice. After you've installed it, you can start the player by opening the Start menu and choosing Programs | Internet Explorer | NetShow Player. NetShow Player will appear as you can see here:

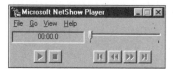

You can use NetShow Player to play files directly available to the computer on which you have installed the player. For example, on the Windows 98 CD-ROM in the \Win98\Content\Audionet folder, you can play the Samp288.asf audio file. To play this kind of file, you can click the file or you can open the File menu, choose Open File, and use the standard Open dialog box. You can also give NetShow an Internet address and filename, as shown below, and have it find the address and file and play it, like the NetShow tutorial shown in Figure 14-21.

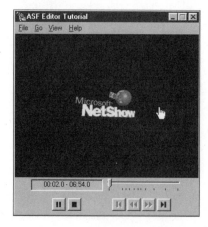

Figure 14-21. *Playing a streaming .asf file over the Internet.*

Third-Party Software

Although we've spent a lot of time covering Microsoft NetMeeting, other similar programs are available from other vendors. Windows 98 supports many of these third-party telephony and videoconferencing products.

CU-SeeME is the best known of the Internet videoconferencing software. CU-SeeME was created at Cornell University in 1992; White Pine Software's Enhanced CU-SeeME, the commercial version, has been included with the Connectix QuickCam, and the inexpensive package has proved very popular. CU-SeeME can be used with dial-up modems or ISDN. When used with White Pine's MeetingPoint conference server, it supports the ITU's H.323 standard and is interoperable with other H.323 compliant systems, including NetMeeting.

Vocaltec's Internet Phone (http://www.vocaltec.com) has been a popular Internet telephony tool. Internet Phone Release 5, which costs about $50, allows you to make calls from your computer to a standard phone using the company's Telephony Gateway technology.

More and more companies, with Microsoft among the vanguard, see the delivery of audio and video over the Internet as an important opportunity for future development. Internet telephony, video conferencing, and audio/video broadcasting are in their relative infancy as Internet technologies. As more bandwidth becomes available, particularly in dial-up connections, the Internet will serve increasingly as a key communications medium.

Windows 98 Networking

Part 6 provides a detailed reference for the installation of a Windows 98 network, as well as how to make the best use of it. Chapter 15 covers the fundamentals of networking, including the types of networks, network hardware, and setting up network interface cards. It then discusses the installation of a Windows 98 network, including using the Network control panel to select the client, adapter, protocol, and service components of the network, and determining what settings are best for your situation. Chapter 16 describes the setup and use of a Windows 98 peer-to-peer network, including how to control resource sharing, how to access resources on other network computers, and how to map network resources.

Networking and Its Installation

Despite all the growth in networking, its installation and management has remained the province of networking professionals. Windows 98 provides an alternative for smaller firms by offering full-featured networking that is relatively easy to install and maintain. Windows 98 can be all the networking software you need, or it can be a well-integrated client in a larger network using other software from Microsoft or other manufacturers. Some of the important networking features in Windows 98 are as follows:

- Full 32-bit networking with 32-bit software, 32-bit file and printer sharing, and 32-bit network card drivers

- Full built-in support for Novell NetWare networking, including a Microsoft 32-bit NetWare client for connecting to either NetWare 3.*x* or 4.*x* servers

- Support for an environment with multiple networks, including simultaneously using multiple network card device drivers

- Full capability for remotely connecting to and using, or even managing, a network including accessing NetWare and UNIX servers

- Support for many industry-standard networking protocols, including TCP/IP and IPX, as well as client support for a number of other networking systems, including Artisoft Lantastic, Banyan Vines, DEC PathWorks, and Sun NFS

The key advantage of Windows 98 networking is that you can take it to any depth that you want. At one extreme, Windows 98 can provide the means for the simple sharing of files or a printer among a couple of computers. At the other extreme, Windows 98 can easily be integrated with several other networking schemes in a large networking complex. In between are the sharing of other devices including CD-ROMs, tape drives, and modems; the implementing of various security and control schemes; and the using of Windows 98 as a Windows NT or NetWare client. Windows 98 has the capability; your needs determine what you do with it.

This chapter will introduce you to networking in general and Windows 98 networking in particular. The chapter will then lead you through the installation and setup of a network using Windows 98, including some of the hardware alternatives and the possible software options.

Networking

Computer networking (or just *networking*) is the connecting of computers in order to share resources, exchange data, and communicate among the users. Resources that can be shared include printers, disk and tape drives, programs, and databases. Exchanging data is the sending of information files from one computer to another, and communicating is the transferring of messages among the computers on the network. The primary reasons for networking are

■ To share and/or control hardware and software

■ To work on common data

■ To improve communication among users

These factors can lead to reduced costs and improved efficiency. Sharing hardware allows you to purchase better, more expensive devices than if each person on the network had one of the devices. Sharing software facilitates its control so that it performs in a consistent way for all users. Sharing software also may allow multiple users to work on common data. Working on common data allows a group of people to maintain a large body of information, like a database or an accounting system. Improved communications with electronic mail, or *e-mail,* facilitates the coordinating of schedules and, often, the more efficient sharing of information.

Types of Networks

Computers in a network can be connected in several different ways including using modems and phone lines. Except for the discussion of remote, or dial-up, networking in Chapter 16, networking in this book refers to a group of computers that each have a network interface card and dedicated cabling (or wireless channel) connecting them and that run Windows 98 or other networking software. Within this framework, there are two classes of networks: wide area networks and local area networks.

Wide area networks (WANs) generally connect other networks or larger computers at some distance from one another using dedicated telephone lines, satellite links, or microwave links. WANs can connect *nodes,* or end points, across the street or around the world from one another. WANs are professionally managed, highly complex networks and are not within the scope of this book.

Local area networks (LANs) generally connect computers or smaller LANs within a single office or building with dedicated cabling or wireless channels. LANs are more common and come in two types that differ in the way they distribute networking tasks: peer-to-peer LANs and client-server LANs.

Peer-to-Peer LANs

In a peer-to-peer LAN, all computers share equally networking tasks and the ability to provide resources and use resources on other computers. Any computer may store programs and data used by others, and any computer may have a printer or other resource shared by all. For example, the peer-to-peer LAN in Figure 15-1 has a shared printer on one computer and a shared tape drive on another.

Peer-to-peer LANs tend to be smaller and more localized to a single workgroup (people working together) than client-server LANs, although this is not a requirement. When a workgroup first decides to utilize a network, it often is a peer-to-peer LAN, because it causes the least disruption and is the least expensive. Workgroup members can continue to do what they previously did on their same computers, and in addition, they can share resources, exchange data, and communicate.

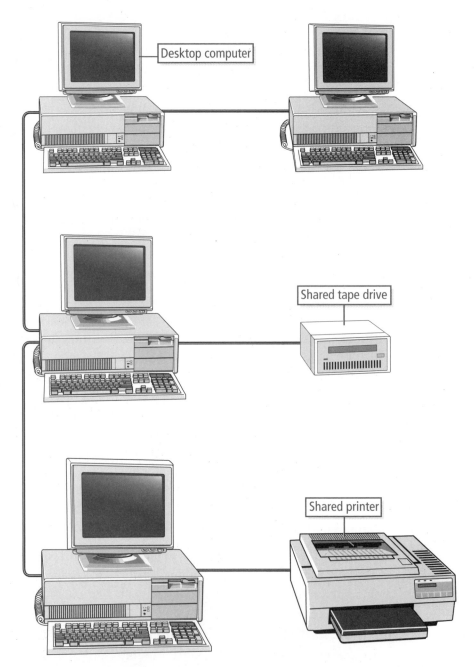

Figure 15-1. *A peer-to-peer LAN with a bus topology.*

A peer-to-peer LAN requires only network interface cards for each computer, cabling to link the computers, and Windows 98. Depending on the topology (see *Network Topology*), you may also need a network hub. Of course, each computer must be able to run Windows 98, so it must have at least a 486/66 MHz processor, 16 MB of memory, and at least 300 MB of free disk space.

Client-Server LANs

In client-server LANs, there are two types of computers: *clients,* or *workstations* for the individual users on the network, and *servers* that provide the central facility for managing the network, storing programs and data, and providing common resources. The network management done by the server includes managing network files, network communications, and network resources such as printers, tape drives, and CD-ROMs. A server is usually dedicated to its task and cannot be used for normal end-user tasks such as word processing. Nevertheless, the server normally is more powerful than the average desktop computer, with more memory, a faster processor, and a lot more disk space. Client workstations, on the other hand, can be less powerful and even may not have a disk, although that is unusual. Workstations usually are normal desktop computers on which normal computing tasks can be run, and they may even have their own peripherals such as a printer (referred to as a *local printer* to distinguish it from a network printer), as shown in Figure 15-2.

Peer-to-peer LANs generally are less expensive than client-server LANs in terms of both hardware and software. Although the workstations may be cheaper in a client-server LAN, a peer-to-peer LAN does not require a dedicated server. Also, the server requires special software and more technical expertise on the part of the people running it. Common server software includes Novell NetWare and Microsoft Windows NT Server. Windows 98, though, works excellently as the client with either server software.

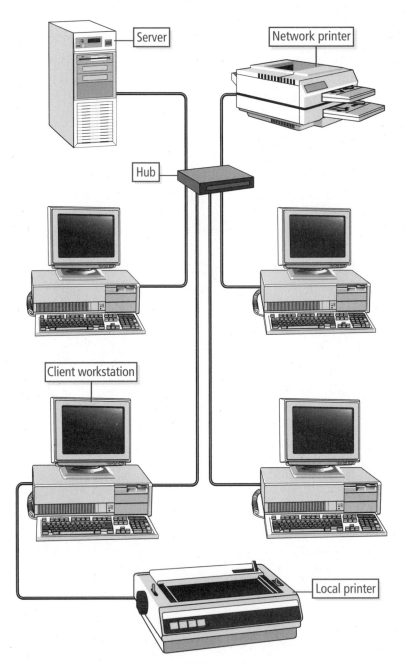

Figure 15-2. *Client-server LAN with a star topology.*

The decision of whether to use a peer-to-peer LAN or a client-server LAN is not black and white. Larger LANs (more than ten nodes) generally tend to be client-server LANs, because at that point the economies of scale allow for the purchase of a reasonable server by having only slightly less capability in each workstation. Nothing prevents larger peer-to-peer LANs, but at about a dozen users, a peer-to-peer LAN is usually too slow in most situations. If you are running a centralized application, like an accounting system, where several people are working on it at one time, a client-server LAN makes a lot of sense. While you can run such a system on a peer-to-peer LAN, one node will be dedicated mostly to the central disk activities, so you might as well make it a server.

Network Hardware

Regardless of the type of network, each node in the network must include a computer (or an intelligent peripheral such as some printers) with a network interface card and the necessary cabling to connect them.

Network Computers

The size and configuration of network computers, over and above the minimum necessary to run Windows 98, depend almost exclusively on what you are going to do with the computers. Look at each workstation or computer in a peer-to-peer LAN, and decide what tasks it will be performing and the hardware required for those tasks. Other than the network interface card and possibly hubs, no special hardware is required for networking.

The server, if one is desired, must also be sized to fit its tasks. The processor does not have to be the absolutely fastest available. A 166 MHz Pentium is a good starting place, and you can go up to a dual or quad processor 300+ MHz Pentium II. The server's memory must be adequate for the software you are running. A practical minimum is 64 MB, although most servers have at least 128 MB, and it is often error-checking-and-correcting (ECC) memory, which is both the most reliable and the most expensive. The disk space must satisfy the storage needs of the applications you are running. In addition, you might want to provide tape backup in the server and an uninterruptible power supply (UPS), so that the server and its files are protected. The only absolute requirement for networking in the server, as in a workstation, is a network interface card.

Network Interface Cards

A *network interface card* (NIC, also called a network card, network board, LAN adapter, or network adapter card) is the electronic interface between your computer and the cabling that joins the network. Network interface cards manage the traffic on the network to make sure that information gets to its destination. The network interface card is plugged into one of the expansion slots on the *motherboard* (main circuit, or system, board) in your computer, and the network cabling plugs into the card.

The network interface card takes information that is to be sent over the network and packages it in *packets,* or *frames,* with an address of where it is going, much like an envelope with an address on the front. The packets are then sent out over the cables and intercepted by the node to which they are addressed. The receiving node then extracts the information and gives it to its computer.

Network interface cards vary in terms of type, the way they connect into slots on the motherboard, and the types of cabling they require.

Types of Network Interface Cards Three common types of network interface cards (NICs) are used in LANs: Ethernet, Token Ring, and ARCnet. ARCnet is typically used in smaller peer-to-peer networks and is being challenged even in that market by Ethernet. Ethernet is common in small to reasonably large networks of both peer-to-peer and client-server LANs. Ethernet is no longer significantly more expensive than ARCnet, and in most situations, it is at least twice as fast. Although ARCnet is slow, it is very reliable. Token Ring is used in larger, more mission-critical client-server networks. Token Ring NICs cost three to four times what an Ethernet NIC costs. They are more than 1.5 times faster than standard Ethernet but less than one-sixth as fast as Fast Ethernet (see *Network Speed* later in this chapter). The other benefits of Token Ring are that it is more reliable than Ethernet and can provide built-in diagnostic and network-management capabilities that are valuable in managing larger networks. The decision on the type of NIC probably points to Ethernet, unless you have a mission-critical situation that makes it worthwhile to pay Token Ring's price.

Types of Motherboard Card Slots The slots on the motherboard are determined by bus architecture. Four bus architectures are in common use today: ISA, EISA, VESA, and PCI. ISA is the oldest bus architecture and can be either 8 or 16 bits (the data path is either 8 or 16 bits wide). ISA network interface cards can also be 8 or 16 bits, with 16-bit cards being twice as fast for a small additional cost. ISA cards can be used in both EISA and VESA slots but without the added benefits of those architectures. EISA, VESA, and PCI are different implementations of a 32-bit bus. EISA is the oldest and the most expensive. VESA is the cheapest and the least sophisticated. PCI is the newest and is the primary bus for high-performance NICs. For many low-demand networking needs, a 16-bit ISA NIC is probably adequate. In situations where you are making full use of the network, you will probably want to go to a 32-bit PCI bus card—the difference in price is not that great.

 IP Windows 98, with its totally 32-bit architecture, can fully utilize a 32-bit network interface card.

Network Speed

The speed at which a network transmits information depends on the type of network and how it handles the information. From slowest to fastest, the speeds of common networks are as follows:

- ARCnet is 2.5 Mbps (megabits per second).
- Type 3 Token Ring is 4 Mbps.
- Standard Ethernet is 10 Mbps.
- Type 1 Token Ring is 16 Mbps.
- Fast Ethernet is 100 Mbps.

Fast Ethernet is being widely implemented today, not just because it is significantly faster than anything else. Fast Ethernet uses the same protocols and data formats as Ethernet, and therefore it is transparent to Windows 98 and other common networking software, which you may be using. Also Fast Ethernet uses the same type of cabling as Ethernet, so if you have reasonably good quality of cabling, you can run Fast Ethernet with what you already have. Finally you can mix Ethernet and Fast Ethernet on the same network. To use Fast Ethernet, you need NICs that support 100 Mbps (most Fast Ethernet NICs support both 10 and 100 Mbps) and hubs that also handle that speed. Because most components of a Fast Ethernet system (software, NICs, hubs, and cabling) can handle both speeds, it is easy to upgrade from 10 to 100 Mbps, one segment at a time. You can also permanently (as permanent as anything is in the computer business) run part of a network at 100 Mbps and another part at 10 Mbps.

To mix 10 Mbps and 100 Mbps, you either need two NICs in the server, one at 10 and one at 100, or you need to have hubs that support both speeds. You can take a slow migration path from 10 Mbps to 100 Mbps by buying 10/100 NICs as you get new equipment and initially run the NICs at 10 Mbps. When you have enough 100 Mbps NICs to warrant it, get a 100 Mbps hub and 100 Mbps NIC for the server and run two NICs in the server (the cheaper approach) or get a hub that supports both speeds. Since Fast Ethernet incorporates the 10 Mbps protocol and can automatically negotiate between the two speeds, it does not require anything special, other than the appropriate NICs and hubs to operate on a network that has segments at both speeds.

There is another way to increase the speed at which a network can operate—by using *multiport switches* instead of hubs. In a normal Ethernet (either standard or Fast) or Token Ring network, all traffic travels throughout the entire network touching every node, but only the node to which it is addressed will accept it and bring it into the computer. That means that the traffic anywhere on the network is a component of the load everywhere on the network. Multiport switches establish dedicated links between the nodes that are communicating, much like a modern phone system that uses a dedicated line, while an unswitched network is similar to the old party-line phone system. The effect of switching is to reduce the traffic throughout the network and give any one transmission the entire capacity of one link. This can have a dramatic increase in throughput (like turning off a gridlocked highway onto a highway where your car is the only vehicle). A switched network can use existing NICs and cabling and only requires switches in place of hubs. Switches, though, are considerably more expensive; for example, a good 8-port 10 Mbps hub costs roughly $150 (the cheapest ones are under $80) compared to roughly $1,500 for an 8-port switch, but this is not a lot more than a 100 Mbps hub, which costs roughly $1,200. One common solution is to use a 100 Mbps link between the switch and the server and then eight or more 10 Mbps links to the clients. In this case, you would need a 100 Mbps NIC in the server and a switch with one 100 Mbps port and eight 10 Mbps ports, which costs roughly $1,800.

 OTE   The prices mentioned here are those in effect in the spring of 1998, and like the prices of most computer products, they are dropping rapidly.

Network Cabling

Two types of cable are used in Ethernet networks: coaxial and twisted pair. Coaxial cable is similar to (but not the same as) television cable. Twisted-pair cabling is similar to four-wire telephone cabling and *might* be the same. You need to check the specifications of the wire that you have (or that is already installed in your building) against those recommended for your network interface cards. Token Ring networks commonly use one of two types of twisted-pair cabling: Type 1, which is shielded and runs at 16 Mbps, and Type 3, which is unshielded and runs at 4 Mbps. Additionally, both Ethernet and Token Ring can use fiber-optic cable with special adapters or converters for particularly long distances—1.2 miles maximum for Ethernet and 2.5 miles maximum for Token Ring. ARCnet uses either twisted-pair or coaxial cable.

 ARNING   Do not use existing telephone twisted-pair cabling without checking its specifications against those recommended for your network interface cards.

Coaxial Cable   Coaxial cable, or *coax*, has wire braid surrounding a central wire with plastic insulation in between and a plastic jacket on the outside. Ethernet coaxial cable can be thin (about 0.2 inch in diameter), called *10Base2* or *ThinNet,* or thick (about 0.4 inch in diameter), called *10Base5* or *Standard* Ethernet. Thick coax, which was the original Ethernet cabling, can connect workstations up to 1640 feet apart versus up to 600 feet for thin coax. Thick coax is several times more expensive than thin, is harder to find, and harder to handle. For these reasons, thick coax is primarily used to connect other networks or over longer distances. Thin coax is generally easy to find and inexpensive. ARCnet cards use a slightly different thin coaxial cable, and you can tell the difference by the number stamped on it. Ethernet thin coax is RG-58A/U; ARCnet is RG-62A/U.

Ethernet thin coax uses a BNC twist-to-lock connector. You can buy the cables with the connectors on them, or you can add the connectors as you install the cable if you have or want to buy the necessary tools. Depending on the network topology (see *Network Topology* later in this chapter) you are using, the cable either connects directly to the network interface card (star topology), or uses a T-connector (bus topology), as shown in Figure 15-3. When you are using a bus topology, the computers in the middle have a cable connected to each end of the T-connector, while the computers on the ends have only one cable and require a 50-ohm terminator on the unused half of the T-connector.

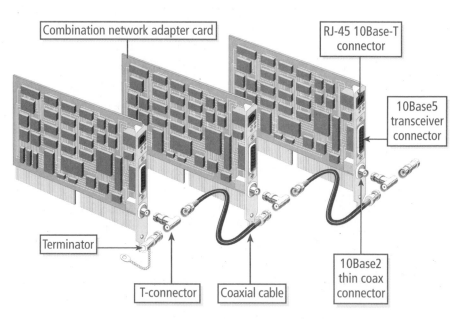

Figure 15-3. *Ethernet thin coax cabling components with a bus topology.*

Twisted-Pair Cable Ethernet twisted-pair cabling (called 10BaseT or UTP for unshielded twisted pair) has four to eight individual wires (two or four pairs—one or two for transmitting and one or two for receiving data). Each wire is insulated and twisted with its mate in a pair, and then the two to four twisted pairs are covered by a plastic outer cover. The twisting of the pairs provides shielding (the more twisting, the more shielding) against electrical and radio interference. If this is insufficient to keep noise off the network, you can get shielded twisted-pair cable that has a foil or braided jacket enclosing each and/or all of the pairs of wires. Twisted-pair cable uses a modular connector, known as an RJ-45 plug, similar to a modular phone plug except that it has eight pins, or conductors, instead of four as in a standard (RJ-11) phone plug.

There are a number of different types of UTP cabling. When you choose UTP, you can specify the inner core, the degree of fire resistance, the number of pairs, and the category grade.

- **The inner core** of each wire can be solid or stranded. Solid wire has less signal loss but breaks more easily. Therefore you should use solid in walls and ceilings, where it has longer runs and is not flexed. Stranded wire should be used between a wall plate and a computer or on a patch panel, where it is frequently flexed.

- **The degree of fire resistance** of the cable can be either *riser* cable (marked "CMR") or *plenum* cable (marked ("CMP"). Riser cable is used out in the open and between floors in a building. It has fire-resistant characteristics, but generally uses a polyvinyl chloride (PVC) outer jacket that can give off fumes if it does burn. Plenum cable is meant to run in air passages such as across a suspended ceiling or beneath a raised floor. It is more fire-resistant and doesn't give off fumes when it does burn. Plenum cable often has a Teflon outer jacket and is several times as expensive as riser cable.

- **The number of twisted pairs** in the cable can range from two to four. Almost all UTP cable installed for data transmission has four pairs of wires.

■ **The category grade** of UTP cable specifies the quality of the transmission characteristics—the higher the category, the better the quality. There are five official categories at the time of this writing, one unofficial category, and one currently going through the standardization process, as follows:

■ **Category 1** includes most telephone wire installed before 1983. It has two twisted pairs and should not be used for data transmission.

■ **Category 2** includes more recent telephone wire. It has four twisted pairs and can handle data transmissions up to 4 Mbps. It should not be used for networking of 10 Mbps and above.

■ **Category 3** was the standard cable used for networking. It has four twisted pairs, three twists per foot, and can handle frequencies up to 16 MHz. It is commonly used for 10 Mbps Ethernet and 4 Mbps Token Ring. Most current telephone installations use this category.

■ **Category 4** was installed in many Token Ring networks. It has four twisted pairs and can handle frequencies up to 20 MHz. It was commonly used for 16 Mbps Token Ring.

■ **Category 5** is the current standard networking cable. It has four twisted pairs, eight twists per foot, and can handle frequencies up to 100 MHz. It is commonly used for Fast Ethernet (100 Mbps) and is installed in the majority of networks today.

■ **Enhanced Category 5** is an unofficial standard with the same specs as Category 5, except that it can handle frequencies up to 200 MHz.

■ **Category 6** is in the standard-setting process and is really shielded twisted-pair cabling with a foil shield wrapped around each pair and another foil shield around all four pairs. Its specifications are not set at the time of this writing, but it is expected that it will handle frequencies up to 400 MHz and be ready when Gigabit Ethernet becomes a reality.

IP If you are installing a network today, it is strongly recommended that you use Category 5 UTP.

For twisted-pair cabling to work, the transmitting pair of wires on one end of the cable must become the receiving pair on the other end. This *crossover* function is handled normally in the hub (see *Network Topology* later in this chapter) in a star topology, which is commonly used with twisted-pair cabling, as shown in Figure 15-4. If you want to network only two computers with 10BaseT, you may do so without a hub by using a special crossover cable, which provides the crossover function.

Unshielded twisted-pair cabling is cheaper and easier to install than co-axial cable, but it is more susceptible to electrical and radio interference. Twisted-pair cable can be shielded, but shielding substantially increases the cost and reduces the availability and ease of installation. Often when you are installing twisted-pair cabling, you can solve most of the interference problems by *not* running the cable alongside any motorized equipment (fans, water coolers, machine tools) or fluorescent light fixtures.

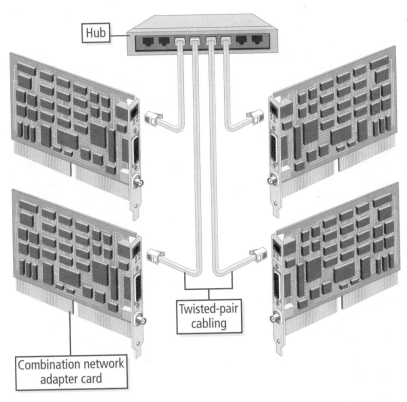

Hub

Twisted-pair
cabling

Combination network
adapter card

Figure 15-4. *Ethernet twisted-pair cabling components with a star topology.*

Cabling Summary Table 15-1 provides a summary of network cabling specifications. It is useful information, but it is to some degree like trying to describe apples and oranges with the same terms. An Ethernet twisted-pair *segment* is the distance between two nodes, and only two nodes can be on it. An Ethernet coaxial *segment* is the maximum length of a single run of coaxial cable and can have up to 30 or 100 nodes depending on the type of coax. A Token Ring *segment* is the length of one ring and can have up to 72 or 260 nodes on it. There is a limit of five Ethernet coaxial segments, and only three of them can have nodes. Therefore, the maximum network length for Ethernet coax is five times the segment length, and the maximum number of network nodes is only three times the number of segment nodes. Both Token Ring and Ethernet twisted pair can be expanded virtually forever. Therefore there is no maximum network length, and for Token Ring, there is no maximum number of nodes. The Ethernet specification itself limits the total number of nodes in the network to 1024, although you can join multiple networks to increase that number many times. There is no specified minimum cable length for Ethernet twisted pair, Token Ring, or ARCnet coax. However, as a practical matter, you should not cut a cable shorter than two feet.

There are many ways to implement a large network and many ways around the limits shown in Table 15-1. These involve various types of hubs, repeaters, and bridges, which are all electronic devices that allow you to expand your network. For more information, see the book *Encyclopedia of Networking* by Tom Sheldon, published in 1998 by Osborne/McGraw-Hill, or the *Black Box Catalog* from Black Box Corporation, 1000 Park Drive, Lawrence, PA 15055, (412) 746-5500.

Network Topology

Network topology describes how the nodes or devices on a network are connected. For Ethernet, there are two topologies: bus and star.

Bus Topology In a *bus topology*, which is used with coaxial cable, each of the devices is connected in a line on a single run of cable. This is a daisy-chain arrangement where the cable goes from device (computer, workstation, printer, or server) to device. With thin coax cable, the T-connector provides the joining of the two cables at each device except on the ends, where a 50-ohm terminator is used on one side of the T-connector, as you can see in Figure 15-5. With thick coax, a clamp-on connector goes over a continuous run of cable and provides the signal to a transceiver, which sends the signal through a separate multiconductor cable to the network interface card, as shown in Figure 15-6. Again, on either end of the thick coax cable, there is a 50-ohm terminator. (This complex, costly configuration, needed with thick coax, is part of the reason that thick coax is not widely used any more.)

Type of Cabling	Max. Segment Length	Max. Network Length	Min. Cable Length	Max. Speed	Max. Network Nodes	Max. Nodes per Segment
Ethernet						
Twisted Pair (10BaseT) Category 3	328 ft			10 Mbps	1024	2
Thin Coax (10Base2)	607 ft	3035 ft	2 ft	10 Mbps	90	30
Thick Coax (10Base5)	1640 ft	8200 ft	8.5 ft	10 Mbps	300	100
Fiber Optic (10BaseF)	1.2 mi			10 Mbps		
Fast Ethernet						
Twisted Pair (100BaseT) Category 5	328 ft			100 Mbps	1024	2
Fiber Optic (100BaseF)	1.2 mi			100 Mbps		
Token Ring						
Type 1 Shielded Category 4 or 5	328 ft			16 Mbps		260
Type 3 Unshielded Category 3	148 ft			4 Mbps		72
Fiber Optic	2.5 mi			16 Mbps		
ARCnet						
Twisted Pair Category 2 or 3	400 ft	4 mi	6 ft	2.5 Mbps	255	10
Thin Coax	1000 ft	4 mi		2.5 Mbps	255	8

Table 15-1.   *Summary of network cabling specifications.*

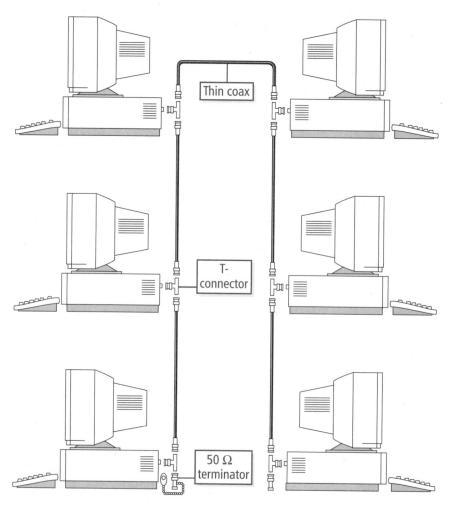

Figure 15-5. *Bus topology with 10Base2 thin coaxial cable.*

Star Topology A *star topology*, which is used by both Ethernet 10BaseT and 100BaseT twisted-pair cabling and Token Ring cabling, uses a hub or switch to fan out the network from one incoming signal to two, four, eight, or more outgoing signals. You can have a server feeding several hubs that each feed several hubs that each feed a number of workstations, allowing you to get very quickly to a large number of nodes, as shown in Figure 15-7. The benefits of a star topology are as follows:

- The loss of one segment generally does not bring down the entire network.

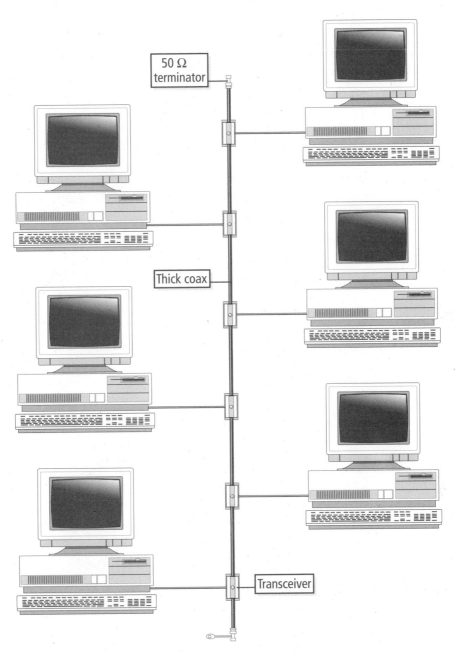

Figure 15-6. *Bus topology with 10Base5 thick coaxial cable.*

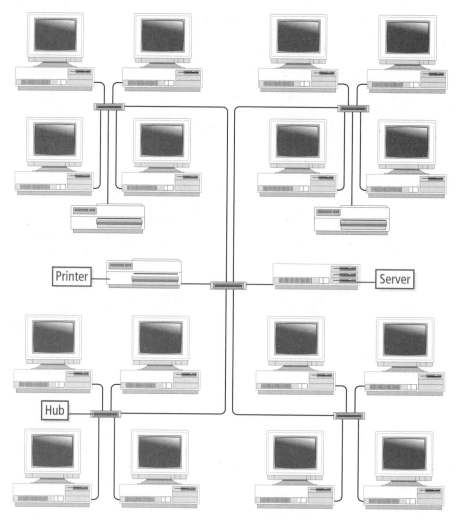

Figure 15-7. *Star topology with 10BaseT or 100BaseT twisted-pair cable.*

■ Some network traffic bottlenecks are avoided by each node having its own cable.

■ Network design is very flexible and is easily expanded.

■ Cable problems are easy to find by observing what is working and what isn't.

> **TIP** In a star topology, you can daisy chain from one star to another and another, creating four or more layers. You will find you improve your reliability if you fan out from one hub to many hubs and have only two, or at the very most three, layers.

On the negative side, hubs are expensive, and if one fails, the entire network will go down. Also, there is a lot of cable in a star topology, and while it is cheaper per foot than coaxial cable, the quantity of it may more than make up for the lower cost per foot.

In summary, Ethernet twisted-pair (10BaseT or 100BaseT) in a star topology is the predominant networking scheme in use today. This means that you will find a large number of competitively priced components on the market and a lot of knowledge about their use.

In all but the simplest network installations, usually a combination of topologies is used. Within a given workgroup, the typical network uses a 10BaseT star topology and then uses a 10Base5 bus topology or recently 100BaseT star topology to form a backbone that runs between workgroups or floors in a building or to the server.

Setting Up Network Interface Cards

For your network interface card to work with your computer, the card must have two or three settings correctly made on it. These settings, which include the interrupt request line (IRQ), the I/O port address, and possibly the upper memory address, determine how the card communicates with the computer, similar to a multimedia card as discussed in Chapter 13. If the NIC is Plug and Play (PnP), these settings are automatically made for you when you install the card or install Windows 98. If the NIC is not PnP, you must physically make some changes to the card. To make these changes, you will need to know the settings for other devices in your computer. To find that out, if you are already running Windows 98, open the Start menu, choose Settings | Control Panel | System, click the Device Manager tab, and then click Print. When the dialog box opens, make sure that System Summary is selected, and then click OK. You will get a list of what device is using which interrupt request line, port address, and upper memory address. With this information, you can see what is available for the network interface card.

As you saw in the section *Installing Multimedia Cards* in Chapter 13, different cards use different methods of changing the settings. You will need to look at the manual for the card and the printout you just made to determine what settings to make for your card. Chapter 13 also discussed the IRQ and port addresses and showed in tables what the common default uses were for various settings. Refer to Chapter 13 when setting the IRQ and I/O port address on your NICs.

 WARNING   A NIC takes 32 (20 hex) address positions, for example, 300h–31Fh. Therefore, if you have a SCSI controller at 340h, you cannot put the network interface card at 330h because it will take up 330h–34Fh, overlapping the SCSI controller and causing serious problems.

Upper Memory Address

The *upper memory address* is an area of upper memory (between 640 KB and 1 MB) that some network interface cards use. Ethernet cards only use this if you have a diskless workstation and boot the computer from a *boot PROM* (programmable read-only memory) in the network interface card. (The boot PROM is a chip that allows you to boot from files on the server.) ARCnet cards use upper memory as buffer memory as well as for a boot PROM. The address, which is a range, is expressed in hexadecimal, like the I/O port address. Table 15-2 shows some default and possible uses of these addresses. Two possible choices for the NIC are CC000h–DBFFFh and E0000h–EFFFFh. Look at what your other devices are using, and then decide what you want to use for this card. Next look at your card's manual, and decide how your choice translates to pins or switches on your card.

Node Address

Each network interface card in a network must have a unique node address. Ethernet cards have this address built into the card, and it cannot be changed. ARCnet cards have a DIP switch that allows you to enter the address for each card. When you do this, be sure to keep a log, so you can see that no two computers have the same address.

Upper Memory Address	Default or Typical Use
A0000h–CBFFFh	Video display adapters
CC000h–DBFFFh	May be available if not used by expanded memory
DC000h–DFFFFh	May be available if not used by SCSI disk controller
E0000h–E7FFFh	Normally available except in PS/2 computers
E8000h–FFFFFh	Used by the system for PnP BIOS

Table 15-2.   *Upper memory addresses and their normal use.*

Setting Up Windows 98 Networking

Under many circumstances, when you set up Windows 98 on a computer properly connected to a network, Setup will detect the network and the NIC you are using and correctly configure Windows to use the network. All you have to do is use the network. Part of the reason that so much of this chapter is devoted to hardware is that 70 to 80 percent of all networking problems are with the hardware.

If your network has either a NetWare or Windows NT server, Setup will often automatically provide the correct client software to run in your computer. If you are upgrading from running Windows for Workgroups or Windows 95 in a peer-to-peer network, or if you are setting up a Windows 98 peer-to-peer network, Setup will again often do all the work for you.

If you add a NIC and a network connection after setting up Windows 98, use the Add New Hardware control panel (open the Start menu and choose Settings | Control Panel | Add New Hardware) to start the Add New Hardware Wizard. This will lead you through the process of identifying and configuring your card and the networking software you are using. Again, in most instances, your task is no greater than clicking Next. Setup should find the card and its resource usage (IRQ and I/O port address) and install the necessary driver software.

If your Windows 98 networking setup did not go perfectly, or if for some reason you want to make a change to your network, the Network control panel provides all of the settings to configure your networking software.

This same set of dialog boxes is used by Setup to enter network settings, so any setup questions you have can be answered by the next series of sections on the Network control panel.

Network Control Panel

You access the Network control panel by opening the Control Panel folder and clicking the Network icon. This opens the Network dialog box, which you can see in Figure 15-8.

IP   You can also open the Network dialog box by right-clicking the Network Neighborhood icon and then choosing Properties in the context menu that appears.

The primary work in the Network dialog box is done in the Configuration tab. Here you can add, remove, and configure components. The components are shown in the list box at the top of the dialog box. By selecting a component, you can remove it (click Remove) or change its properties (click Properties). You can also add components by clicking Add. When

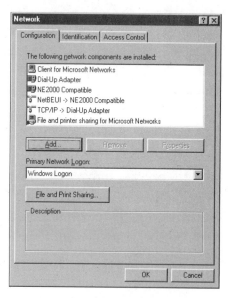

Figure 15-8.   *Network dialog box.*

you do that, a list of the four components is displayed in the Select Network Component Type dialog box, as shown below. Each of these components is discussed next.

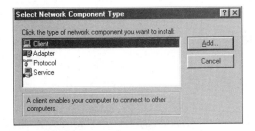

Network Clients

A network client is the primary software component necessary for your computer to operate on a network. It provides the ability within Windows 98 to access files and print to printers located on other computers. Windows 98 comes with a number of network clients that allow you to connect to and utilize different networks. If you are physically connected to a network when you run Setup, it is likely that Setup will detect the network and install the appropriate client. If, for whatever reason, Setup cannot determine what client to install, or if you want to install a client, you do so through the Select Network Client dialog box, which is shown in Figure 15-9. You open the Select Network Client dialog box by choosing Client and clicking Add in the Select Network Component Type dialog box discussed above.

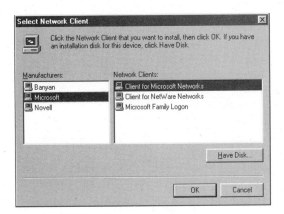

Figure 15-9. *Select Network Client dialog box.*

Selecting a Network Client If you want to create a Windows 98 peer-to-peer network, connect to or replace a Windows 95 or Windows for Workgroups network, or if you want to be a client on a Windows NT or LAN Manager network, you need to use the Client for Microsoft Networks. If you want to be a client on a Novell NetWare network, you can use either the Microsoft Client for NetWare Networks or one of the Novell clients. If you are on another manufacturer's network, you need to select the manufacturer and appropriate client for your network.

 OTE Both Novell and Microsoft have NetWare clients, and you should probably try both to see which works best for you.

The Select Network Client dialog box lists the manufacturers that have contributed clients to operate within Windows 98, as well as the clients Microsoft has written for Windows 98. If you want to use other client software that you got separately from Windows 98, you may do so by clicking Have Disk. Otherwise, select the manufacturer and client software you want to use, and then click OK.

Setting Client Properties After you have installed a client, you can set its properties by double-clicking it in the Network dialog box or selecting it and clicking Properties. Each type of client has its own set of properties, as shown in Figures 15-10 and 15-11.

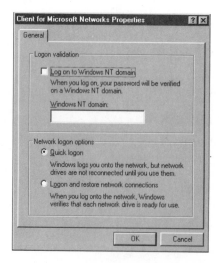

Figure 15-10. *Client for Microsoft Networks Properties dialog box.*

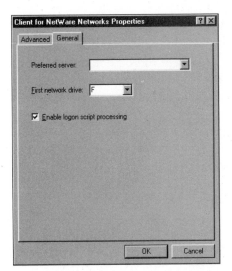

Figure 15-11. *Client for NetWare Networks Properties dialog box.*

The Client for Microsoft Networks Properties dialog box allows you to specify whether you will log on to an identified Windows NT domain and to determine how much checking you want to do of available network drives at logon. If your network drives (those that you have mapped to your computer) are mandatory for your work, then you probably want to do the more time-consuming Logon And Restore Network Connections. If you have several network drives that are often not up when you start up, you will want to use the Quick Logon. If you don't use Quick Logon in the latter case, you will be asked about each network drive that is not available. After you have done that several times, you'll want to switch to Quick Logon.

Network Adapters

A network adapter connects your computer to a network. This can be a NIC that connects to a dedicated cable or wireless link using Ethernet, Token Ring, or ARCnet, or it can be a Virtual Private Networking adapter (see Chapter 16) or even a modem that allows you to connect to a telephone line. When you run through Setup or the Add New Hardware Wizard, the system will try to determine what type of adapter you have and its settings (IRQ, I/O port address, and so on). Also, if you install a network interface card after setting up Windows 98, Windows may detect the new card on startup. In any case (Setup, Add New Hardware Wizard, or startup), if the card adheres to the Plug and Play standard, Windows 98 will be able to identify it and its settings; otherwise, you will have to manually do the identification. From within Setup or the Add Hardware Wizard, you'll be shown the Select Network Adapters dialog box, which you see in Figure 15-12. You can open the same dialog box by selecting Add from the Network dialog box, choosing Adapter, and clicking Add.

Selecting a Network Adapter The Select Network Adapters dialog box lists many of the manufacturers of network interface cards as well as their various models. If you are using a generic network interface card that is NE1000 (8-bit), NE2000 (16-bit), or NE3200 (32-bit) compatible, you can find these adapters under Novell/Anthem, as shown in Figure 15-12. If you want to use a network interface card not on the list and for which you have a floppy disk or a CD, you may do so by clicking Have Disk. Otherwise, select the manufacturer and network adapter you want to use, and then click OK.

Setting Network Adapter Properties While running Setup or the Add New Hardware Wizard, after selecting a network interface card, a Properties dialog box appears. It is similar to the one you see in Figure 15-13 but specific to your adapter card. The settings in the dialog box will vary for each type of card, but the NE2000 settings are representative. All cards have Driver Type and Bindings tabs; cards that are not Plug and Play also have Resources and/or Advanced tabs. The Driver Type tab allows you to

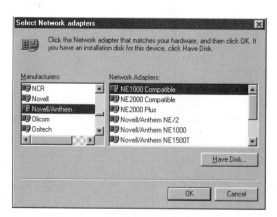

Figure 15-12. *Selecting a network adapter.*

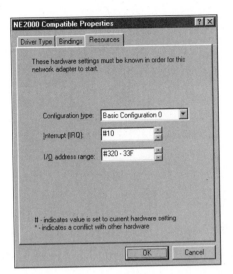

Figure 15-13. *A sample network adapter Properties dialog box.*

select between enhanced mode and real mode drivers. Enhanced mode drivers are by far the best choice. Bindings allows you to attach ("bind") one or more protocols to a particular adapter. See the discussion later in this chapter about protocols. In the Resources tab, you tell Windows the IRQ and I/O port address to use for this card. With some Plug and Play–compliant cards, resource information is automatically provided to Windows, so a Resource tab is not necessary. The Advanced tab allows you to set values for specific properties, which vary among adapter cards.

Network Protocols

A network protocol is the method of communication used on the network. For the network to function, all computers on the network must employ the same protocol. A protocol is like a human language—to communicate, people must speak the same language. When you choose a client and an adapter, or they are selected for you by Setup, one or more protocols are installed and attached, or "bound," to the adapter. You can add a protocol by clicking Add in the Network control panel, selecting Protocol, and then clicking Add again. The Select Network Protocol dialog box opens, as shown in Figure 15-14.

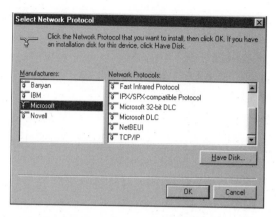

Figure 15-14. *Select Network Protocol dialog box.*

Selecting a Network Protocol Many protocols were developed for specific types of networks, such as IPX/SPX for Novell NetWare. Over time these protocols have evolved and are now being used on several types of networks. With Windows 98, you can simultaneously use several protocols, but each takes loading time and computer resources. Windows 98 includes several protected mode (able to address large memory space with multitasking) Microsoft-implemented protocols as follows:

- **ATM Call Manager, ATM Emulated LAN, and ATM LAN Emulation Client** are Asynchronous Transfer Mode, new high-speed protocols.

- **Fast Infrared Protocol** is used to communicate short distances (within a room) without cables.

- **IPX/SPX** stands for Internetwork Packet Exchange/Sequenced Packet Exchange, developed by Novell for NetWare.

- **Microsoft DLC and 32-bit DLC** are Data Link Control protocols, used primarily to connect to IBM mainframe computers.

- **NetBEUI** stands for Network basic input/output system (NetBIOS) Enhanced User Interface, developed by IBM and Microsoft.

- **TCP/IP** means Transmission Control Protocol/Internet Protocol, developed for UNIX and the Internet.

Additionally, Windows 98 includes several protocols contributed by other vendors such as Banyan, EICON, and Novell. The question becomes which protocol is best under different circumstances. For the Microsoft protocols, their primary use and considerations are as follows:

- **ATM** is used for very fast (up to 10 Gbps), high-demand WANs.

- **Infrared** is used for laptop to network, laptop to printer, and where cables cannot be used.

- **IPX/SPX** is used with Novell NetWare and combined NetWare–Windows NT networks; it is slower, with more overhead than NetBEUI on smaller LANs.

- **DLC** is used to connect IBM mainframe computers to computers running Windows 98; it is also used to provide connectivity to printers connected directly to the network.

- **NetBEUI** is used with smaller (100 or fewer nodes) IBM and Microsoft networks. It offers fast, small memory usage, and good error protection, but poor performance over WANs.

- **TCP/IP** is used with Internet, UNIX, and multiple hardware/operating system platforms. This is the most widely accepted protocol and is good for most LANs and WANs.

 OTE TCP/IP is set up by default by Windows 98 Setup if you are not using a Novell network. It is, under most circumstances, your best choice.

The Select Network Protocol dialog box lists some of the manufacturers of network protocols as well as the protocols they provide. If you want to use a network protocol that is not on the list and for which you have a floppy disk or a CD, you may do so by clicking Have Disk. Otherwise, select the manufacturer and protocol you want to use, and then click OK.

Setting Network Protocol Properties Each protocol has a unique set of properties and a unique Properties dialog box, as you can see in Figures 15-15 and 15-16. All of the dialog boxes have at least two tabs: Bindings, where you identify where the protocol will be used, and Advanced, where you make detailed settings. Other tabs are unique to specific protocols. The default settings work under most circumstances.

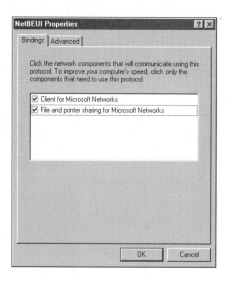

Figure 15-15.   *NetBEUI Properties dialog box.*

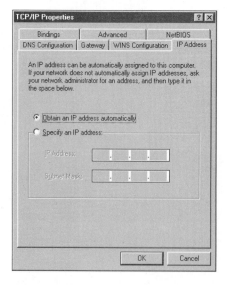

Figure 15-16.   *TCP/IP Properties dialog box.*

IP   If you are using TCP/IP, be sure to check the IP Address in the TCP/IP Properties dialog box, and if you are not connected to a server that automatically assigns you an address, be sure to specify an IP address. If you don't, you'll find that the system will pause periodically for a couple of seconds while it tries to get an IP address from a nonexistent server source.

Network Services

Network services provide the means for you to share the disks, files, folders, and printers on your computer with others on the network (to perform the server function in a peer-to-peer network). From the Select Network Component Type dialog box, you can select Service and Add to open the Select Network Service dialog box, shown in Figure 15-17. Microsoft provides file and printer sharing for both Microsoft and NetWare networks, although you can install only one at a time, and support for NetWare Directory Services (NDS). Other manufacturers provide other services such as system backup. If you have a network service on a floppy disk or CD, click Have Disk. Otherwise, select the service you want to use, and click OK.

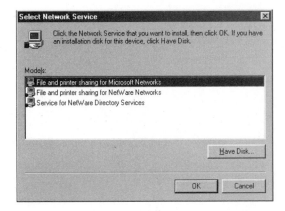

Figure 15-17.   *Select Network Service dialog box.*

Each service has a unique set of properties and a unique Properties dialog box, as you can see in Figure 15-18. As with network protocols, the property defaults are a good place to start with network services.

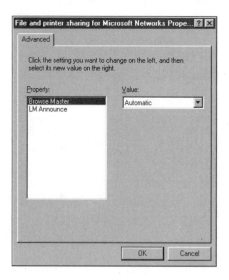

Figure 15-18. *File And Printer Sharing For Microsoft Networks Properties dialog box.*

Using a Windows 98 Network

You can use a network in many ways. You can share the resources (files, folders, disks, CD-ROMs, and printers) on or connected to your computer with others in your workgroup. You can utilize the resources on other computers in your workgroup or on servers to which you have access, and you can transfer files and send messages to anyone to whom you are connected. You can also share certain software on a network and use *groupware,* which is software that is meant to be used by several people in a workgroup. Examples of groupware are Lotus Notes, which defined this type of software, and Microsoft Outlook.

In this chapter, you will see how to share your resources and how to control that sharing. You will also see how to find and utilize resources elsewhere on the network to which you are connected, including transferring files. This chapter also covers dial-up or remote networking, virtual private networking, and the networking accessories that are part of Windows 98.

Sharing Your Resources

You can share most of the hardware, software (programs), and data that are on your computer. For your protection and the protection of your programs and data, you have a reasonable degree of control over how these resources are shared and by whom. Two levels of sharing control are available in Windows 98: a *summary level* where you can turn sharing on or off for your entire computer and all of its resources, and a *detail level* where you can turn sharing on or off individually for each specific disk, folder, and printer.

Turning Resource Sharing On or Off

In order to share any of the resources on your computer, you must turn on sharing at a summary level. Windows 98 allows you to control the sharing of files and folders, and separately, control the sharing of printers. The *sharing of files and folders* means that others on your network can read and potentially modify the files in the disks and folders that you have identified as being shared. The *sharing of printers* means that others on your network can print their documents on the printer(s) that you have identified as being shared. You manage the summary-level enabling of file and printer sharing through the Network control panel with the following steps:

1. Open the Start menu and choose Settings | Control Panel | Network. The Network dialog box opens, as you can see in Figure 16-1.

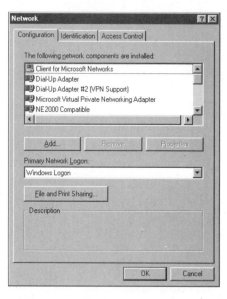

Figure 16-1.   *Network dialog box.*

2. Click the File And Print Sharing button just below the middle of the Network dialog box. The File And Print Sharing dialog box opens, as shown here:

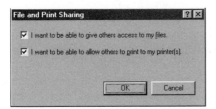

3. To share your resources, select either or both of the check boxes. Select the top box to share disks, folders, and files; select the bottom box to share the printer devices connected to or on your computer (such as a fax).

4. If the check boxes are selected (check marks in them) and you don't want to share either or both types of resources, click the boxes to turn off sharing.

5. Click OK after you have set the summary-level sharing status the way you want it. You'll have to restart your computer for the changes to take effect.

Sharing Individual Resources

Although you may have turned on file and/or printer sharing on your computer at a summary level, nothing is shared until you specifically enable sharing for a particular resource. You must do this on a resource-by-resource basis except that if you share a disk, all folders and files on that disk are automatically shared.

 ARNING If you do not want to share all the files on a disk, do not share the disk drive. You must specifically share the individual folders to which you want to provide access.

Sharing Disks and Folders

Disks and folders are shared through either My Computer or Windows Explorer using these steps:

1. Open either My Computer or Windows Explorer, and right-click the disk or folder you want to share. The context menu for that object opens, as you can see here:

2. Select Sharing from the context menu. The resource's Properties dialog box opens with the Sharing tab selected, as shown in Figure 16-2.

3. Select Shared As to share a disk or folder, and either accept the default name or enter a new name, which will be what the object is called on other computers. You can also enter a comment that will help identify your computer. You can see the comment in the Details view of the Windows Explorer view of Network Neighborhood.

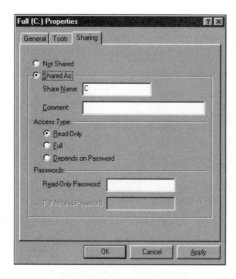

Figure 16-2.   *Sharing tab in a disk's or folder's Properties dialog box.*

4. Select the type of access you want to provide from among the following choices:

   ■ **Read-Only** access allows people to read and copy files but not to modify or delete them.

   ■ **Full** access allows people to modify and delete files as well as add and read them.

   ■ **Depends On Password** access allows you to give different individuals different passwords, some of which allow full access and some read-only access.

5. Enter the passwords you want to use for the type of access you have chosen, and click OK.

Repeat this process for each disk or folder that you want to share.

 OTE The Windows 98 installation default is that all disks, folders, and printers are *not* shared, so if you do nothing, people will not have access to your resources. You must specifically share what you want others to use.

 IP You can tell if a disk, folder, or printer is shared in My Computer or Windows Explorer because if it is, it will have an open hand beneath it, like this:

Sharing Printers

 Sharing a printer is similar to sharing a disk or a folder except that it begins in the Printers folder. Use the following steps:

1. Open the Start menu, and choose Settings | Printers. The Printers dialog box opens.

2. Right-click the printer you want to share, and in the context menu that opens, click Sharing. The Sharing tab of the printer's Properties dialog box opens, as shown in Figure 16-3.

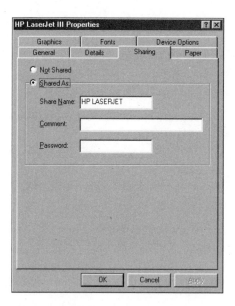

Figure 16-3.   *Sharing tab of a printer's Properties dialog box.*

3. Select Shared As, and either accept the Share Name or enter a new one. Enter a comment if you want to provide one and a password if you want password protection on the use of the printer.

4. When you are satisfied that the dialog box is the way you want it, click OK.

Using Resources on Other Computers

A major benefit of networking to you personally is that you now have access to all of the resources that have been shared on your network. To realize this benefit, you must locate the resources and utilize them. You can do that through Network Neighborhood or by mapping the resources to your computer.

Accessing Resources through Network Neighborhood

Network Neighborhood is the primary path to network resources. It performs the same functions for your network resources as My Computer does for the resources on your computer. When you open Network Neighborhood, you see the computers in your immediate workgroup as well as an icon representing the rest of your network, as you can see in Figure 16-4.

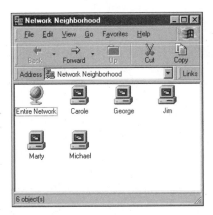

Figure 16-4. *Network Neighborhood.*

If you open the Entire Network icon, you'll see the other workgroups and servers that you can access. If you open these workgroups, you'll see the individual computers that are available within them.

If you click a computer, either directly in Network Neighborhood or within a workgroup under Entire Network, you will see the resources that have been shared on that computer, as shown in Figure 16-5. By clicking a disk resource, you can open it and see the folders and files that are available within it, just as you can by clicking a disk in My Computer. Depending on how the disks and folders are shared, you will be able to read and copy files and possibly modify and delete them. If you want to copy a file onto your own computer, you need only drag it from its original folder to one on a disk in your computer. Use the following steps for that purpose:

 IP Dragging a file between disks copies it, unlike dragging a file between locations on the same disk, which moves the file.

1. Open Network Neighborhood from the desktop, and select the network computer from which you want to copy the file.

2. Open the network computer, and select the disk and folder containing the file. You should be able to see the file. If not, use the scroll bar until you see the file.

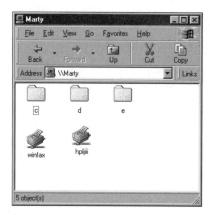

Figure 16-5. *Resources shared on a particular computer.*

3. Open My Computer, and select first the disk and then the folder that are to receive the file. You should now be able to see both the receiving folder and the file you want to copy. If not, drag and size the windows until you can see both, as shown in Figure 16-6.

4. Drag the file from the network computer's folder to your computer's folder. A copy of the file will be on your computer for you to use as you want.

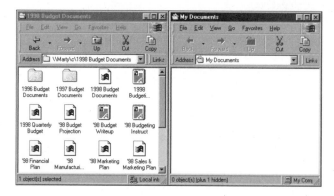

Figure 16-6. *Windows setup for copying between a network computer and yours.*

Using Windows Explorer with Network Neighborhood

Windows Explorer provides full access to the computers, disks, folders, and files within Network Neighborhood, as you can see in Figure 16-7. This makes searching for and copying files easier, because you can get at and align the sending and receiving folders more simply. Compare the following steps with those that have just preceded:

1. Open Network Neighborhood in the left pane of Windows Explorer, and select the computer, drive, and folder from which you want to copy the file.

2. Adjust the right pane so you can see the file you want to copy.

3. Adjust the left pane so you can see the folder to which you are going to copy the file, opening the necessary parent disks and folders. The Windows Explorer window shown in Figure 16-8 is set up for the same source and destination as the windows in Figure 16-6.

4. Drag the file in the right pane to the correct folder in the left pane.

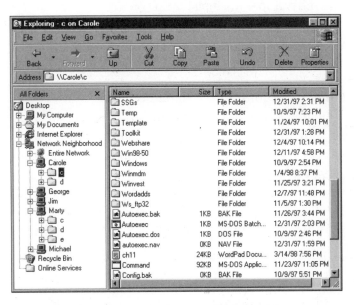

Figure 16-7.   *Network Neighborhood within Windows Explorer.*

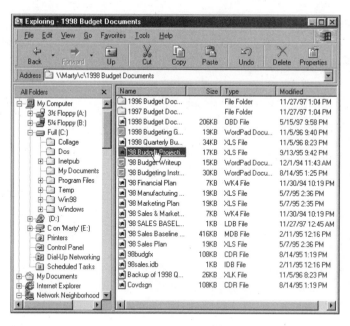

Figure 16-8. *Windows Explorer setup for copying between a network computer and yours.*

While the number of steps for the Windows Explorer approach and the Network Neighborhood/My Computer windows approach are the same, the Windows Explorer method is significantly easier to carry out and is more intuitive.

Printing through Network Neighborhood

In a manner similar to the copying of a file by dragging it between the Network Neighborhood and My Computer windows, you can print by dragging a printable document file to a network printer. Use the following steps to do that:

1. Open Network Neighborhood, and select the computer with the printer you want to use.

2. Open My Computer, and select the disk and folder containing the file you want to print.

3. Adjust the windows so you can see both the file and the printer.

4. Drag the file to the printer, as shown in Figure 16-9. The file will be printed on the printer you chose.

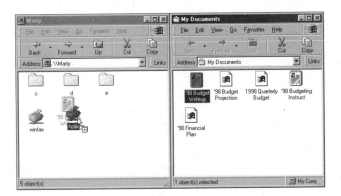

Figure 16-9. *Dragging a file to print it on a network printer.*

 OTE For drag-and-drop printing to work, the file to be printed must be associated with a program that is registered in Windows with a print action. See *Associating Files* in Chapter 6.

Using Find over a Network

Finding a file over a simple network, such as those shown in the figures here, is fairly simple, but in a large network you may have a difficult time finding the correct computer, let alone the correct file. You can use the Find option on the Start menu to locate computers and find folders and files on a network. The Computer option, which you can select immediately after choosing Find from the Start menu, allows you to enter a computer name and, optionally, a disk or folder. Windows will tell you the workgroup the computer is in and any comments associated with that computer, as you can see in Figure 16-10. You can enter either the full network path name (see tip below) if you want to specify a disk or folder, or just a computer name without any backslashes. If you search for a computer by itself within your workgroup, you will get Network Neighborhood as the Location.

 IP A network path name that includes the computer name has the following format: *computer name\drive letter\folder name\filename.*

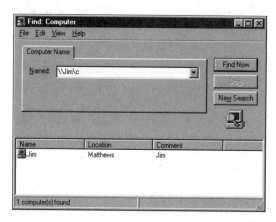

Figure 16-10. *Finding a network computer gives you the workgroup it is in.*

To search for a file or a folder on a network computer, you must know the computer it is on, or the network drive must be mapped to your computer (see the next section). With a known computer, you can use Network Neighborhood from within Find to locate the computer and then search for the file on that computer. The steps to do that are as follows:

1. Open the Start menu, and choose Find | Files or Folders. The Find: All Files dialog box opens.

2. Click Browse, scroll the list until you see Network Neighborhood, and then open Network Neighborhood and, if necessary, the Entire Network.

3. Select the workgroup and the computer, as you see in Figure 16-11, and then click OK.

4. Enter the file or folder name to search for, and click Find Now. The results are displayed as in any other Find, like those shown in Figure 16-12.

Mapping Network Resources to Your Computer

If you use the same network resources often, you will find that the above procedures become cumbersome, and you will want a more direct approach. Mapping network resources to your computer, which you first read about in Chapter 2, is such an approach. Mapping creates a pseudoresource on your computer that you can treat just as if it were physically there. You can do this for both disks and printers.

Figure 16-11. *Selecting a network computer to search.*

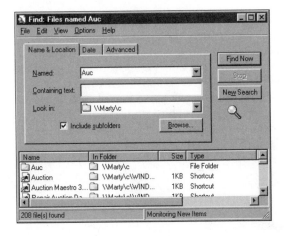

Figure 16-12. *Results of a network search.*

 OTE Windows 98 has menu options for mapping network disk drives, but a similar procedure for printers is called *capturing a printer port.*

Mapping a Network Drive

One of the major benefits of mapping a network drive is that you can directly address the drive from within all applications, just as if it were a drive on your computer. To map a network drive to your computer, use the following instructions:

1. From Network Neighborhood, or Network Neighborhood within Windows Explorer, open the computer that has the drive you want

to map, and right-click that drive. In the context menu, select Map Network Drive. The Map Network Drive dialog box opens, as you see here:

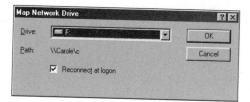

2. Make sure the drive letter and the path are the way you want them, decide whether to reconnect each time you log on (it slows down booting), and then click OK. The new drive letter will be available on your computer, and it will refer to the network drive.

IP   A more difficult approach to mapping a network drive is to open the Tools menu in Windows Explorer and choose Map Network Drive. The Map Network Drive dialog box will appear, but you must select the drive letter and type in the path without being able to browse for it. But, if you have recently mapped the drive, it will be on the list that appears when you click the down arrow at the right of the Path text box, like this:

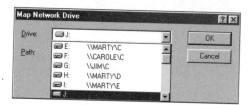

Mapping a Network Printer

In Chapter 7, you saw how to add a network printer to your computer, allowing you to print directly to it. This provides a printer path such as \\Sales3\HpLJ4 where *Sales3* is the computer name and *HpLJ4* is the printer name. With certain situations and applications, especially DOS applications, you cannot use a printer path like this. Instead you need to specify a port address, such as *LPT2*. Windows 98 allows you to map network printers to an unused port address. As noted earlier, this is called *capturing a printer port*. You can do this in two different ways. The first is at the end of adding a new printer (started by clicking Add Printer in the

Printers folder) where the Add Printer Wizard displays a Capture Printer Port button, as shown in Figure 16-13. The second way is in the printer's Properties dialog box, where the Details tab also has a similar button. In both cases, the Capture Printer Port dialog box opens, as shown below. The Add Printer Wizard has the added benefit of having the path already filled in.

In the Capture Printer Port dialog box, open the Device drop-down list box, and choose the port address you want to use. If you have a local printer attached to your computer, it probably will be using LPT1 (although this dialog box will not alert you to that). In this case, you would not want to use LPT1 for a network printer. If you have already mapped other network printers, they will be displayed like this:

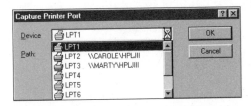

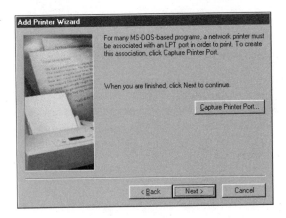

Figure 16-13. *Add Printer Wizard with the Capture Printer Port button active.*

If you entered the Capture Printer Port through the Properties dialog box, you will need to enter a printer path. See the discussion at the start of this section on printer paths. When the port and path are the way you want them, click OK to complete the network printer mapping. You can then refer to the port address from MS-DOS or Windows to use the network printer.

Dial-Up Networking

Dial-up networking, or *remote access* (*RAS*—pronounced "razz"), allows you to remotely access a network over a modem and phone lines or other communications links. With RAS, you can be on the road with your laptop, dial into your office computer, and not only access that computer but the entire network to which it is connected, just as if you were using your office computer. As long as your laptop and office computers are running Windows 98 and are both configured for dial-up networking, you can access any network (peer-to-peer, client-server, NetWare, or Windows NT) to which your office computer is connected. You can get and send mail, access shared data, print remotely, and transfer shared files. Dial-up networking also allows you to connect to public networks, such as the Internet, that are not running Windows 98, as you read in Chapter 11. With the explosion of mobile computing, dial-up networking is a significant part of Windows 98.

To use dial-up networking, you need to set up your mobile or remote computer (the *remote client*) with a dial-up connection to your office or connecting computer (the *dial-up server*). You also need to set up your office or connecting computer to be a server so it will receive incoming calls and serve as a gateway to the network to which it is connected.

 OTE   You may have already set up a dial-up networking client to connect to the Internet, as discussed in Chapter 11. That client is good only to connect to the server maintained by your ISP. You must create a separate dial-up networking client for each server to which you want to connect.

Setting Up a Remote Client

 You set up dial-up networking through the Dial-Up Networking folder in My Computer or Windows Explorer. To create on your computer a remote client that can call in and connect to another computer, use these instructions:

1. Open My Computer, and then open the Dial-Up Networking folder. My folder looks like this with an Internet connection named WhidbeyNet; yours will reflect any connections you have:

2. Click the Make New Connection icon. The Make New Connection dialog box opens, as shown in Figure 16-14.

3. Type in a name for the computer you are calling; make it a name that is meaningful to you.

 OTE The name you give the computer you are dialing appears as an icon label in the Dial-Up Networking folder.

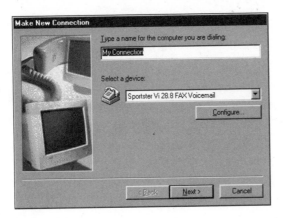

Figure 16-14. *Make New Connection wizard.*

4. If your modem is not displayed in the Select A Device drop-down list, you need to install your modem in Windows 98. See Chapter 10 on how to do this. The Configure button allows you to make settings pertaining to your modem. These settings are also described in Chapter 10.

5. Click Next, and enter the area code and telephone number of the computer you want to call.

6. Click Next again. You'll be told that you have successfully created a new connection. Click Finish to complete the process. The Dial-Up Networking folder reappears with an icon for your new connection, as you can see in Figure 16-15.

Setting Up a Dial-Up Server

Any computer with a modem running Windows 98 can be set up to act as a dial-up server. It can receive one call at a time and provide access to both its own resources as well as those on the network to which it is attached. Use the following instructions to set up a dial-up server:

 OTE The Dial-Up Server is not installed in a Typical install. If you do not have it installed, you can install it by opening the Add/Remove Programs control panel, selecting the Windows Setup tab, and choosing Communications | Dial-Up Server.

Figure 16-15. *Dial-Up Networking folder with connection icons.*

1. If the Dial-Up Networking folder is not already open, reopen it by opening the Start menu and choosing Programs | Accessories | Communications | Dial-Up Networking. From the Dial-Up Networking folder, open the Connections menu and choose Dial-Up Server. The Dial-Up Server dialog box opens, as you see in Figure 16-16.

2. Click Allow Caller Access to enable that function.

3. If you want to define a password for remote access, click Change Password, enter the old and new passwords, and click OK. The default password is a null, the absence of any password.

4. If you want a comment displayed when someone connects to the server, enter that in the Comment text box.

5. Click Server Type for access to several advanced settings, which you can see below. Under most circumstances, you should keep the default settings shown here. Click Cancel to return to the Dial-Up Server dialog box.

Figure 16-16. *Dial-Up Server dialog box.*

6. Click Apply to turn on the Dial-Up Server. You will see the Status change from Idle to Monitoring, as you see in Figure 16-17. Click OK to close the dialog box.

Using Dial-Up Networking

After you have the client and server set up, using dial-up networking is as easy as clicking a connection icon. When you do that, the Connect To dialog box opens, as shown in Figure 16-18. This should reflect the entries that you made when you set up the connection. One important new aspect of this dialog box is that it lets you establish and utilize various locations from which you can call. This way you can have places from which you frequently call already established with their particular settings, such as area code and digits to get an outside line. You can establish new locations and their characteristics through the Dial Properties button as described in Chapter 10.

When the Connect To dialog box is the way you want it, click Connect. You will hear your modem dialing, and a dialog box will appear indicating your progress. When a connection is made, the Connection Established message appears, as you can see in Figure 16-19. Also, the connection icon appears on the right of the taskbar. If you double-click this icon, the Connected To dialog box appears and shows the speed and duration of connection, like this:

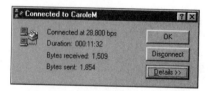

In addition to using a dial-up connection explicitly by clicking it, you can do it implicitly by trying to use a remote resource that requires a dial-up connection, for example, a mapped disk drive or a network printer. In any case, after you have connected to a dial-up server, you can

- Access information on the disk drives attached to either the server or its network

- Print on the printers attached to either the server or its network

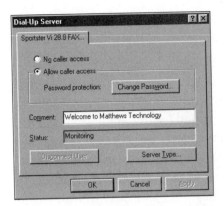

Figure 16-17. *Dial-Up Server waiting for an incoming call.*

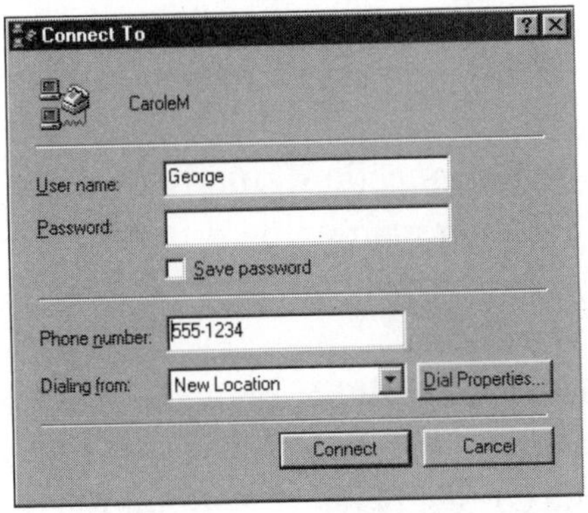

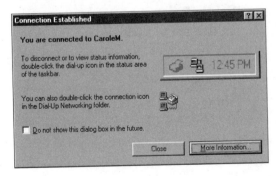

Figure 16-18. *Connect To dialog box.*

Figure 16-19. *The Connection Established message appears when you are connected.*

Accessing Remote Disk Drives

To access individual disk drives on either the computer to which you are connected or its network, you must map those drives to drive letters on your computer as described earlier in this chapter. The difficult part is knowing the correct network path of the drive you want to use. The path has the same format as described earlier, namely *computer name**drive name*. If you know the computer name, you can open the Start menu and choose Find | Computer, then click the found computer to see the drives and printers that are connected to that computer. After you have mapped the drive(s) to your computer, you can use Windows Explorer or My Computer to access files over the dial-up connection, just as if you were directly using the server computer, with the only penalty being the slowness of the modem.

Printing on Remote Printers

To use a printer over a dial-up connection, simply establish the connection, and then use the Add Printer icon in the Printers folder to create a new network printer using that connection. You can then print to that printer as you would to any network printer. If you are not physically connected when you print, the output will be spooled to your disk until you are next connected, at which time it will print. As with remote drives, the difficult part is knowing the correct network path for the printer. The format is *computer name**printer name*.

Disconnecting from a Dial-Up Server

To disconnect from a dial-up server, double-click the dial-up connection icon on the right of the taskbar. Then in the Connected To dialog box, click Disconnect.

Controlling a Dial-Up Server

Whenever you have an enabled modem on a computer that is receptive to calls, as is the case with a dial-up server, you need to be concerned with security. The first step is to turn off caller access in the Dial-Up Server dialog box whenever you do not need it. The second step is to use password protection. You can do this at both the dial-up server level as well as at the drive- and folder-sharing levels, giving you double protection. As with any passwords, keep them secure and change them often. The final (and not always possible) step is to watch who is using the server. You can do this through the Dial-Up Server dialog box, as you can see in Figure 16-20, as well as in Net Watcher, which is described at the end of this chapter.

 ARNING Be sensitive to the security needs of a dial-up server.

Virtual Private Networking

Virtual private networking (VPN) uses dial-up networking with the Point-to-Point Tunneling Protocol (PPTP) over the Internet to provide secure remote access to a private or corporate network. You can be in a remote location, dial a local phone number to connect to the Internet, and then connect to the private network through the Internet. Both your Internet communications and the private network are secure. Windows 98 can only be a client with VPN; the server must run Windows NT or another operating system that supports PPTP.

 OTE Virtual private networking is not installed with a Typical install. If you do not have it installed, you can do so by opening the Add/Remove Programs control panel, selecting the Windows Setup tab, and choosing Communications | Virtual Private Networking.

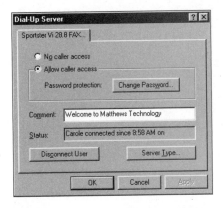

Figure 16-20. *Dial-Up Server dialog box showing someone connected to your computer.*

To set up a VPN client, you must know the IP address or host name of the PPTP server. Assuming that you already have some way to connect to the Internet, you can use the following steps to set up and connect to the PPTP server using VPN:

1. Open the Dial-Up Networking folder by opening the Start menu and choosing Programs | Accessories | Communications | Dial-Up Networking.

2. Click Make New Connection to open the Make New Connection wizard. Enter the name that you want to use for the connection. This name will appear under the icon in the Dial-Up Networking folder.

3. In the Select A Device drop-down list, select Microsoft VPN Adapter, as shown in Figure 16-21, and click Next.

4. Enter the host name or IP address of the server to which you want to connect, and again click Next.

5. Confirm that the entries you have made are correct, use Back to make any necessary changes, and then click Finish.

6. If you want to change the VPN connection, right-click its icon and choose Properties. The connection's dialog box opens, where you can change the host name or IP address and the Connect Using device.

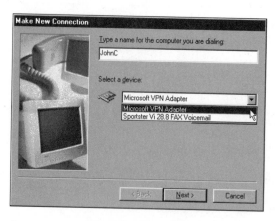

Figure 16-21. *Setting up a virtual private network.*

7. To connect to the VPN server, first establish a connection to the Internet in your normal way, just as if you were going to browse the Web.

8. When you have a connection to the Internet, click the new VPN Dial-Up connection you completed in step 5. The Connect To dialog box opens, where you can enter a user name and password, confirm the settings you made in steps 3 and 4, and then click Connect. The Connecting To message appears followed by a Connected To message.

9. After you are connected, you can use the drives, folders, files, printers, and other devices for which you have permission, just as if you were connected through a LAN.

Protocols to Use with Dial-Up Networking

Depending on the network behind the dial-up server to which you want to connect, and what you want to do on that network, you will need to have different protocols bound to the dial-up adapters in *both* the server and the remote client. Chapter 15, under *Network Protocols,* discusses this topic and how to install, or bind, protocols to an adapter. For dial-up networking, use the guidelines in Table 16-1 for selecting the protocols that are correct for your situation. Other than when you want to access a NetWare network, TCP/IP is the best choice. Also, you can have multiple protocols bound to the dial-up adapter, but it will slow down the loading time.

Protocol	Circumstances
Any	Accessing only the resources in the dial-up server
TCP/IP	Accessing the Internet, Windows NT, Windows 95 or 98, or other networks
IPX/XPX	Accessing a NetWare network
NetBEUI	Accessing a Windows NT, Windows 95 or 98, or other Microsoft or IBM network

Table 16-1.   *Protocols to use in Dial-Up Networking.*

Networking Accessories

Windows 98 includes three networking accessories; however, the first two accessories discussed in the following sections are not part of the Typical install, and the third can be started only by typing its name in the Run command line or by clicking its icon in the Windows folder. The networking accessories are

- **Hearts,** a card game that can be played by as many as four people on the network

- **Net Watcher,** a utility that allows you to see who on the network is accessing your resources and what they are accessing

- **WinPopup,** a utility that allows you to send a quick message to someone on the network and have it pop up on the recipient's computer

 OTE   If Hearts and Net Watcher are not installed on your computer, install them by opening the Add/Remove Programs control panel, clicking the Windows Setup tab, and choosing Accessories | Games for Hearts or System Tools | Net Watcher.

Using Hearts

You start Hearts by opening the Start menu and choosing Programs | Accessories | Games | Hearts. This opens the Hearts Network window and a dialog box that asks your name and whether you want to join another game or start your own and be the dealer, as shown below. If you elect to join another game, you will be asked for the dealer's computer name. If you elect to be the dealer, Hearts will then wait for others to join the game. When you are ready to start, press F2 or choose New Game from the Game menu. You may have from zero to three other players. The computer will play the hands not taken by live participants. When the game begins, the Hearts window looks like that shown in Figure 16-22.

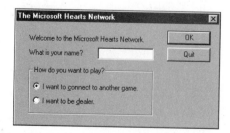

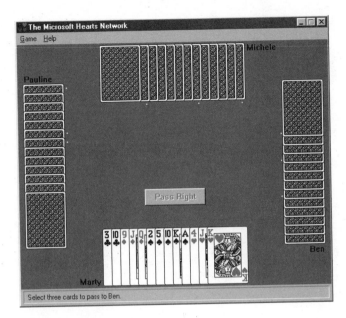

Figure 16-22. *Hearts window.*

The objective of the game is to have the lowest score by *not* taking tricks with hearts or the queen of spades in them *unless* you can take all such tricks. You take a trick by playing the highest card in the suit led for that trick. You begin the game by passing three cards from your hand to one of the other players. Every fourth hand, no cards are passed. Normally you want to pass your highest hearts or any spade queen or above (select a card to play by clicking it). Then the person with the two of clubs leads with that card. You must follow suit if you can. If you can't follow suit, you may throw away your high hearts or spades or any other card you want. Whoever takes a trick plays the first card for the next trick. Play continues until all cards have been played. At the end of a game, one point is assessed for each heart in the tricks you took plus 13 for the queen of spades. If you get all of the hearts plus the queen of spades, you get zero points, and all other players get 26 points.

Using Net Watcher

You start Net Watcher by opening the Start menu and choosing Programs | Accessories | System Tools | Net Watcher. This opens the Net Watcher window, shown in Figure 16-23. This initial window shows users currently connected to your computer and the folders and files they have open. Two other views are available in Net Watcher: one showing shared resources, as you see in Figure 16-24, and the other showing files opened by network users, as shown in Figure 16-25. Net Watcher, through the toolbar buttons or the Administer and View menus, allows you to perform the functions shown in Table 16-2.

 OTE To view the contents of another computer, that computer must be set up for remote administration. See *Remote Administration Permission* in Chapter 5 for information on remotely administering networked computers.

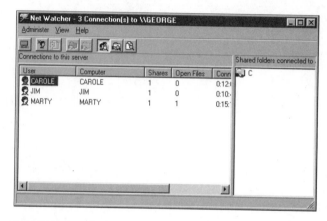

Figure 16-23. *Net Watcher showing the activity of users on your computer.*

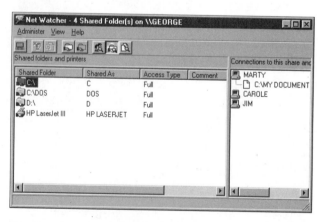

Figure 16-24. *Net Watcher showing shared resources on your computer.*

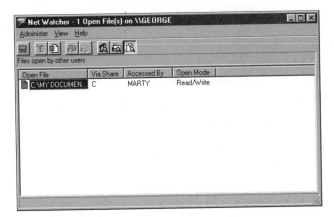

Figure 16-25. *Net Watcher showing files opened by others on the network.*

Button	Name	Function
	Select Server	Changes the computer ("server") that you are looking at
	Disconnect User	Terminates someone who is currently logged on to your computer
	Close File	Closes a file that is opened by a network user
	Add/Stop Share	Shares or stops sharing a resource
	Show Users	Displays view shown in Figure 16-23
	Show Shared Folders	Displays view shown in Figure 16-24
	Show Files	Displays view shown in Figure 16-25

Table 16-2. *Net Watcher toolbar buttons.*

Using WinPopup

You start WinPopup by opening the Start menu, selecting Run, typing
Winpopup, and clicking OK. Alternatively, you can open the Windows
Explorer, display the Windows folder, and click Winpopup.exe. If you click
the Send button or choose Send from the Messages menu, the Send Message
window opens, as shown in Figure 16-26. Here you can send a message to

one person (computer) or to everyone in a workgroup. If you are sending it to just one person, you must type in the computer name; to send it to your workgroup, click Workgroup, and then type in the name of the workgroup. In either case, type the message and click OK. The person(s) receiving the message must have WinPopup running in order to receive the message. If WinPopup is loaded but minimized and you have checked Messages | Options | Pop Up Dialog On Message Receipt, when a message is received, the window will open ("pop up") with the message, as shown in Figure 16-27.

  IP   You can automatically start WinPopup every time you start Windows 98 by putting a shortcut to WinPopup in your \Windows\Start Menu\Programs\StartUp folder. The program file for WinPopup, Winpopup.exe, is in your \Windows folder.

Figure 16-26.   *WinPopup Send Message dialog box.*

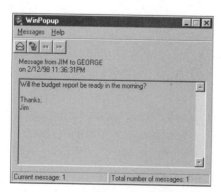

Figure 16-27.   *WinPopup window with a message that has been received.*

Note to the reader: Italicized page numbers refer to figures, tables, and illustrations.

About the Author

Martin Matthews (Marty) has used computers for over 30 years, beginning with some of the earliest mainframe computers to the most recent personal computers and servers. He has done this as a programmer, system analyst, manager, vice president, and president of a software firm. As a result, he has first-hand knowledge of not only how to program and use a computer, but also how to make the best use of the information a computer can produce.

While at the software firm, Marty, with his wife, wrote a small book on how to buy mini-computers. In 1983, this book caught the eye of a publisher who gave them a contract to write a book on word processing. In the next 15 years, they wrote 50 editions of 31 computer book titles on topics as diverse as Microsoft Windows 95, Excel, FrontPage, Access, Office, and networking.

In this same 15-year period, Marty beta tested most versions of MS-DOS, Microsoft Windows, Word, Excel, and Office, as well as many other software products. He has also used most of what has come to be called personal computers, from the earliest Apple and IBM PCs to machines with the latest Pentium processors.

Marty, his wife, and their son live on a island in Puget Sound where, on the rare instances when they can look up from their computers, they look west over seven miles of water to the snow-capped Olympic mountains.

The manuscript for this book was prepared and submitted to Microsoft Press in electronic form. Text files were prepared using Microsoft Word 97 for Windows 95. Pages were composed by Microsoft Press using Adobe PageMaker 6.51 for Windows, with text in Melior and display type in Frutiger Condensed. Composed pages were delivered to the printer as electronic prepress files.

Cover Designer
Patrick Lanfear

Interior Graphic Designer
Kim Eggleston

Interior Graphic Artist
Travis Beaven

Principal Compositor
Sybil Ihrig, Helios Productions

Principal Proofreader/Copy Editor
Deborah O. Stockton/
Harriet O'Neal, Margaret Berson

Indexer
James Minkin

Microsoft Press has titles to help everyone— from new users to seasoned developers—

Step by Step Series
Self-paced tutorials for classroom instruction or individualized study

Starts Here™ Series
Interactive instruction on CD-ROM that helps students learn by doing

Field Guide Series
Concise, task-oriented A–Z references for quick, easy answers— anywhere

Official Series
Timely books on a wide variety of Internet topics geared for advanced users

All User Training   All User Reference

Quick Course® Series
Fast, to-the-point instruction for new users

Select Editions Series
A comprehensive curriculum alternative to standard documentation books

At a Glance Series
Quick visual guides for task-oriented instruction

start faster and go farther!

The wide selection of books and CD-ROMs published by Microsoft Press contain something for every level of user and every area of interest, from just-in-time online training tools to development tools for professional programmers. Look for them at your bookstore or computer store today!

Professional Select Editions Series
Advanced titles geared for the system administrator or technical support career path

Microsoft Certified Professional Training
The Microsoft Official Curriculum for certification exams

Best Practices Series
Candid accounts of the new movement in software development

Microsoft Programming Series
The foundations of software development

Professional   Developers

Microsoft Press® Interactive
Integrated multimedia courseware for all levels

Strategic Technology Series
Easy-to-read overviews for decision makers

Microsoft Professional Editions
Technical information straight from the source

Solution Developer Series
Comprehensive titles for intermediate to advanced developers

Microsoft® Press

mspress.microsoft.com

Take the
whole family
siteseeing!

For Microsoft® Windows® 95 and Windows NT®

The Reference for Everyday Use in Home, School, and Office

1998 Edition
Regular Online Updates

Official
Microsoft® Bookshelf®
Internet Directory

Searchable on CD-ROM—with direct links to thousands of the best and most useful Internet sites

Microsoft Press

U.S.A.	**$39.99**
U.K.	£37.49 [V.A.T. included]
Canada	$55.99
ISBN 1-57231-617-9	

Want to update your stock portfolio? Explore space? Recognize consumer fraud? Find a better job? Trace your family tree? Research your term paper? Make bagels? Well, go for it! The OFFICIAL MICROSOFT® BOOKSHELF® INTERNET DIRECTORY, 1998 EDITION, gives you reliable, carefully selected, up-to-date reviews of thousands of the Internet's most useful, entertaining, and functional Web sites. The searchable companion CD-ROM gives you direct, instant links to the sites in the book—a simple click of the mouse takes you wherever you want to go!

Developed jointly by Microsoft Press and the Microsoft Bookshelf product team, the OFFICIAL MICROSOFT BOOKSHELF INTERNET DIRECTORY, 1998 EDITION, is updated regularly on the World Wide Web to keep you informed of our most current list of recommended sites. Microsoft Internet Explorer 4.0 is also included on the CD-ROM.

Microsoft® *Press*

Get the most from the *Internet!*

U.S.A. **$14.99**
U.K.   £13.99
Canada $21.99
ISBN 1-57231-804-X

For new and experienced Internet users, QUICK COURSE® IN MICROSOFT® INTERNET EXPLORER 4 shows you the most efficient ways to use Internet Explorer 4 to get just what you need from the Internet. This book will help you:

- Learn concepts, learn Microsoft Internet Explorer, and get on the World Wide Web right away

- Efficiently search for, print, and save the information you need

- Use Outlook™ Express to exchange e-mail with other Internet users

- Participate in newsgroups, save articles to read offline, and post articles of interest to others

- Explore all the cool new stuff available with Internet Explorer, including FrontPage® Express

Quick Course® books offer you streamlined instruction in the form of no-nonsense, to-the-point tutorials and learning exercises. The core of each book is a logical sequence of straightforward, easy-to-follow instructions for building useful business documents—the same documents you create and use on the job.

Microsoft®*Press*

Register Today!

Return this
Microsoft® Windows® 98 Companion
registration card for
a Microsoft Press® catalog

U.S. and Canada addresses only. Fill in information below and mail postage-free. Please mail only the bottom half of this page.

1-57231-931-3   *MICROSOFT® WINDOWS® 98 COMPANION*   *Owner Registration Card*

NAME

INSTITUTION OR COMPANY NAME

ADDRESS

CITY   STATE   ZIP

Microsoft *Press*
Quality Computer Books

**For a free catalog of
Microsoft Press® products, call
1-800-MSPRESS**